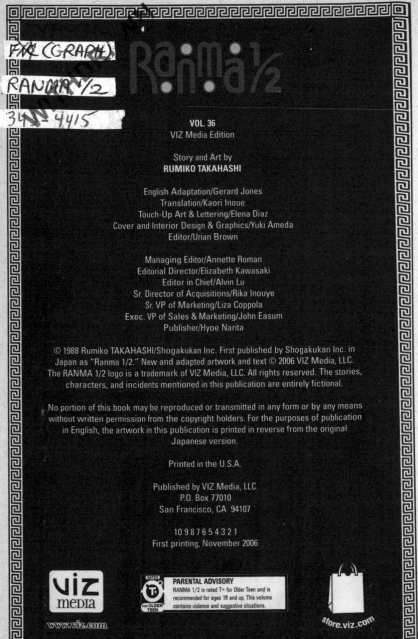

Ranma 1/2

VOL. 36
VIZ Media Edition

Story and Art by
RUMIKO TAKAHASHI

English Adaptation/Gerard Jones
Translation/Kaori Inoue
Touch-Up Art & Lettering/Elena Diaz
Cover and Interior Design & Graphics/Yuki Ameda
Editor/Urian Brown

Managing Editor/Annette Roman
Editorial Director/Elizabeth Kawasaki
Editor in Chief/Alvin Lu
Sr. Director of Acquisitions/Rika Inouye
Sr. VP of Marketing/Liza Coppola
Exec. VP of Sales & Marketing/John Easum
Publisher/Hyoe Narita

Published by VIZ Media, LLC
P.O. Box 77010
San Francisco, CA 94107

10 9 8 7 6 5 4 3 2 1
First printing, November 2006

www.viz.com

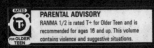
PARENTAL ADVISORY
RANMA 1/2 is rated T+ for Older Teen and is recommended for ages 16 and up. This volume contains violence and suggestive situations.

store.viz.com

Ranma 1/2

VOL. 36   VIZ Media Edition

STORY & ART BY
RUMIKO TAKAHASHI

STORY THUS FAR

The Tendos are an average, run-of-the-mill Japanese family—on the surface, that is. Soun Tendo is the owner and proprietor of the Tendo Dojo, where "Anything Goes Martial Arts" is practiced. Like the name says, anything goes, and usually does.

When Soun's old friend Genma Saotome comes to visit, Soun's three lovely young daughters—Akane, Nabiki and Kasumi—are told that it's time for one of them to become the fiancée of Genma's teenage son, as per an agreement made between the two fathers years ago. Youngest daughter Akane—who says she hates boys—is quickly nominated for bridal duty by her sisters.

Unfortunately, Ranma and his father have suffered a strange accident. While training in China, both plunged into one of many "cursed" springs at the legendary martial arts training ground of Jusenkyo. These springs transform the unlucky dunkee into whomever—or whatever—drowned there hundreds of years ago.

From then on, a splash of cold water turns Ranma's father into a giant panda, and Ranma becomes a beautiful, busty young woman. Hot water reverses the effect...but only until next time. As it turns out, Ranma and Genma aren't the only ones who have taken the Jusenkyo plunge—and it isn't long before they meet several other members of the Jusenkyo "cursed."

Although their parents are still determined to see Ranma and Akane marry and assume ownership of the training hall, Ranma seems to have a strange talent for accumulating surplus fiancées...and Akane has a few stubbornly determined suitors of her own. Will the two ever work out their differences and get rid of all these "extra" people, or will they just call the whole thing off? What's a half-boy, half-girl (not to mention all-girl, *angry* girl) to do...?

CAST OF CHARACTERS

THE SAOTOMES

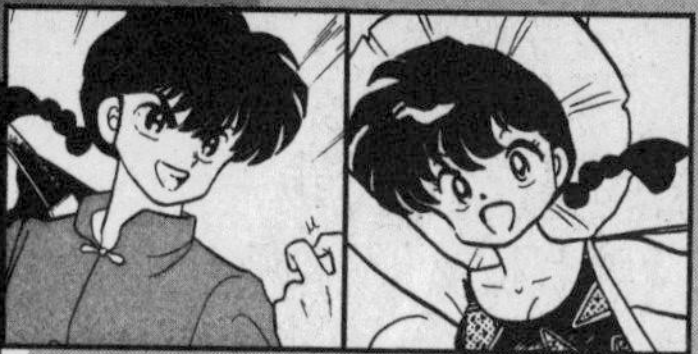

RANMA SAOTOME
Martial artist with far too many fiancées, and an ego that won't let him take defeat. Changes into a girl when splashed with cold water.

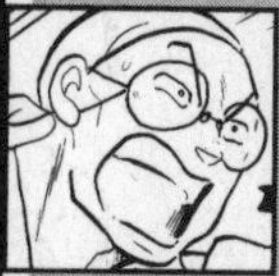

GENMA SAOTOME
Ranma's lazy father, who left his wife and home years ago with his young son (Ranma) to train in the martial arts. Changes into a panda.

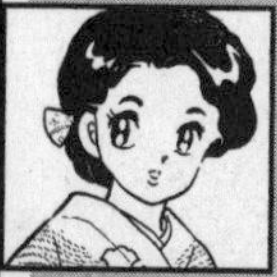

NODOKA SAOTOME
The wife of Genma and mother of Ranma, who doesn't know of their curse or where they are, as they always disguise themselves in their panda and girl forms whenever she is around...

THE MASTERS

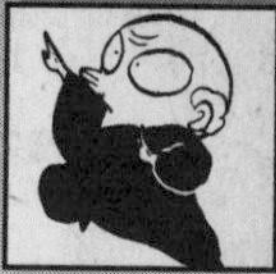

HAPPOSAI
Happosai is the founding father of Anything-Goes Martial Arts, and is a dirty old man with a penchant for stealing girls underwear.

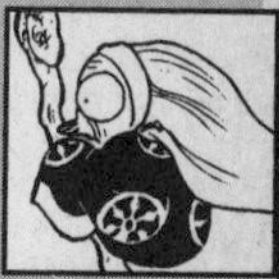

COLOGNE
Grumpy old granny of Shampoo who wants to see her dear granddaughter do well. Is she a better martial arts coach than Genma and Soun?

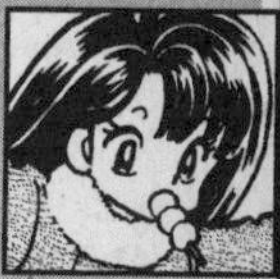

HINAKO NINOMIYA
An English teacher at Furinkan High who switches between the form of a child and an adult woman (by draining an opponent's energy).

THE TENDOS

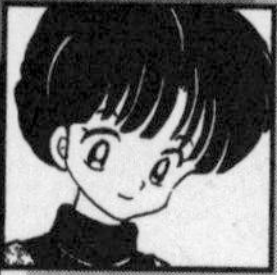

AKANE TENDO
Martial artist, tomboy, and Ranma's reluctant fiancée. Has no clue how much Ryoga likes her, or what relation he might have to her pet black pig, P-chan.

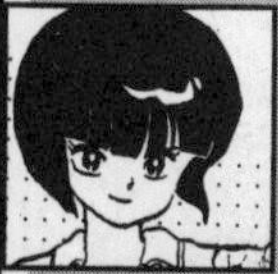

NABIKI TENDO
Always ready to "make a buck" off the suffering of others, cold-hearted capitalist Nabiki is the middle Tendo daughter.

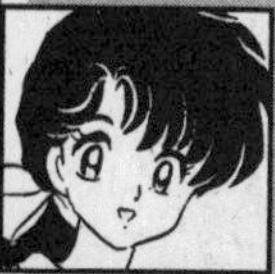

KASUMI TENDO
Sweet-natured eldest Tendo daughter and substitute mother figure for the Tendo family.

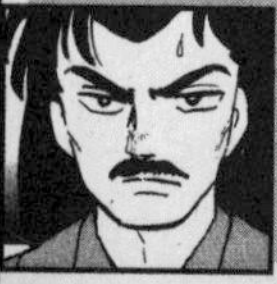

SOUN TENDO
Head of the Tendo household and owner of the Tendo Dojo. Father of three daughters.

THE SUITORS

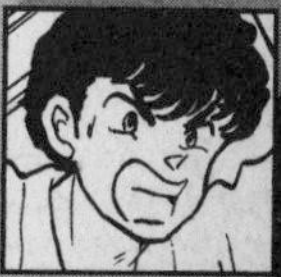

TATEWAKI KUNO
Poetry spouting Tatewaki is the school's Kendo captain and is one of Ranma's major rivals. He is in love with both girl-type Ranma and Akane...

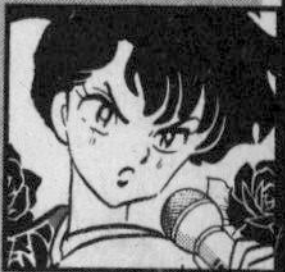

KODACHI KUNO
Twisted sister of Tatewaki. An expert in Martial Arts Rhythmic Gymnastics, she's determined to use her ribbon-whipping skills to tame Ranma.

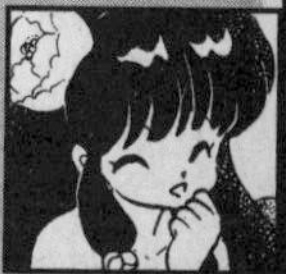

SHAMPOO
Works at the Cat Café and fell into one of the accursed springs. Has a thing for Ranma, and definitely doesn't have a thing for Mousse or Akane. Mee-yow!

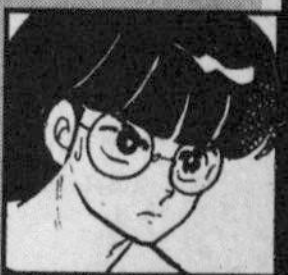

MOUSSE
Nearsighted quacker who fell into one of the accursed springs and has a thing for Shampoo.

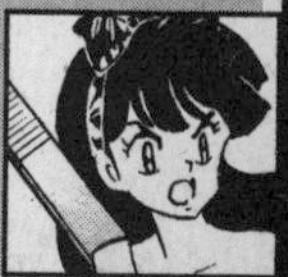

UKYO KUONJI
Okonomiyaki chef Ukyo's grudge against Ranma goes way back to when their fathers agreed to have them become engaged to each other as little children but stole their okonomiyaki cart and left her behind.

CONTENTS

PART 1
THE PHOENIX AND THE DRAGON

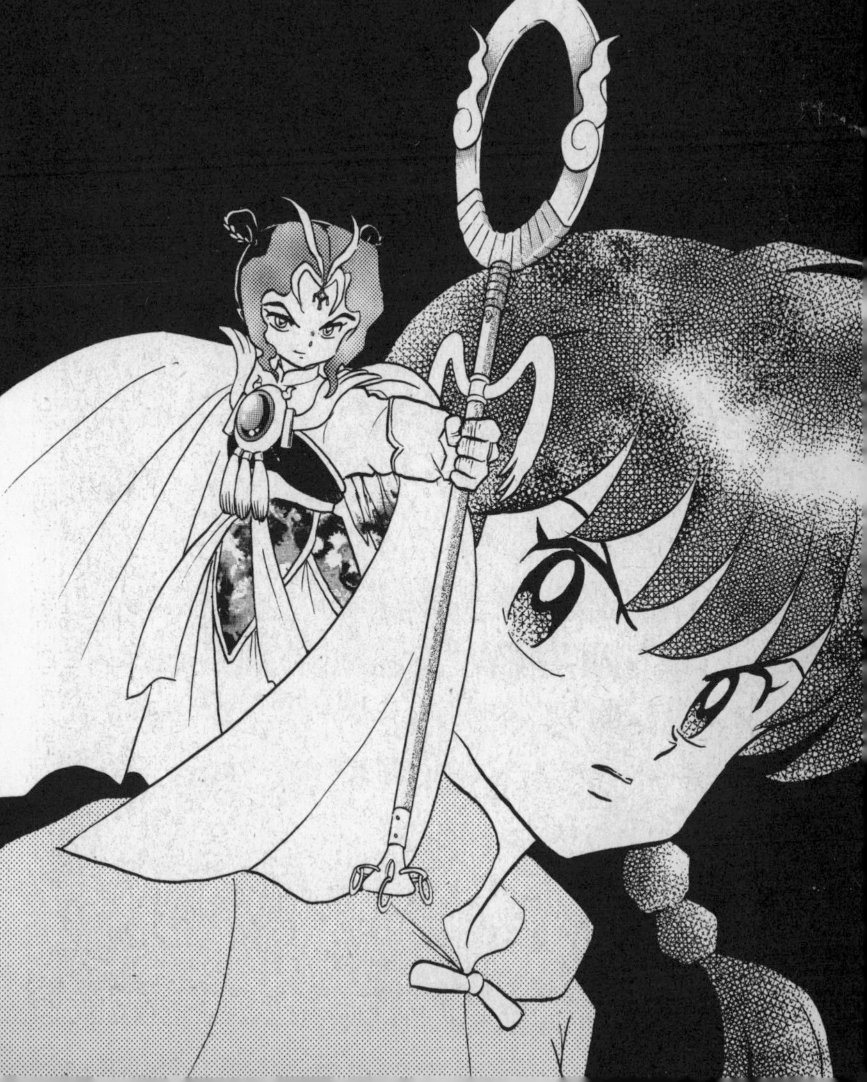

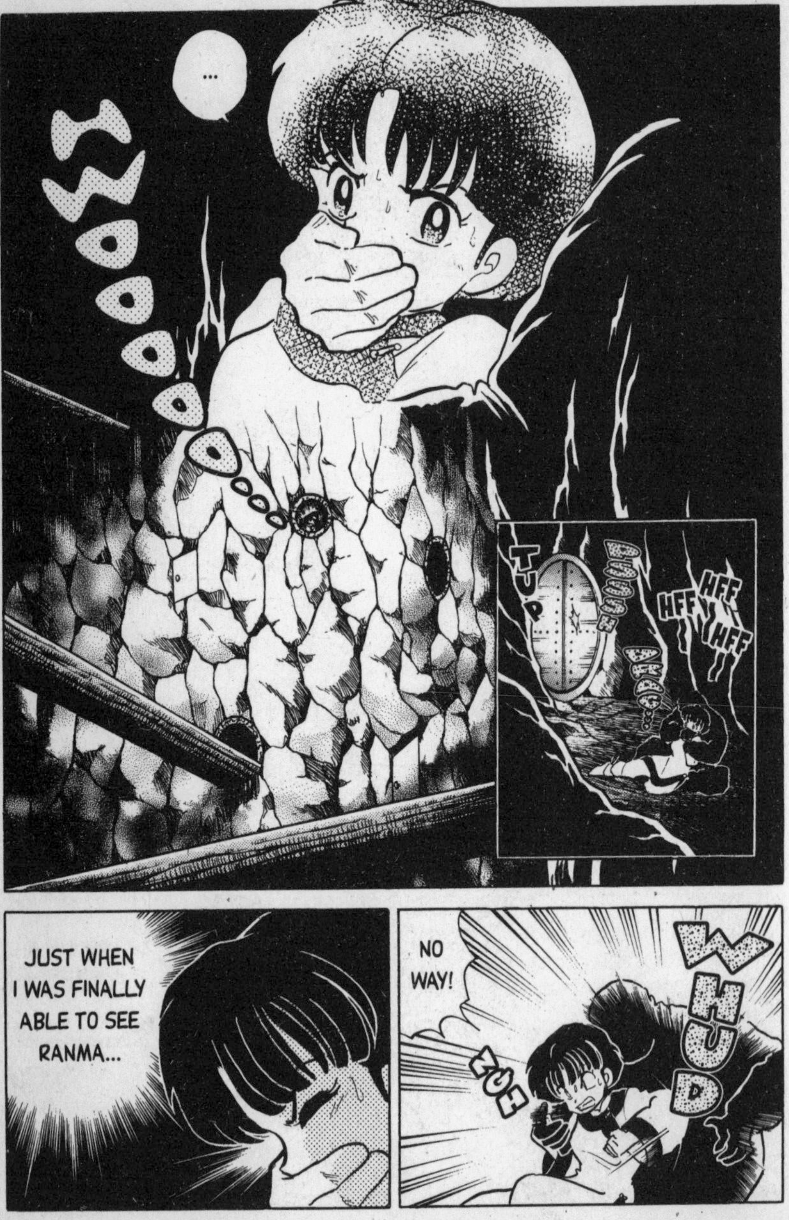
...
TUP
HFF
HFF
HFF
JUST WHEN I WAS FINALLY ABLE TO SEE RANMA...
NO WAY!
WHUD

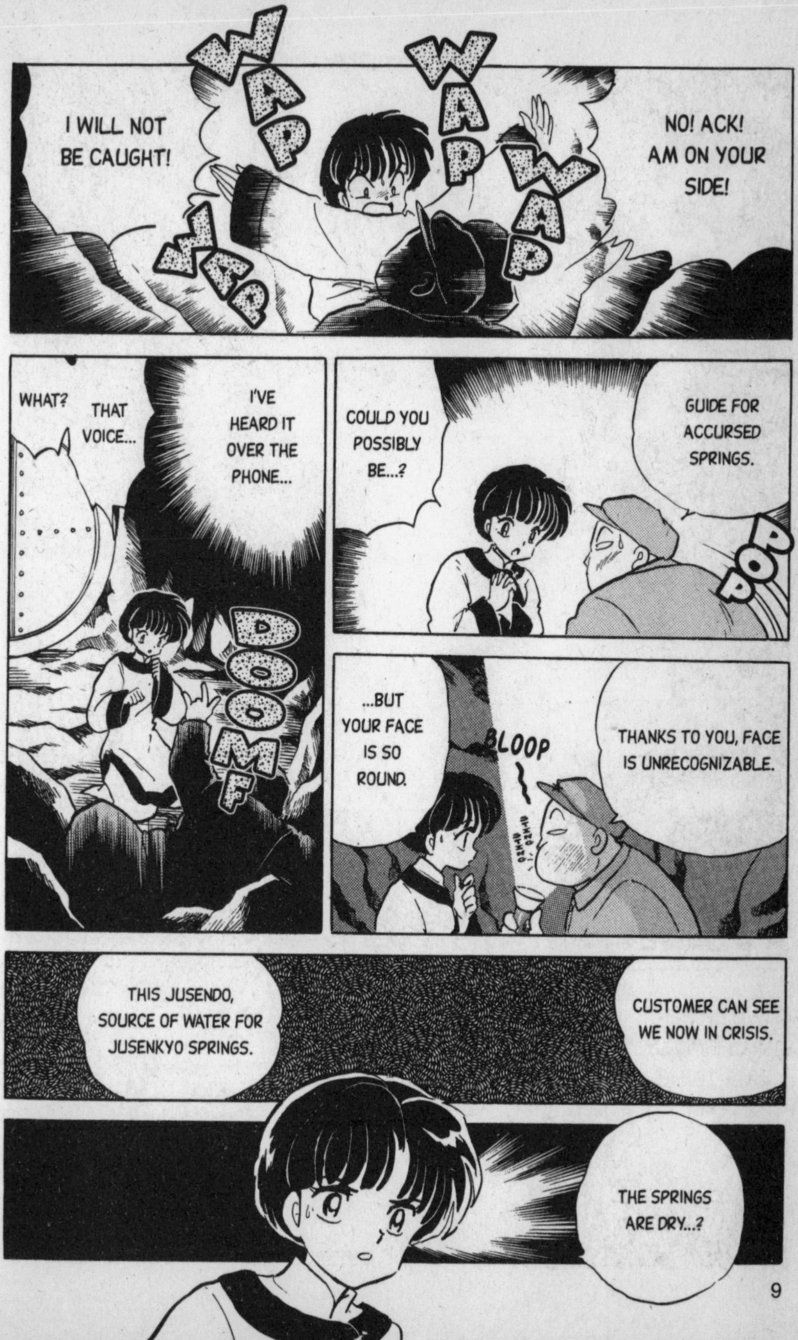
I WILL NOT BE CAUGHT!
WAP WAP WAP WAP
NO! ACK! AM ON YOUR SIDE!
WHAT?
THAT VOICE...
I'VE HEARD IT OVER THE PHONE...
DOOMF
COULD YOU POSSIBLY BE...?
GUIDE FOR ACCURSED SPRINGS.
POP
...BUT YOUR FACE IS SO ROUND.
BLOOP
THANKS TO YOU, FACE IS UNRECOGNIZABLE.
THIS JUSENDO, SOURCE OF WATER FOR JUSENKYO SPRINGS.
CUSTOMER CAN SEE WE NOW IN CRISIS.
THE SPRINGS ARE DRY...?

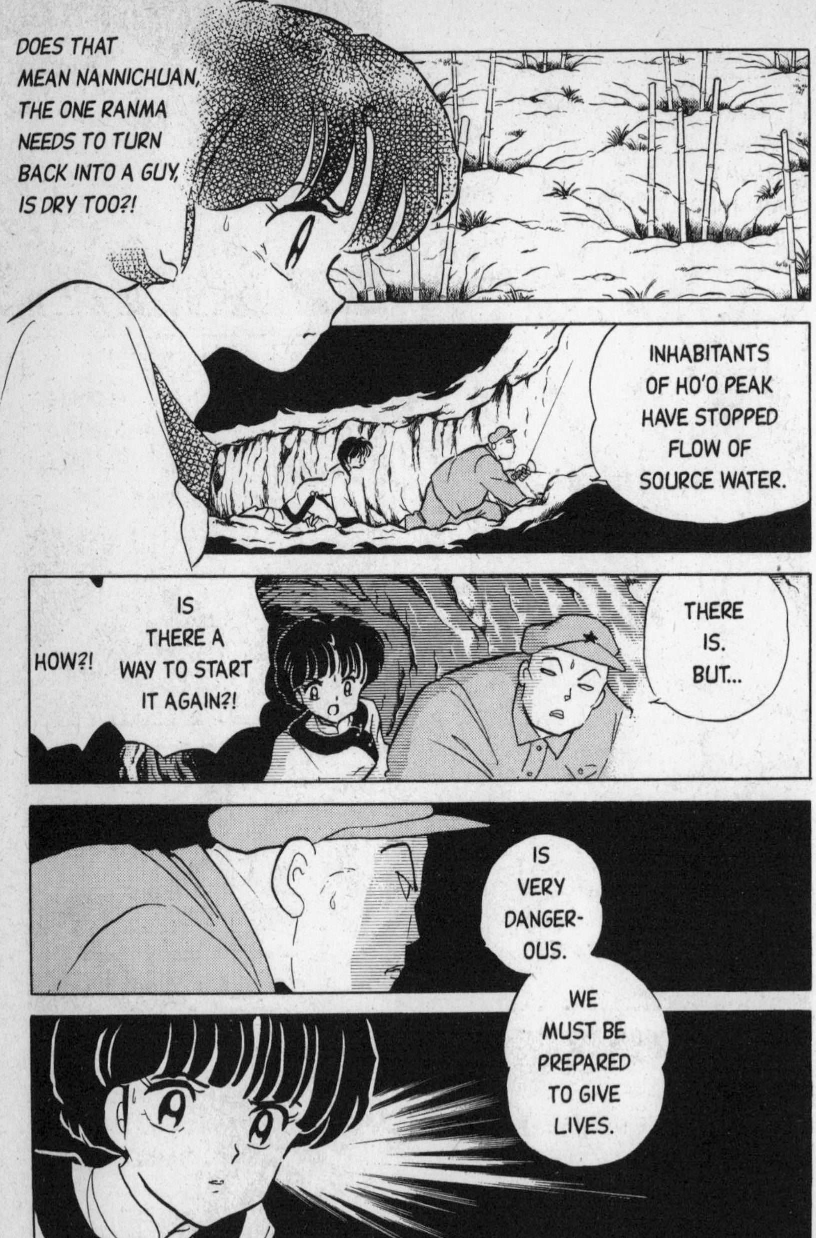
DOES THAT MEAN NANNICHUAN, THE ONE RANMA NEEDS TO TURN BACK INTO A GUY, IS DRY TOO?!
INHABITANTS OF HO'O PEAK HAVE STOPPED FLOW OF SOURCE WATER.
HOW?!
IS THERE A WAY TO START IT AGAIN?!
THERE IS. BUT...
IS VERY DANGER-OUS.
WE MUST BE PREPARED TO GIVE LIVES.

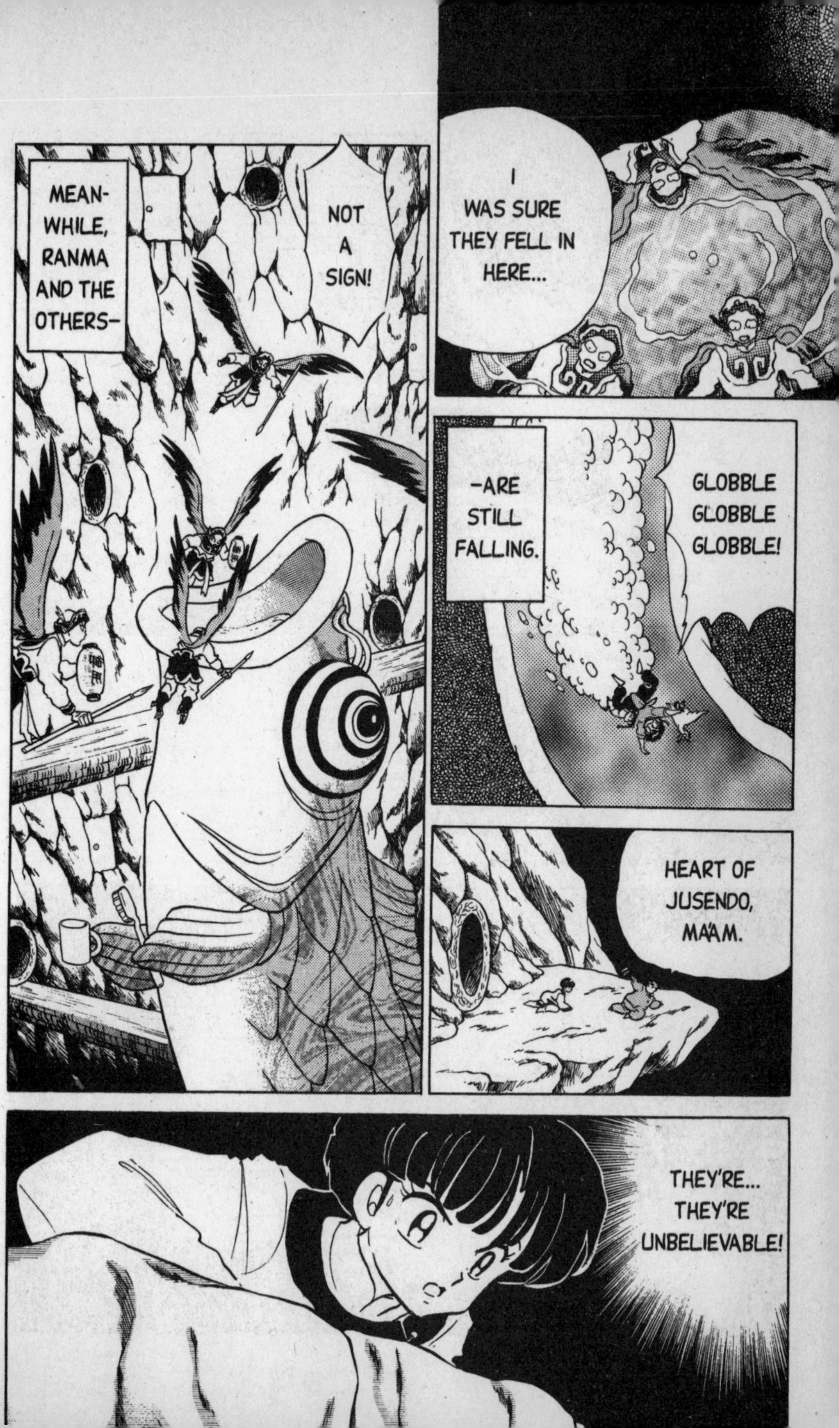
MEAN-WHILE, RANMA AND THE OTHERS—
NOT A SIGN!
I WAS SURE THEY FELL IN HERE...
—ARE STILL FALLING.
GLOBBLE GLOBBLE GLOBBLE!
HEART OF JUSENDO, MA'AM.
THEY'RE... THEY'RE UNBELIEVABLE!

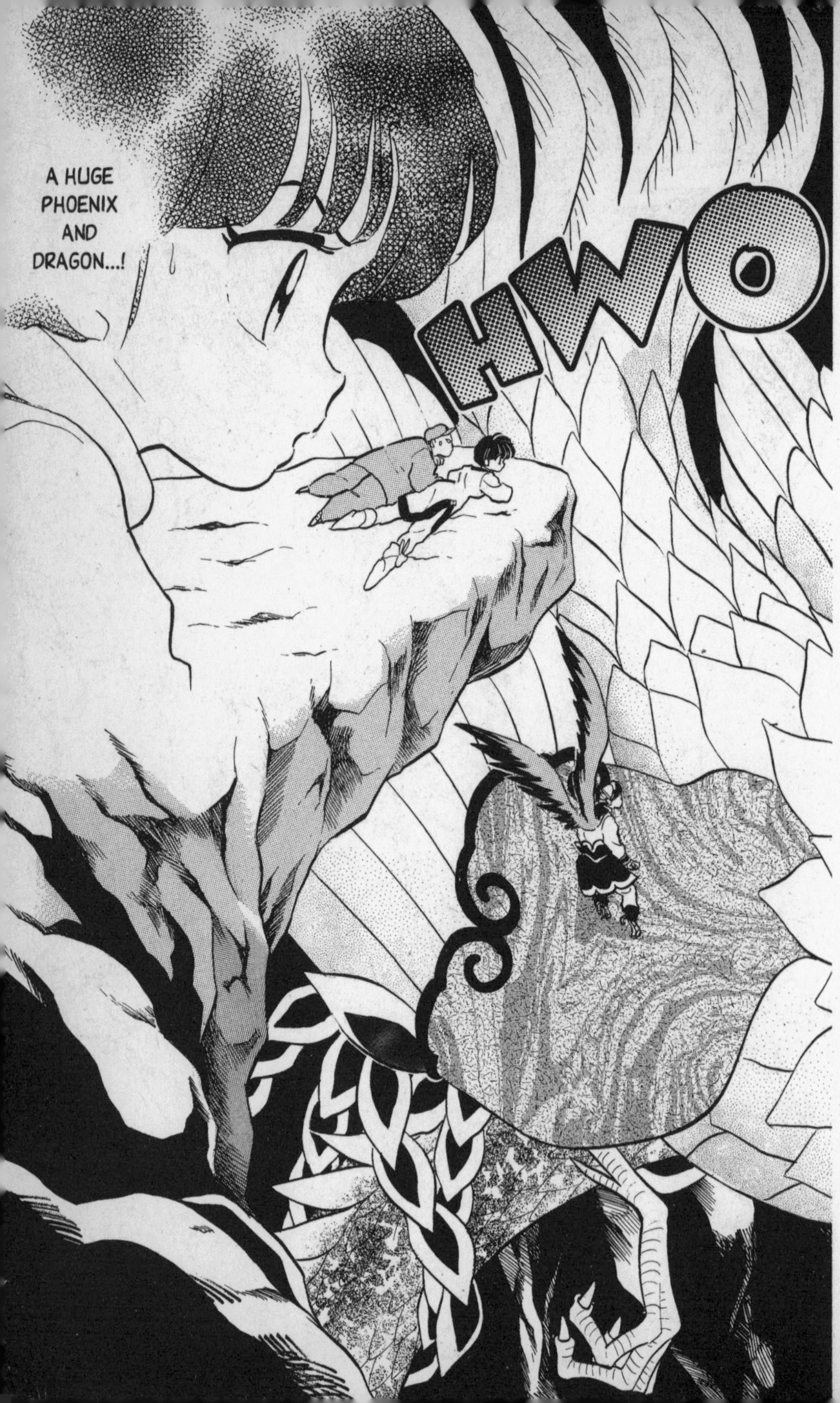
A HUGE PHOENIX AND DRAGON...!
HWO

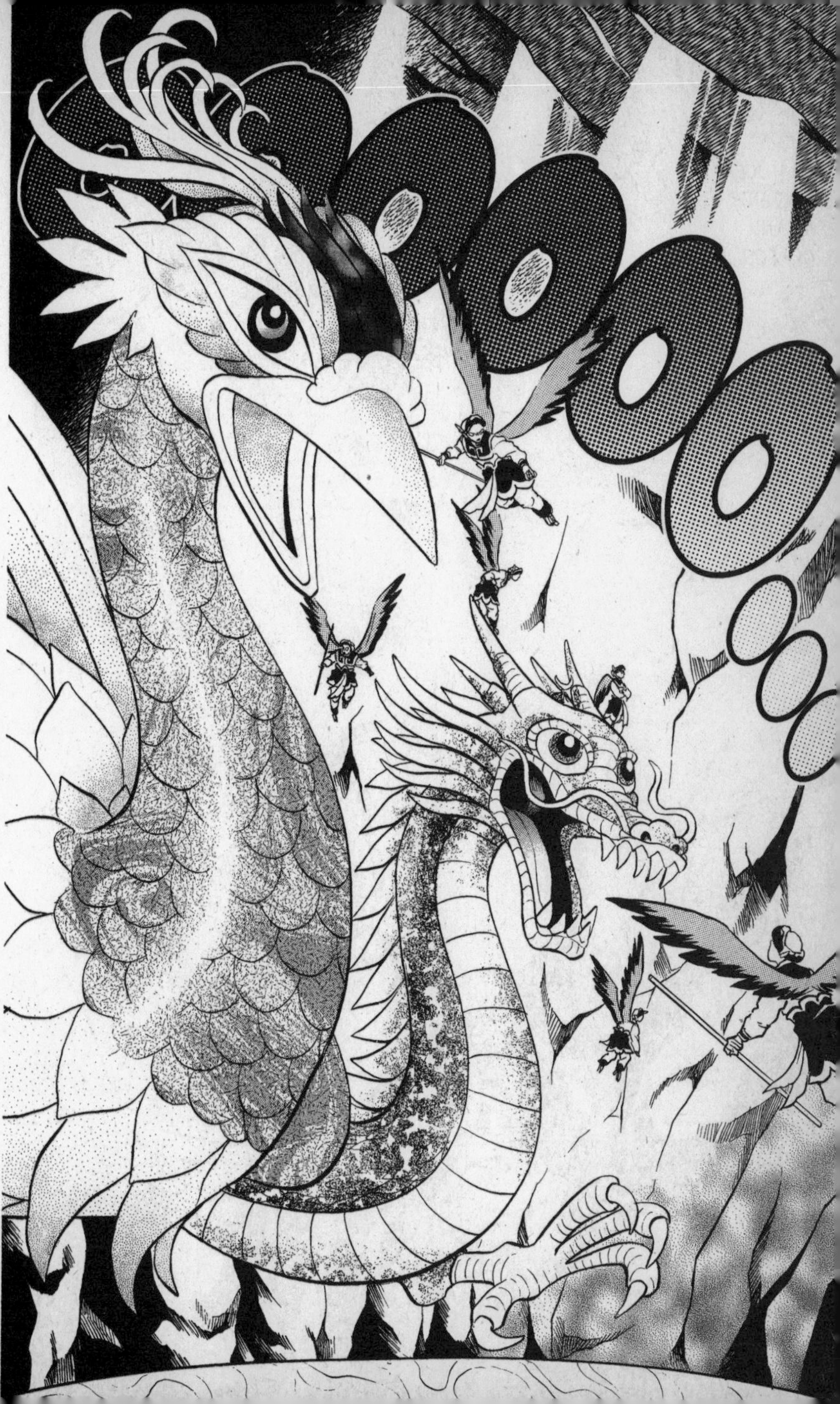
OOOOOO...

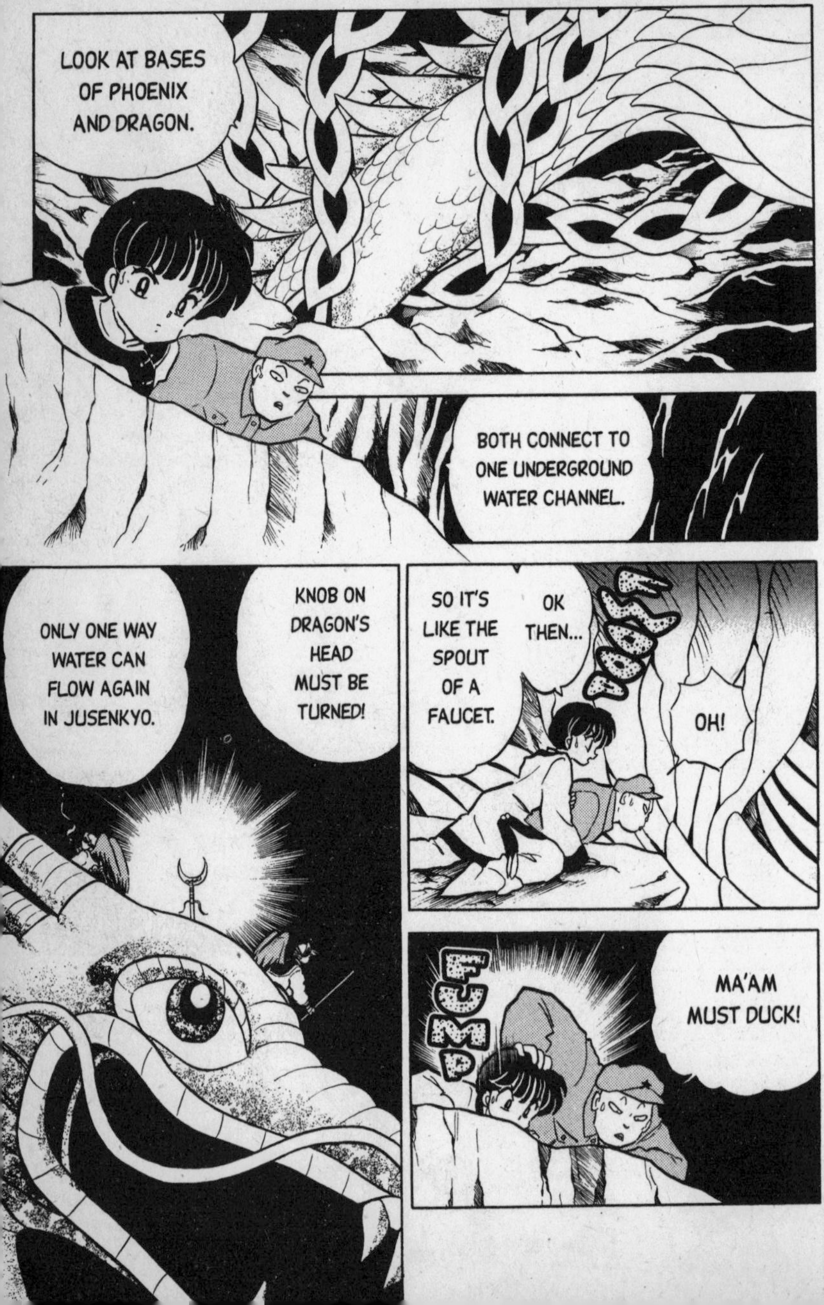

LOOK AT BASES OF PHOENIX AND DRAGON.
BOTH CONNECT TO ONE UNDERGROUND WATER CHANNEL.
ONLY ONE WAY WATER CAN FLOW AGAIN IN JUSENKYO.
KNOB ON DRAGON'S HEAD MUST BE TURNED!
SO IT'S LIKE THE SPOUT OF A FAUCET.
OK THEN...
OH!
FUMP
MA'AM MUST DUCK!

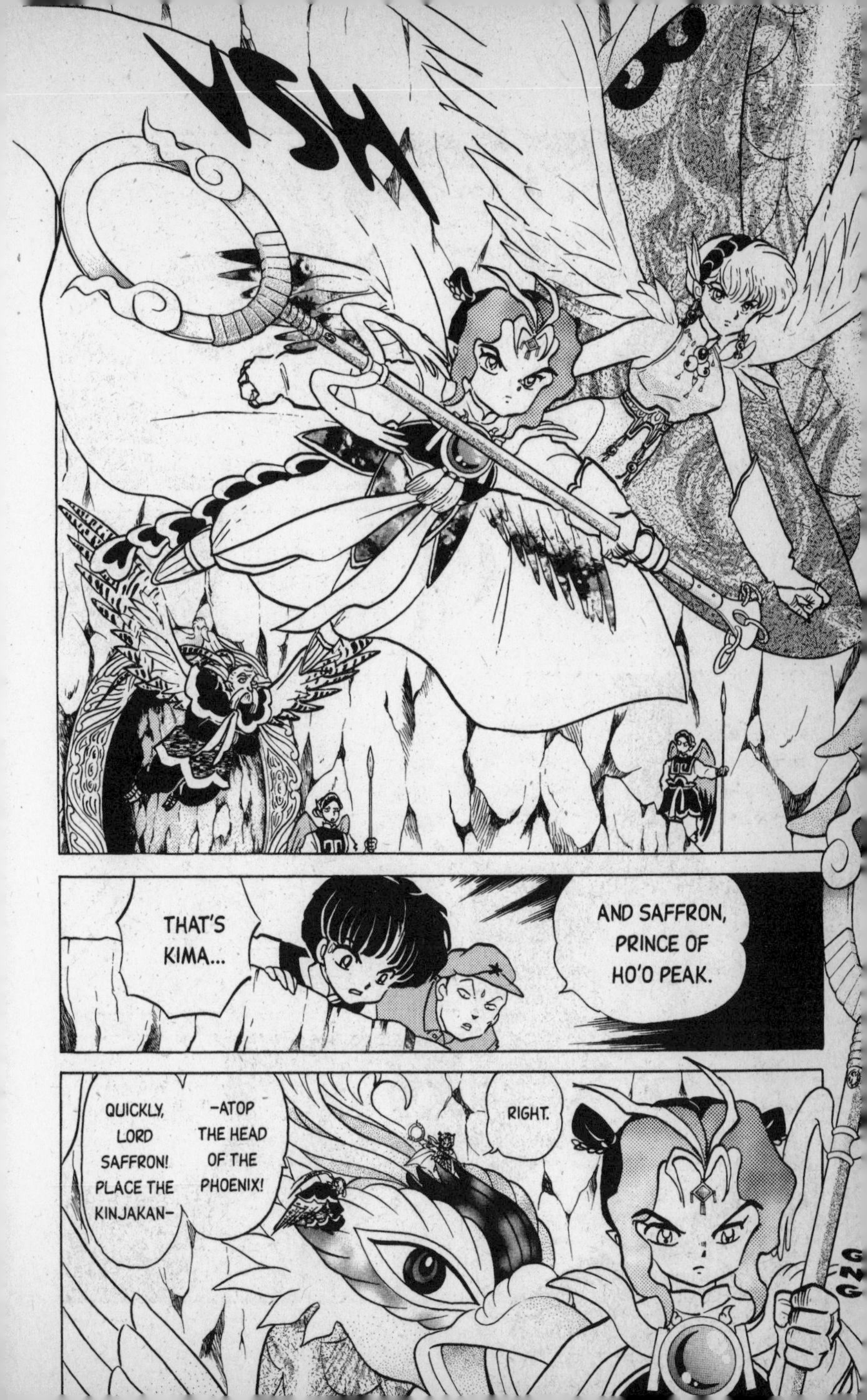
VSHH
THAT'S KIMA...
AND SAFFRON, PRINCE OF HO'O PEAK.
QUICKLY, LORD SAFFRON! PLACE THE KINJAKAN-
-ATOP THE HEAD OF THE PHOENIX!
RIGHT.
GNG

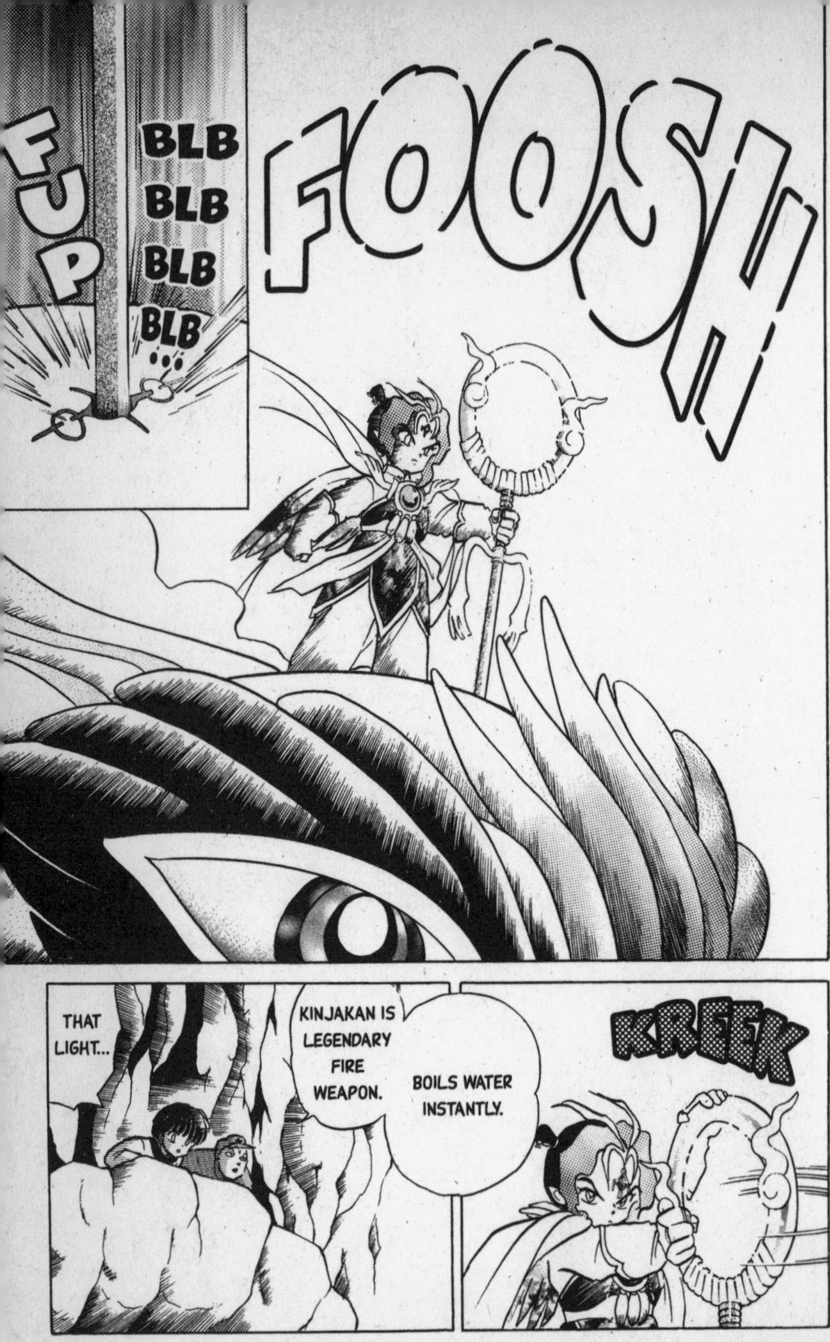
FUP
BLB BLB BLB BLB ...
FOOSH
THAT LIGHT...
KINJAKAN IS LEGENDARY FIRE WEAPON.
BOILS WATER INSTANTLY.
KREEK

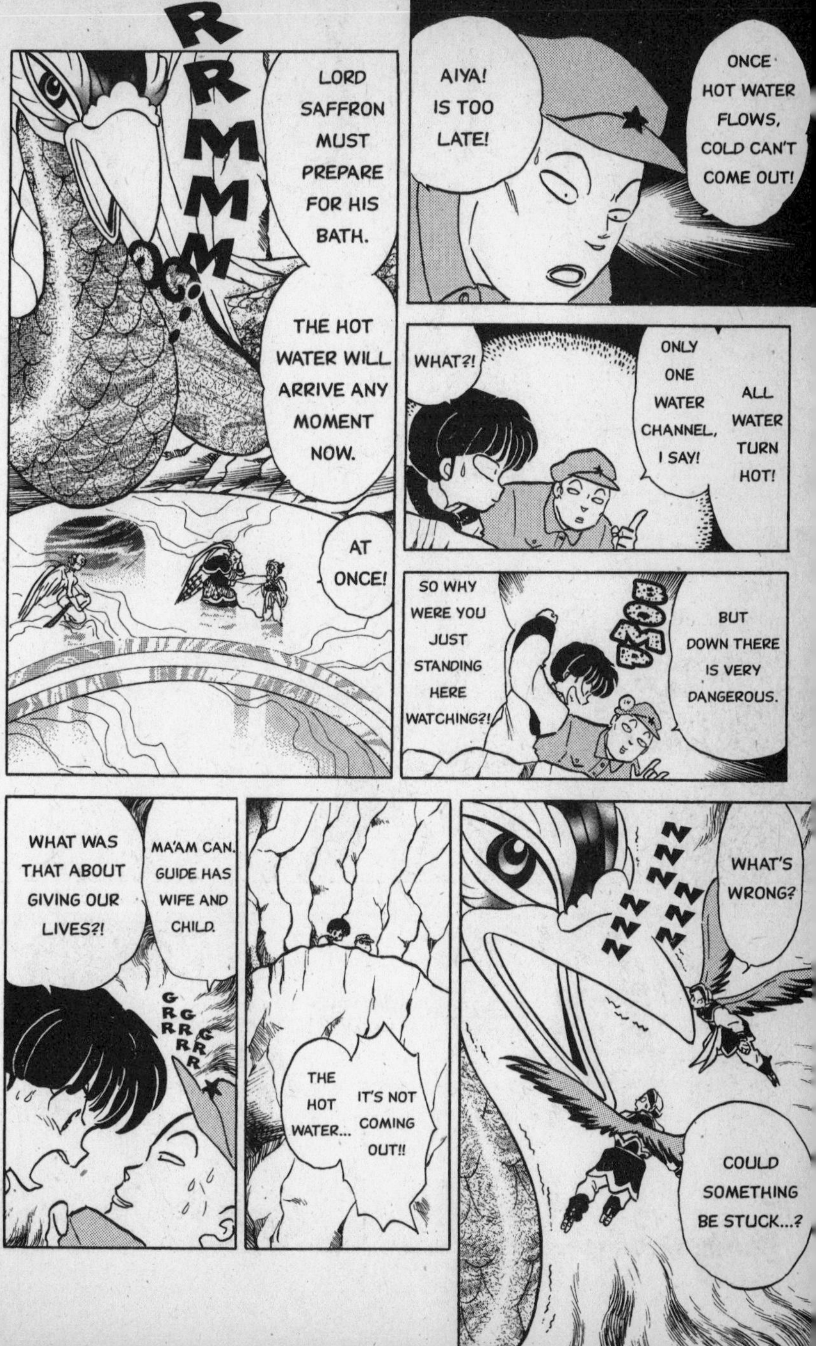
RRRMMM
LORD SAFFRON MUST PREPARE FOR HIS BATH.
THE HOT WATER WILL ARRIVE ANY MOMENT NOW.
AT ONCE!
AIYA! IS TOO LATE!
ONCE HOT WATER FLOWS, COLD CAN'T COME OUT!
WHAT?!
ONLY ONE WATER CHANNEL, I SAY!
ALL WATER TURN HOT!
SO WHY WERE YOU JUST STANDING HERE WATCHING?!
BOMP
BUT DOWN THERE IS VERY DANGEROUS.
WHAT WAS THAT ABOUT GIVING OUR LIVES?!
MA'AM CAN. GUIDE HAS WIFE AND CHILD.
GRR GRR GRR
THE HOT WATER...
IT'S NOT COMING OUT!!
NNNNN NNNNN
WHAT'S WRONG?
COULD SOMETHING BE STUCK...?

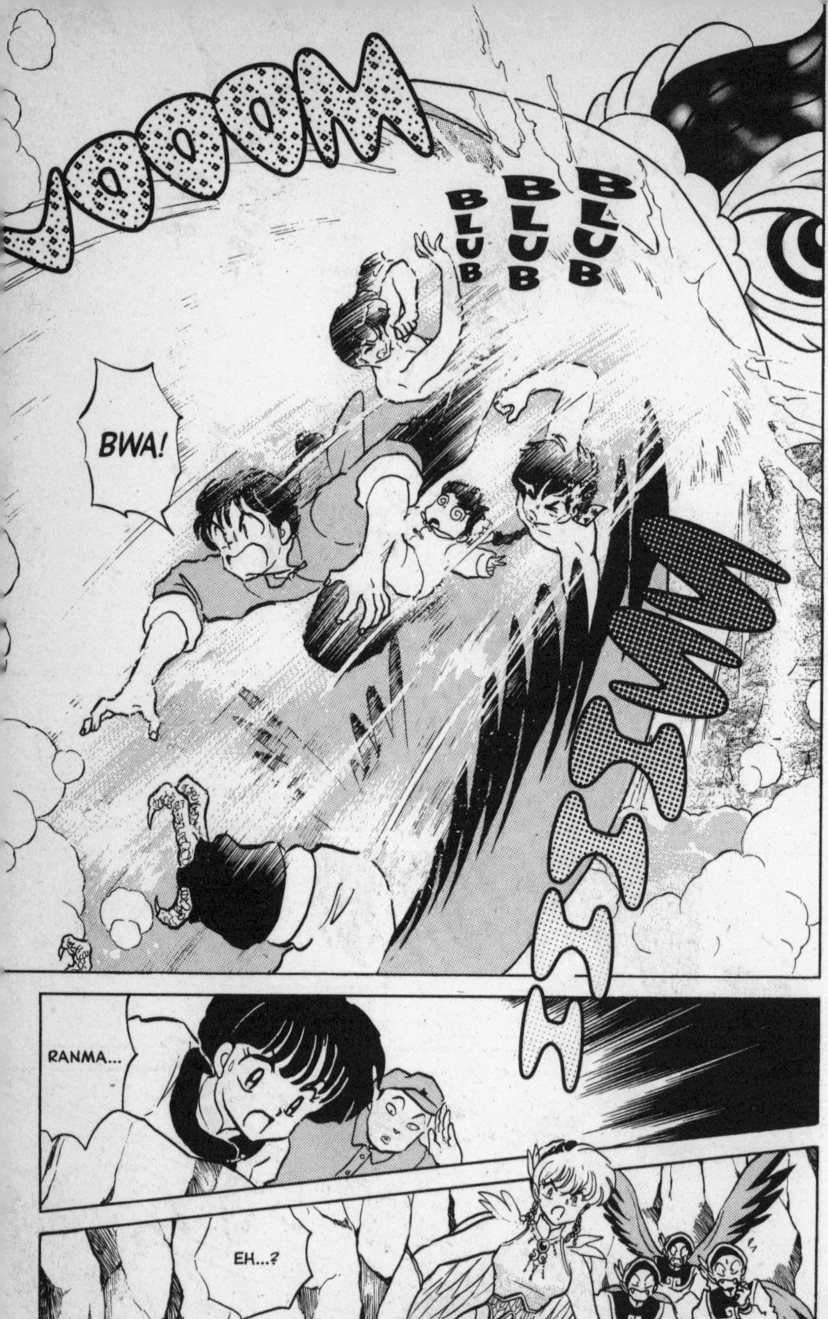
VOOOM
BLUB BLUB BLUB
BWA!
RANMA...
EH...?

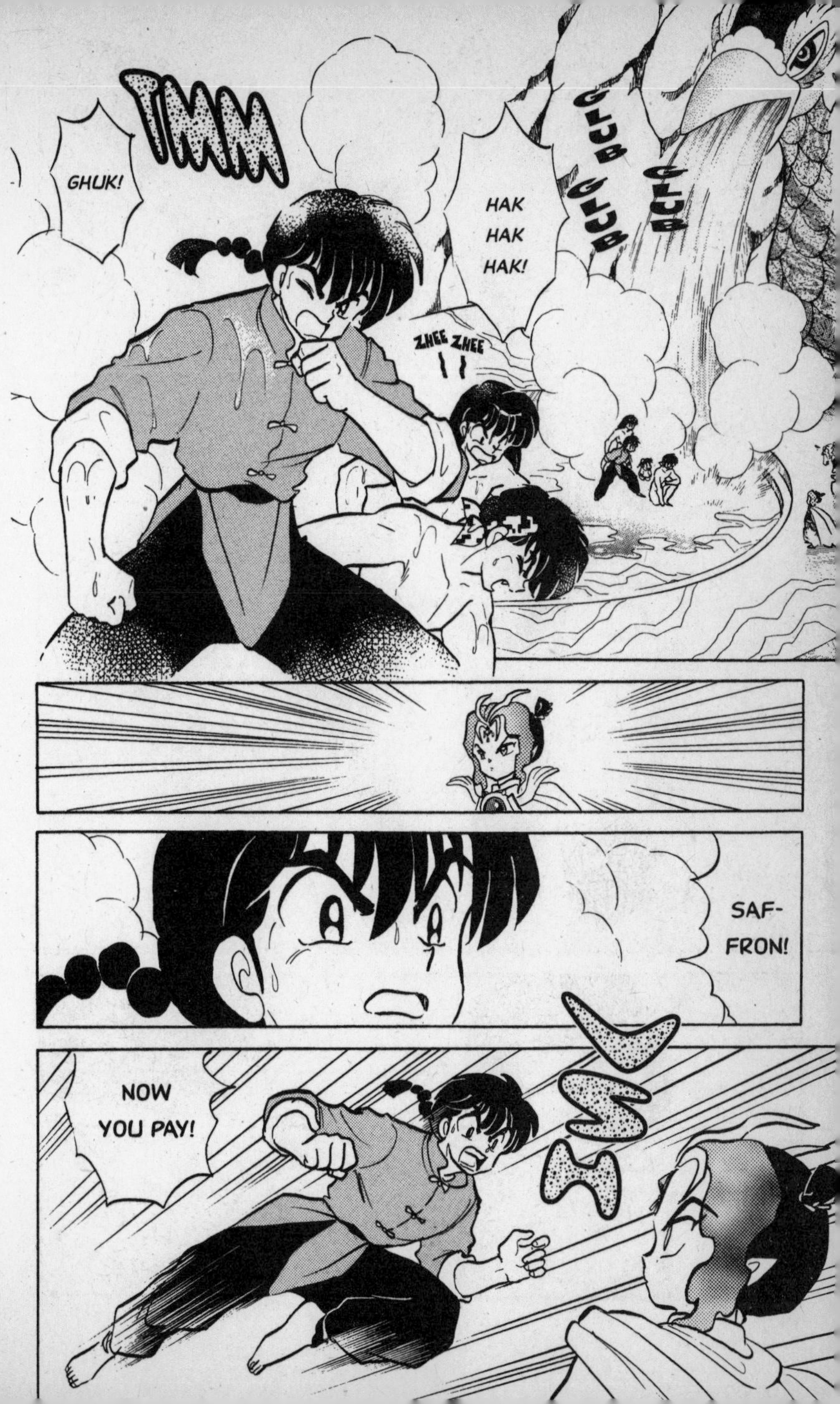
GHUK!
TMMM
HAK HAK HAK!
ZHEE ZHEE
GLUB GLUB
GLUB GLUB
SAF-FRON!
NOW YOU PAY!

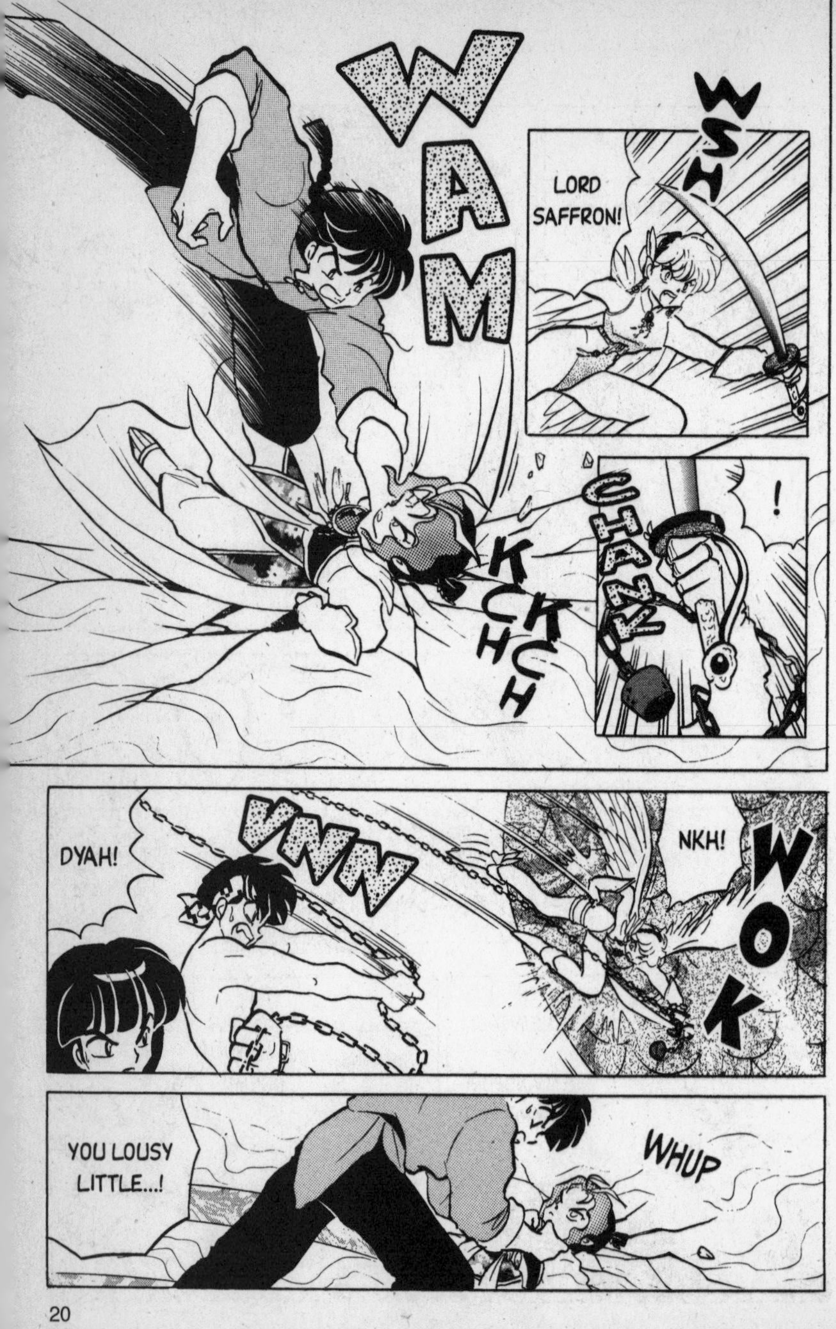
WAM
KACHH
KACHH
WSH
LORD SAFFRON!
CHANK
!
DYAH!
VNN
NKH!
WOK
YOU LOUSY LITTLE...!
WHUP

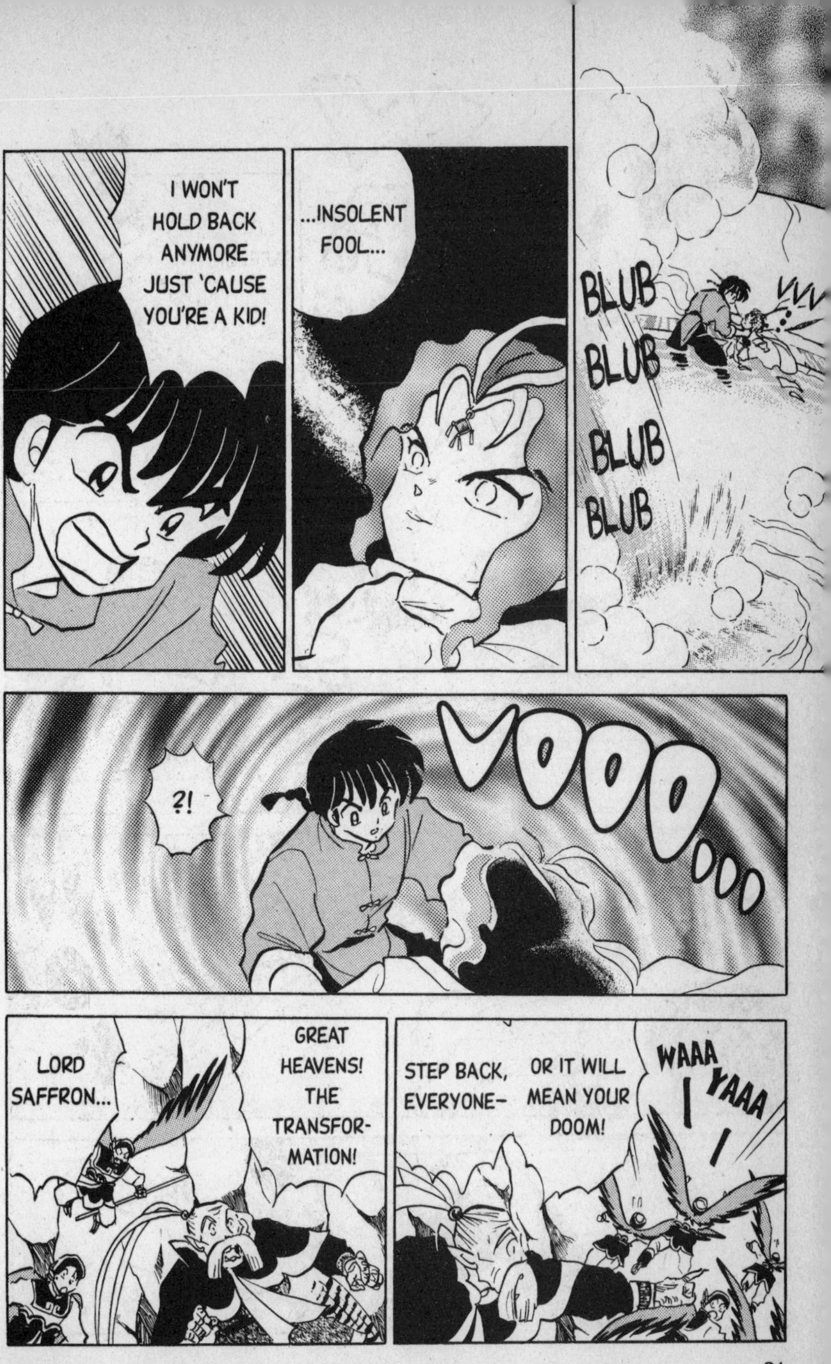
I WON'T HOLD BACK ANYMORE JUST 'CAUSE YOU'RE A KID!
...INSOLENT FOOL...
BLUB BLUB BLUB BLUB
?!
VOOO...OOO
LORD SAFFRON...
GREAT HEAVENS! THE TRANSFORMATION!
STEP BACK, EVERYONE—
OR IT WILL MEAN YOUR DOOM!
WAAA YAAA

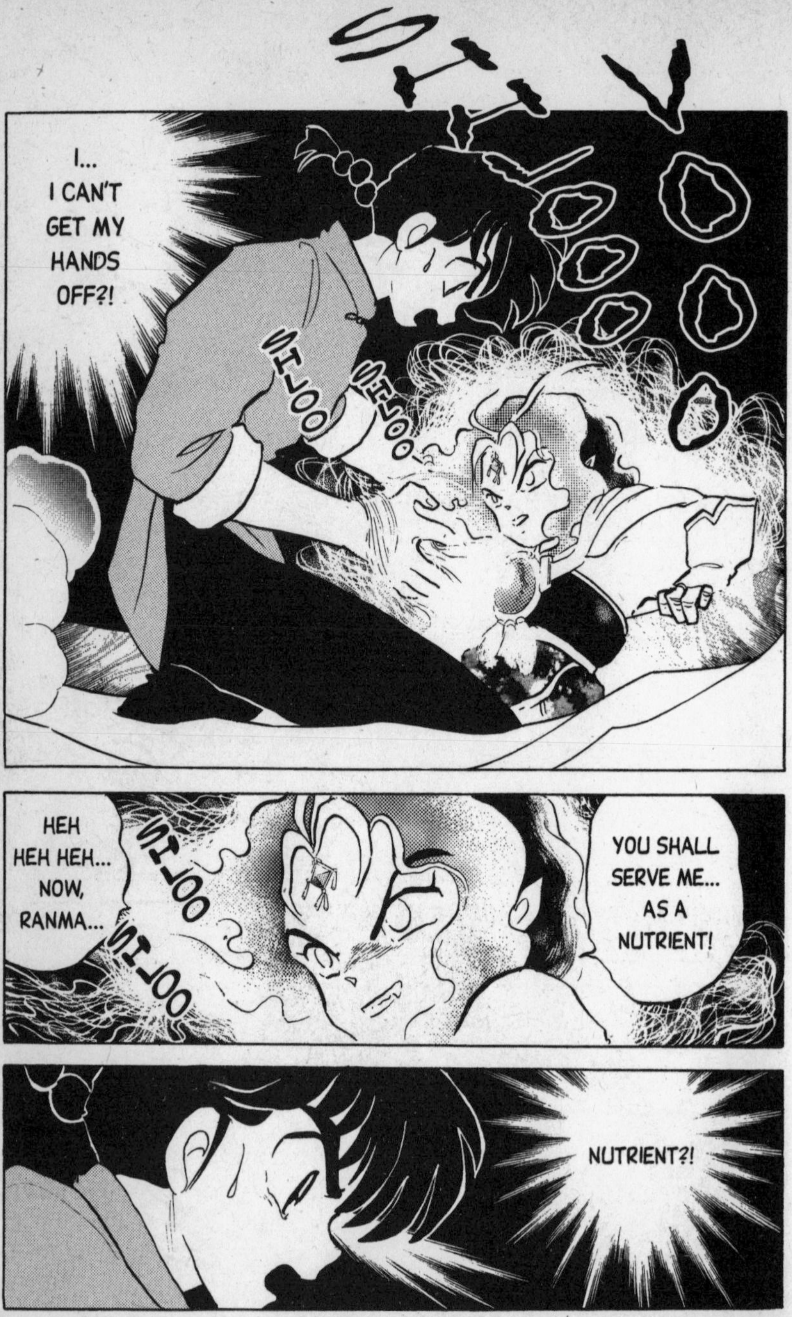
I... I CAN'T GET MY HANDS OFF?!
SHLOO
SHLOO
HEH HEH HEH... NOW, RANMA...
SHLOO
SHLOO
YOU SHALL SERVE ME... AS A NUTRIENT!
NUTRIENT?!

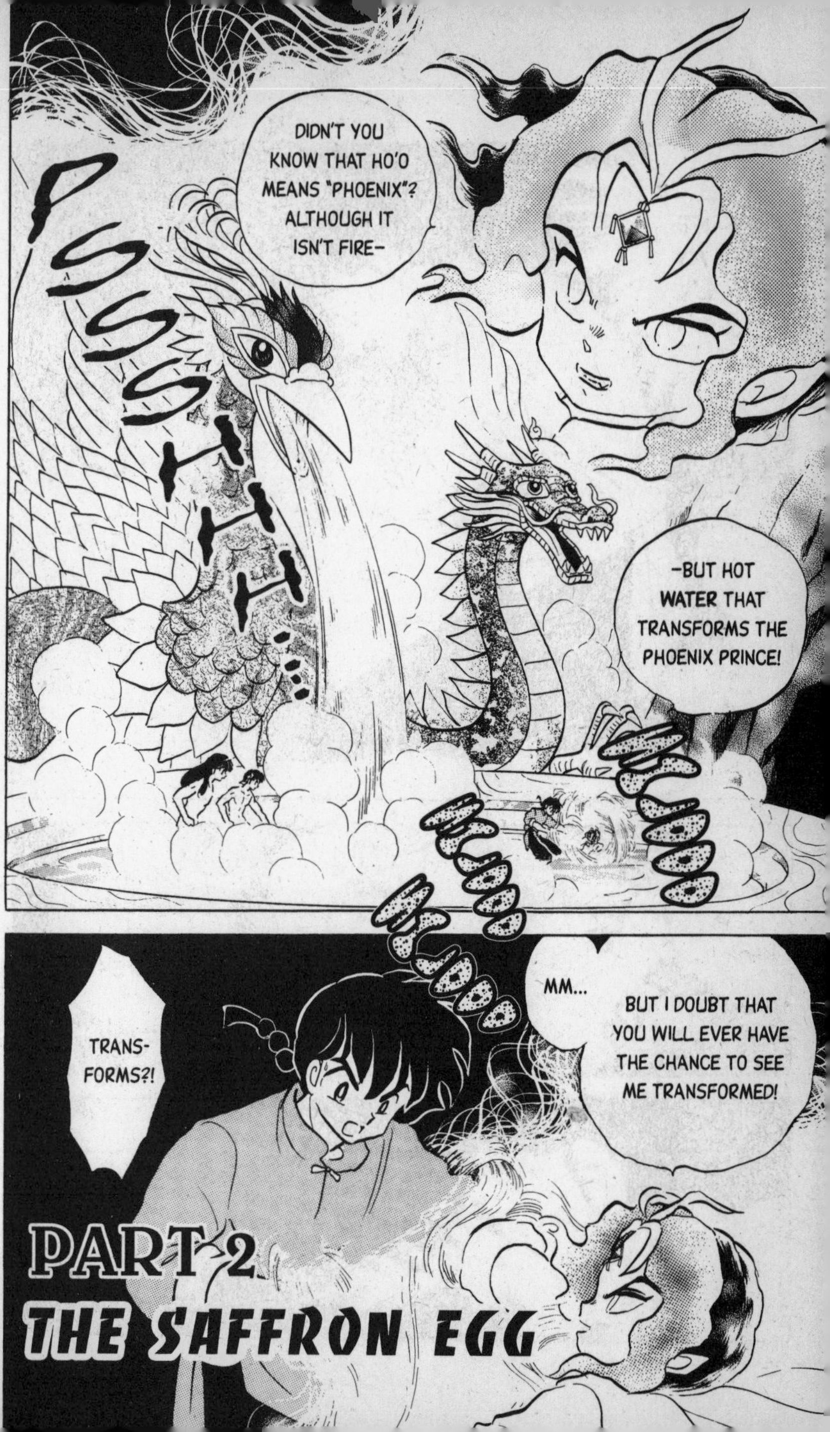
DIDN'T YOU KNOW THAT HO'O MEANS "PHOENIX"? ALTHOUGH IT ISN'T FIRE-
PSSSHHH...
-BUT HOT WATER THAT TRANSFORMS THE PHOENIX PRINCE!
WHOOO
WHOOO
WHOOO
TRANS-FORMS?!
MM...
BUT I DOUBT THAT YOU WILL EVER HAVE THE CHANCE TO SEE ME TRANSFORMED!
PART 2
THE SAFFRON EGG

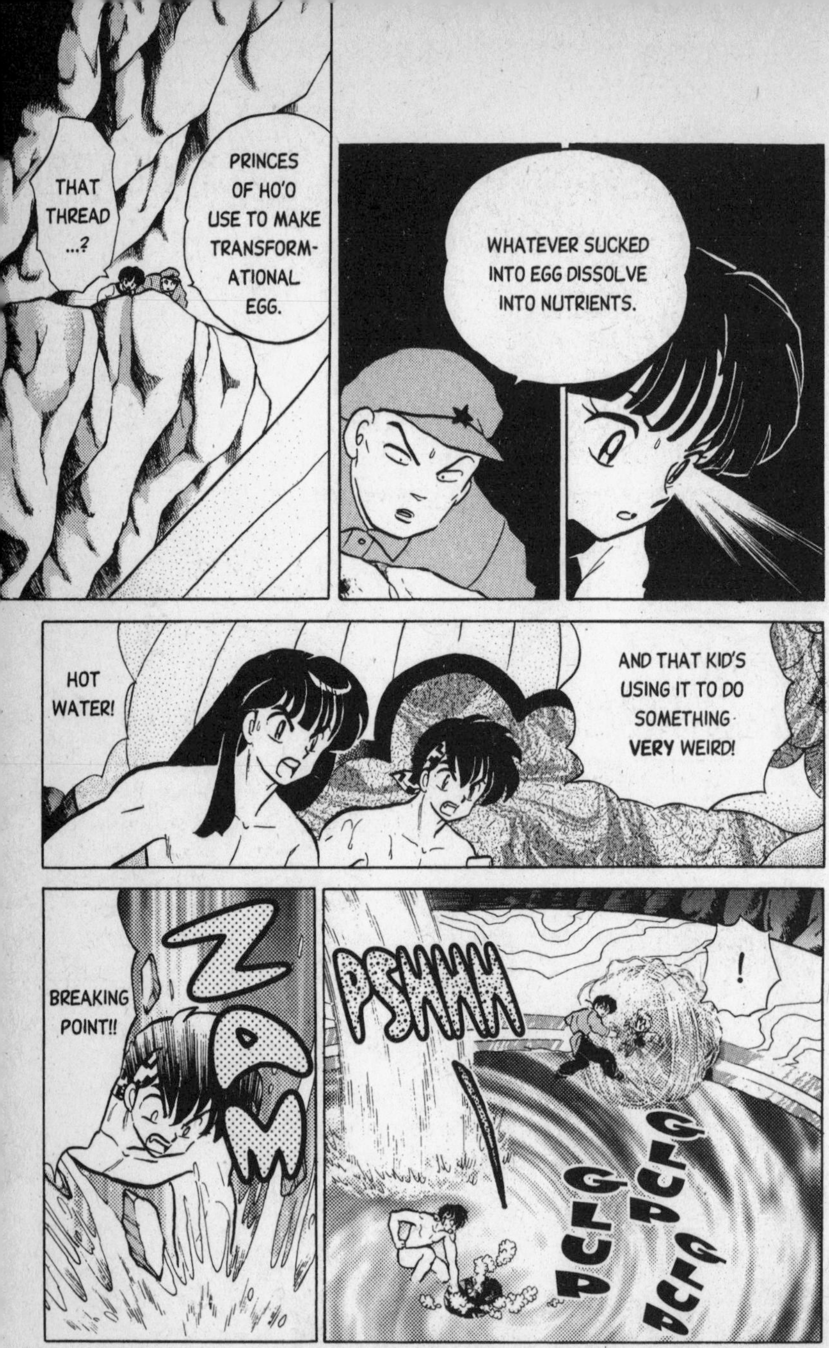
THAT THREAD ...?
PRINCES OF HO'O USE TO MAKE TRANSFORM-ATIONAL EGG.
WHATEVER SUCKED INTO EGG DISSOLVE INTO NUTRIENTS.
HOT WATER!
AND THAT KID'S USING IT TO DO SOMETHING VERY WEIRD!
BREAKING POINT!!
PSHHH
!
GLUP GLUP
GLUP GLUP

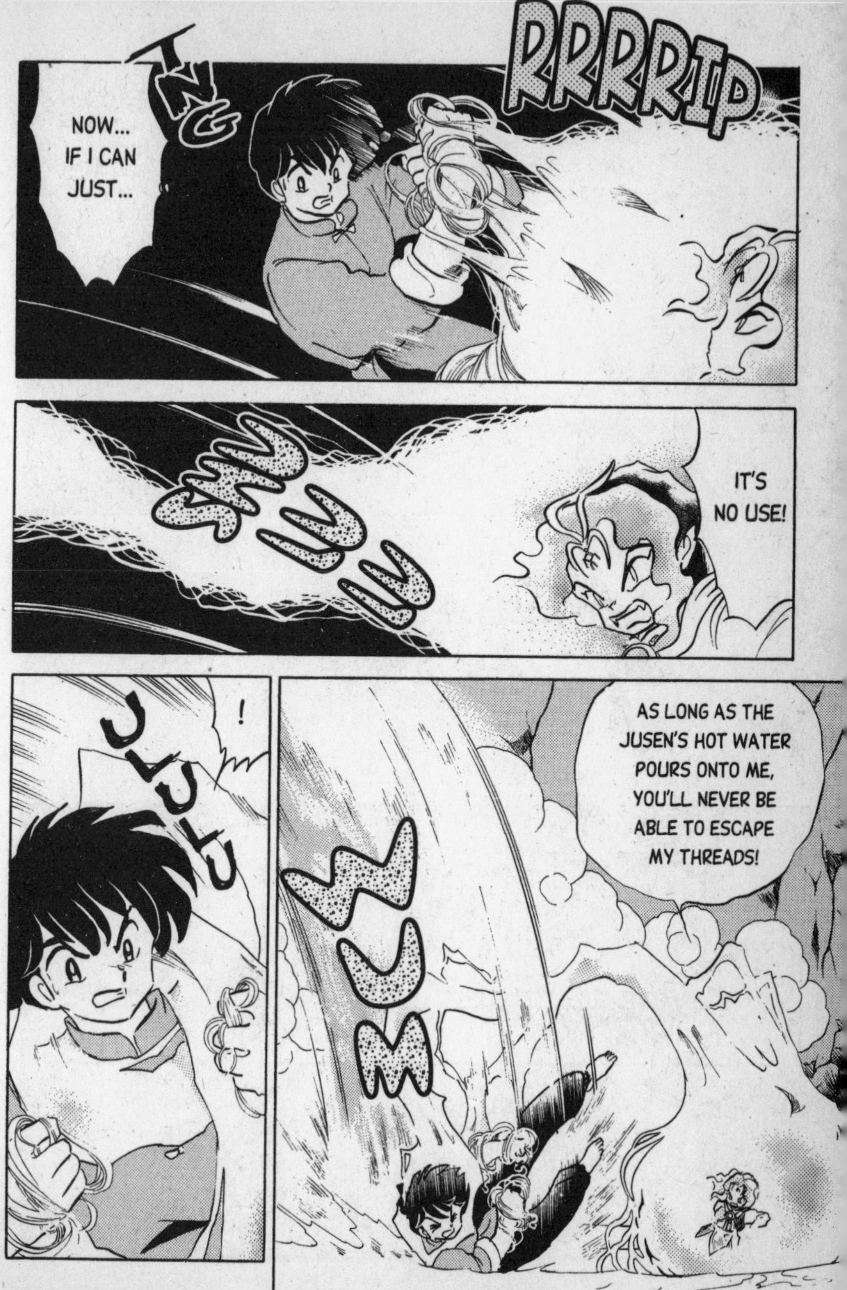

NOW... IF I CAN JUST...
TNG
RRRRIP
SWISH
IT'S NO USE!
JUTU
!
AS LONG AS THE JUSEN'S HOT WATER POURS ONTO ME, YOU'LL NEVER BE ABLE TO ESCAPE MY THREADS!
WUM

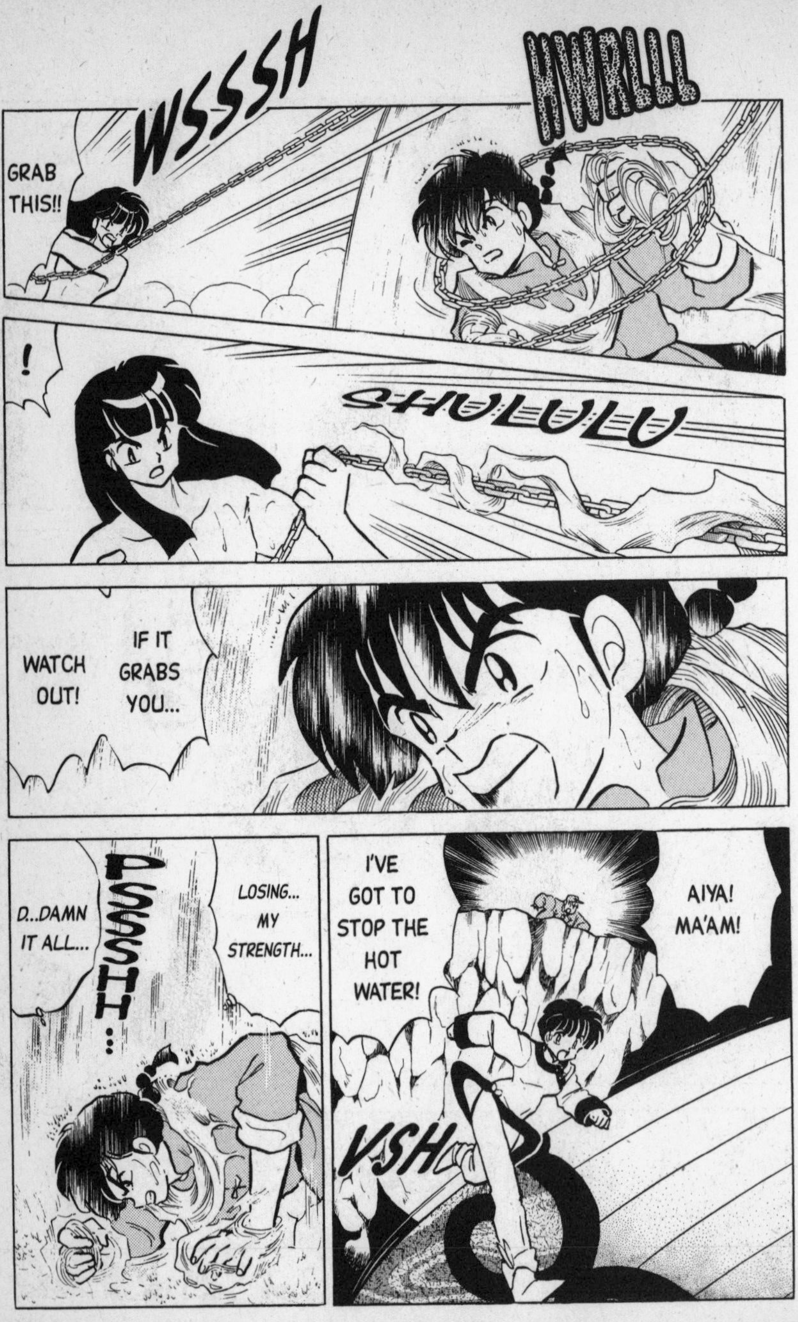
WSSSH
HWRLLL
GRAB THIS!!
!
SHULULU
WATCH OUT!
IF IT GRABS YOU...
D...DAMN IT ALL...
PSSSHH...
LOSING... MY STRENGTH...
I'VE GOT TO STOP THE HOT WATER!
AIYA! MA'AM!
VSH

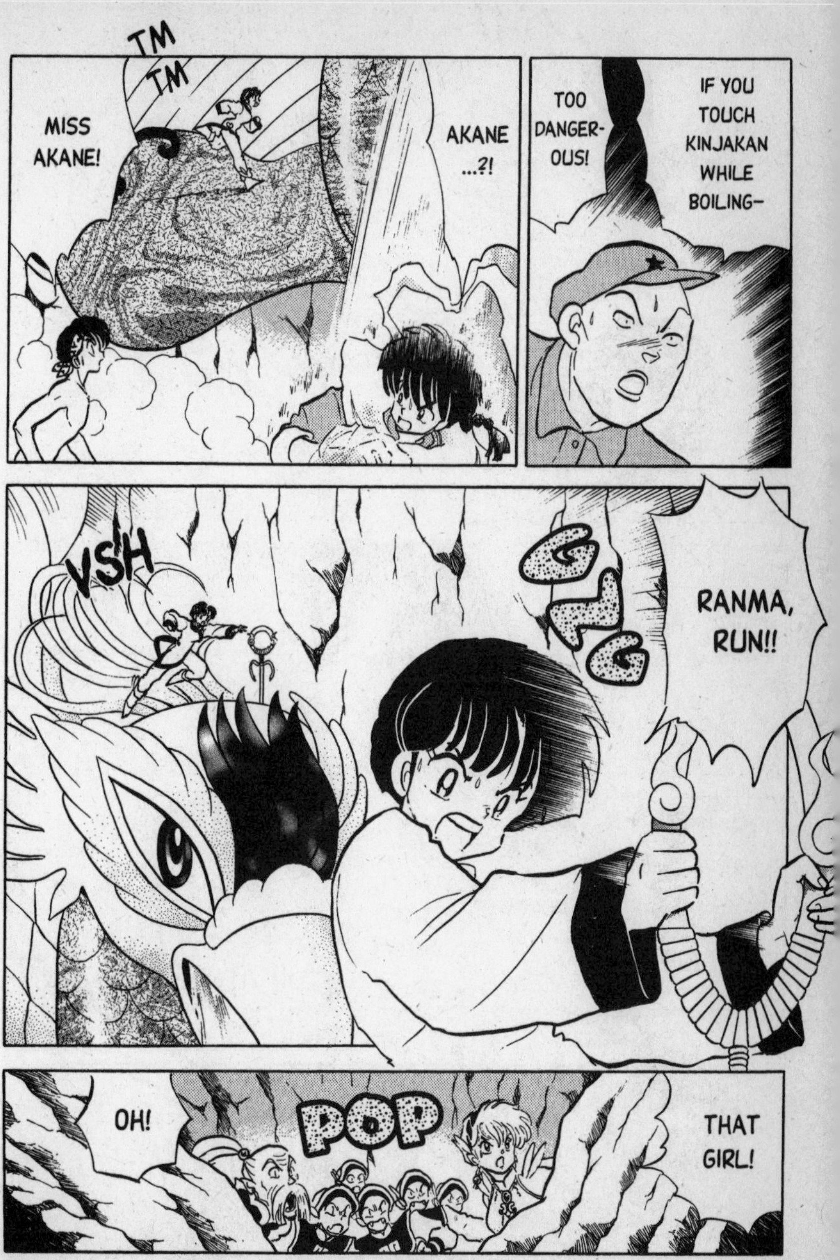
TM
TM
MISS AKANE!
AKANE ...?!
TOO DANGER-OUS!
IF YOU TOUCH KINJAKAN WHILE BOILING—
VSH
GYG
RANMA, RUN!!
OH!
POP
THAT GIRL!

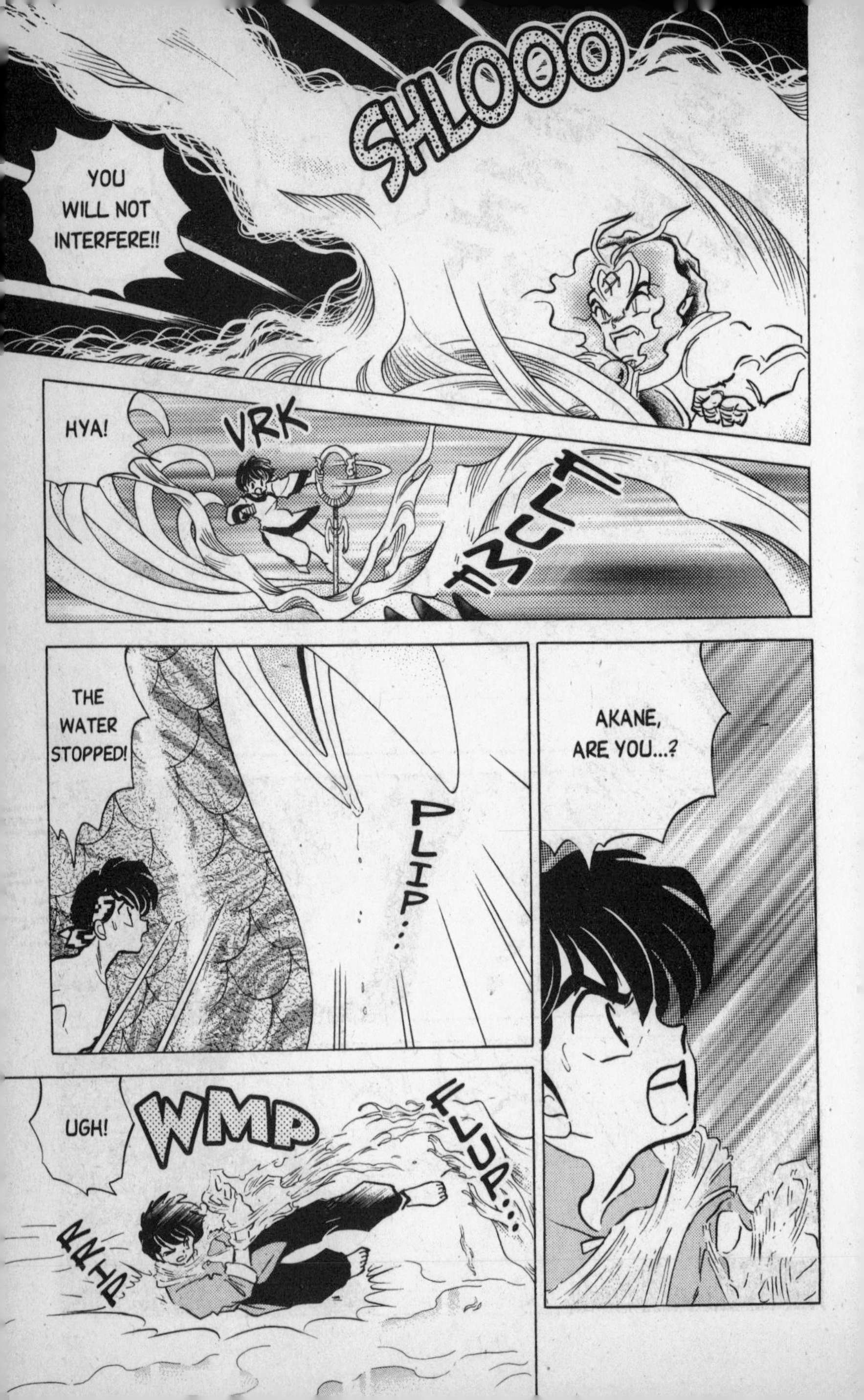
SHLOOO
YOU WILL NOT INTERFERE!!
HYA!
VRK
FLUMF
THE WATER STOPPED!
PLIP...
AKANE, ARE YOU...?
UGH!
WMP
FLUUP...
THRR

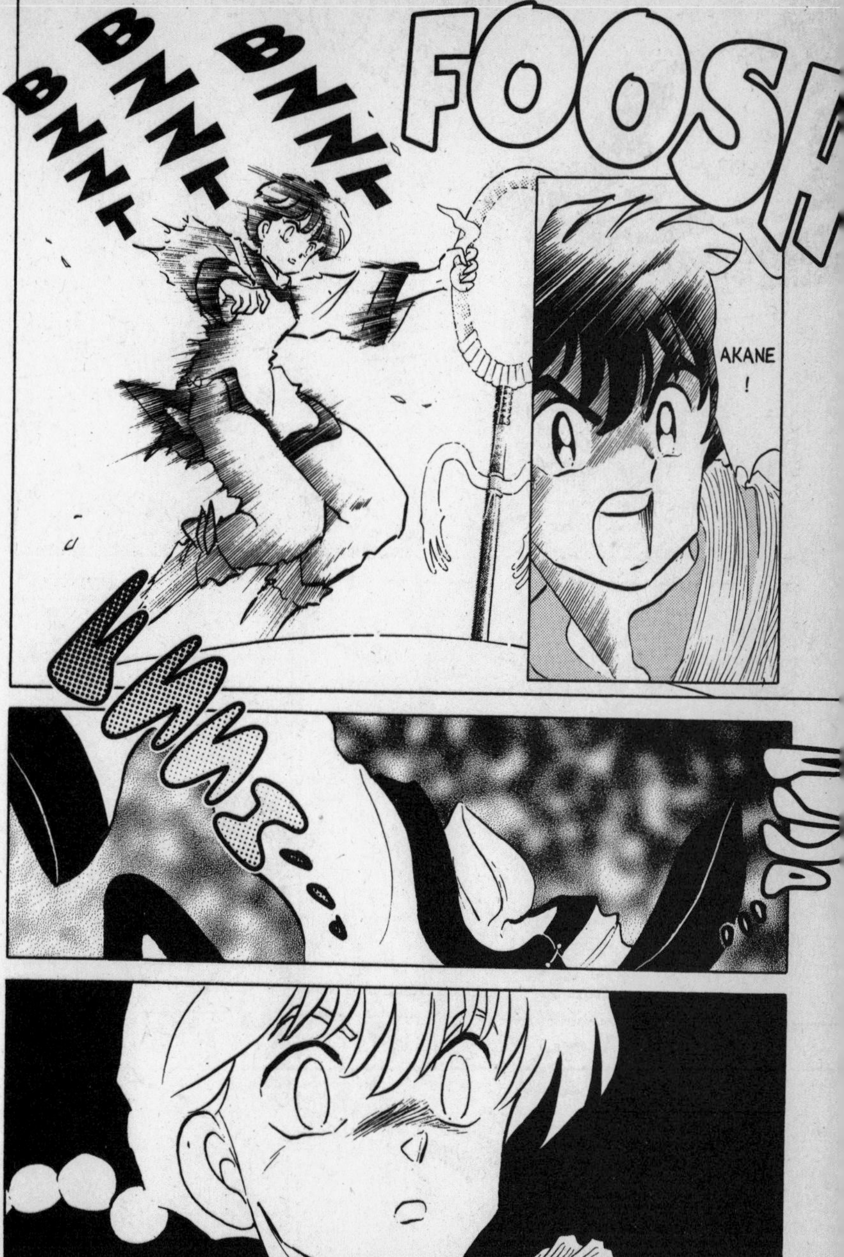
BZZT
BZZT
BZZT
FOOSH
AKANE !

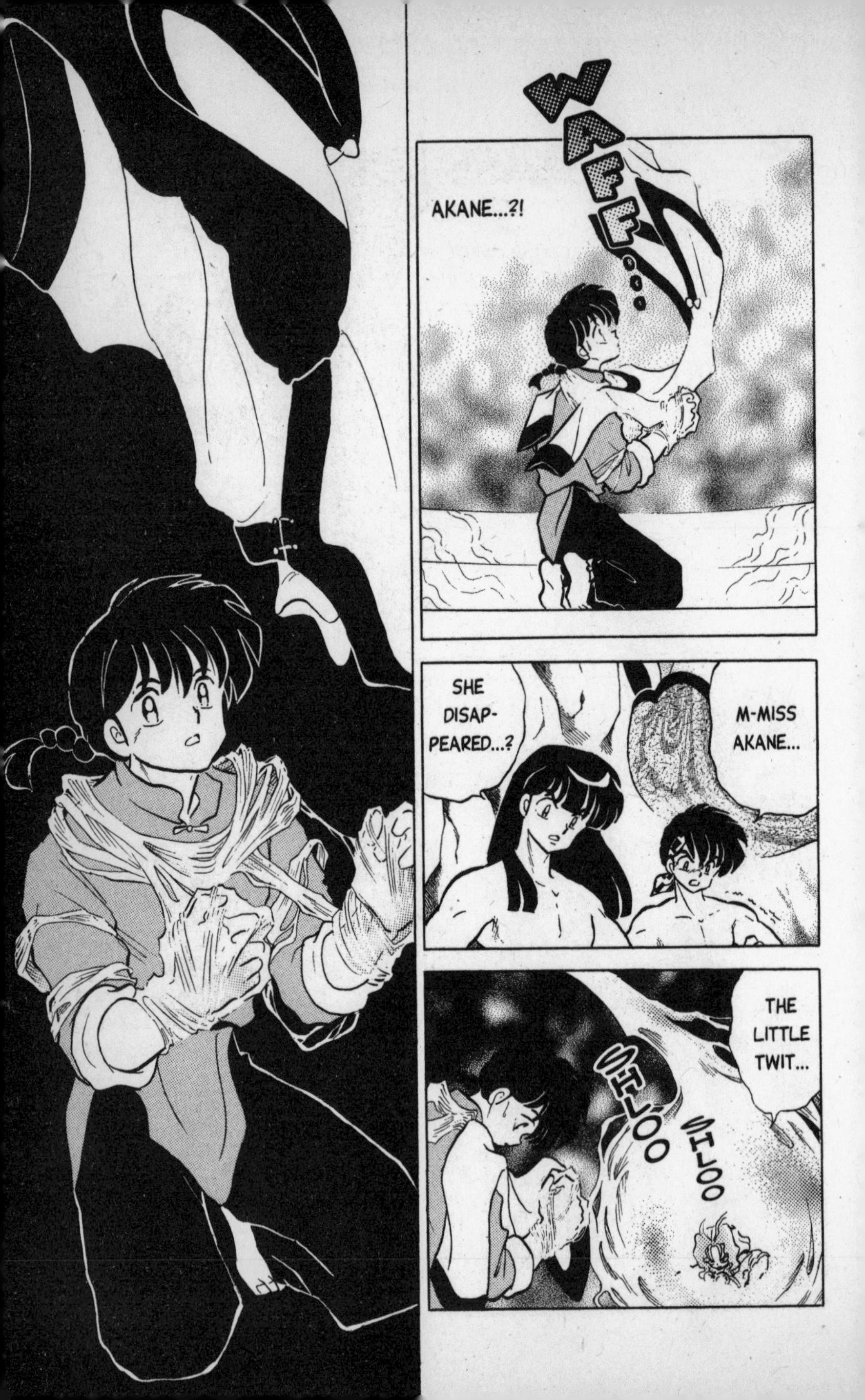

WAFF...
AKANE...?!
SHE DISAP-PEARED...?
M-MISS AKANE...
THE LITTLE TWIT...
SHLOO
SHLOO

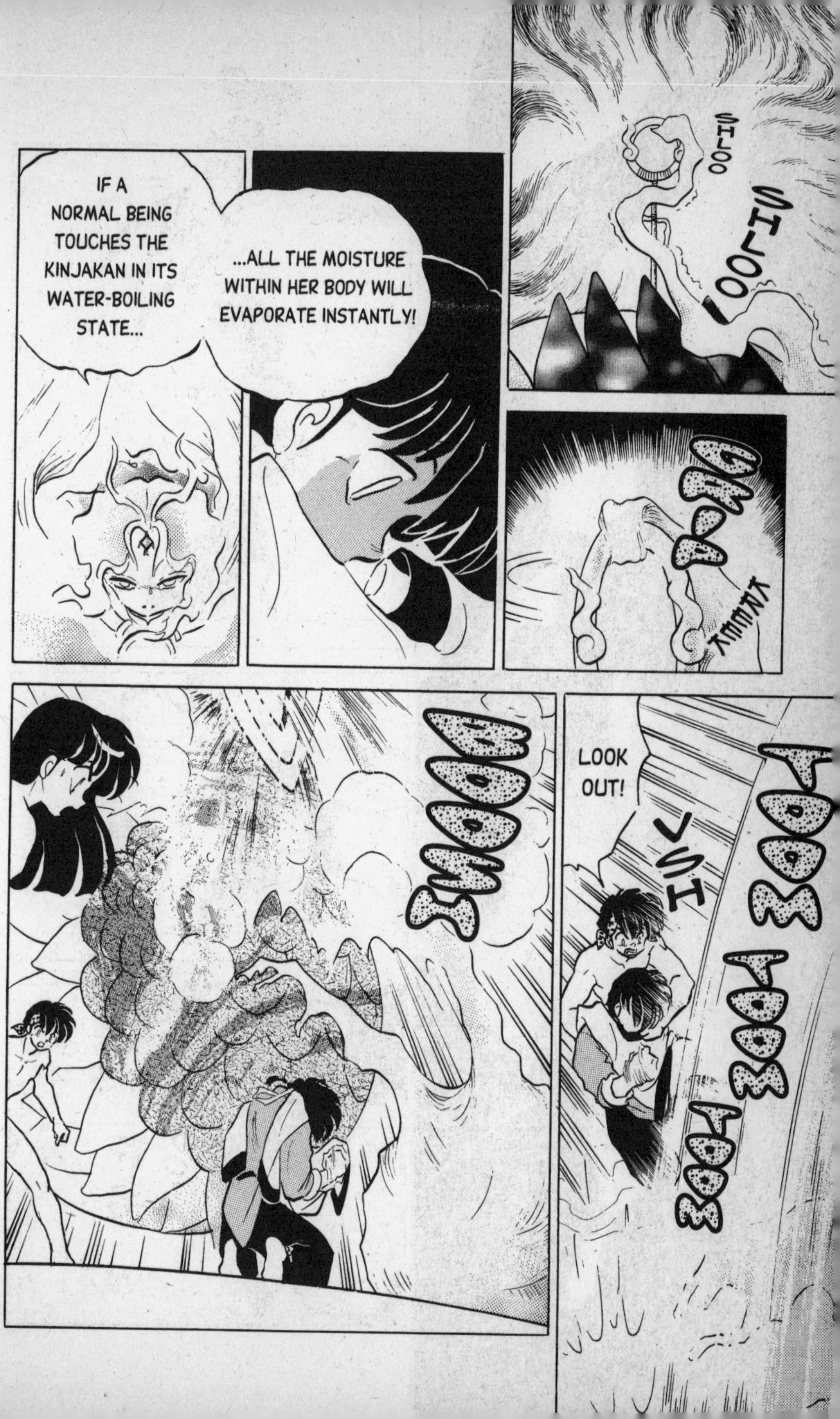
IF A NORMAL BEING TOUCHES THE KINJAKAN IN ITS WATER-BOILING STATE...
...ALL THE MOISTURE WITHIN HER BODY WILL EVAPORATE INSTANTLY!
SHLOO
SHLOO
BOOM!
LOOK OUT!

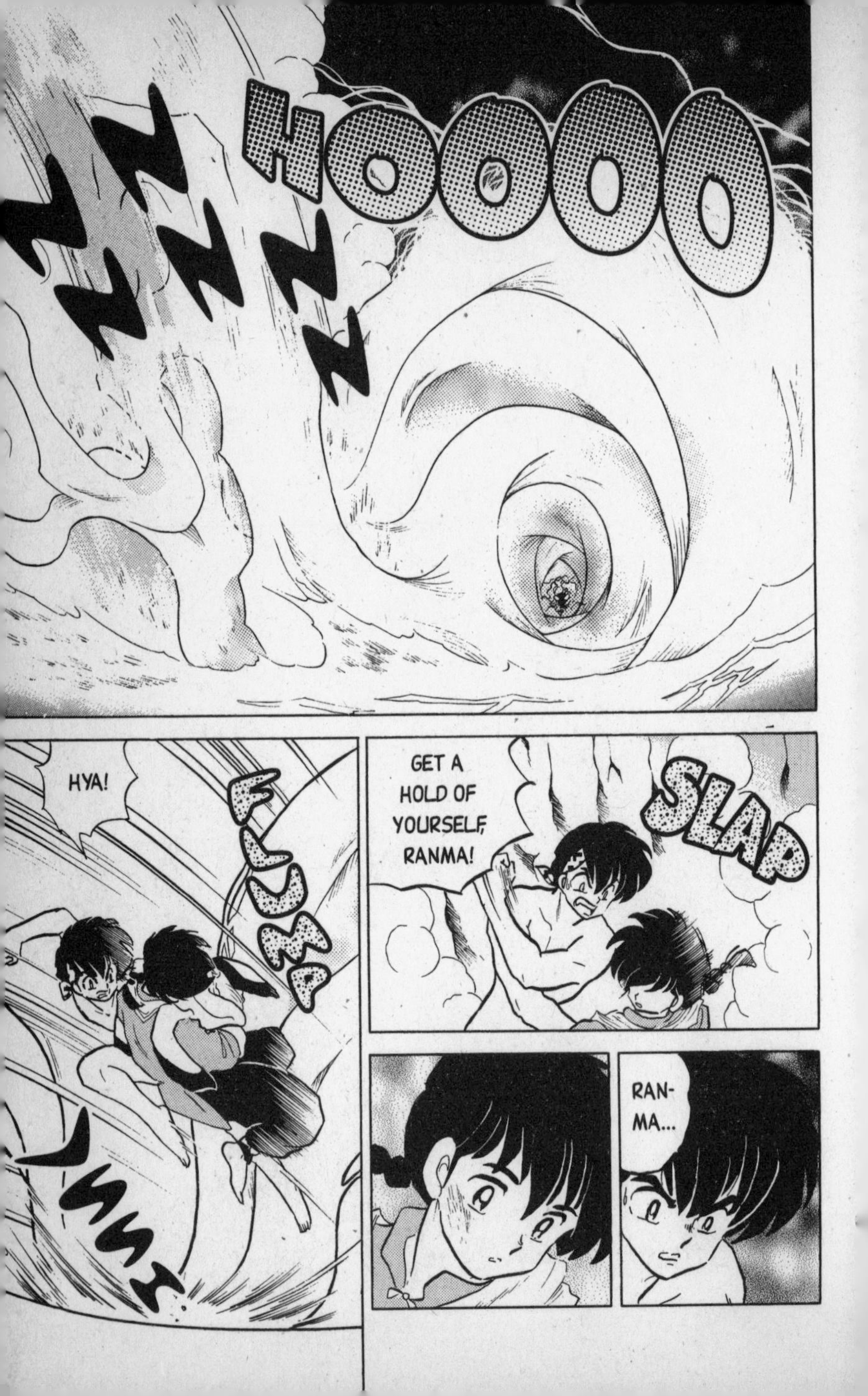
HOOOOO
HYA!
FLUMP
WM
GET A HOLD OF YOURSELF, RANMA!
SLAP
RAN-MA...

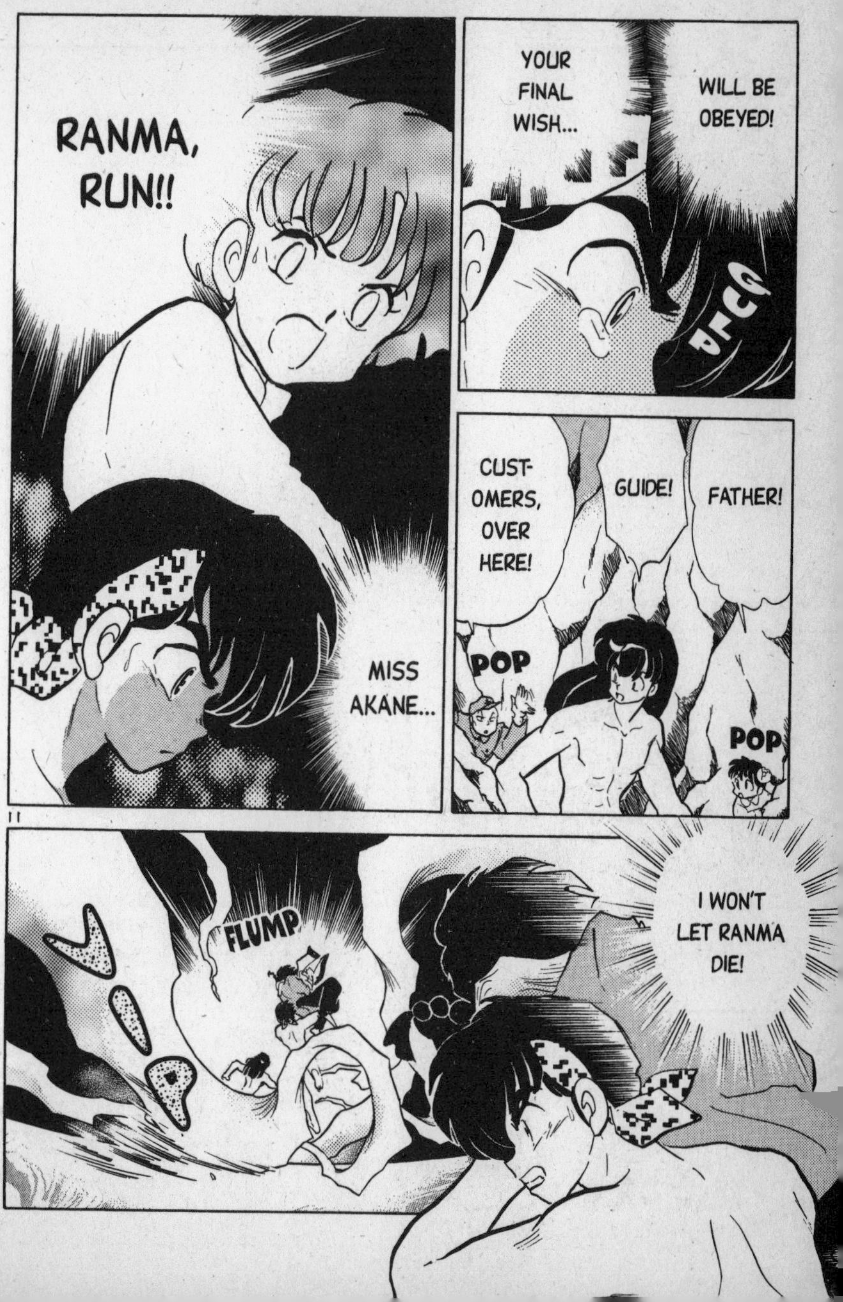
RANMA, RUN!!
MISS AKANE...
YOUR FINAL WISH...
WILL BE OBEYED!
GULP
CUST-OMERS, OVER HERE!
GUIDE!
FATHER!
POP
POP
FLUMP
I WON'T LET RANMA DIE!

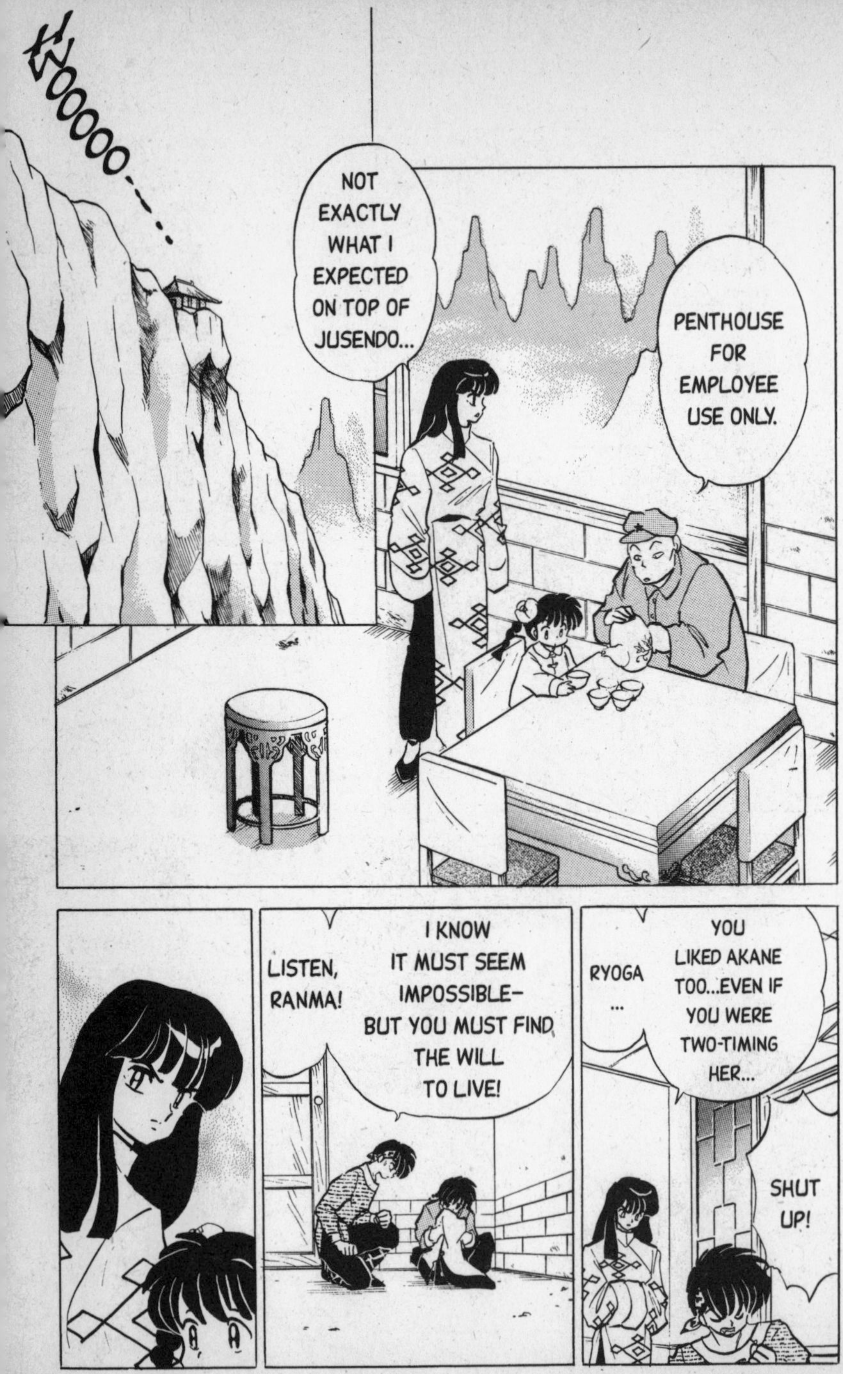

WOOOOO...
NOT EXACTLY WHAT I EXPECTED ON TOP OF JUSENDO...
PENTHOUSE FOR EMPLOYEE USE ONLY.
LISTEN, RANMA!
I KNOW IT MUST SEEM IMPOSSIBLE-- BUT YOU MUST FIND THE WILL TO LIVE!
RYOGA...
YOU LIKED AKANE TOO...EVEN IF YOU WERE TWO-TIMING HER...
SHUT UP!

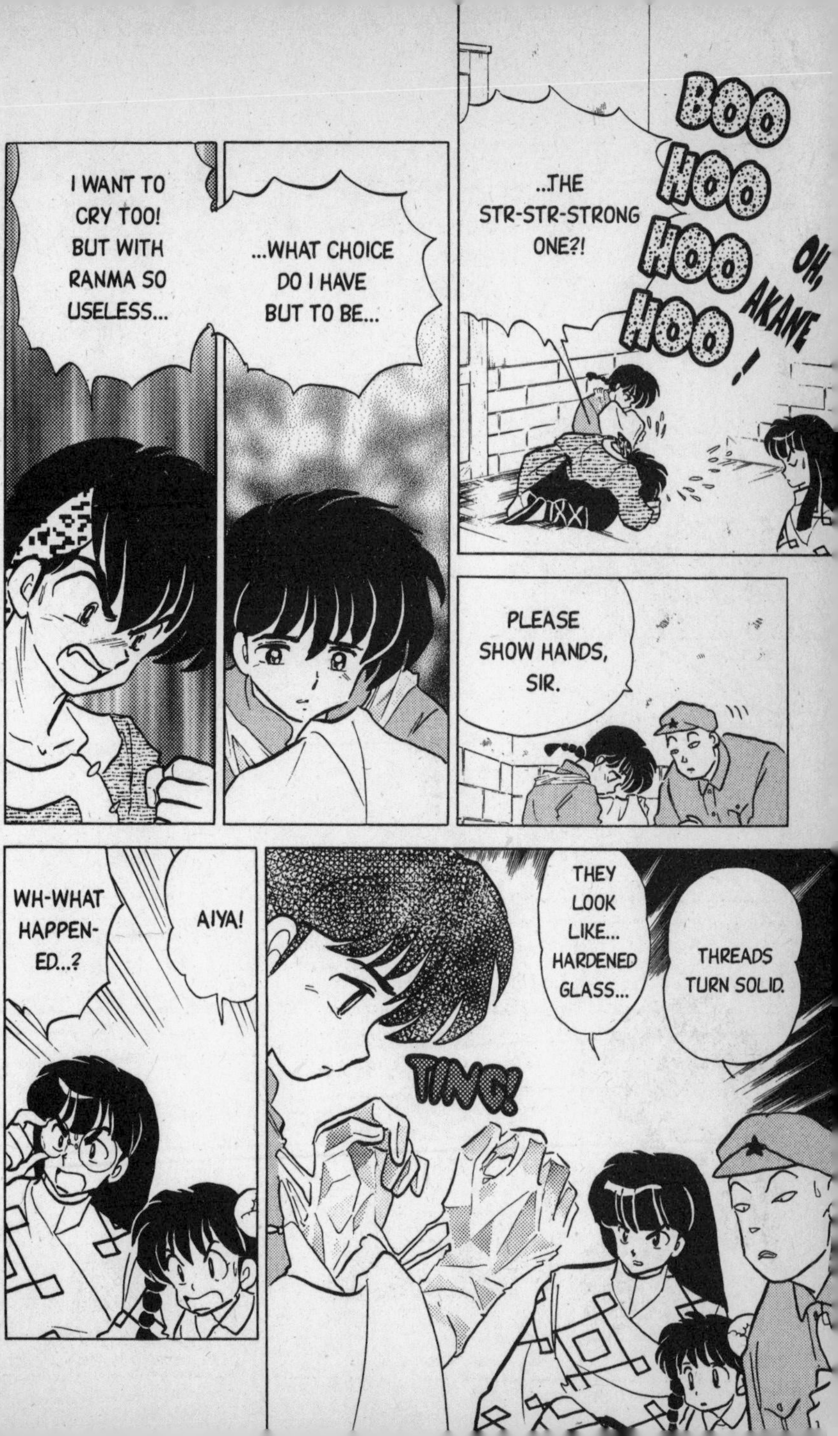
I WANT TO CRY TOO! BUT WITH RANMA SO USELESS...
...WHAT CHOICE DO I HAVE BUT TO BE...
...THE STR-STR-STRONG ONE?!
BOO HOO HOO HOO
OH, AKANE!
PLEASE SHOW HANDS, SIR.
WH-WHAT HAPPEN-ED...?
AIYA!
THEY LOOK LIKE... HARDENED GLASS...
THREADS TURN SOLID.
TING!

SIR IS LUCKY FOR FROZEN HANDS.

WITH GOOD GRIP, SIR WOULD BE NUTRIENT NOW.

G...

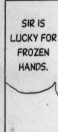

FSH

PWIK

GIVE THAT BACK!

WSH

AIYA!

KWOOMP

KLONG

TUNK TUNK TUNK

OHH...

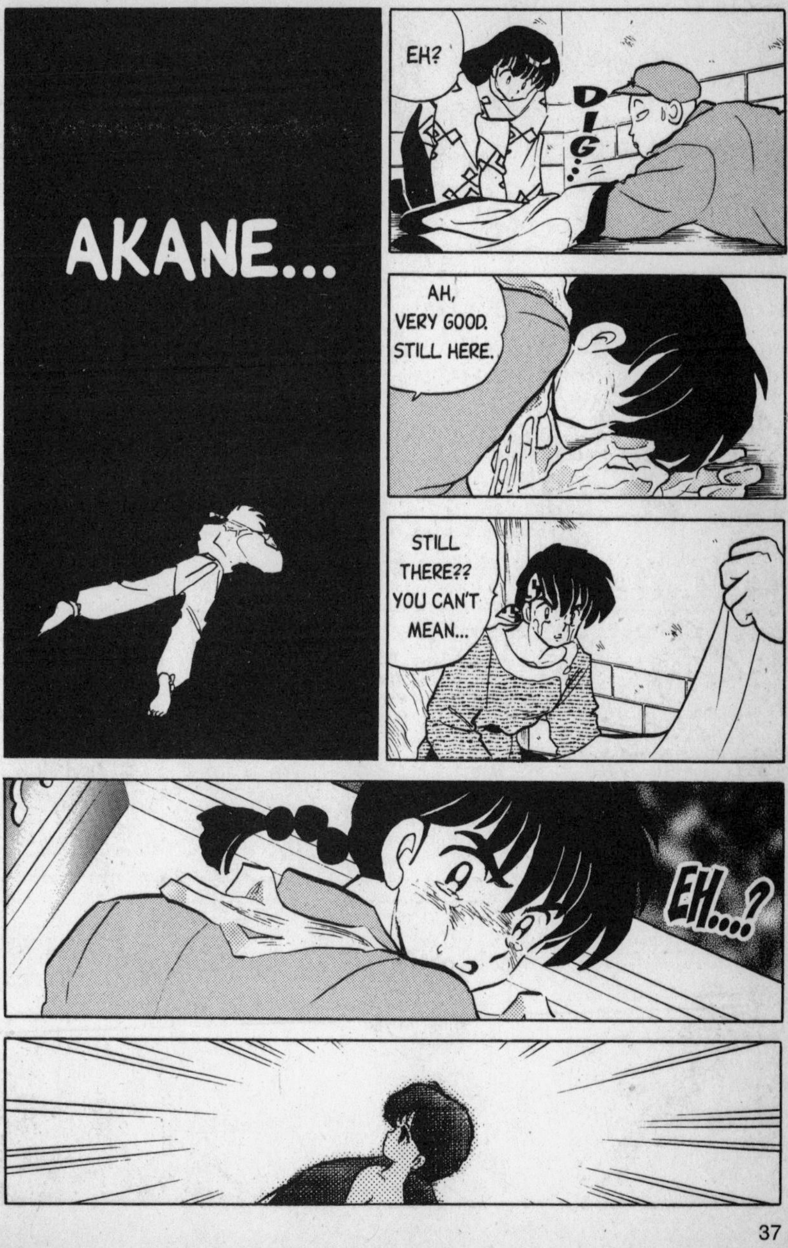
AKANE...
EH?
DIG...
AH, VERY GOOD. STILL HERE.
STILL THERE?? YOU CAN'T MEAN...
EH...?

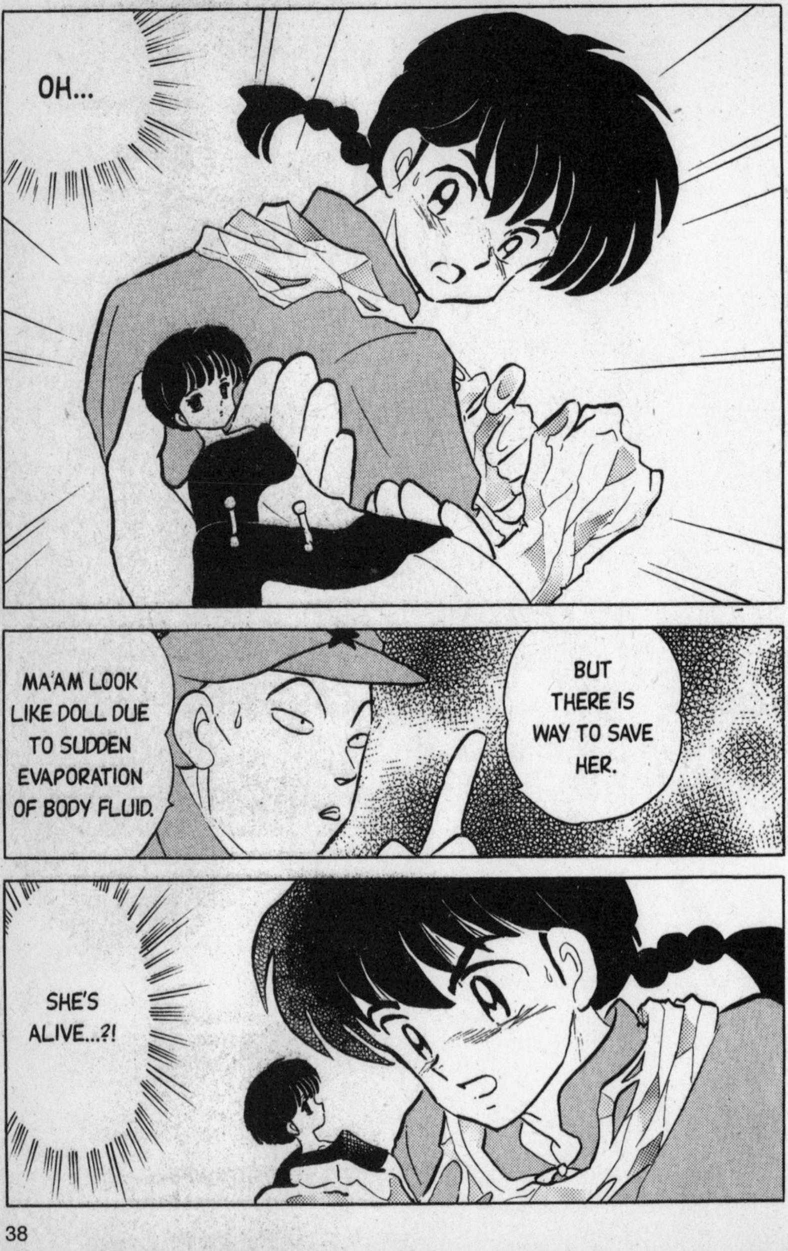
OH...
MA'AM LOOK LIKE DOLL DUE TO SUDDEN EVAPORATION OF BODY FLUID.
BUT THERE IS WAY TO SAVE HER.
SHE'S ALIVE...?!

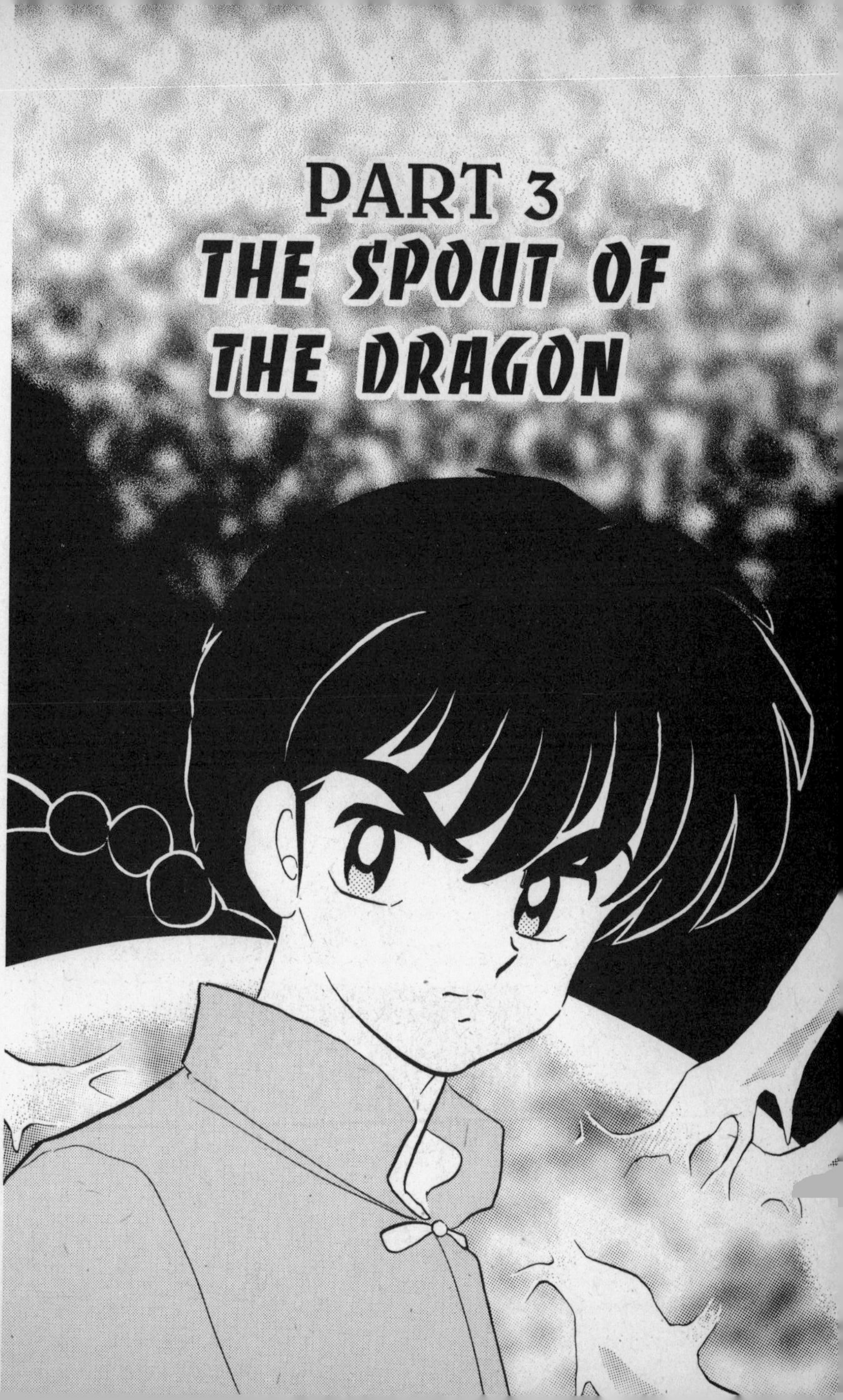
PART 3
THE SPOUT OF THE DRAGON

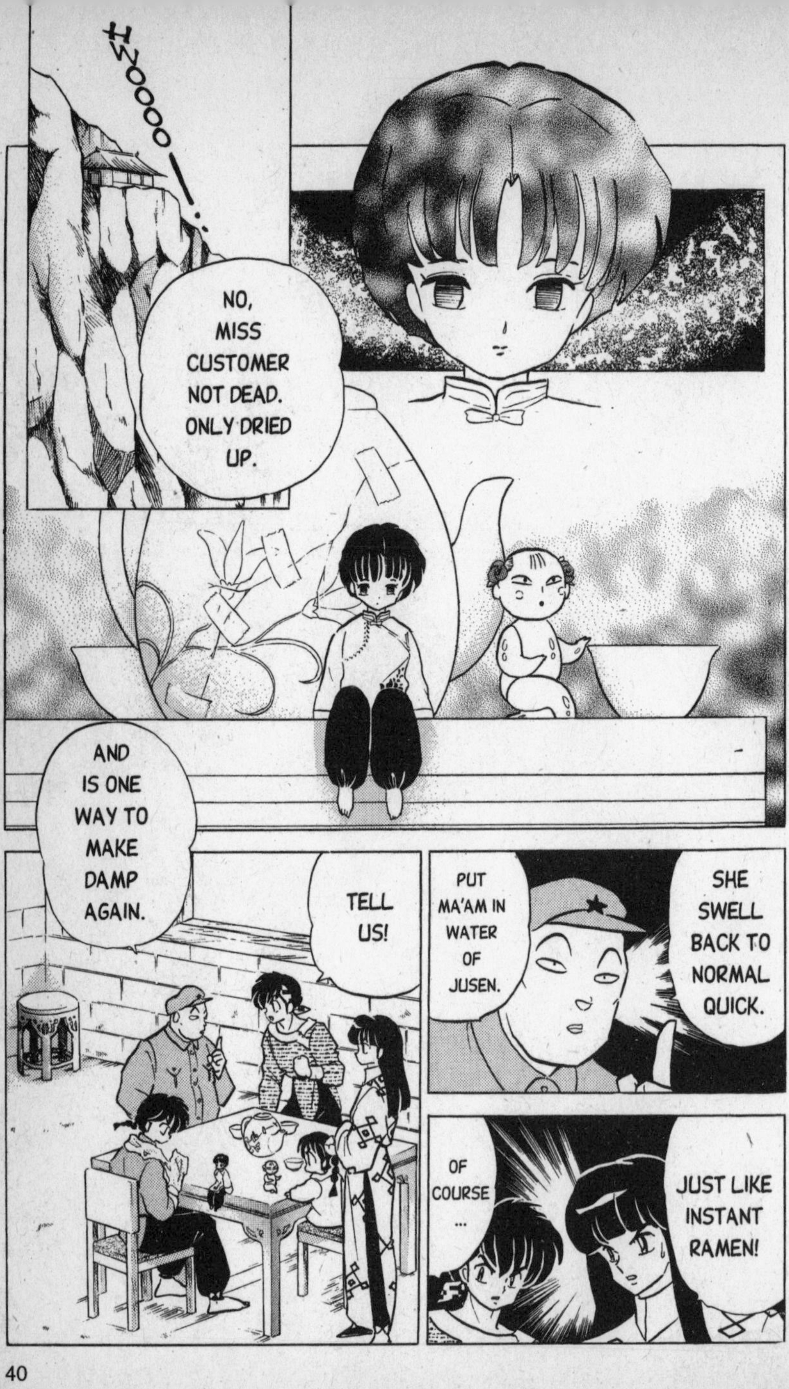
HWOOOO
NO, MISS CUSTOMER NOT DEAD. ONLY DRIED UP.
AND IS ONE WAY TO MAKE DAMP AGAIN.
TELL US!
PUT MA'AM IN WATER OF JUSEN.
SHE SWELL BACK TO NORMAL QUICK.
OF COURSE ...
JUST LIKE INSTANT RAMEN!

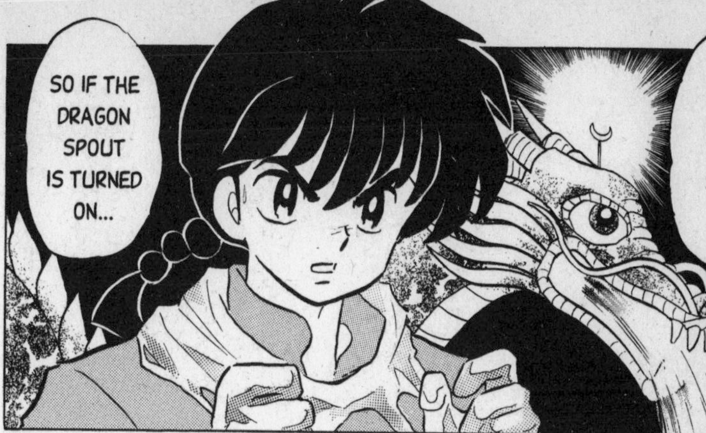
SO IF THE DRAGON SPOUT IS TURNED ON...
AKANE CAN BE SAVED?!

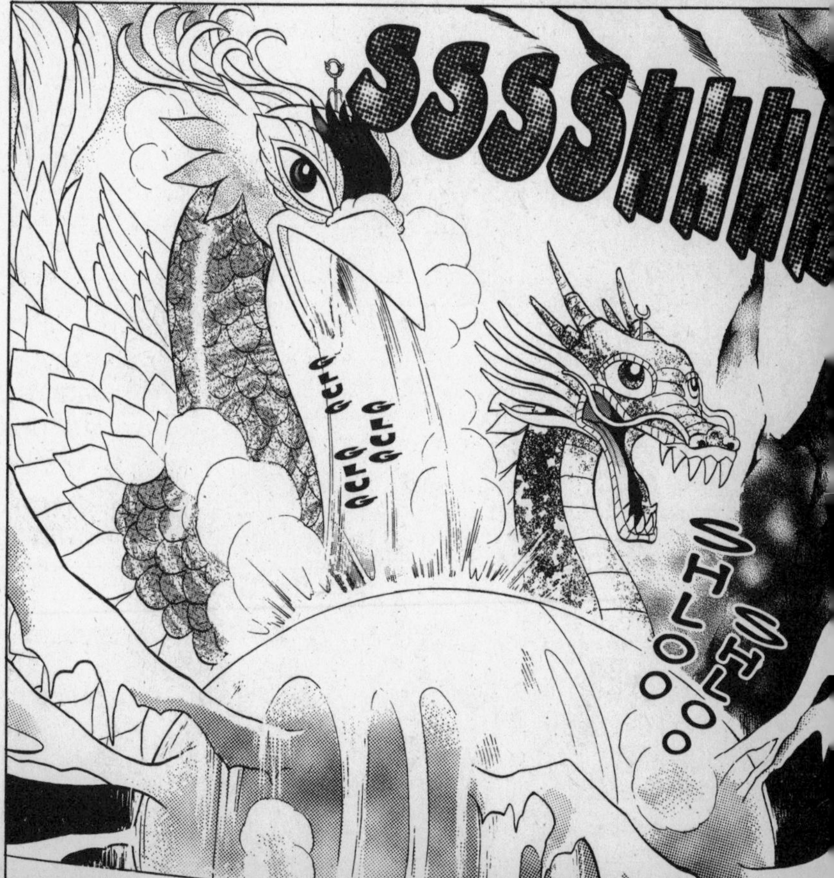
SSSSHHHH
GLUG GLUG
GLUG GLUG
SHLOOO
SHLOOO

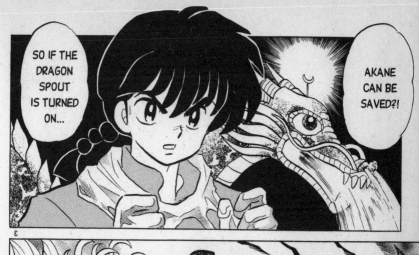

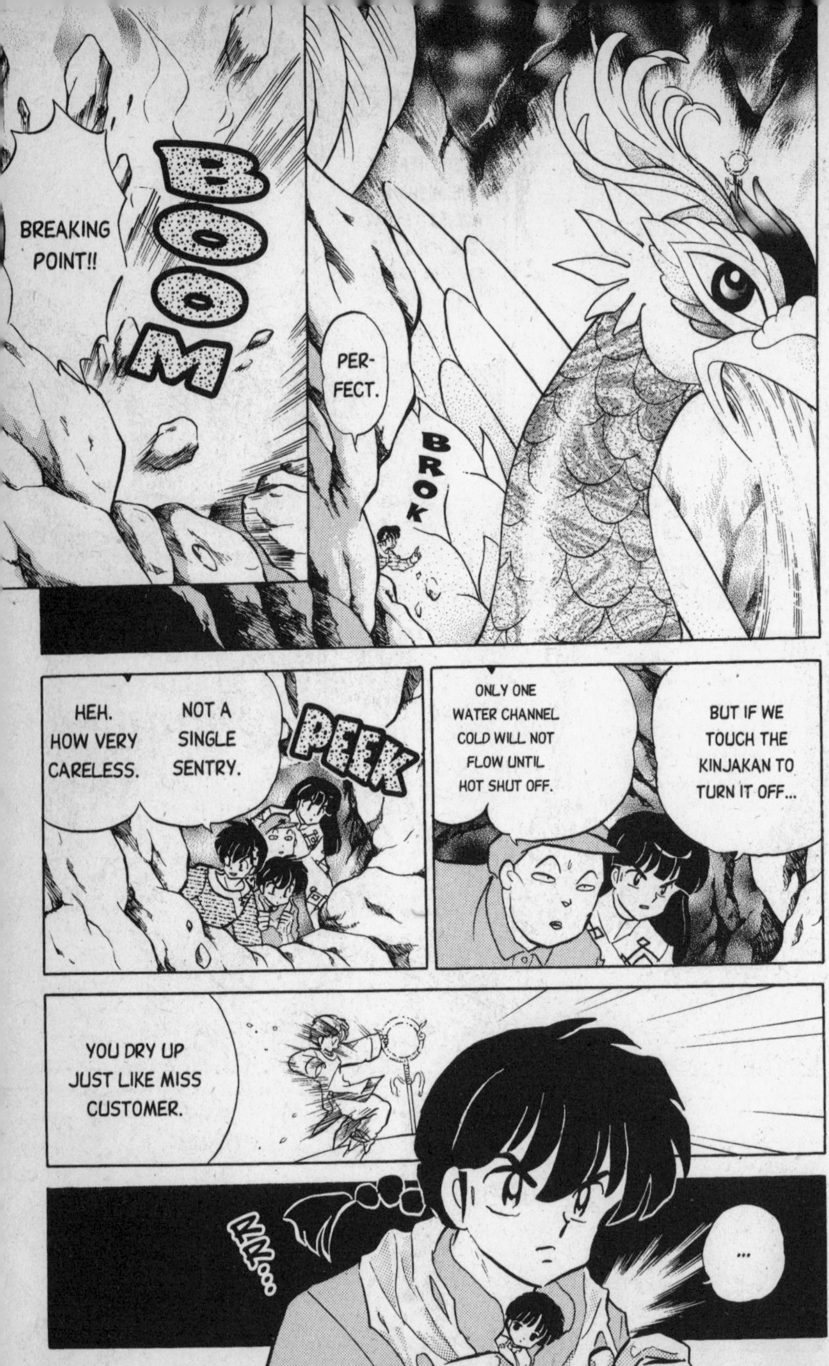
BOOM
BREAKING POINT!!
PER-FECT.
BROK
HEH. HOW VERY CARELESS.
NOT A SINGLE SENTRY.
PEEK
ONLY ONE WATER CHANNEL COLD WILL NOT FLOW UNTIL HOT SHUT OFF.
BUT IF WE TOUCH THE KINJAKAN TO TURN IT OFF...
YOU DRY UP JUST LIKE MISS CUSTOMER.
...

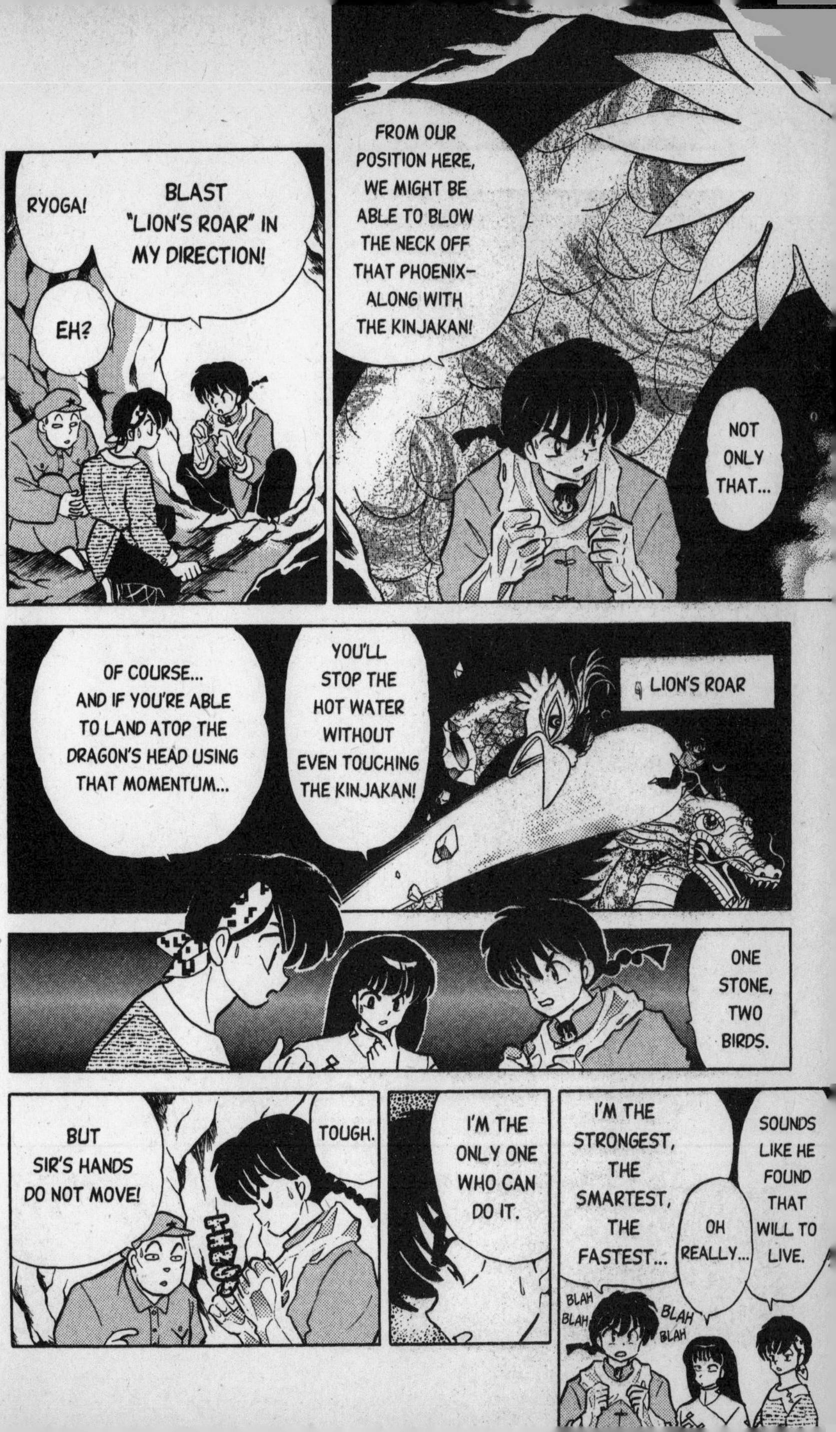
RYOGA!
BLAST "LION'S ROAR" IN MY DIRECTION!
EH?
FROM OUR POSITION HERE, WE MIGHT BE ABLE TO BLOW THE NECK OFF THAT PHOENIX-ALONG WITH THE KINJAKAN!
NOT ONLY THAT...
OF COURSE... AND IF YOU'RE ABLE TO LAND ATOP THE DRAGON'S HEAD USING THAT MOMENTUM...
YOU'LL STOP THE HOT WATER WITHOUT EVEN TOUCHING THE KINJAKAN!
LION'S ROAR
ONE STONE, TWO BIRDS.
BUT SIR'S HANDS DO NOT MOVE!
TOUGH.
I'M THE ONLY ONE WHO CAN DO IT.
I'M THE STRONGEST, THE SMARTEST, THE FASTEST...
OH REALLY...
SOUNDS LIKE HE FOUND THAT WILL TO LIVE.
BLAH BLAH
BLAH BLAH

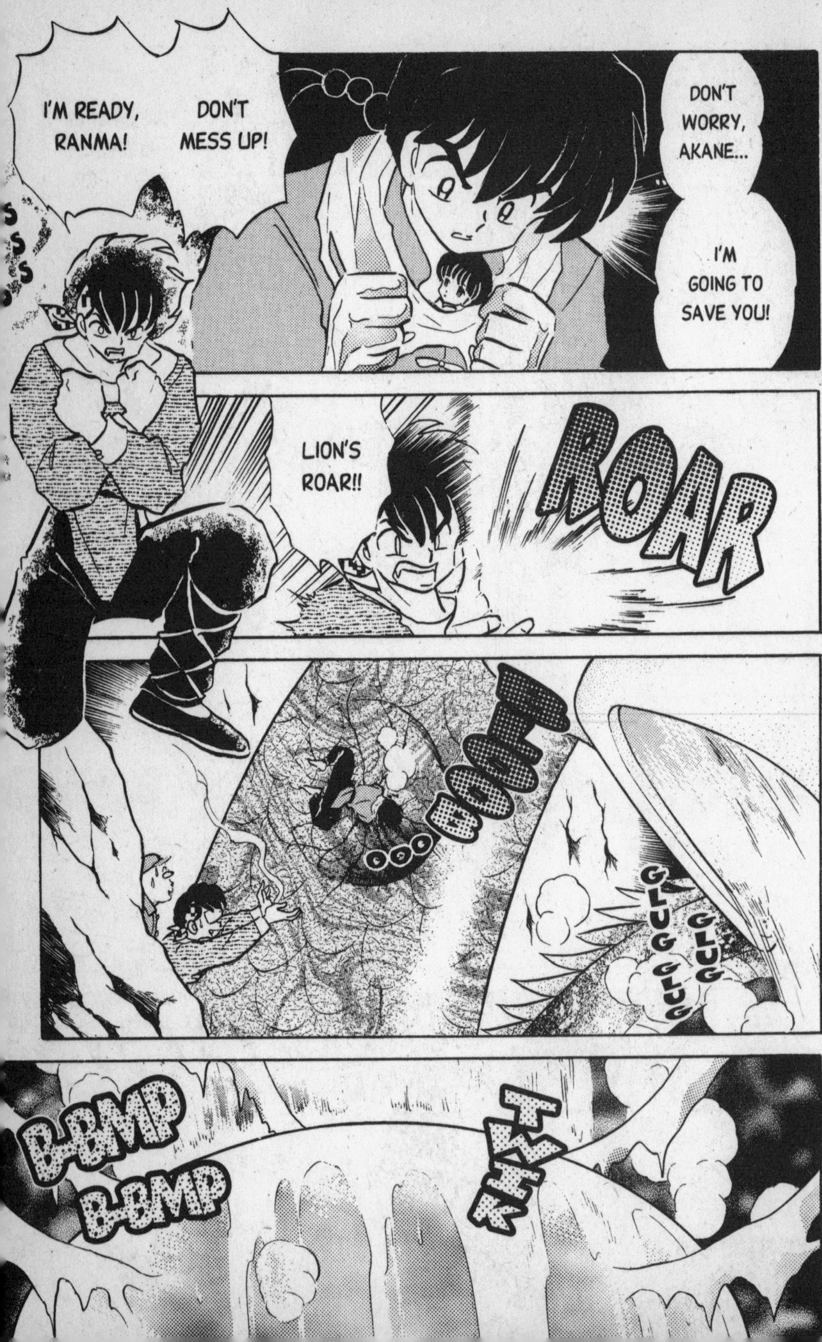
I'M READY, RANMA!
DON'T MESS UP!
SSS
DON'T WORRY, AKANE...
I'M GOING TO SAVE YOU!
LION'S ROAR!!
ROAR
...BOOM
GLUG GLUG GLUG GLUG
B-BMP B-BMP
TWIK

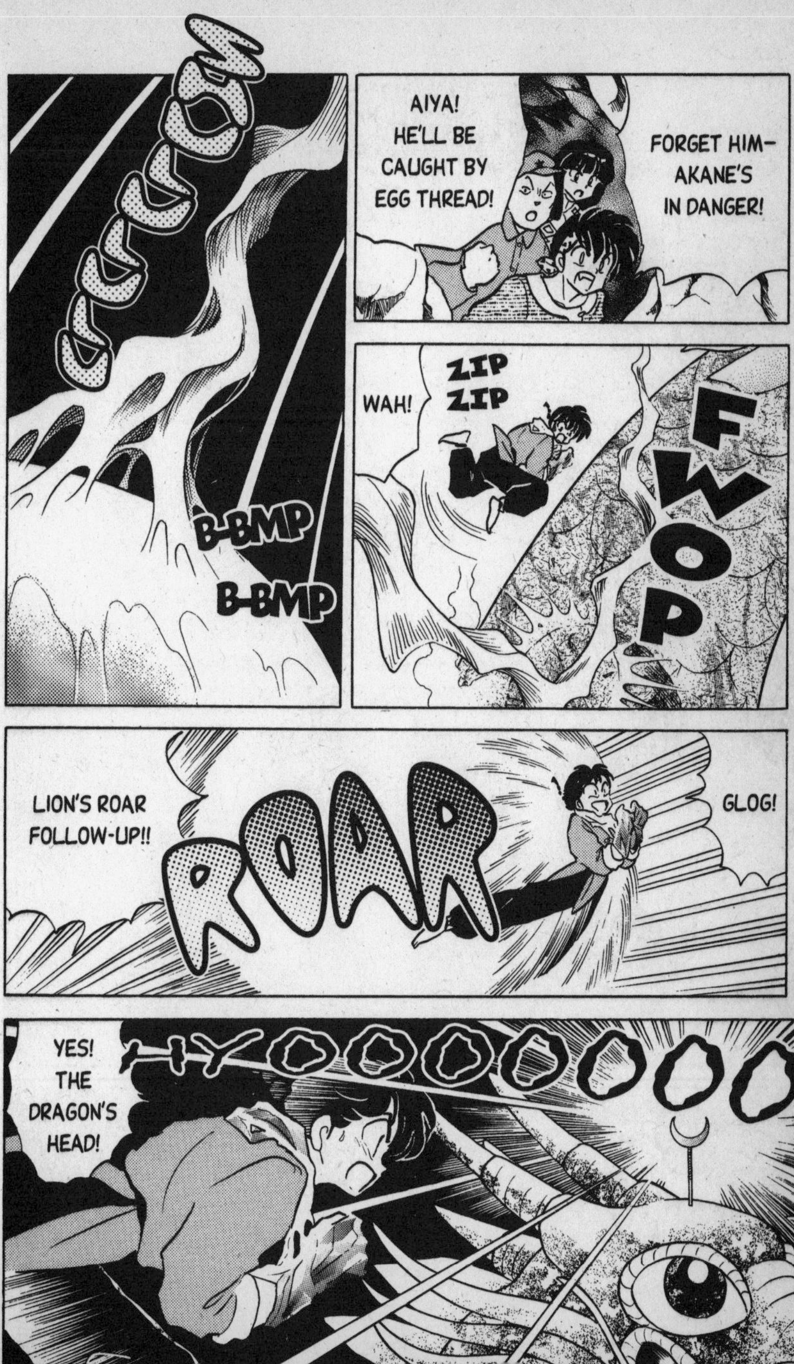
B-BMP
B-BMP
AIYA! HE'LL BE CAUGHT BY EGG THREAD!
FORGET HIM-AKANE'S IN DANGER!
WAH!
ZIP ZIP
FWOP
LION'S ROAR FOLLOW-UP!!
ROAR
GLOG!
YES! THE DRAGON'S HEAD!
HYOOOOOOOO

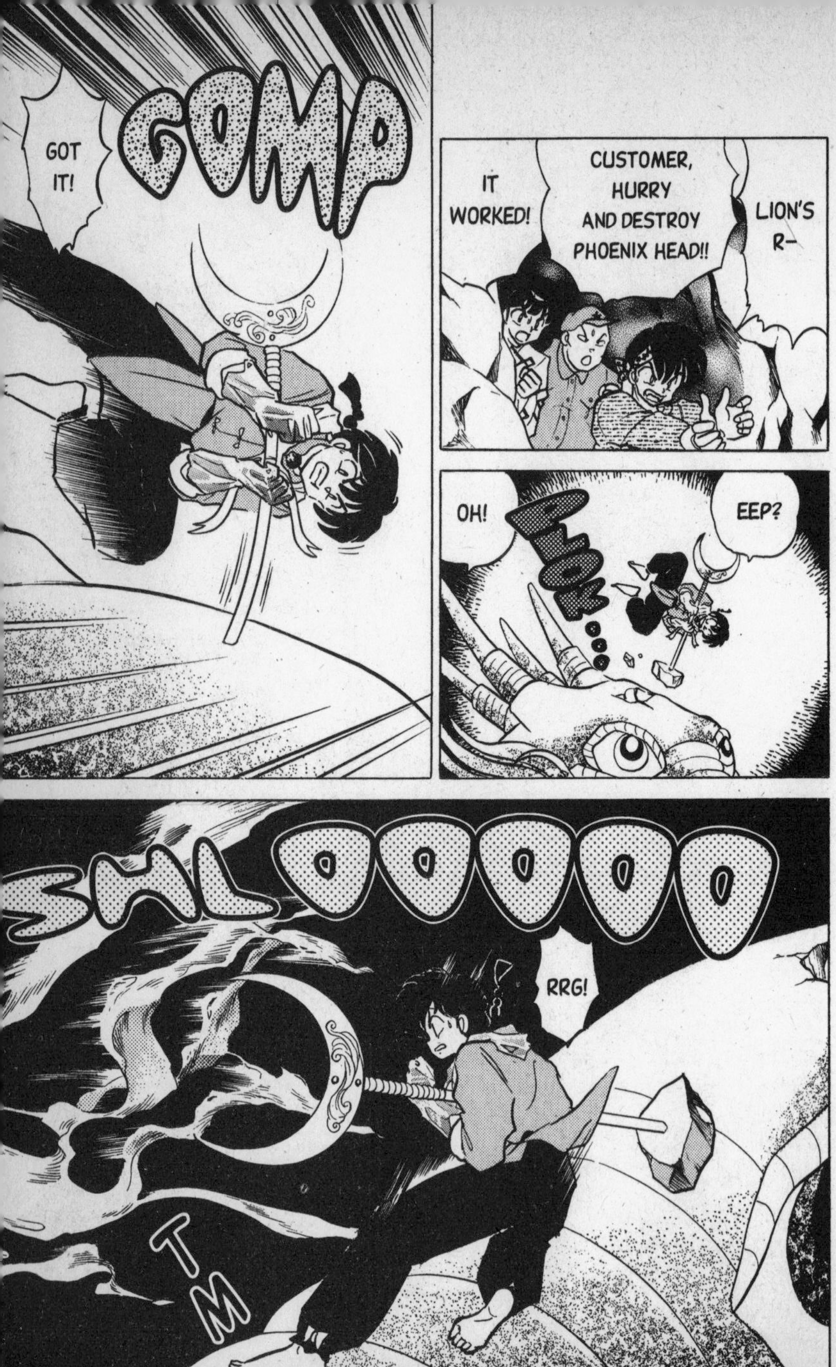
GOT IT!
GOMP
IT WORKED!
CUSTOMER, HURRY AND DESTROY PHOENIX HEAD!!
LION'S R–
OH!
EEP?
RRG!

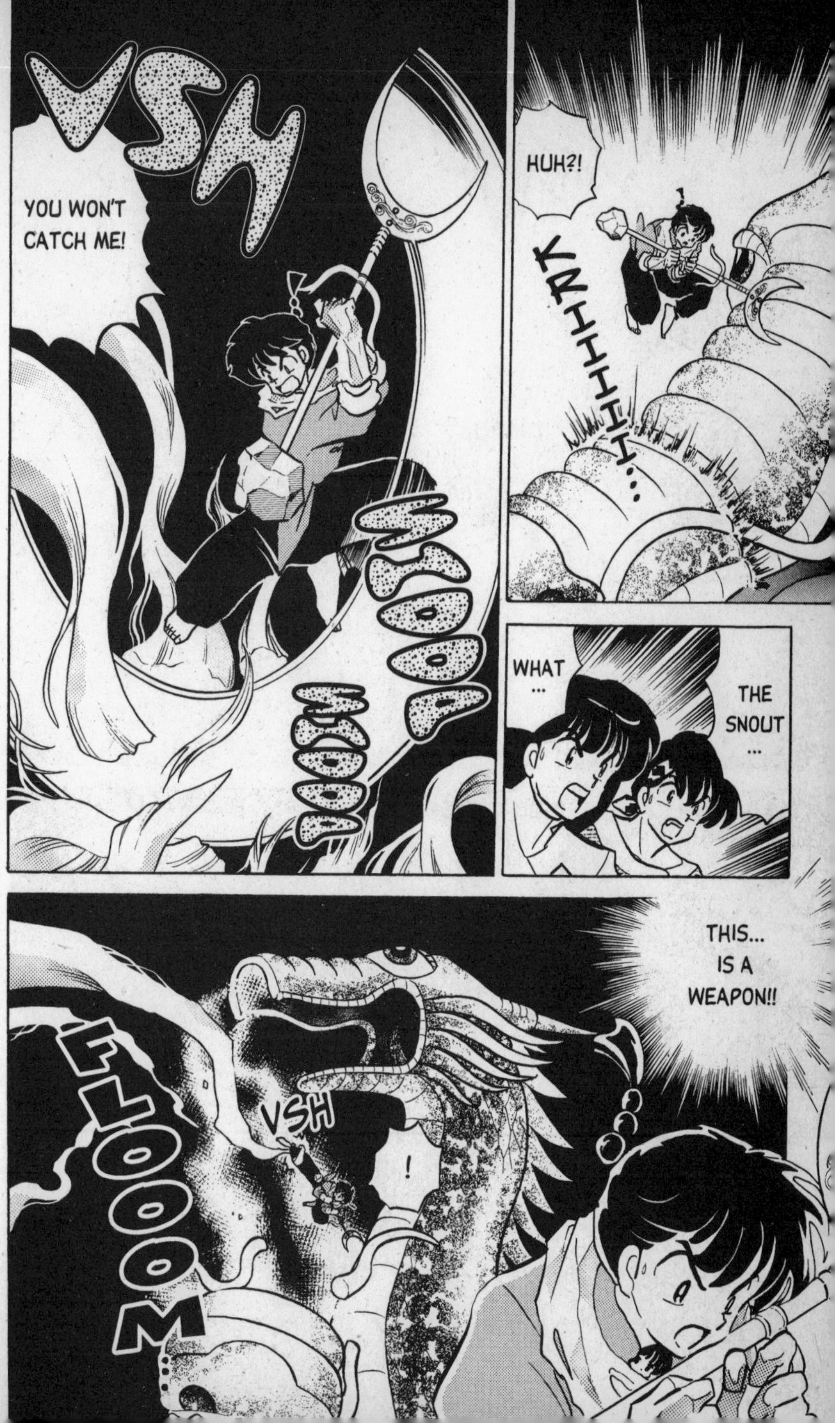
VSH
YOU WON'T CATCH ME!
WHOOA
WHOOA
HUH?!
KRIIIIII...
WHAT ...
THE SNOUT ...
THIS... IS A WEAPON!!
FLOOOM...
VSH
!

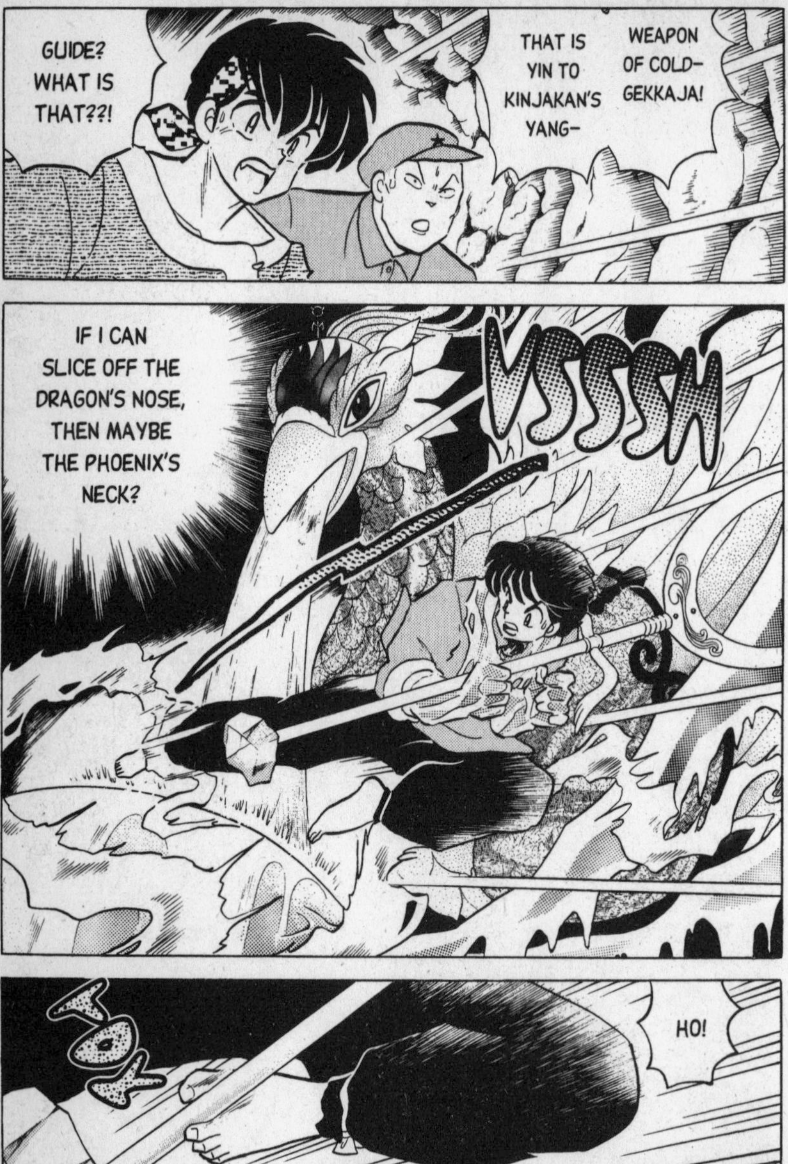
GUIDE? WHAT IS THAT??!
THAT IS YIN TO KINJAKAN'S YANG—
WEAPON OF COLD— GEKKAJA!
IF I CAN SLICE OFF THE DRAGON'S NOSE, THEN MAYBE THE PHOENIX'S NECK?
VSSSH
VOK
HO!

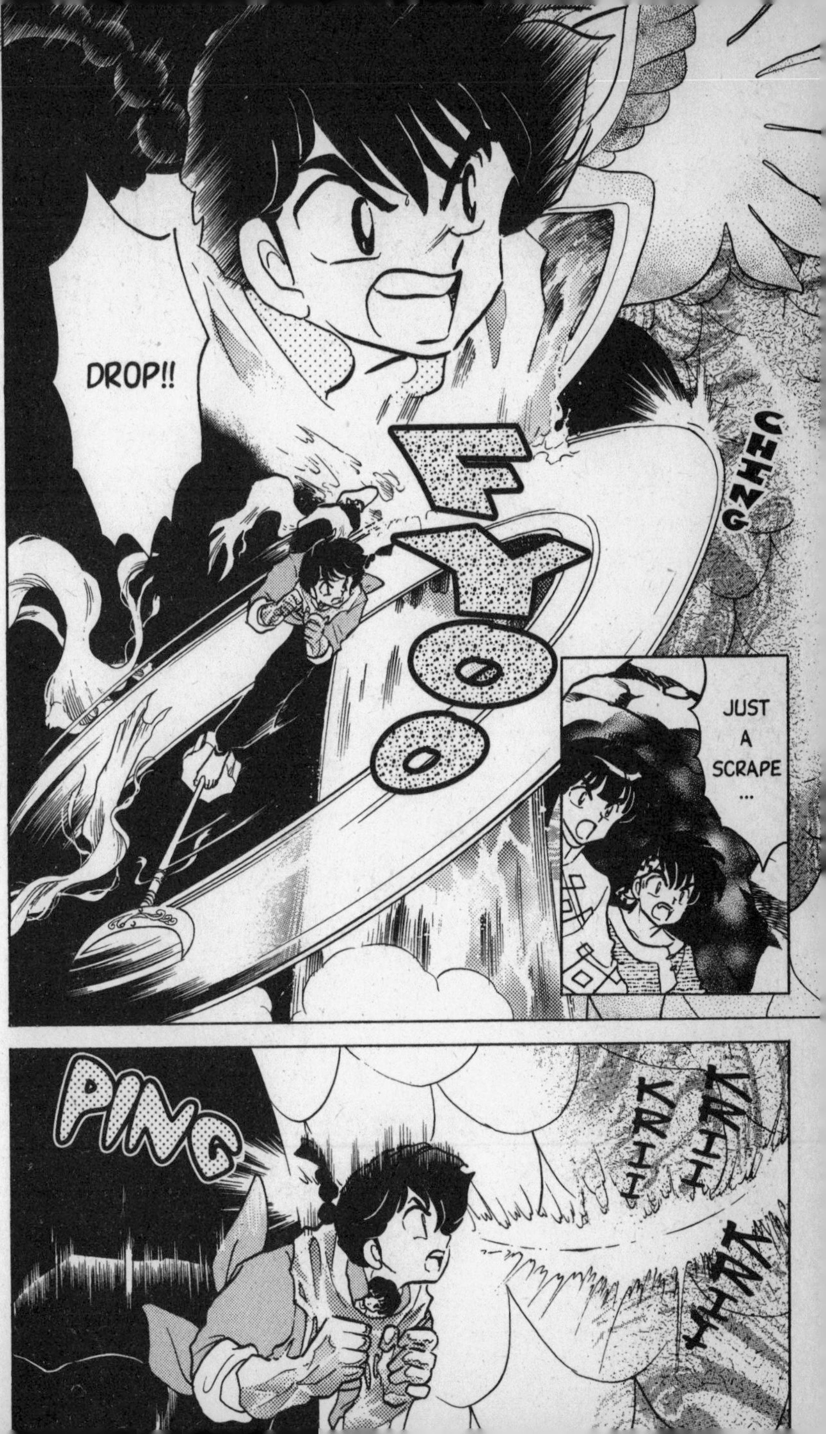
DROP!!
CHING
JUST A SCRAPE ...
PING
KRIII
KRIII
KRIII

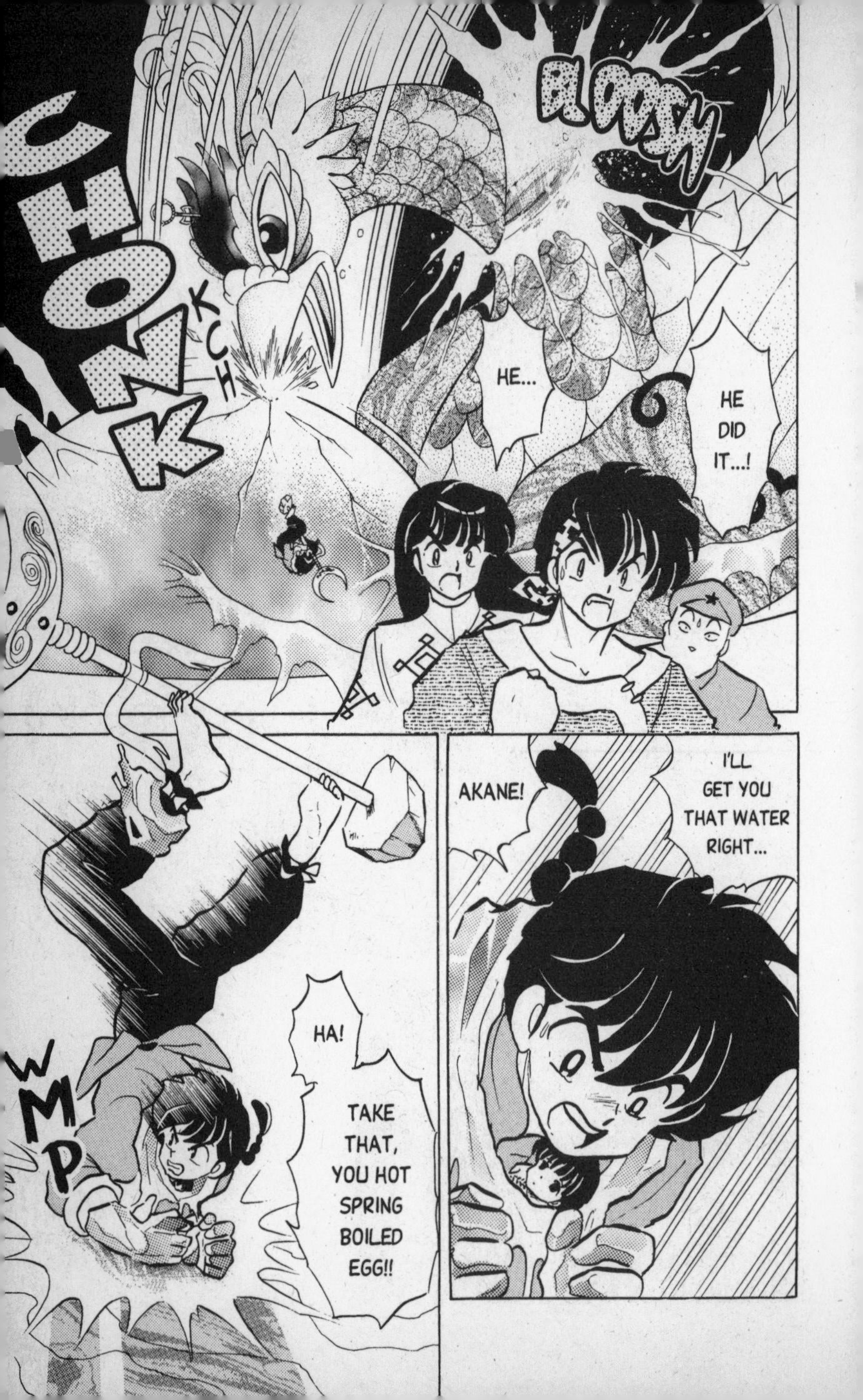
CHONK
KCH
HE...
HE DID IT...!
WMP
HA!
TAKE THAT, YOU HOT SPRING BOILED EGG!!
AKANE!
I'LL GET YOU THAT WATER RIGHT...

B-BMP

K K K K

B-BMP

PING

AGH!

WD XO

KLAK KLAK KLAK

SHHH

RANMA... MISS AKANE!

N...

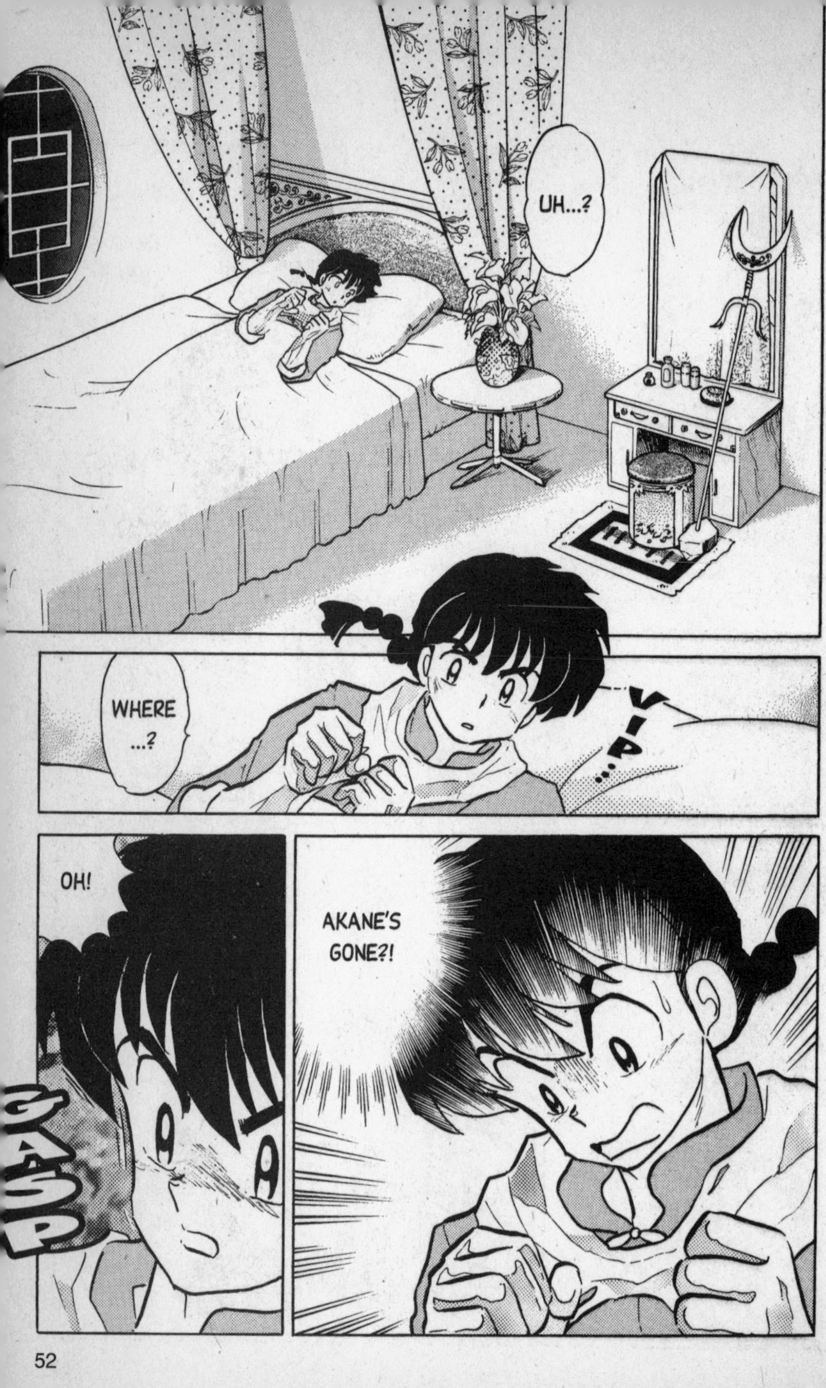
UH...?
WHERE ...?
VIP...
OH!
GASP
AKANE'S GONE?!

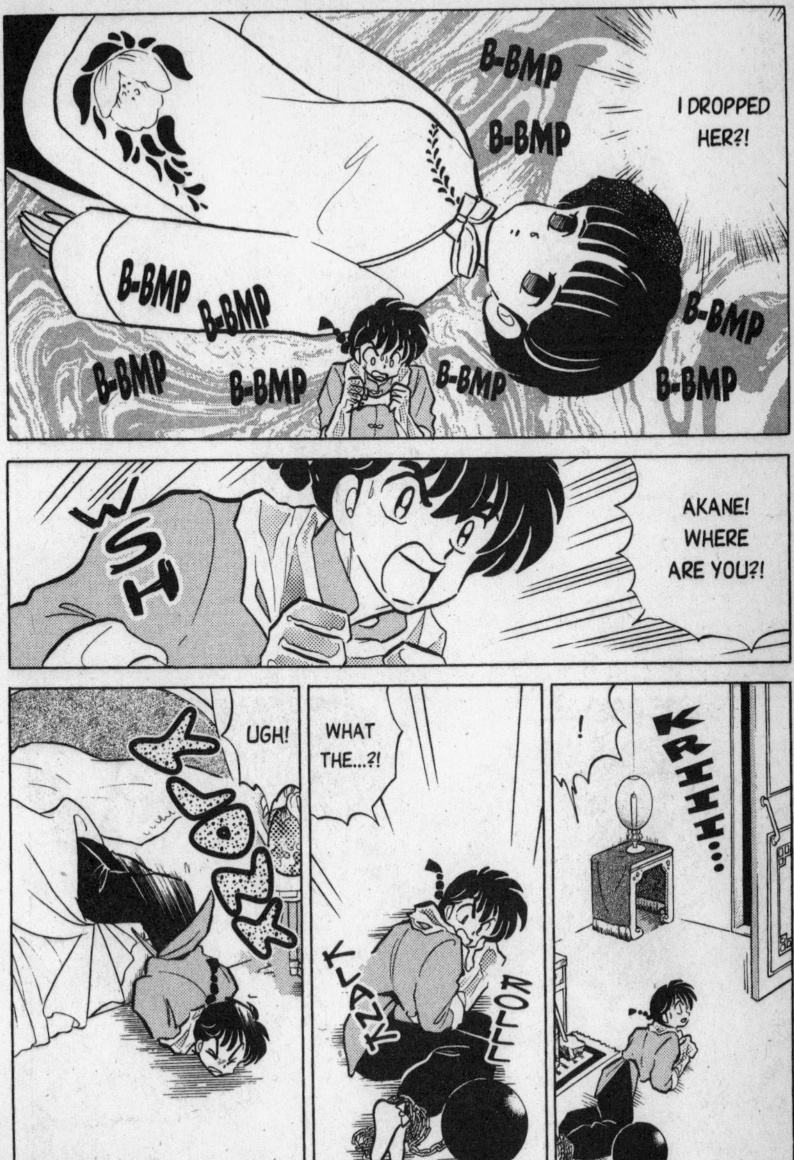
B-BMP
B-BMP
B-BMP
B-BMP
B-BMP
B-BMP
B-BMP
B-BMP
B-BMP
I DROPPED HER?!
WSH
AKANE! WHERE ARE YOU?!
UGH!
WHAT THE...?!
KLANK
ROLL
!
KRIIII...

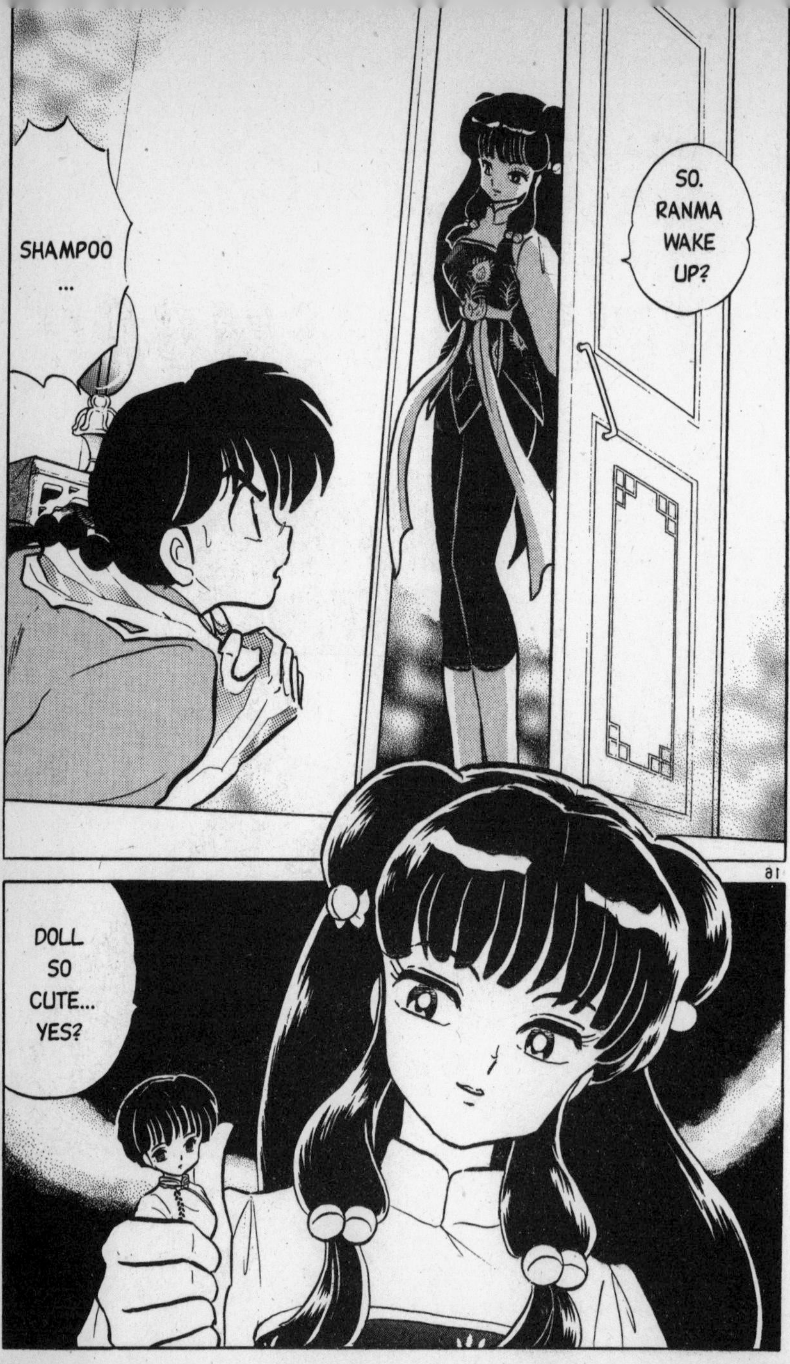
SHAMPOO ...
SO. RANMA WAKE UP?
DOLL SO CUTE... YES?

PART 4

A LAST, SWEET MEMORY

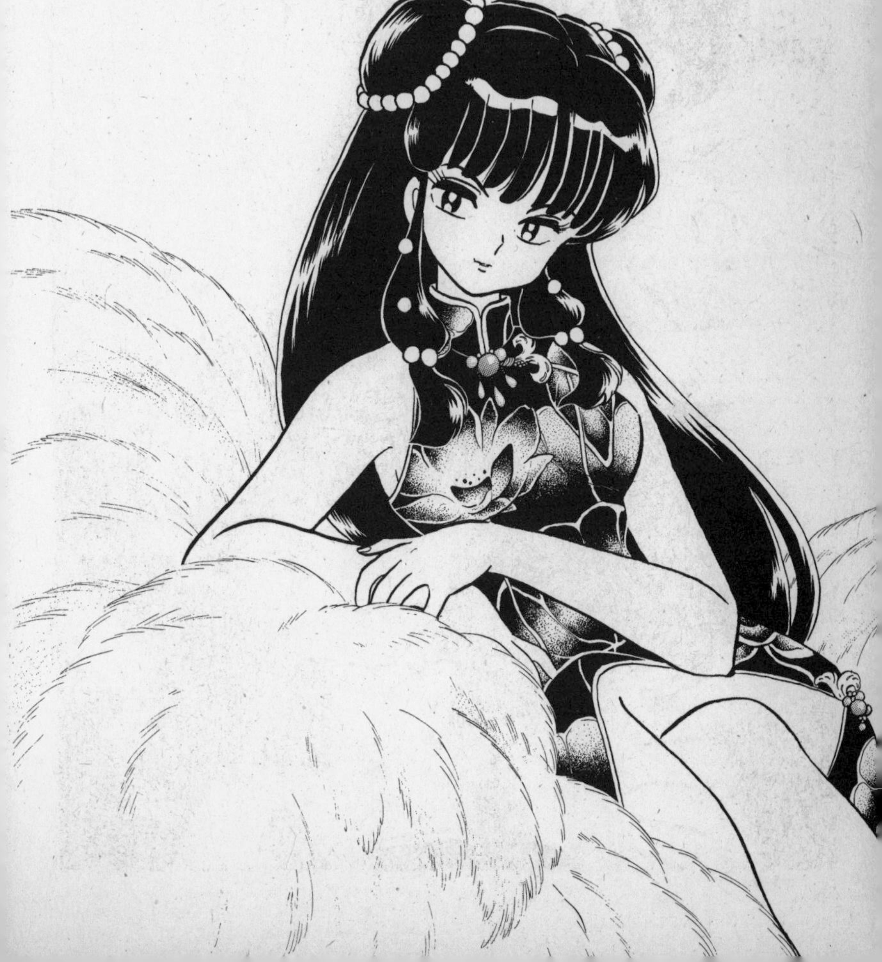

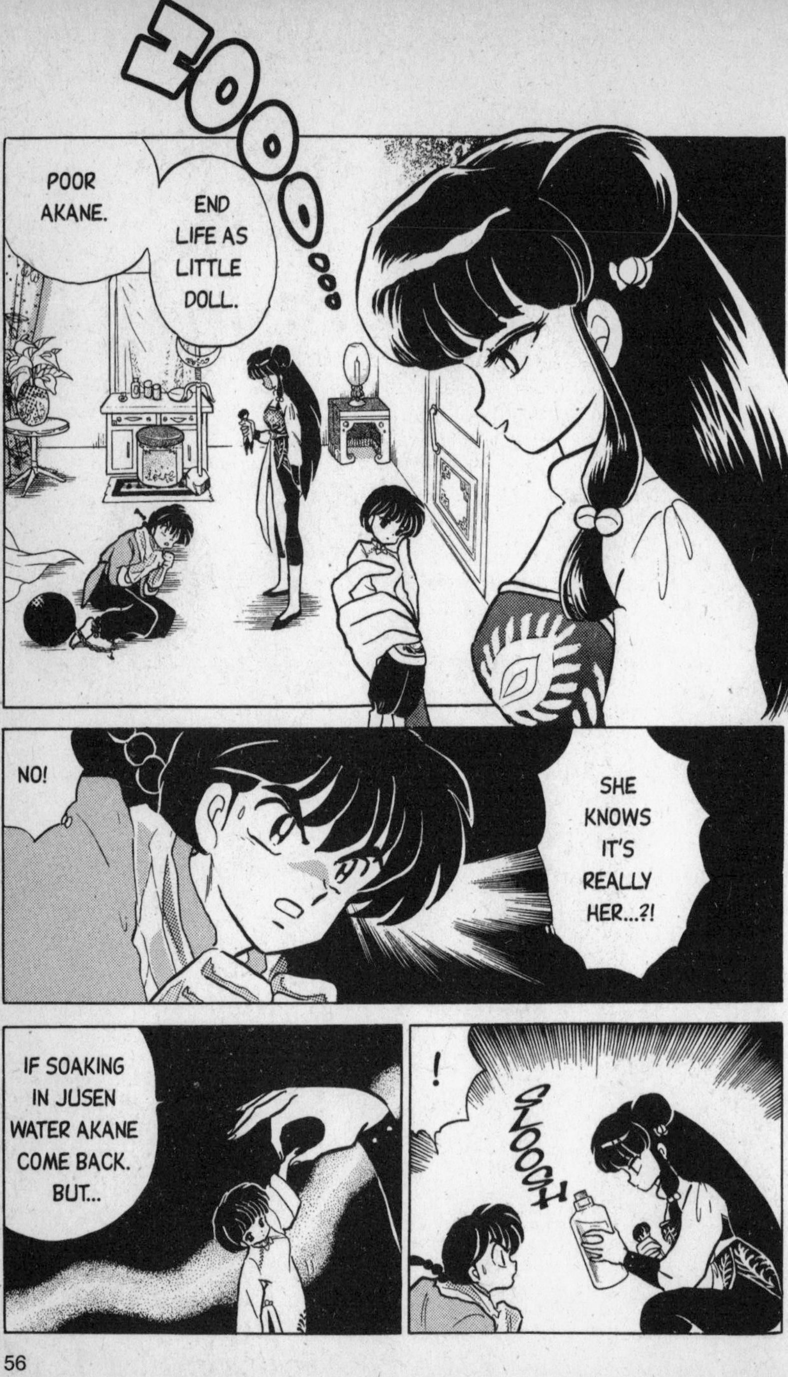
ZOOOOOOOO
POOR AKANE.
END LIFE AS LITTLE DOLL.
NO!
SHE KNOWS IT'S REALLY HER...?!
IF SOAKING IN JUSEN WATER AKANE COME BACK. BUT...
!
GLOOGH

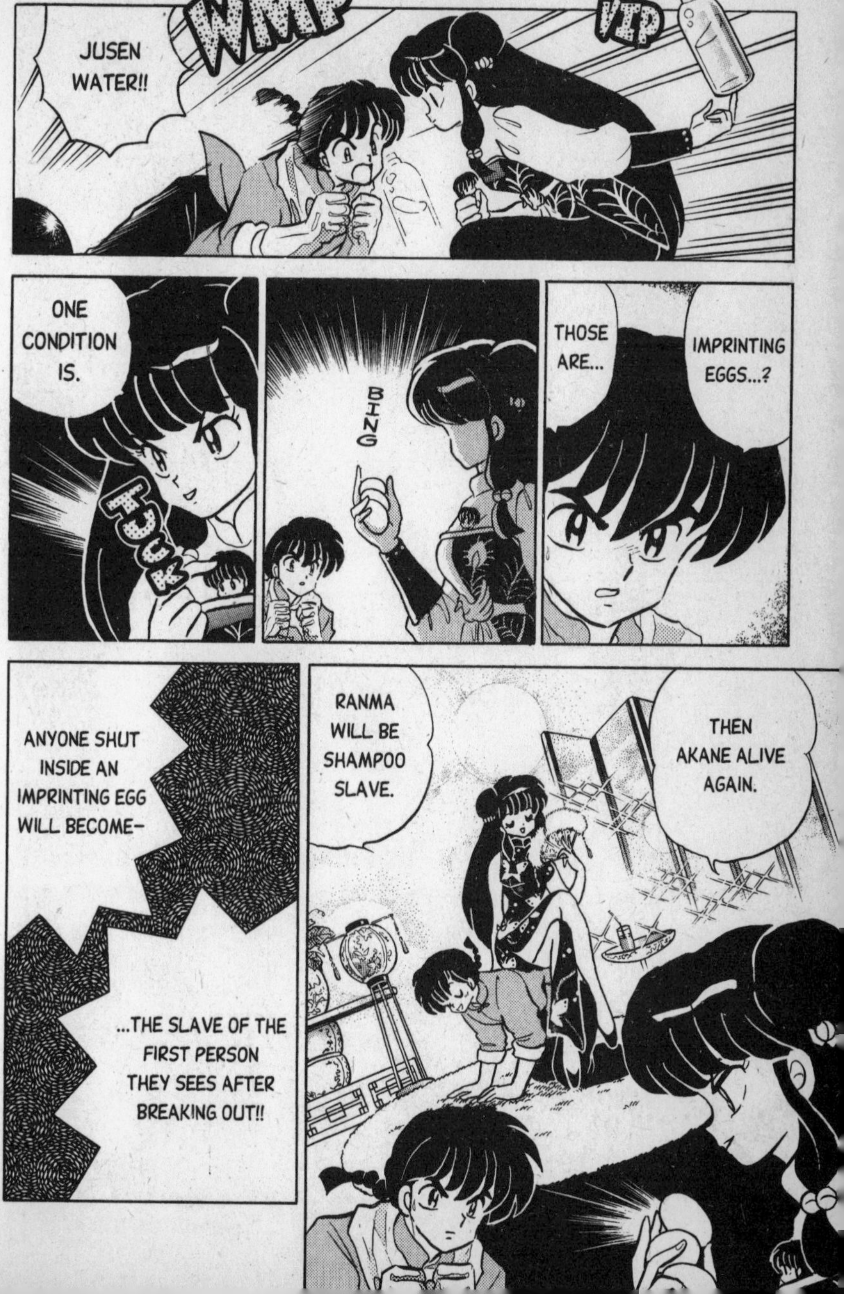
WMP
VIP
JUSEN WATER!!
ONE CONDITION IS.
TUCK
BING
THOSE ARE...
IMPRINTING EGGS...?
ANYONE SHUT INSIDE AN IMPRINTING EGG WILL BECOME—
...THE SLAVE OF THE FIRST PERSON THEY SEES AFTER BREAKING OUT!!
RANMA WILL BE SHAMPOO SLAVE.
THEN AKANE ALIVE AGAIN.

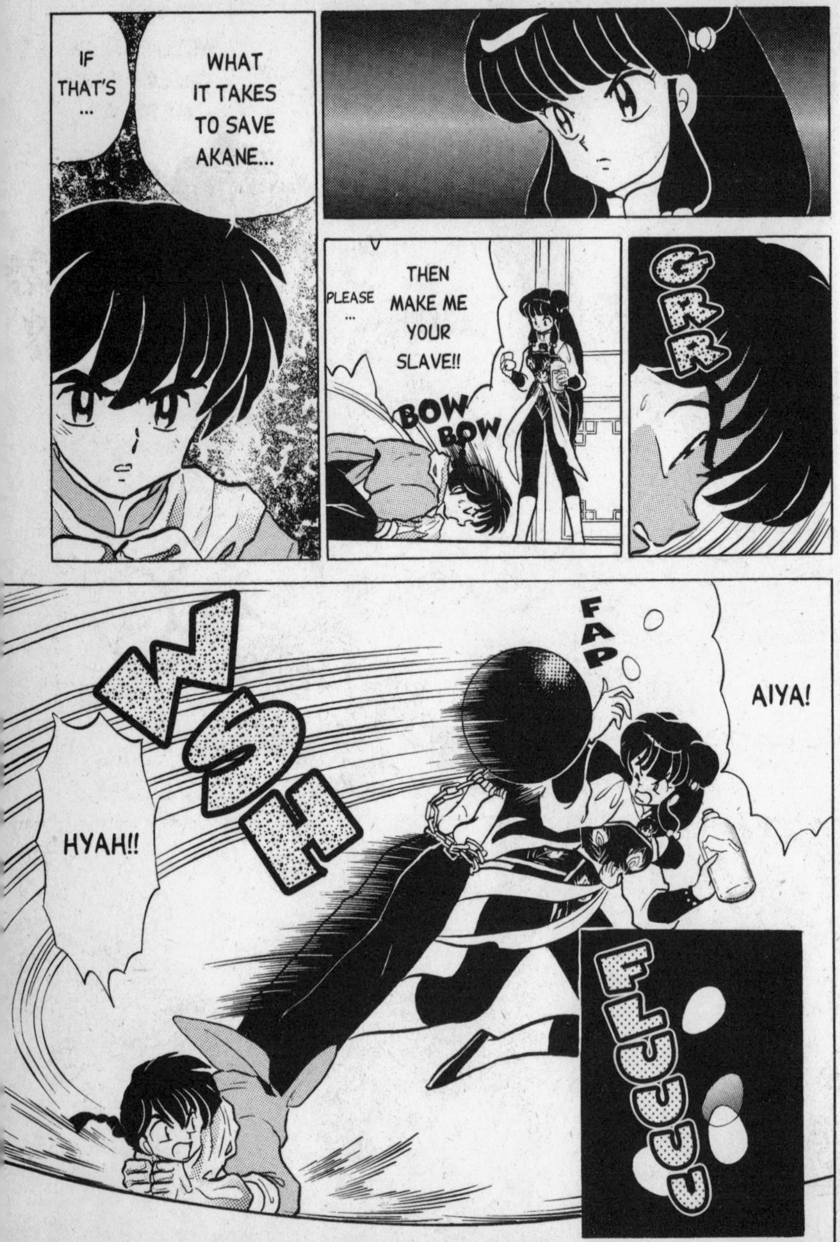
IF THAT'S ...
WHAT IT TAKES TO SAVE AKANE...
PLEASE ...
THEN MAKE ME YOUR SLAVE!!
BOW BOW
GRR
HYAH!!
WSSH
FAP
AIYA!
FLUUUU

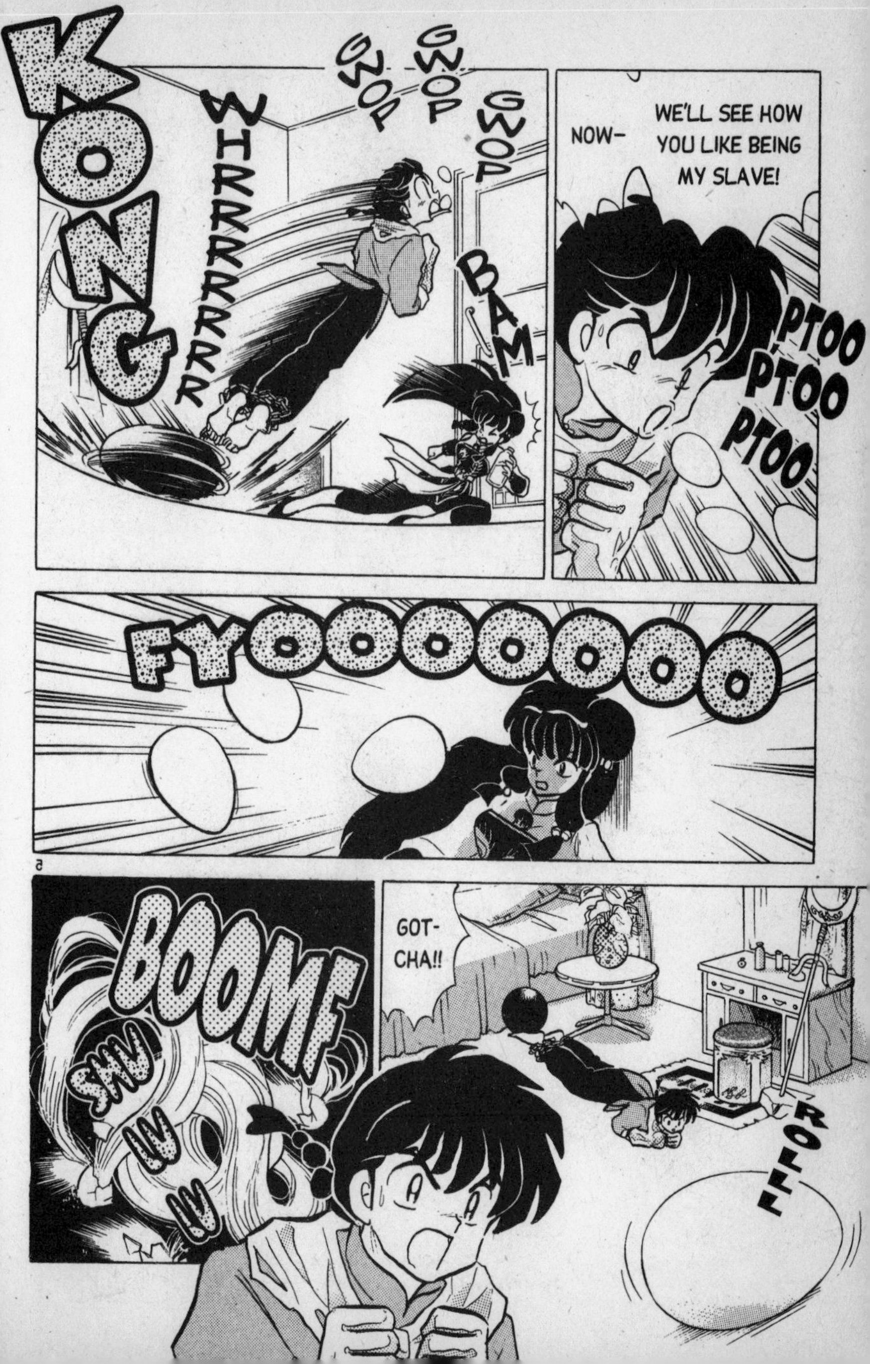
KONG
WHRRRRRRRR
GWOP GWOP GWOP
BAM
NOW—
WE'LL SEE HOW YOU LIKE BEING MY SLAVE!
PTOO PTOO PTOO
FYOOOOOOO
BOOMF
GOT-CHA!!
ROLL

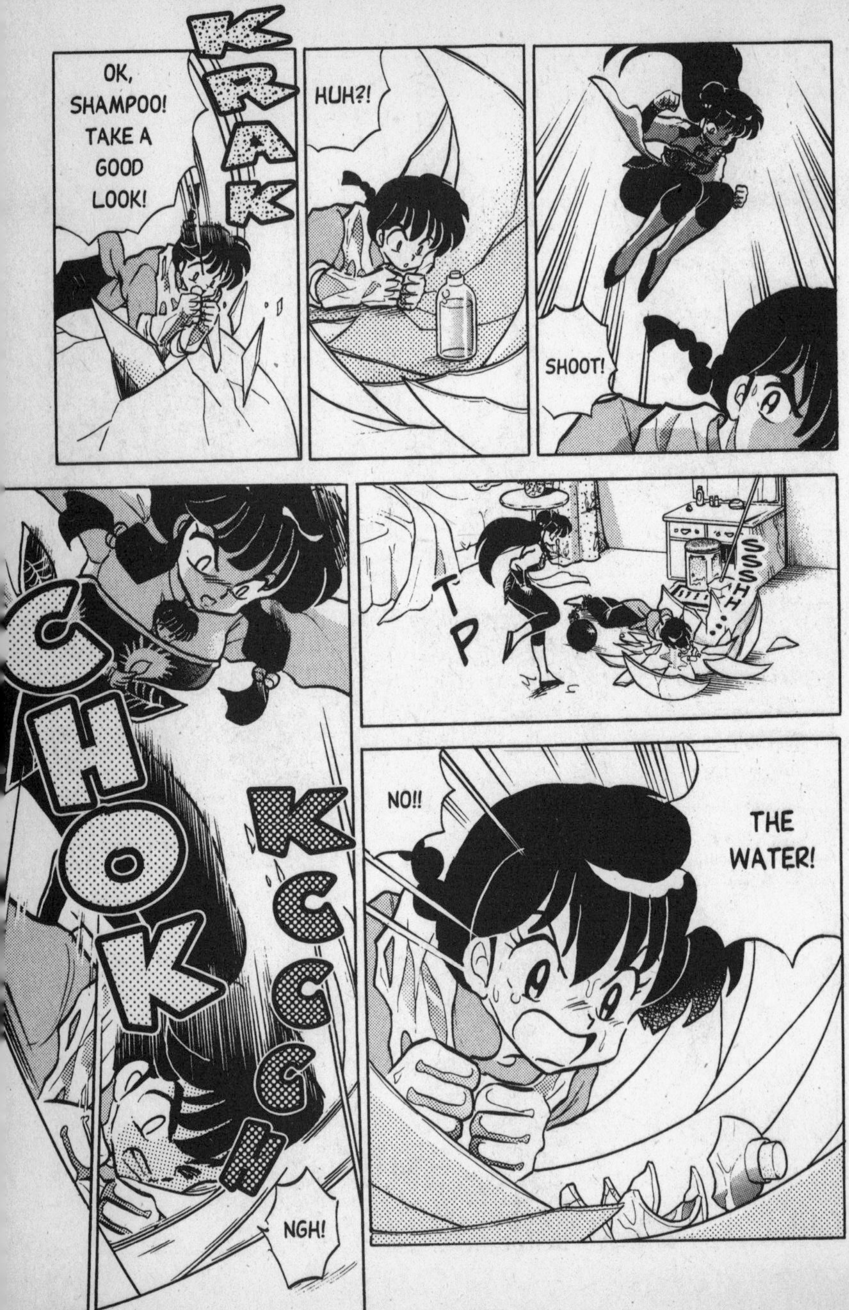
OK, SHAMPOO! TAKE A GOOD LOOK!
KRAK
HUH?!
SHOOT!
CHOK
KCCCR
NGH!
TP
SSSSH...
NO!!
THE WATER!

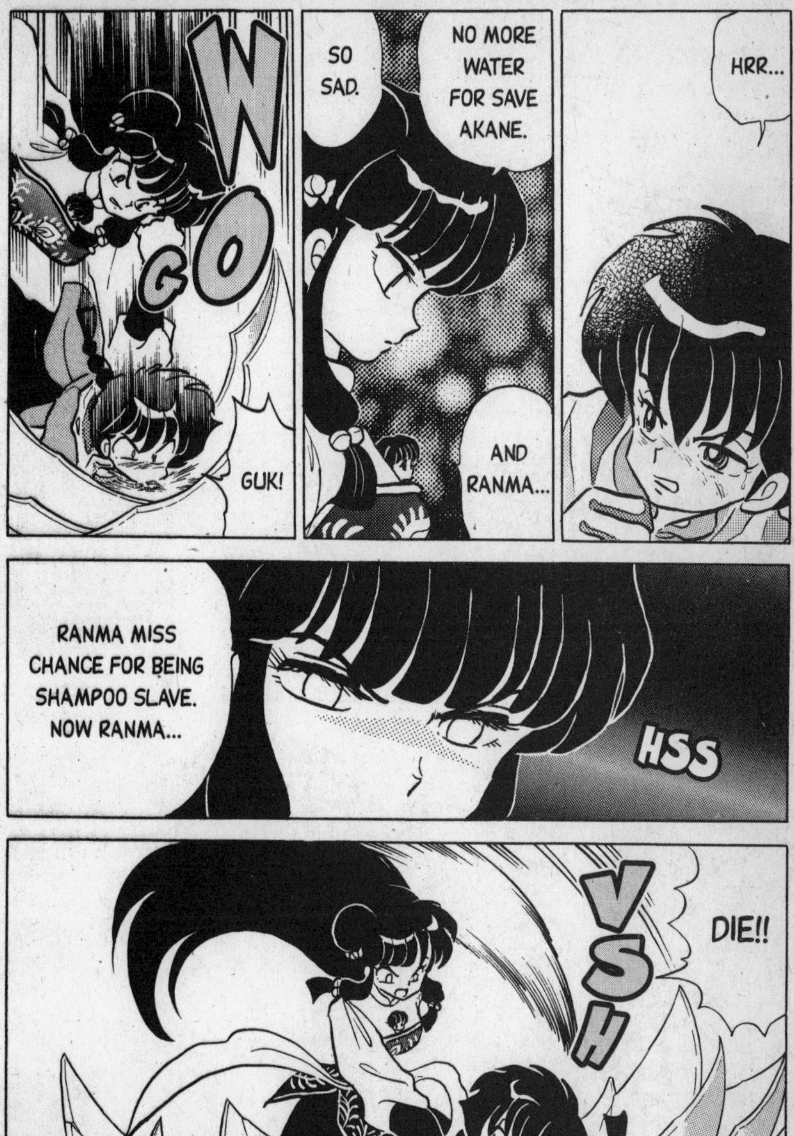
WGO
GUK!
SO SAD.
NO MORE WATER FOR SAVE AKANE.
AND RANMA...
HRR...
RANMA MISS CHANCE FOR BEING SHAMPOO SLAVE. NOW RANMA...
HSS
VSH
DIE!!

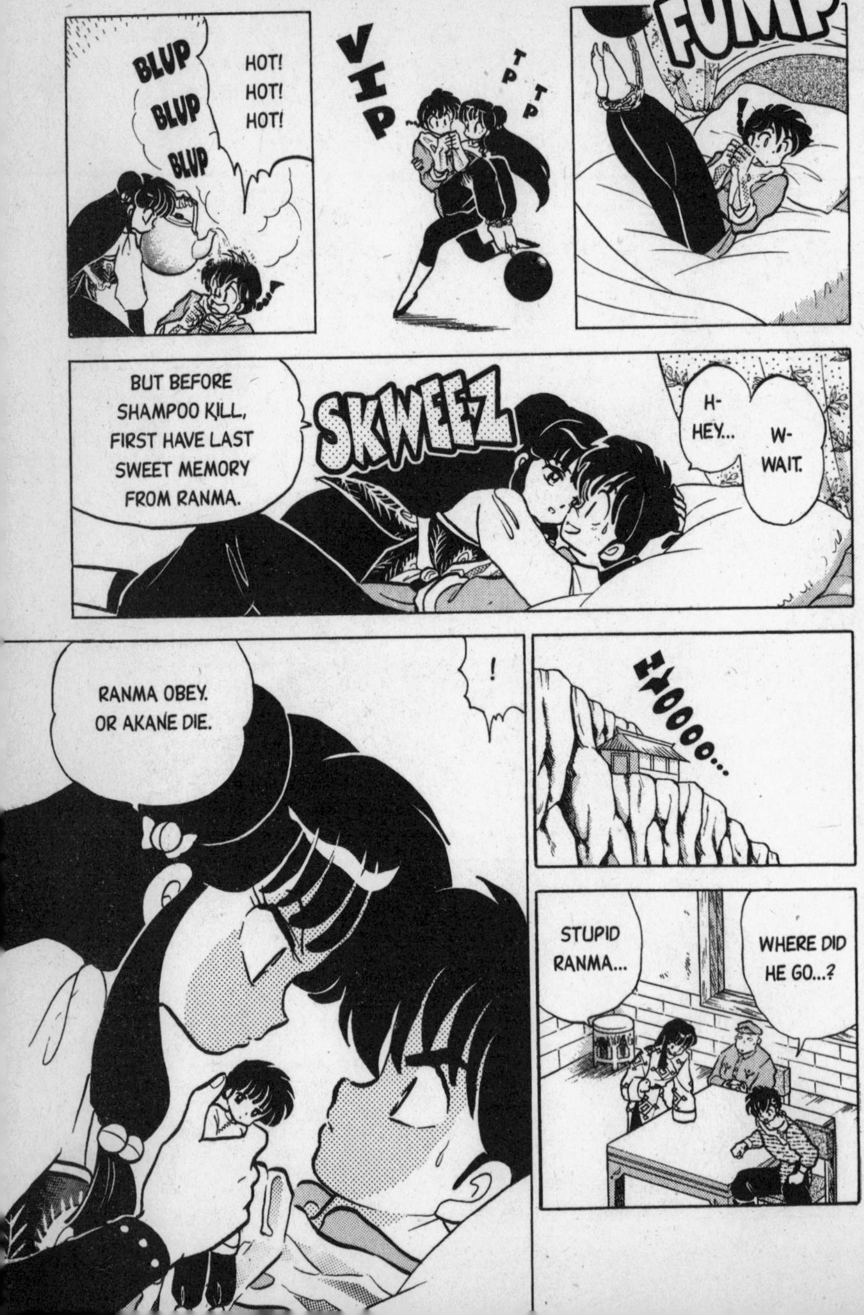
BLUP
BLUP
BLUP
HOT! HOT! HOT!
VIP
TP TP
FUMP
BUT BEFORE SHAMPOO KILL, FIRST HAVE LAST SWEET MEMORY FROM RANMA.
SKWEEZ
H-HEY...
W-WAIT.
RANMA OBEY. OR AKANE DIE.
!
HYOOOOO...
STUPID RANMA...
WHERE DID HE GO...?

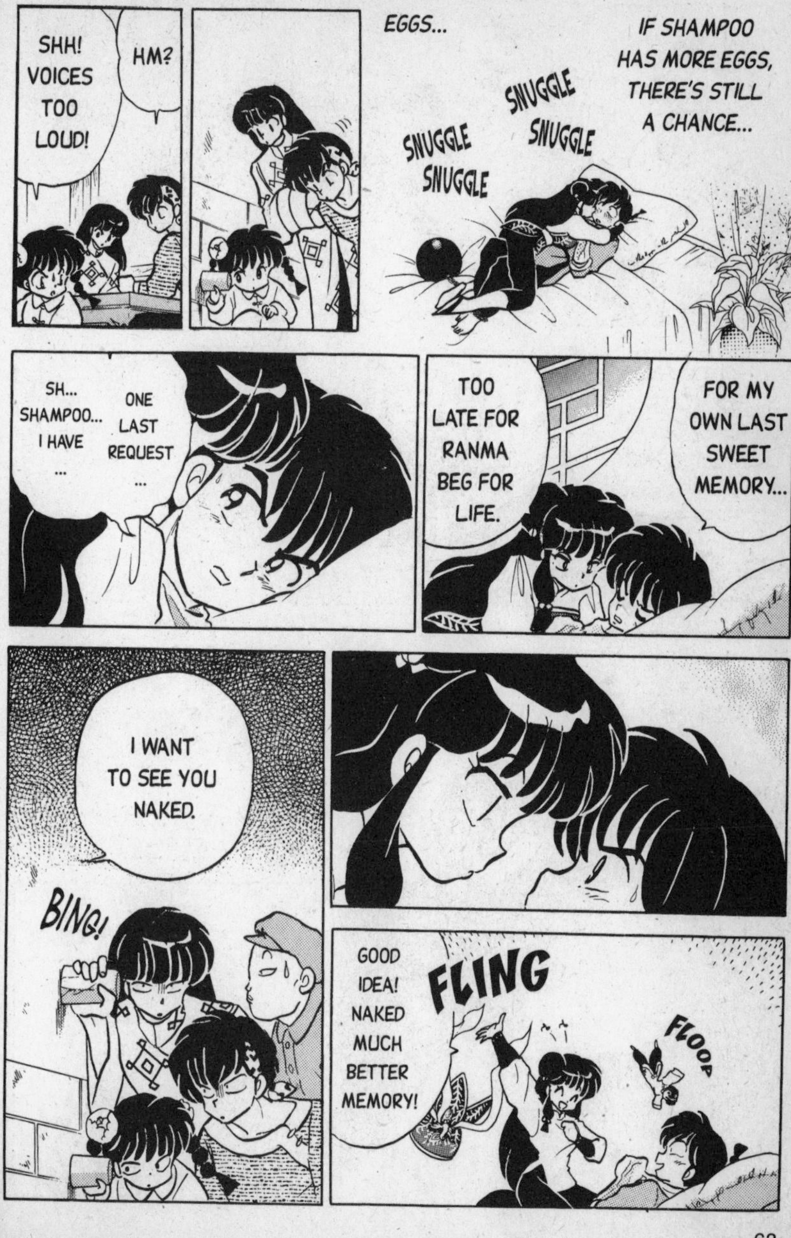
SHH! VOICES TOO LOUD!
HM?
EGGS...
IF SHAMPOO HAS MORE EGGS, THERE'S STILL A CHANCE...
SNUGGLE SNUGGLE
SNUGGLE SNUGGLE
SH... SHAMPOO... I HAVE ...
ONE LAST REQUEST ...
TOO LATE FOR RANMA BEG FOR LIFE.
FOR MY OWN LAST SWEET MEMORY...
I WANT TO SEE YOU NAKED.
BING!
GOOD IDEA! NAKED MUCH BETTER MEMORY!
FLING
FLOOP

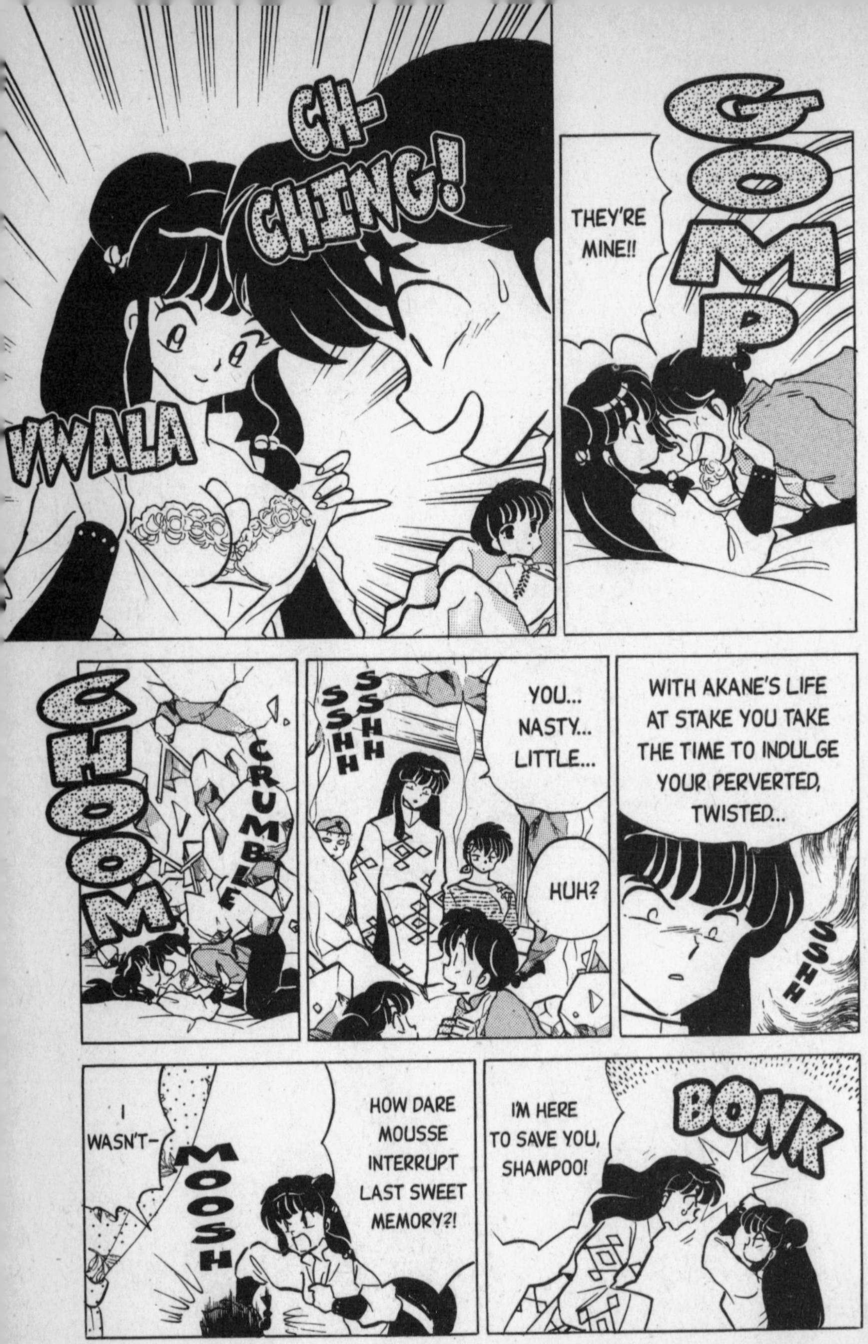
VWALA
CH-CHING!
THEY'RE MINE!!
GOMP
CHOOM
CRUMBLE
SSHH
SSHH
YOU... NASTY... LITTLE...
HUH?
WITH AKANE'S LIFE AT STAKE YOU TAKE THE TIME TO INDULGE YOUR PERVERTED, TWISTED...
SSHH
I WASN'T-
MOOSH
HOW DARE MOUSSE INTERRUPT LAST SWEET MEMORY?!
I'M HERE TO SAVE YOU, SHAMPOO!
BONK

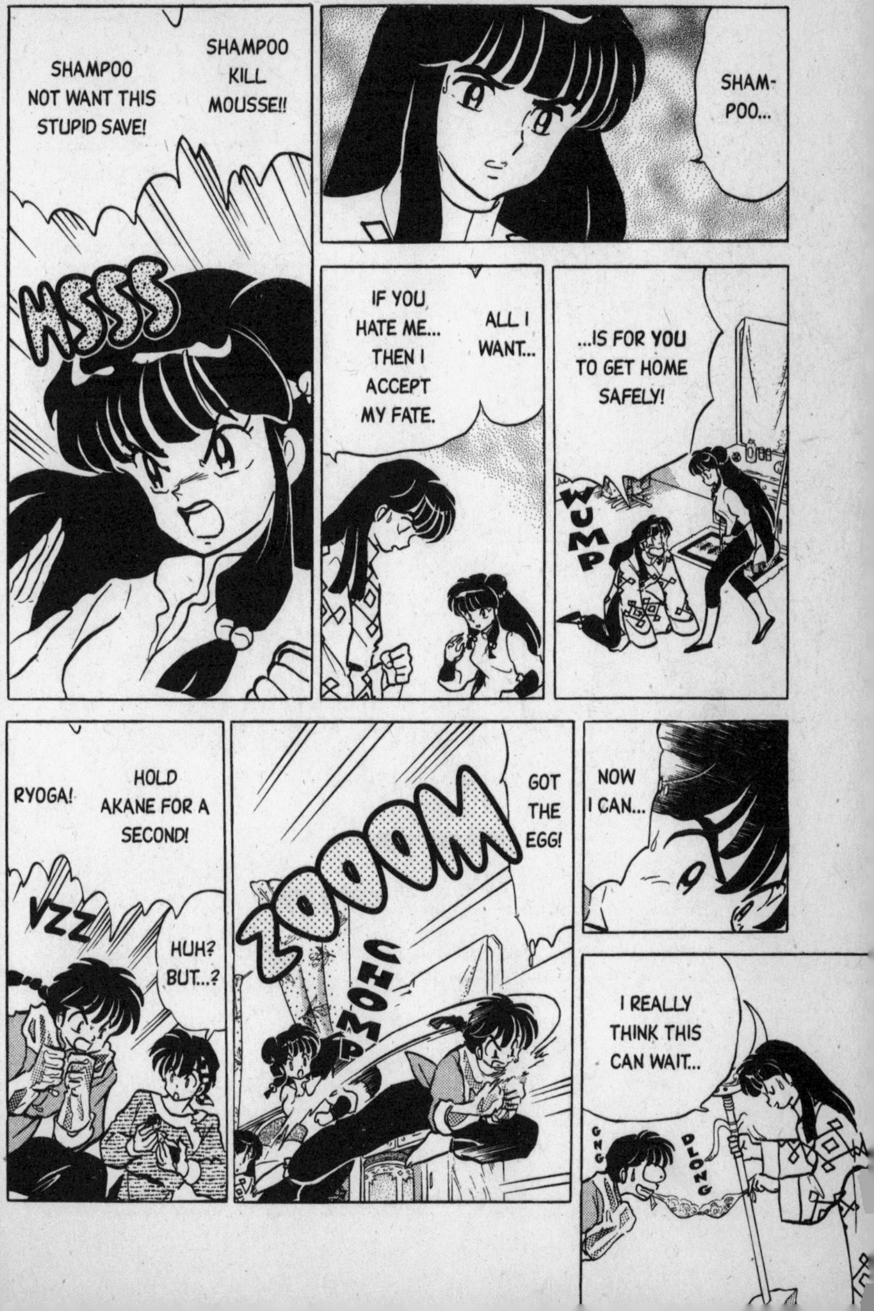
SHAMPOO NOT WANT THIS STUPID SAVE!
SHAMPOO KILL MOUSSE!!
HSSS
SHAM-POO...
IF YOU HATE ME... THEN I ACCEPT MY FATE.
ALL I WANT...
...IS FOR YOU TO GET HOME SAFELY!
WUMP
RYOGA!
HOLD AKANE FOR A SECOND!
VZZ
HUH? BUT...?
GOT THE EGG!
ZOOOM
CHOMP
NOW I CAN...
I REALLY THINK THIS CAN WAIT...
GNG
DLONG

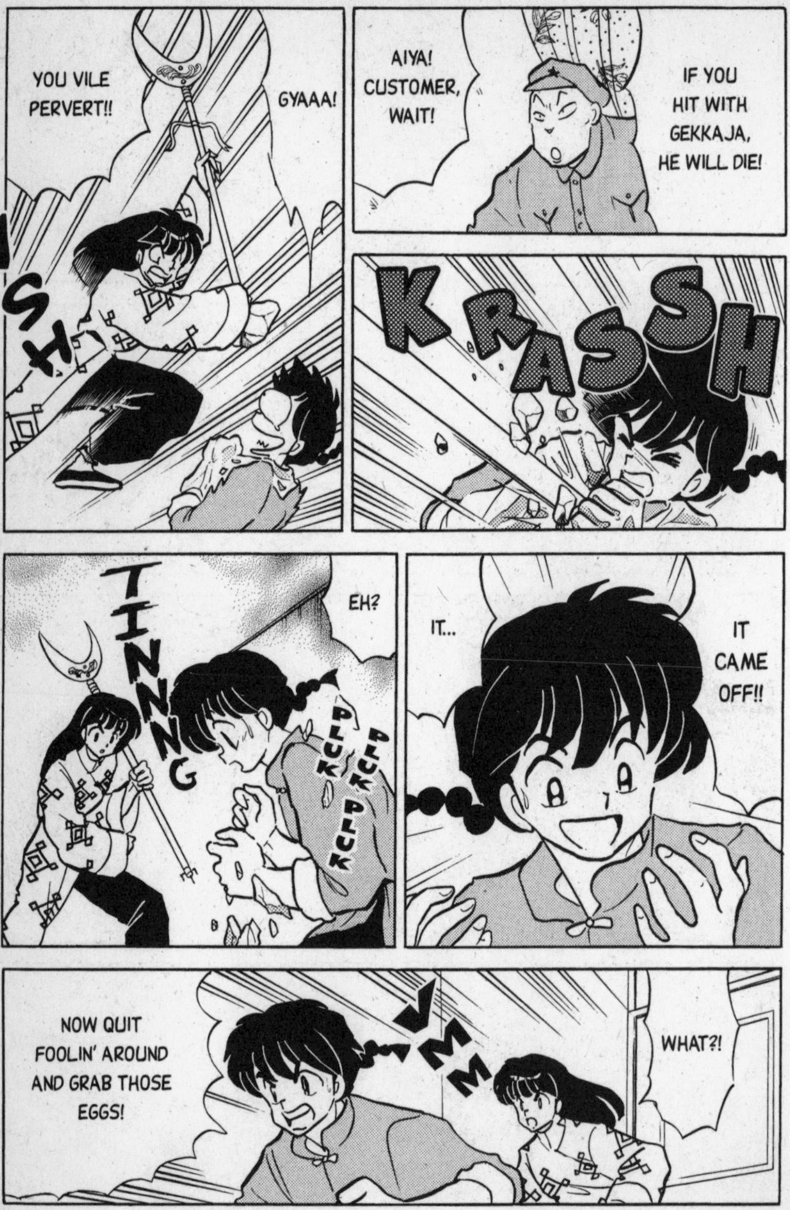
YOU VILE PERVERT!!
GYAAA!
VSH
AIYA! CUSTOMER, WAIT!
IF YOU HIT WITH GEKKAJA, HE WILL DIE!
KRASSH
TINNNG
EH?
PLUK PLUK PLUK PLUK
IT...
IT CAME OFF!!
NOW QUIT FOOLIN' AROUND AND GRAB THOSE EGGS!
VMM
WHAT?!

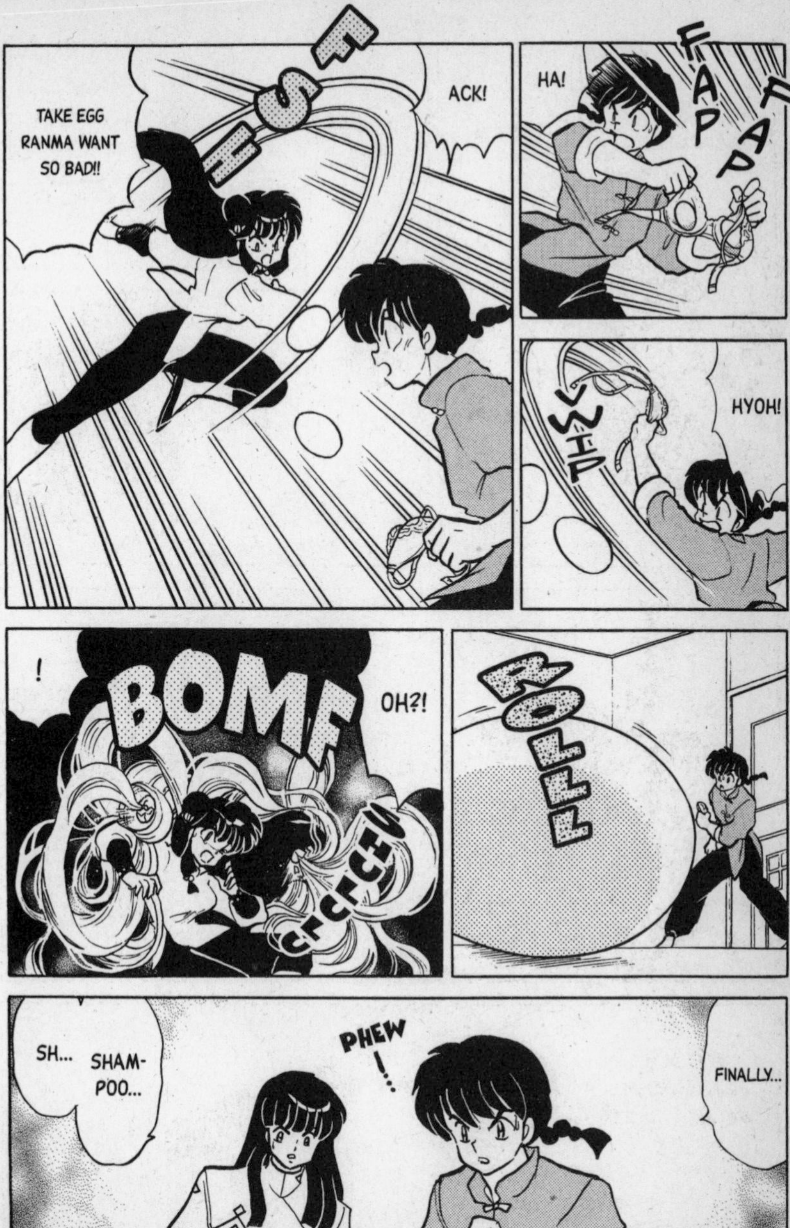
TAKE EGG RANMA WANT SO BAD!!
HISS
ACK!
HA!
FAP
FAP
FAP
WHIP
HYOH!
!
BOMF
OH?!
ROLLL
SH...
SHAM-POO...
PHEW...!
FINALLY...

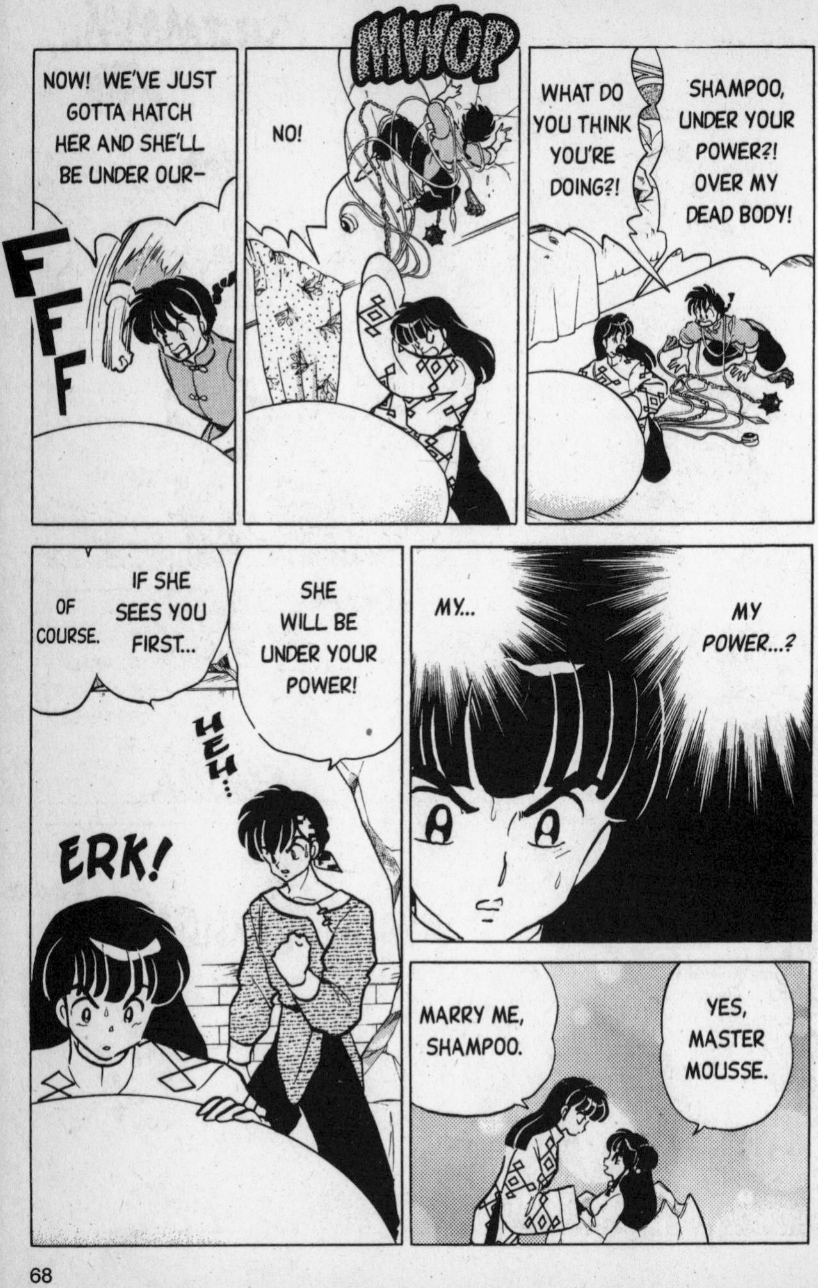
NOW! WE'VE JUST GOTTA HATCH HER AND SHE'LL BE UNDER OUR-
FFF
MWOP
NO!
WHAT DO YOU THINK YOU'RE DOING?!
SHAMPOO, UNDER YOUR POWER?! OVER MY DEAD BODY!
OF COURSE.
IF SHE SEES YOU FIRST...
SHE WILL BE UNDER YOUR POWER!
HEH...
ERK!
MY...
MY POWER...?
MARRY ME, SHAMPOO.
YES, MASTER MOUSSE.

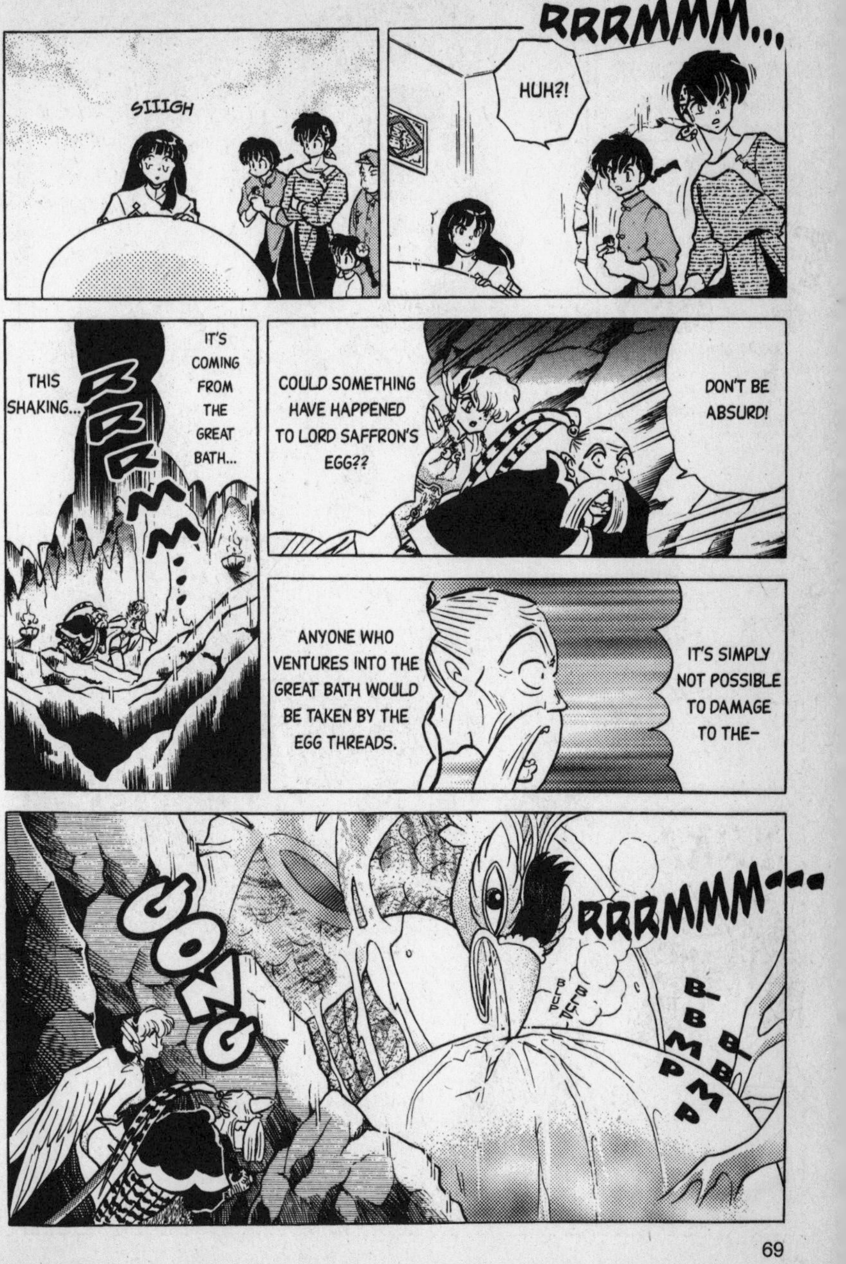
SIIIGH
RRRMMM...
HUH?!
THIS SHAKING...
RRRMMM...
IT'S COMING FROM THE GREAT BATH...
COULD SOMETHING HAVE HAPPENED TO LORD SAFFRON'S EGG??
DON'T BE ABSURD!
ANYONE WHO VENTURES INTO THE GREAT BATH WOULD BE TAKEN BY THE EGG THREADS.
IT'S SIMPLY NOT POSSIBLE TO DAMAGE TO THE–
GONG
RRRMMM...
BLUP BLUP
B-BMMP
B-BMMP

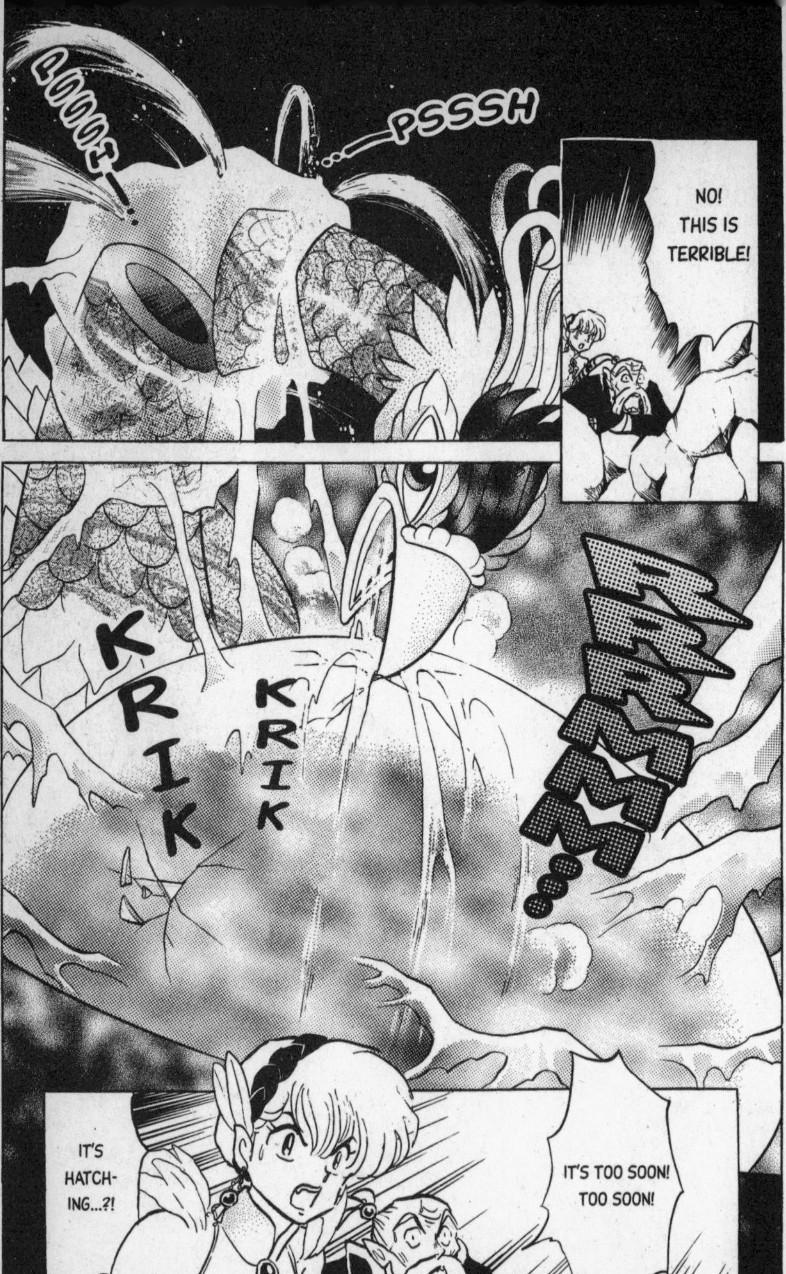
POOSSH!!
...PSSSH
NO! THIS IS TERRIBLE!
KRIK
KRIK
RRRMMMM...
IT'S HATCH-ING...?!
IT'S TOO SOON! TOO SOON!

PART 5
SAFFRON REBORN

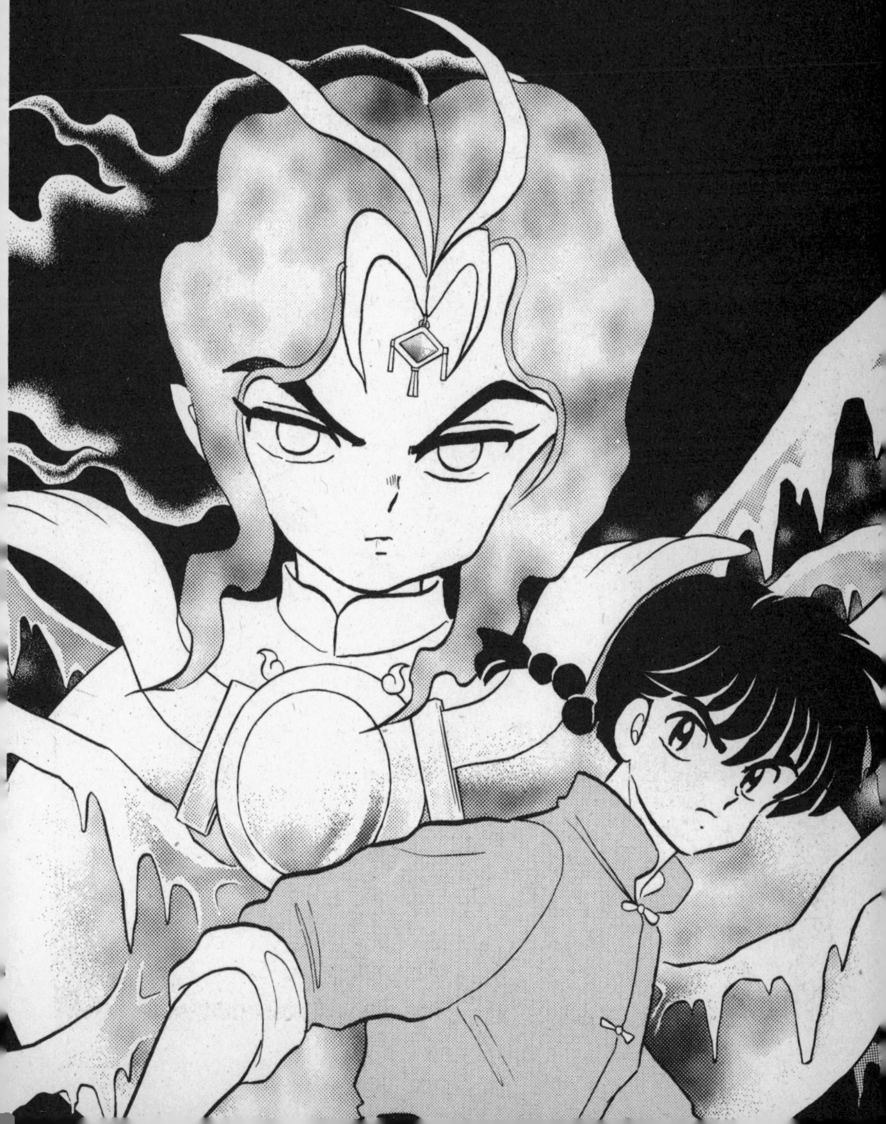

TOO
SOON?!

SIGNIFICANTLY!
A PROPER
TRANSFORMATION
CALLS FOR ANOTHER
3 DAYS OF GESTATION!

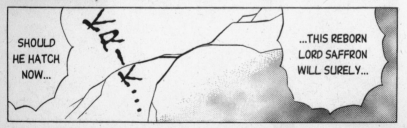

SHOULD
HE HATCH
NOW...

...THIS REBORN
LORD SAFFRON
WILL SURELY...

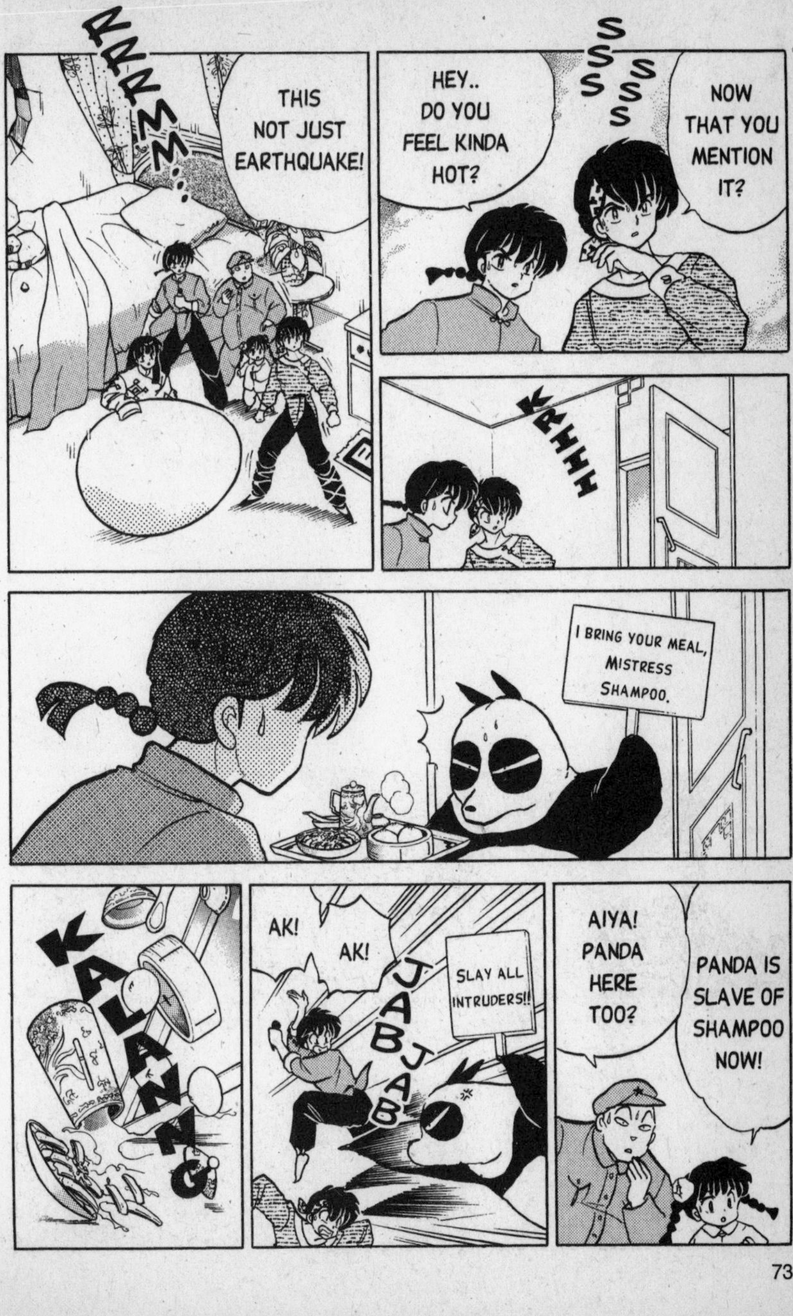
RRRRMM...
THIS NOT JUST EARTHQUAKE!
HEY.. DO YOU FEEL KINDA HOT?
SSSSSS
NOW THAT YOU MENTION IT?
KRIIIH
I BRING YOUR MEAL, MISTRESS SHAMPOO.
KALANNG
AK!
AK!
JABJABJAB
SLAY ALL INTRUDERS!!
AIYA! PANDA HERE TOO?
PANDA IS SLAVE OF SHAMPOO NOW!

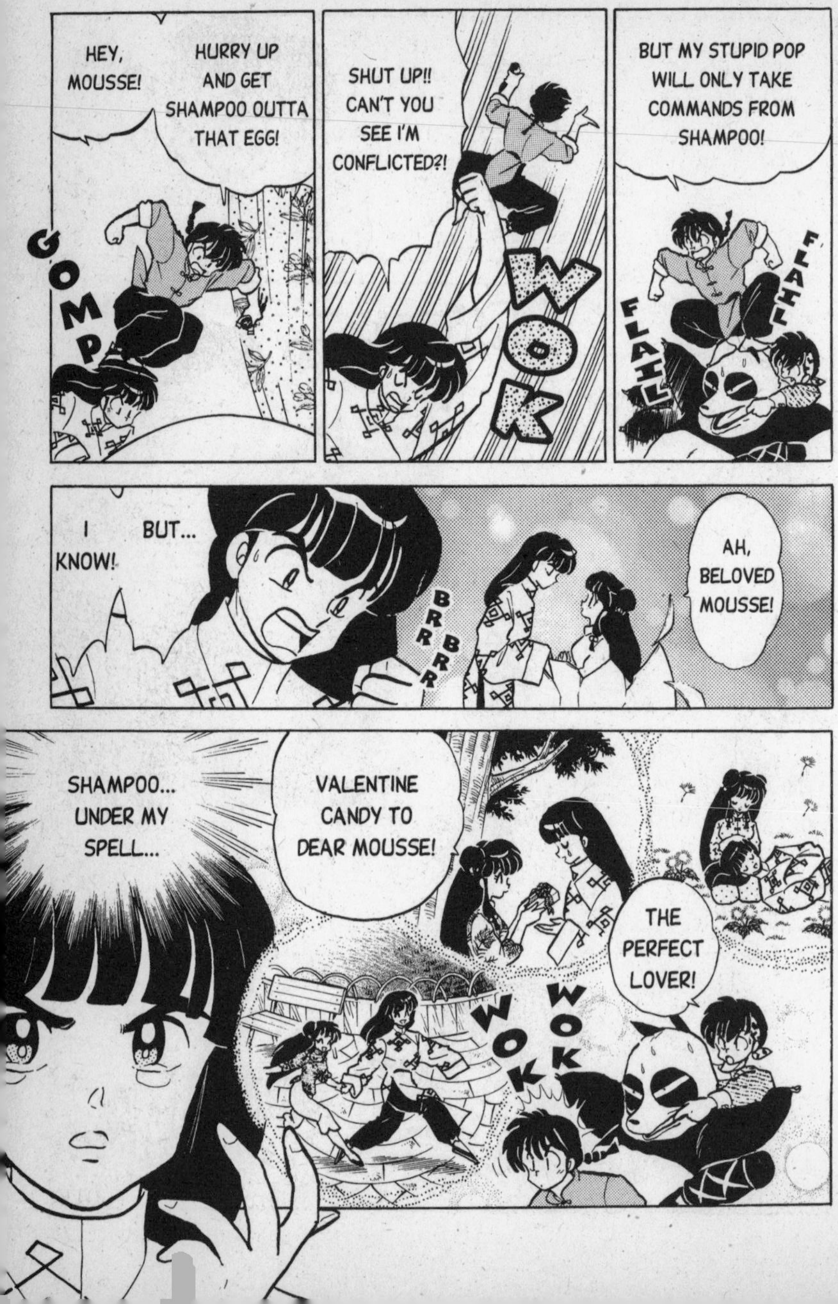
HEY, MOUSSE!
HURRY UP AND GET SHAMPOO OUTTA THAT EGG!
GOMP
SHUT UP!! CAN'T YOU SEE I'M CONFLICTED?!
WOK
BUT MY STUPID POP WILL ONLY TAKE COMMANDS FROM SHAMPOO!
FLAIL
FLAIL
I KNOW!
BUT...
BRRR
BRRR
AH, BELOVED MOUSSE!
SHAMPOO... UNDER MY SPELL...
VALENTINE CANDY TO DEAR MOUSSE!
THE PERFECT LOVER!
WOK
WOK

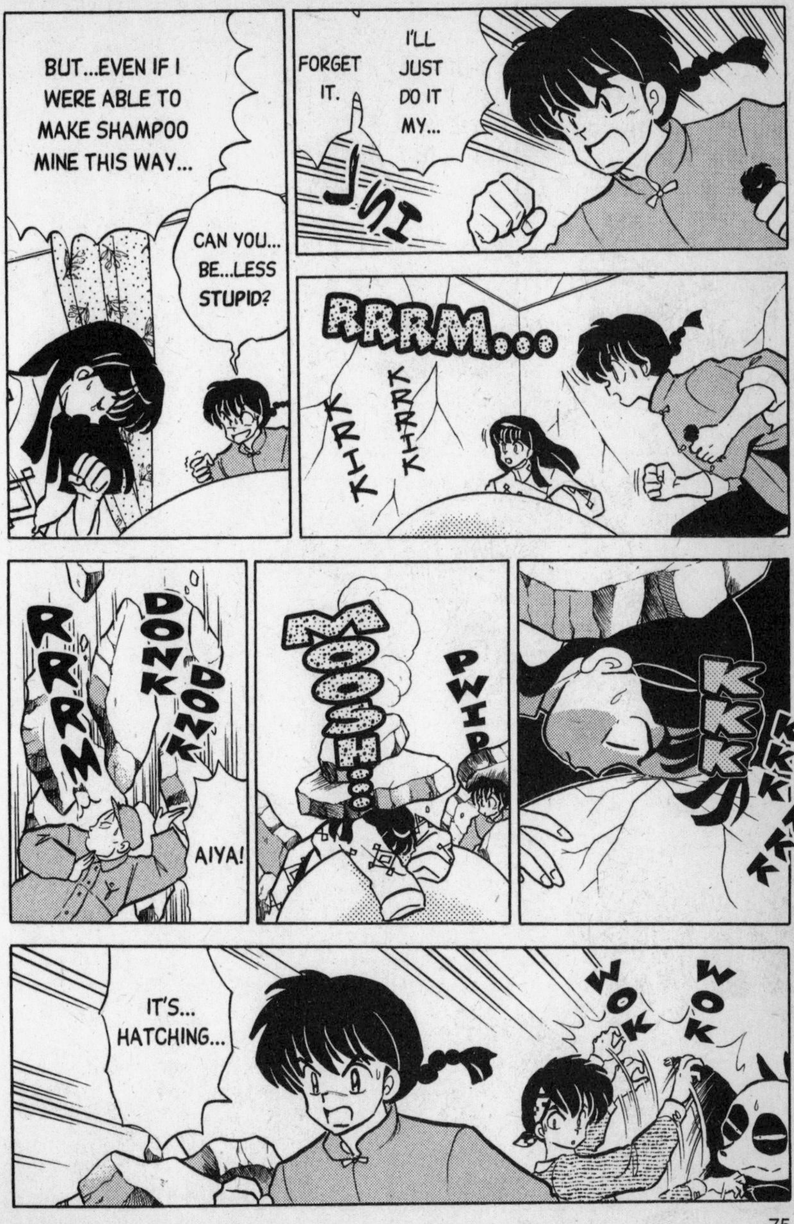
BUT...EVEN IF I WERE ABLE TO MAKE SHAMPOO MINE THIS WAY...
CAN YOU... BE...LESS STUPID?
FORGET IT.
I'LL JUST DO IT MY...
ISLJ
RRRM...
KRIK
KRRIK
RRRM
DONK
DONK
AIYA!
MOOSH...
PWIP
KKK
KKKKKKK
IT'S... HATCHING...
WOK
WOK

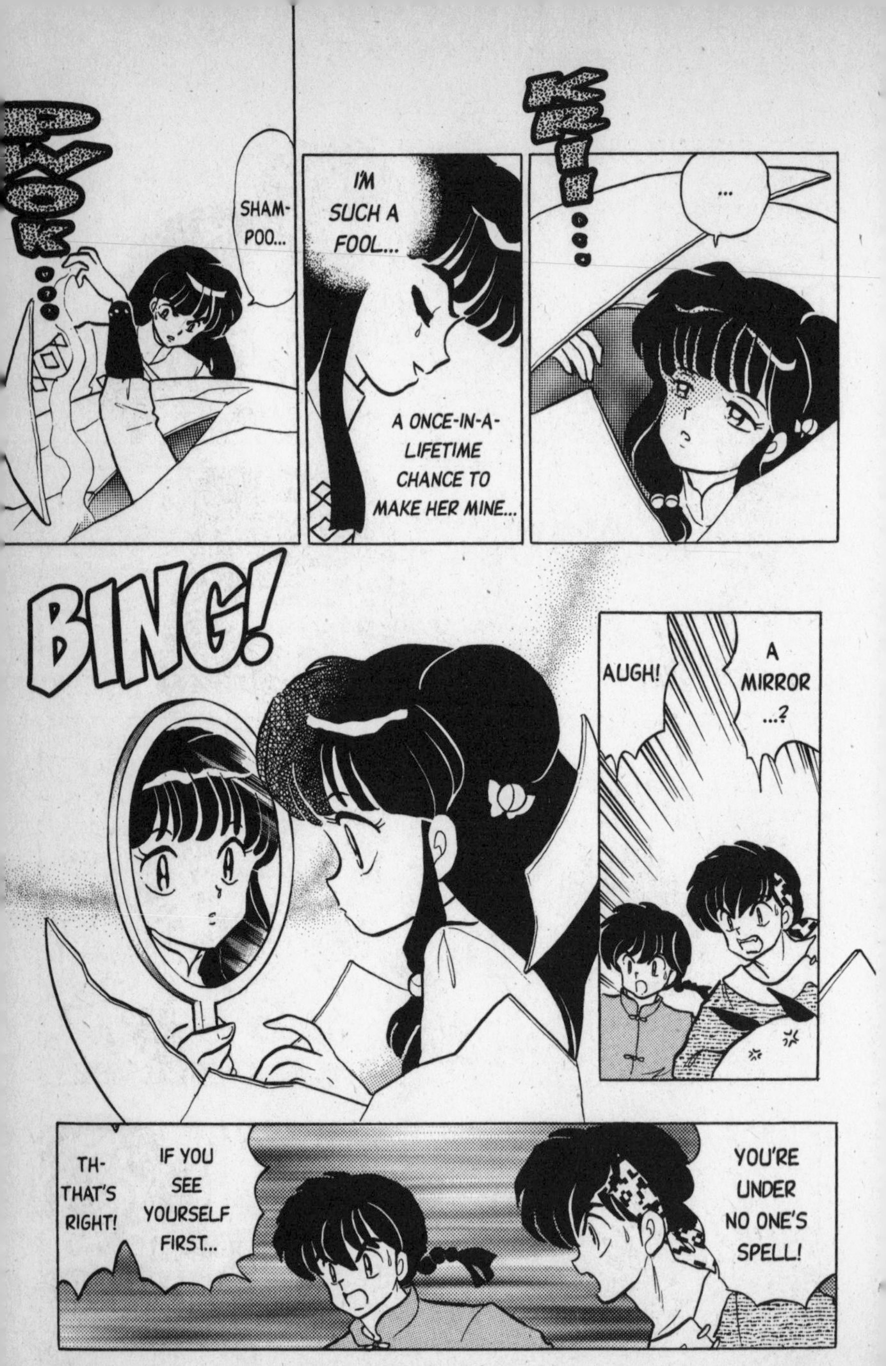
PYOK...
SHAMPOO...
I'M SUCH A FOOL...
A ONCE-IN-A-LIFETIME CHANCE TO MAKE HER MINE...
...
BING!
AUGH!
A MIRROR ...?
TH-THAT'S RIGHT!
IF YOU SEE YOURSELF FIRST...
YOU'RE UNDER NO ONE'S SPELL!

WHAT SHAMPOO DOING...?

SHAMPOO... I'M GLAD...

MOUSSE...?

POP

THIS... IS THE RIGHT THING.

SIGH

IF I'M TO HAVE YOUR LOVE, IT MUST BE...

AIYA, RANMA! SO SCARY FOR SHAMPOO!

EEE!

EEE!

YOU DIDN'T EXACTLY LOOK SCARED!

GRRR

GRRR

HURRY UP AND GIVE THIS PANDA AN ORDER!

YES, MIST-RESS!

SSHH

SSHH

OOOOOO@@@@@@

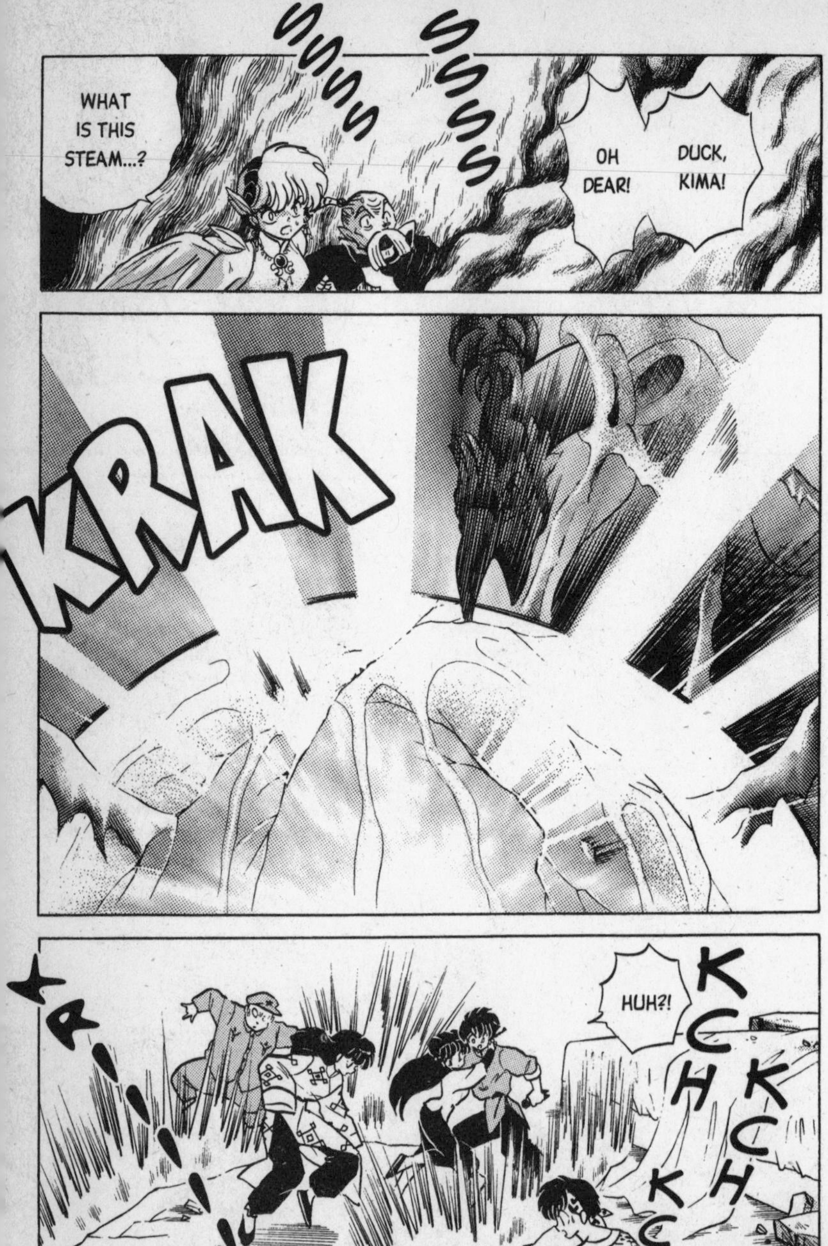

WHAT IS THIS STEAM...?
SSSSS
SSSSS
OH DEAR! DUCK, KIMA!
KRAK
HUH?!
KCHKCH
KCH

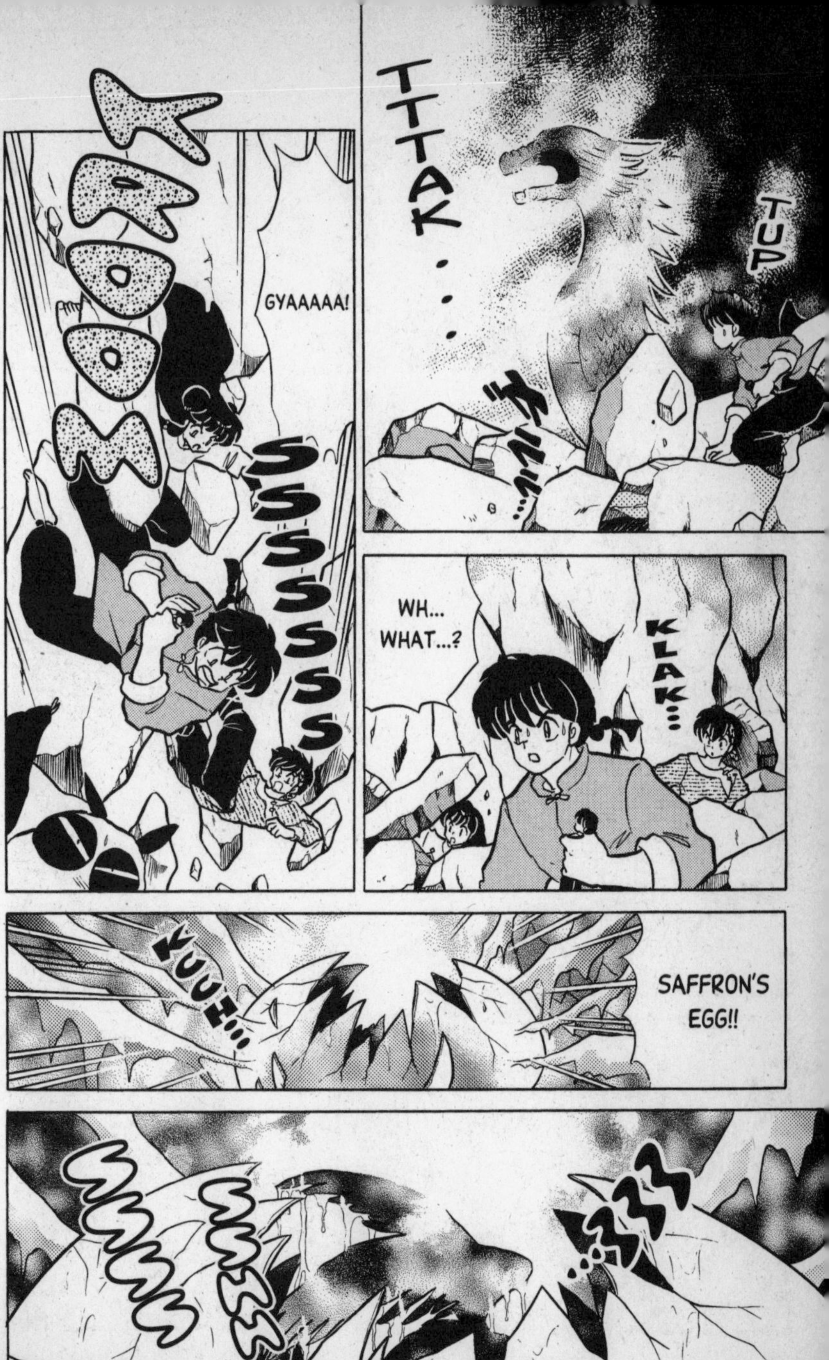
KABOOM
GYAAAAA!
SSSSSSS
TTTAK...
TUP
WH... WHAT...?
KLAK...
KUUH...
SAFFRON'S EGG!!

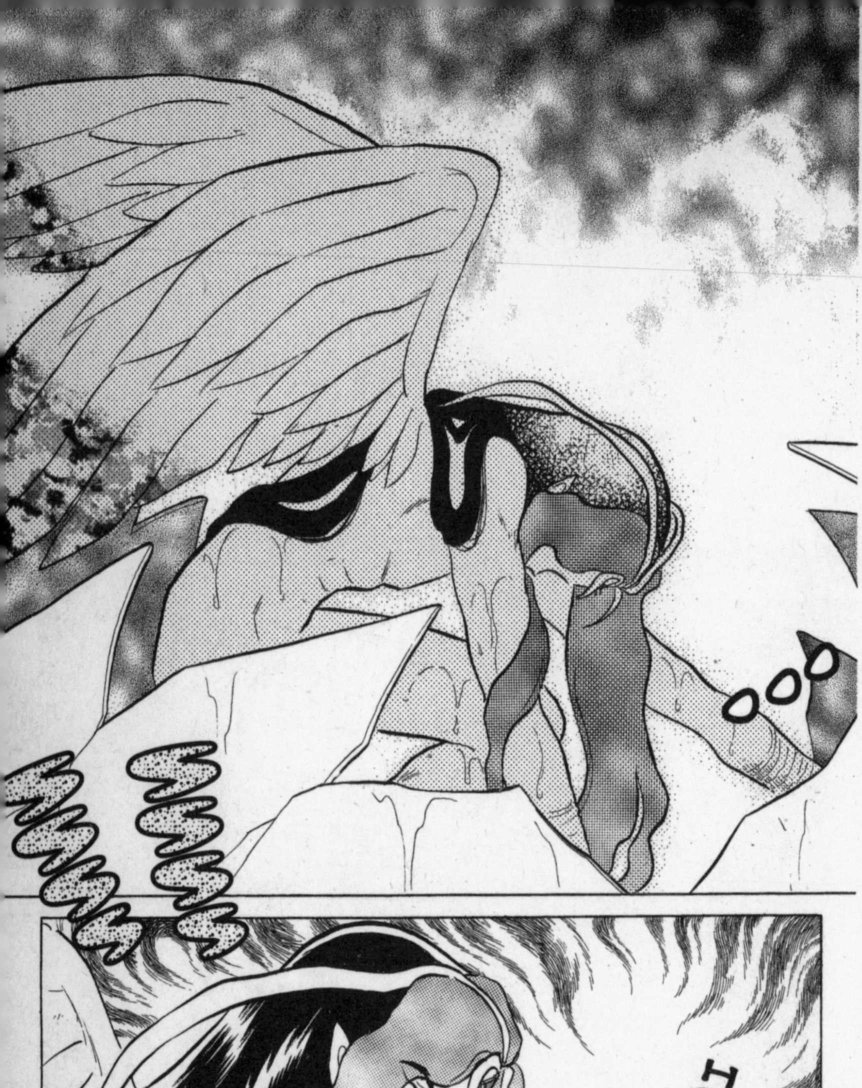
OOO

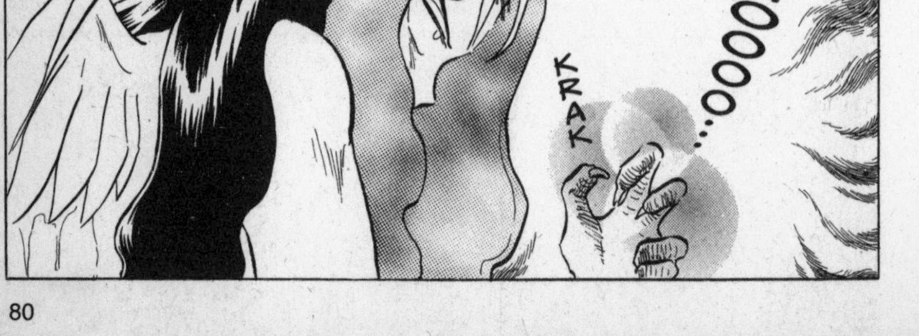
KRAK
HOOOOO...

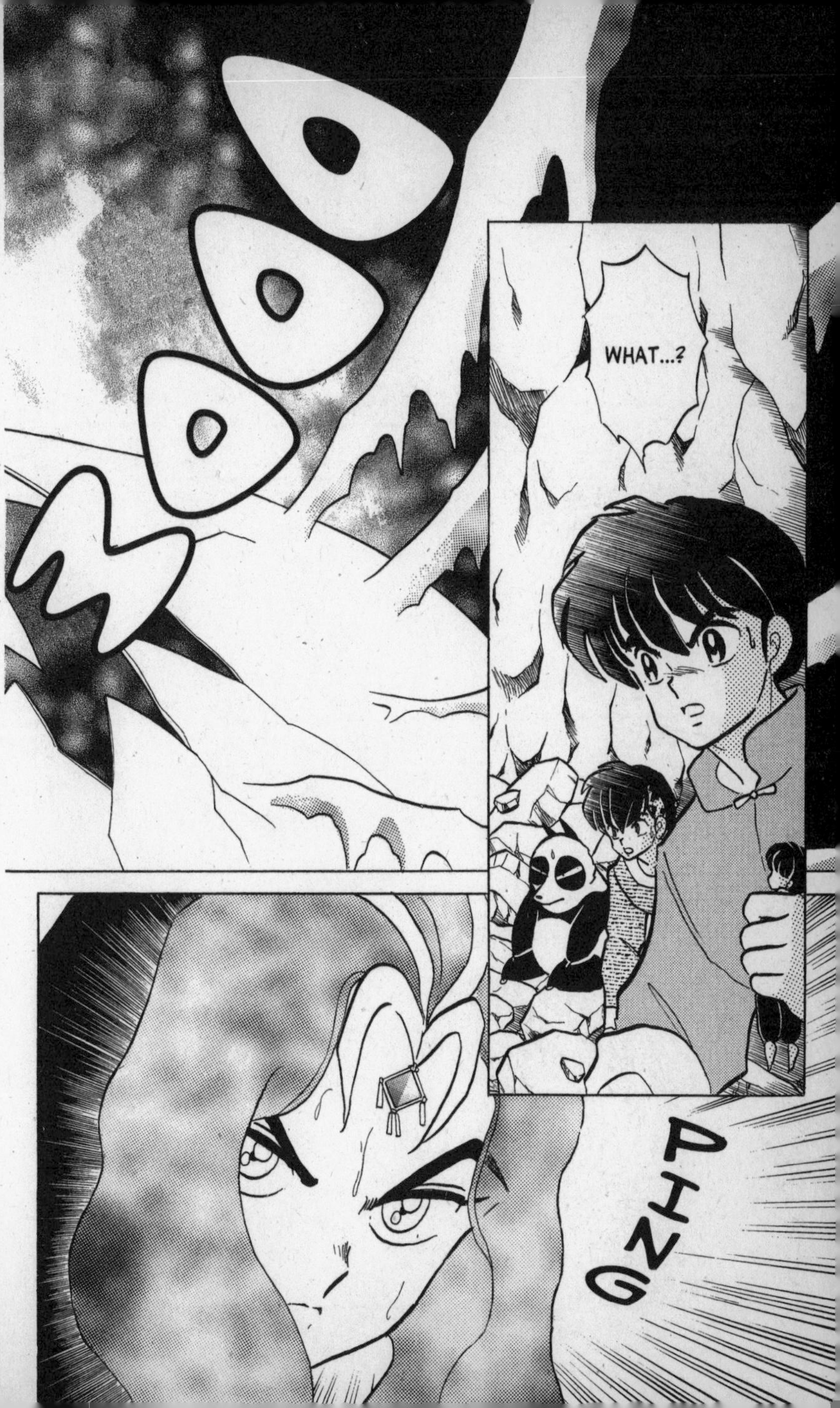
WHAT...?
PING

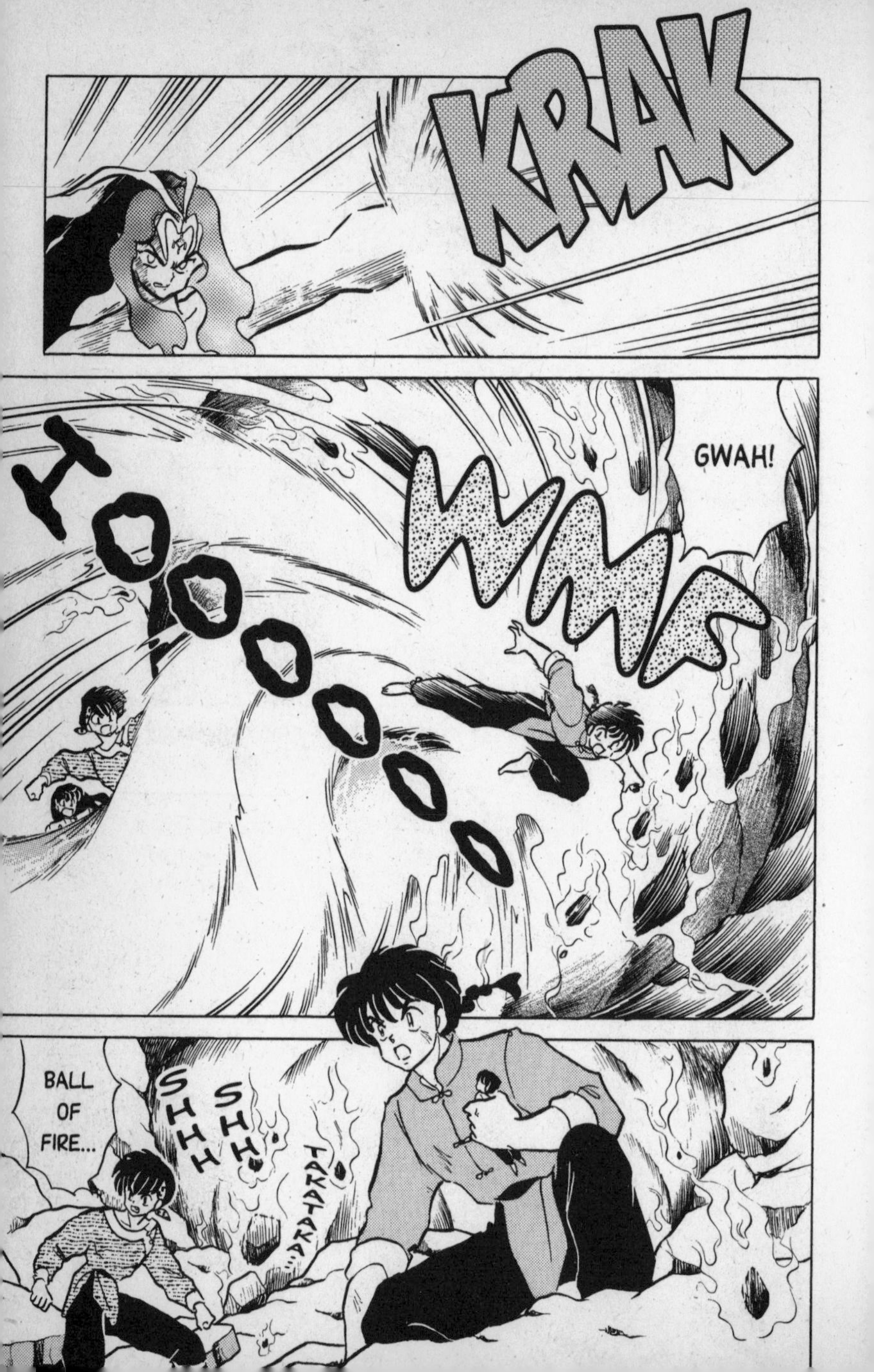
KRAK
HOOOOOOOO
WHAM
GWAH!
BALL OF FIRE...
SHHH
SHHH
TAKATAKA...

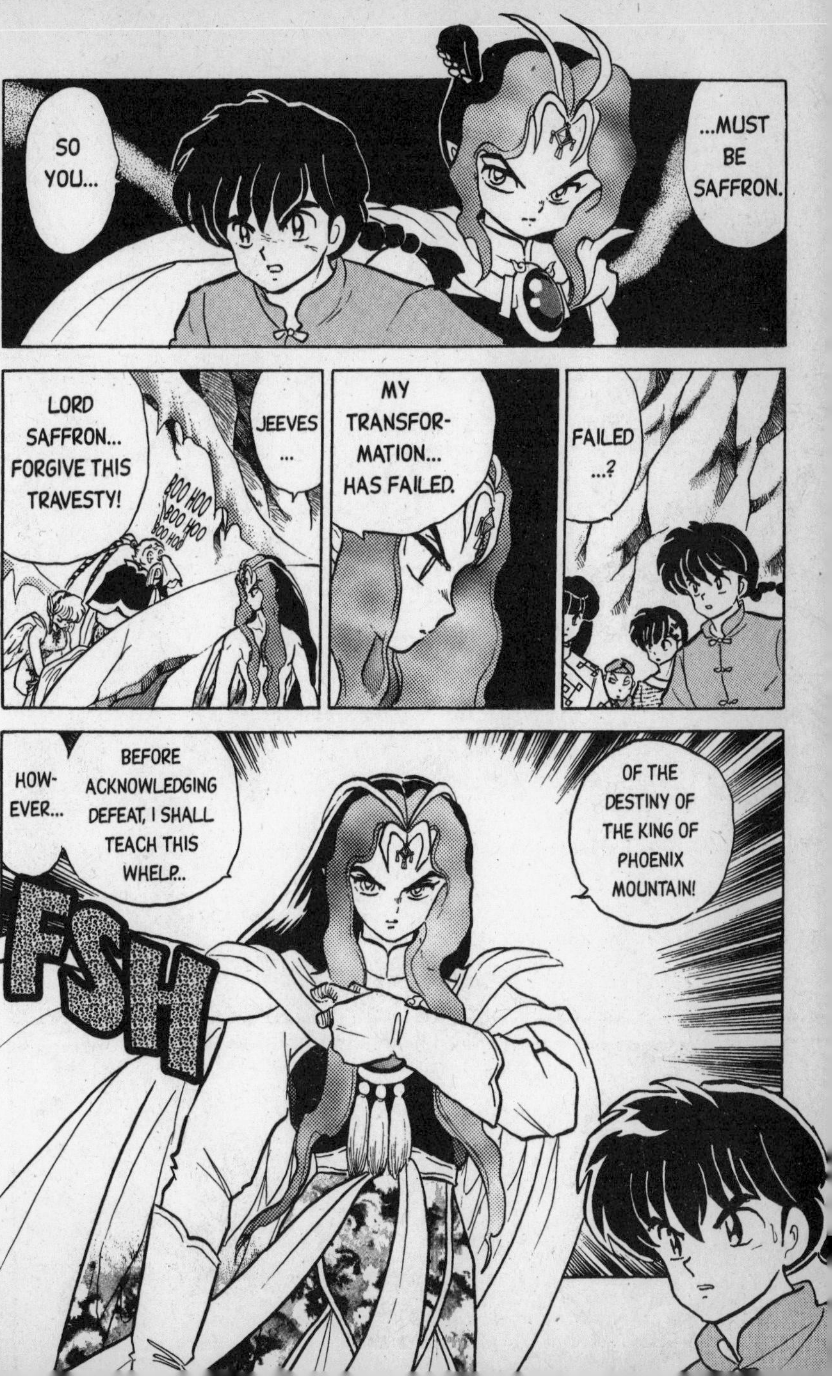
SO YOU...
...MUST BE SAFFRON.
LORD SAFFRON... FORGIVE THIS TRAVESTY!
BOO HOO BOO HOO BOO HOO
JEEVES ...
MY TRANSFOR-MATION... HAS FAILED.
FAILED ...?
HOW-EVER...
BEFORE ACKNOWLEDGING DEFEAT, I SHALL TEACH THIS WHELP...
OF THE DESTINY OF THE KING OF PHOENIX MOUNTAIN!
FSH

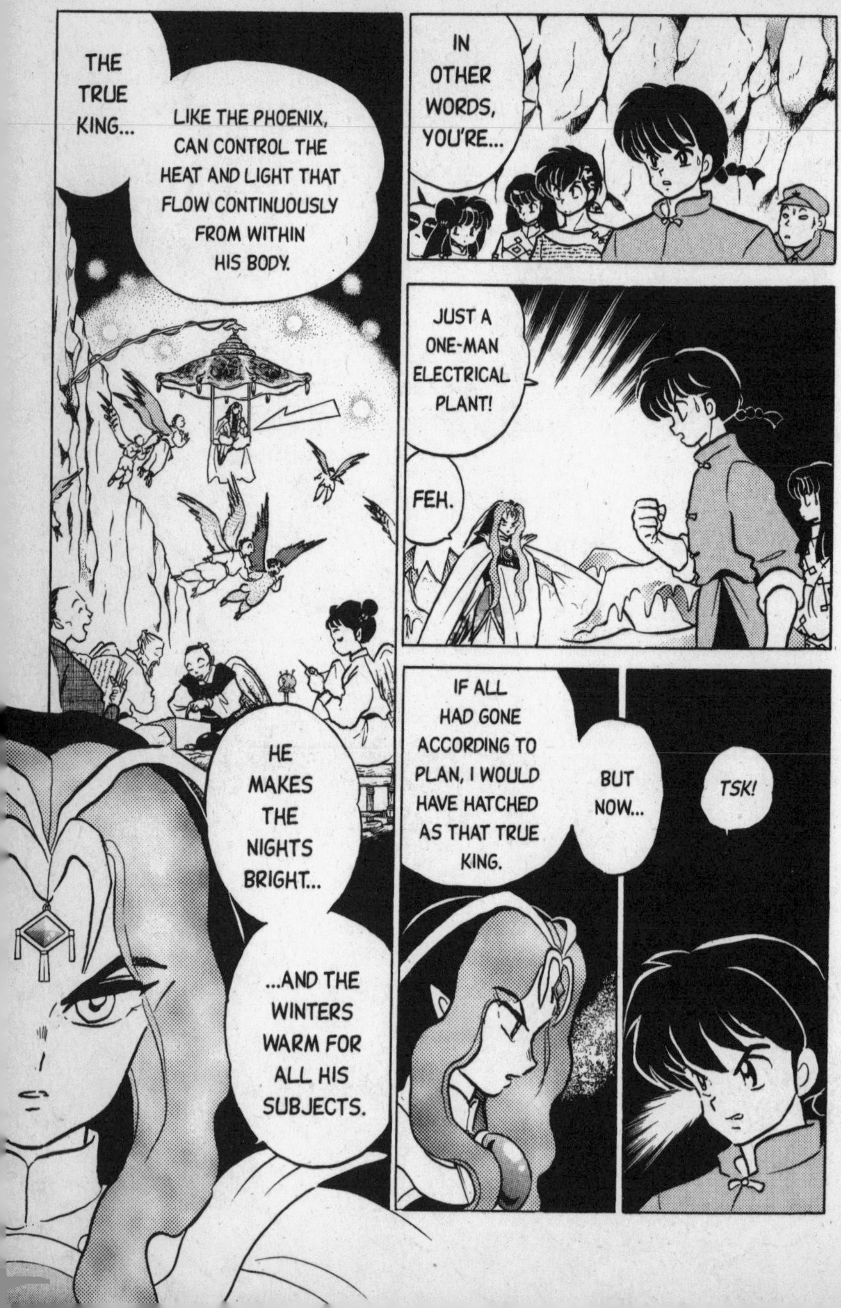
THE TRUE KING...
LIKE THE PHOENIX, CAN CONTROL THE HEAT AND LIGHT THAT FLOW CONTINUOUSLY FROM WITHIN HIS BODY.
HE MAKES THE NIGHTS BRIGHT...
...AND THE WINTERS WARM FOR ALL HIS SUBJECTS.
IN OTHER WORDS, YOU'RE...
JUST A ONE-MAN ELECTRICAL PLANT!
FEH.
IF ALL HAD GONE ACCORDING TO PLAN, I WOULD HAVE HATCHED AS THAT TRUE KING.
BUT NOW...
TSK!

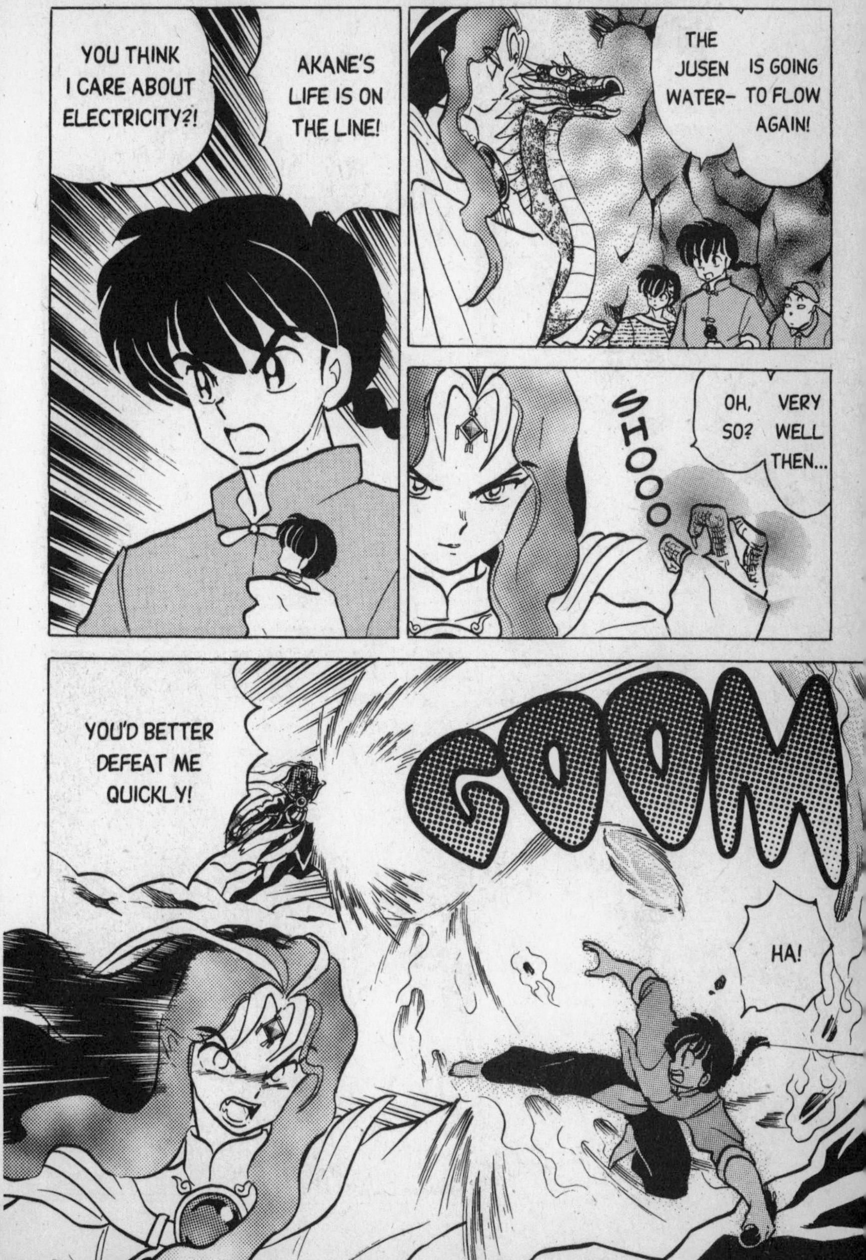
YOU THINK I CARE ABOUT ELECTRICITY?!
AKANE'S LIFE IS ON THE LINE!
THE JUSEN WATER– IS GOING TO FLOW AGAIN!
SHOOOO
OH, SO? VERY WELL THEN...
YOU'D BETTER DEFEAT ME QUICKLY!
GOOM
HA!

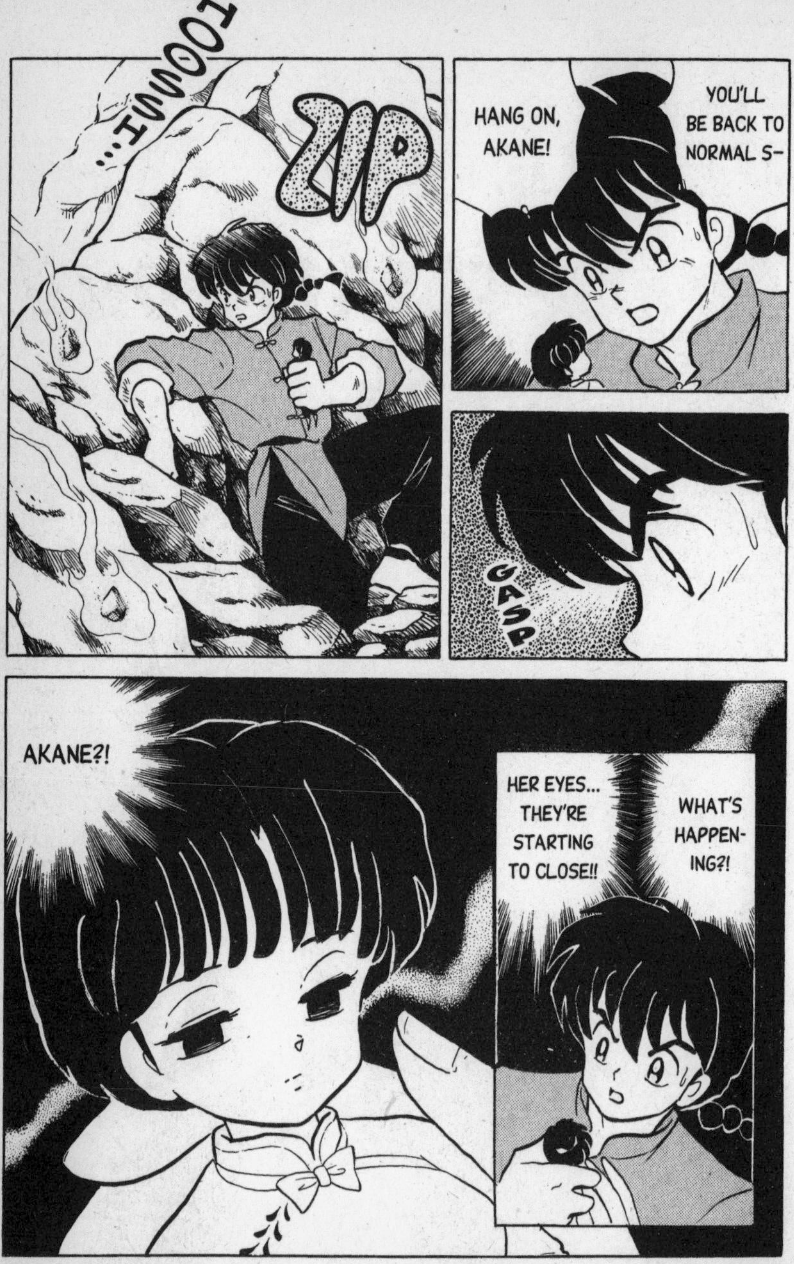
FOOOSSH...!!
ZIP
HANG ON, AKANE!
YOU'LL BE BACK TO NORMAL S—
GASP
AKANE?!
HER EYES... THEY'RE STARTING TO CLOSE!!
WHAT'S HAPPEN-ING?!

PART 6

RANMA BATTLES SAFFRON!!

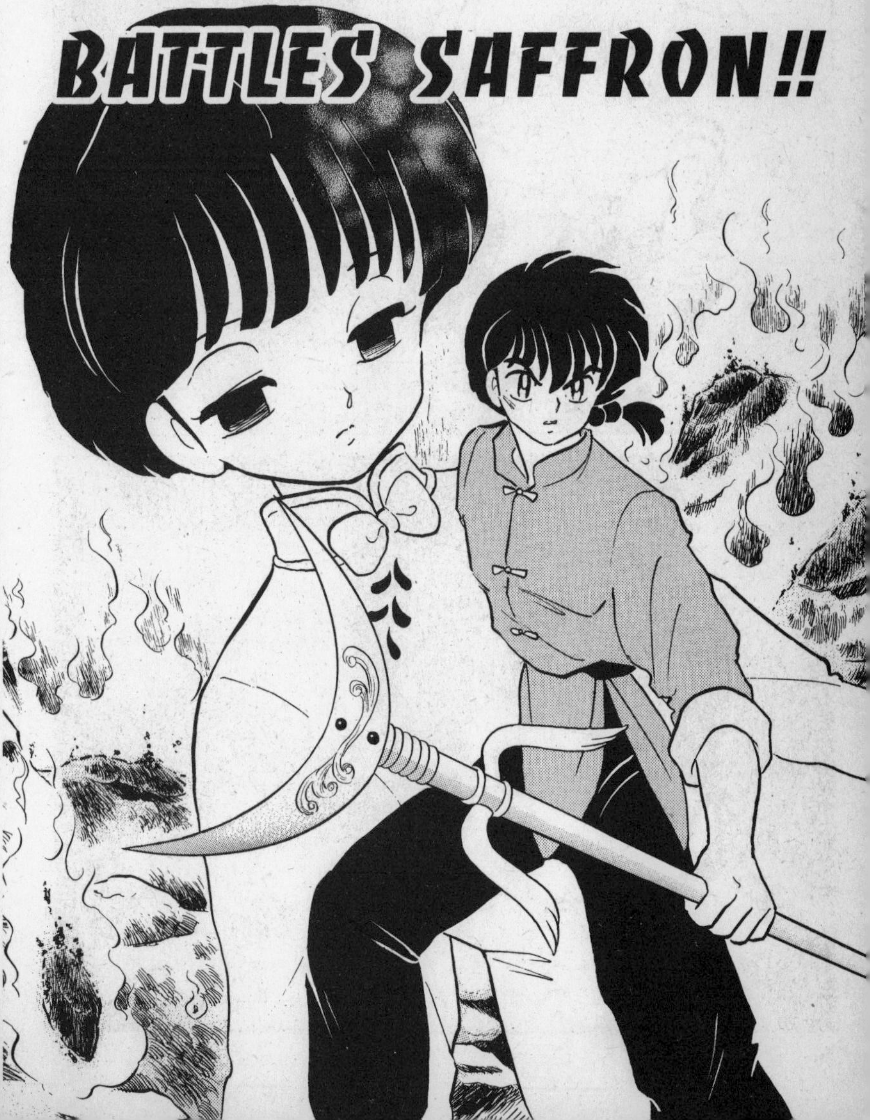

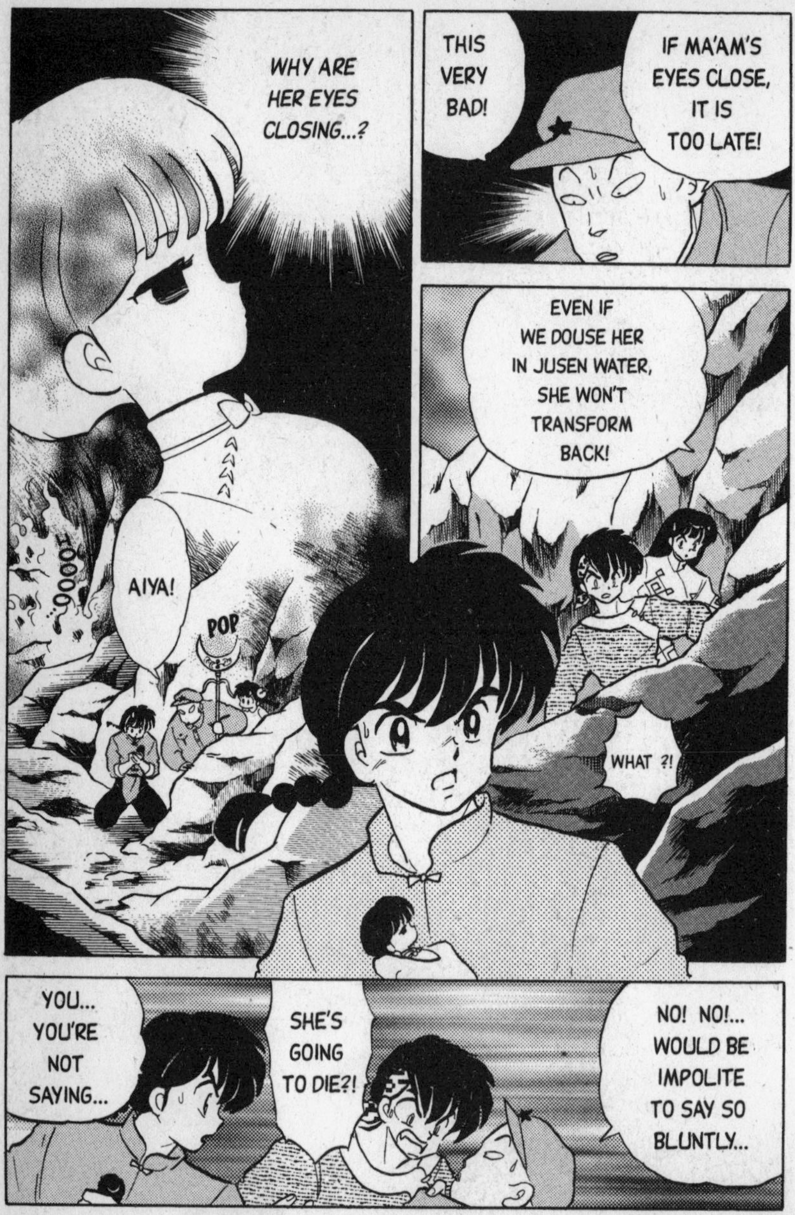
WHY ARE HER EYES CLOSING...?
AIYA!
POP
THIS VERY BAD!
IF MA'AM'S EYES CLOSE, IT IS TOO LATE!
EVEN IF WE DOUSE HER IN JUSEN WATER, SHE WON'T TRANSFORM BACK!
WHAT ?!
YOU... YOU'RE NOT SAYING...
SHE'S GOING TO DIE?!
NO! NO!... WOULD BE IMPOLITE TO SAY SO BLUNTLY...

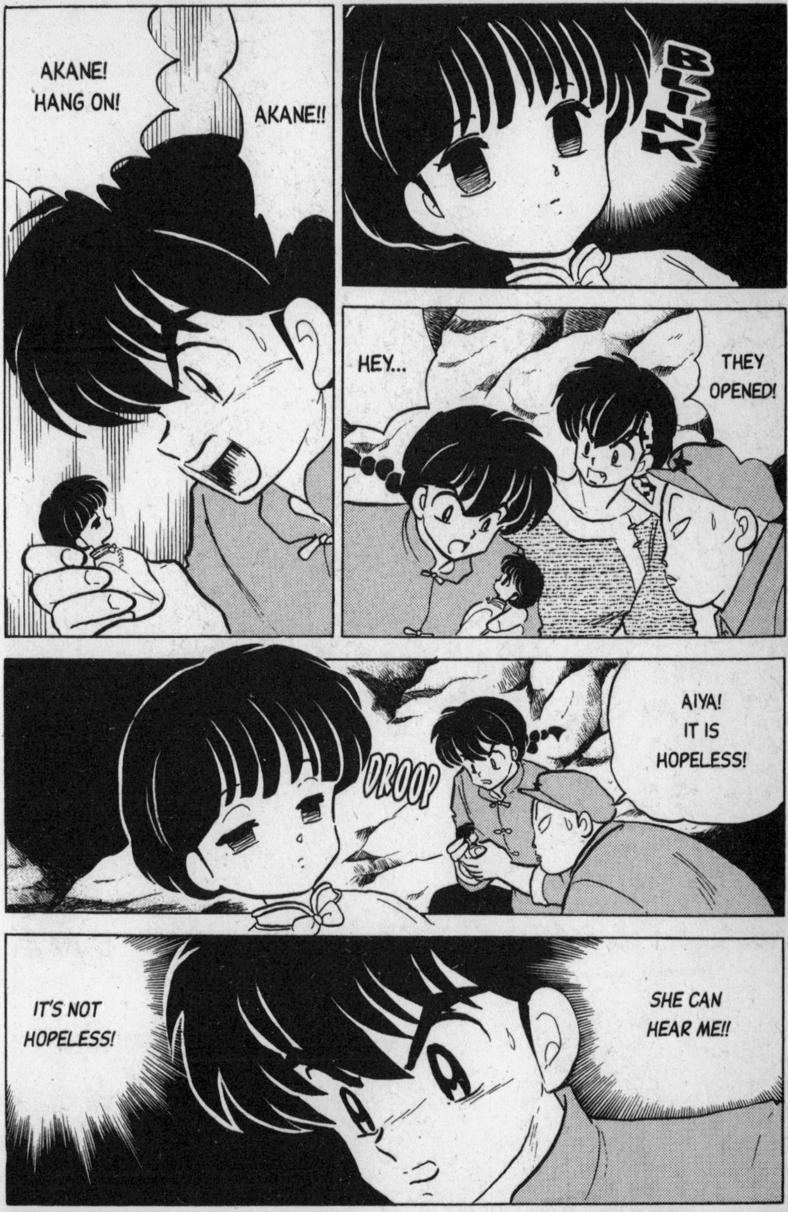
AKANE!
HANG ON!
AKANE!!
BLINK
HEY...
THEY OPENED!
DROOP
AIYA!
IT IS
HOPELESS!
IT'S NOT
HOPELESS!
SHE CAN
HEAR ME!!

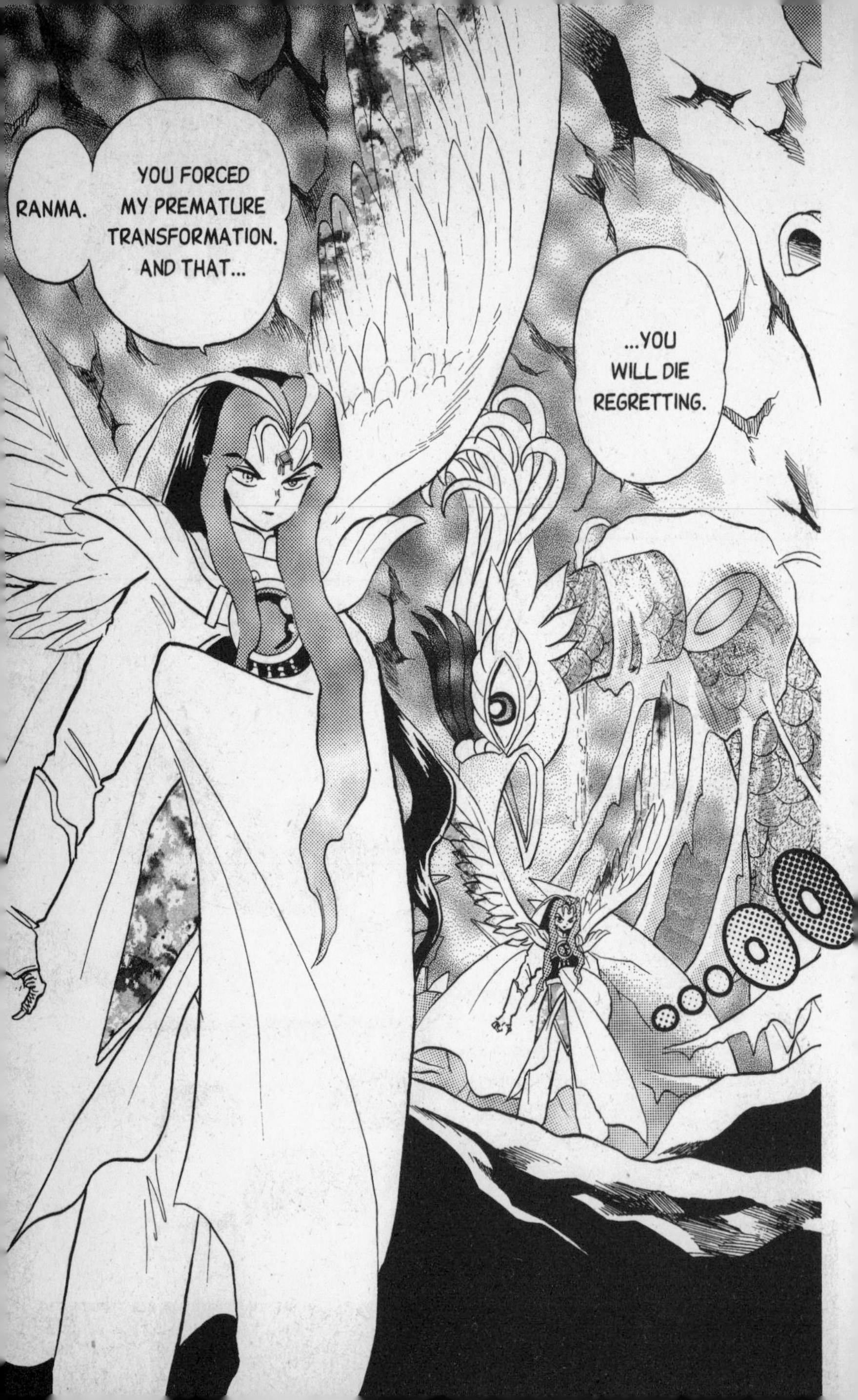
RANMA.
YOU FORCED MY PREMATURE TRANSFORMATION. AND THAT...
...YOU WILL DIE REGRETTING.

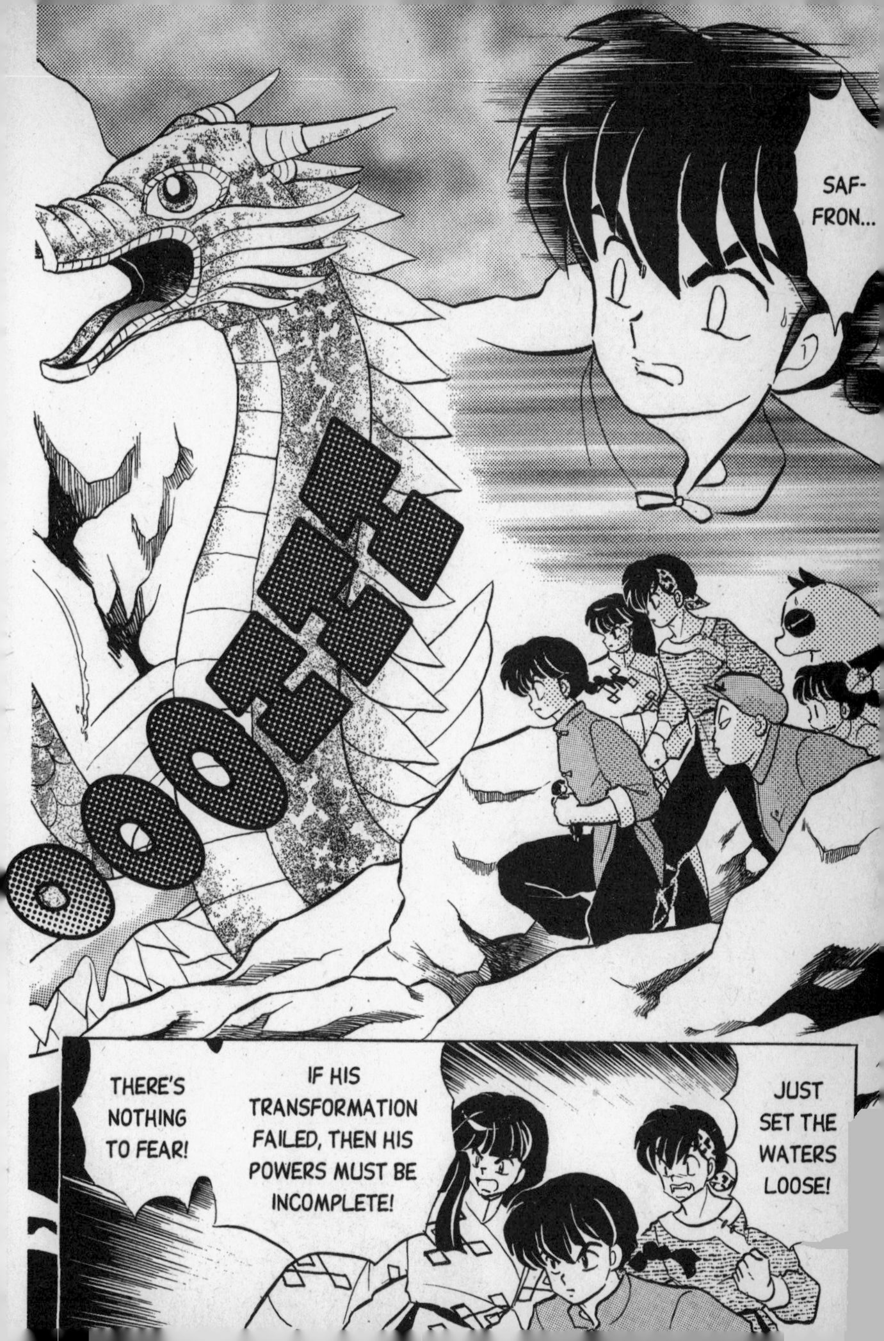
OOOHHH
SAF-
FRON...
THERE'S NOTHING TO FEAR!
IF HIS TRANSFORMATION FAILED, THEN HIS POWERS MUST BE INCOMPLETE!
JUST SET THE WATERS LOOSE!

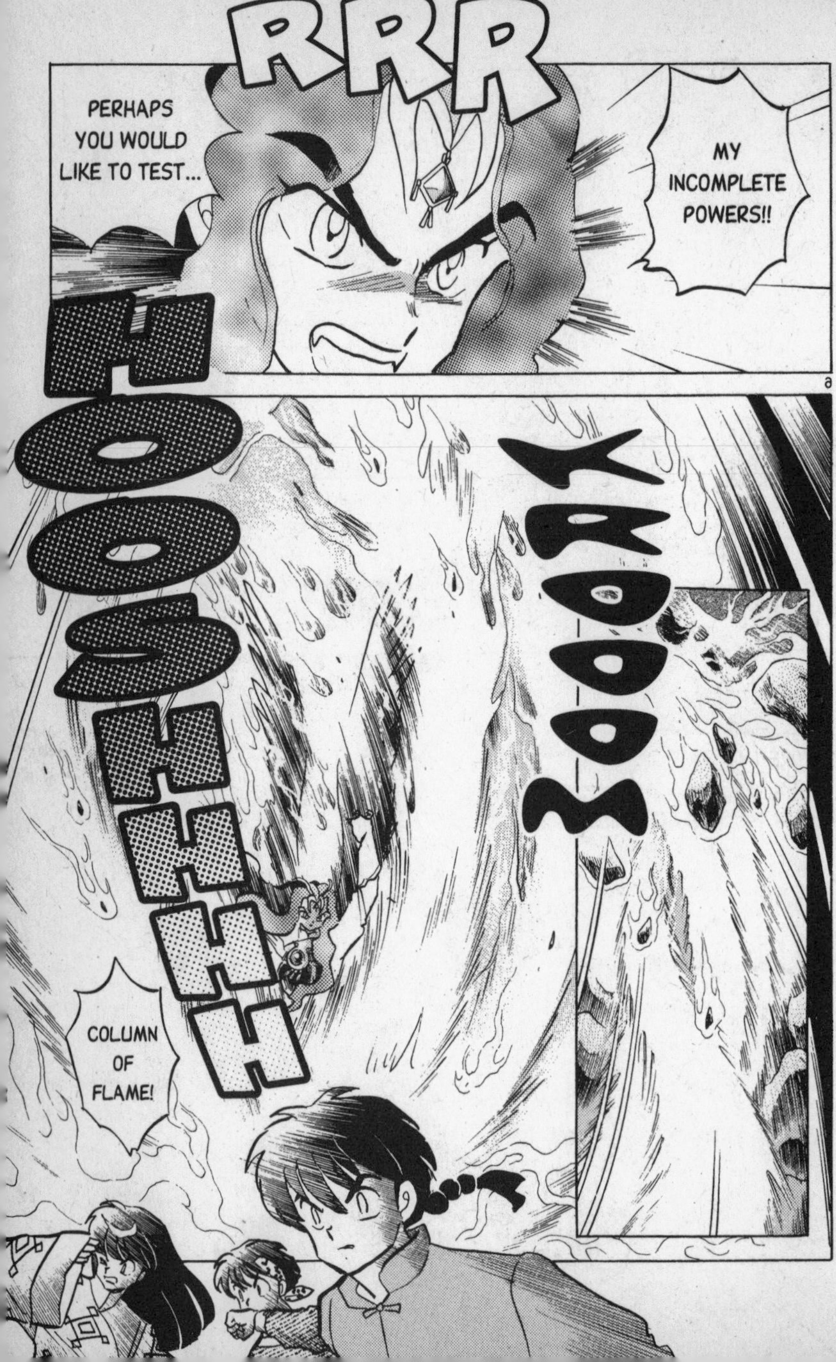
RRR
PERHAPS YOU WOULD LIKE TO TEST...
MY INCOMPLETE POWERS!!
HOOSHHHH
KROOOM
COLUMN OF FLAME!

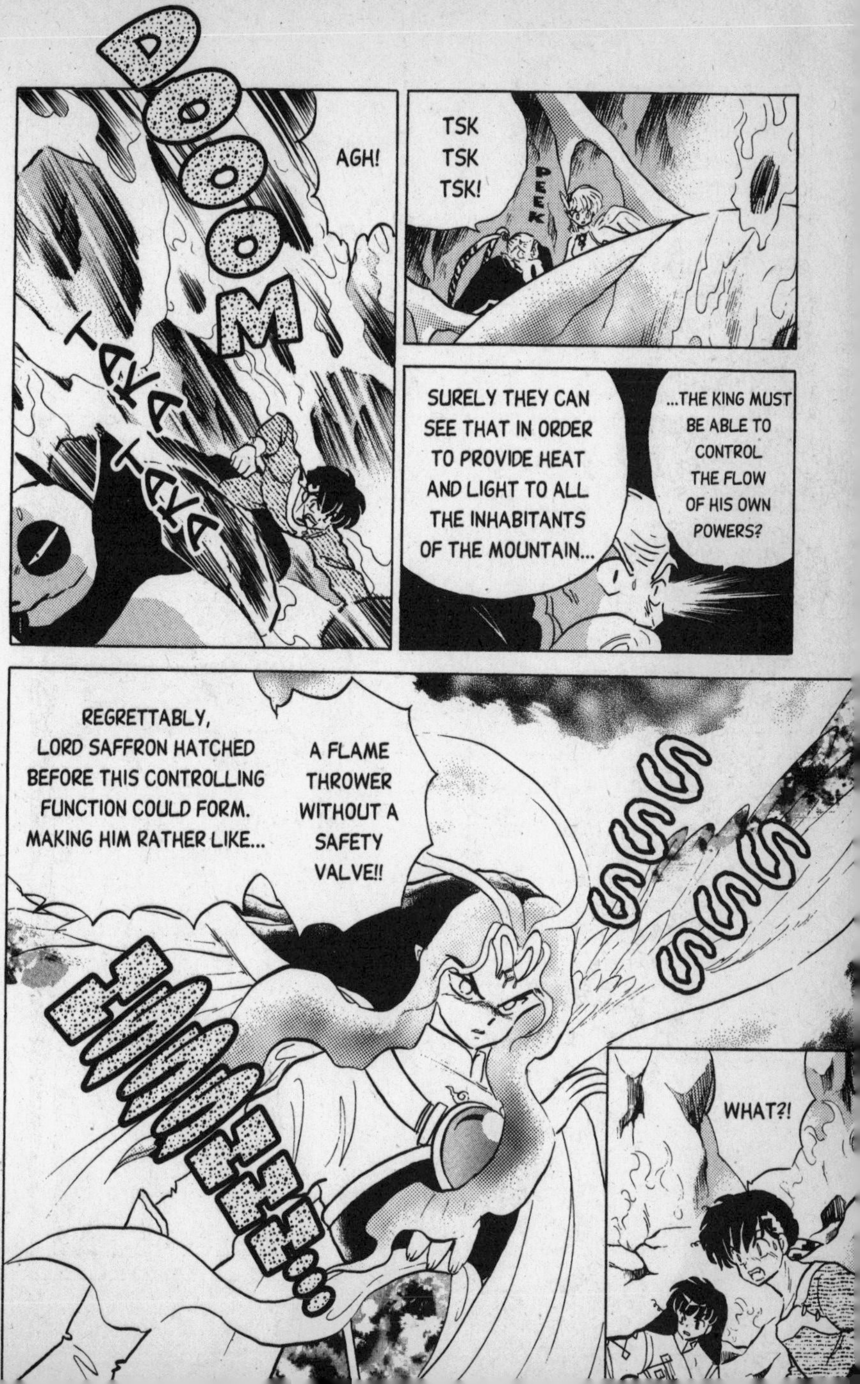
DOOOOM
AGH!
TAKA TAKA TAKA
TSK TSK TSK!
PEEK
SURELY THEY CAN SEE THAT IN ORDER TO PROVIDE HEAT AND LIGHT TO ALL THE INHABITANTS OF THE MOUNTAIN...
...THE KING MUST BE ABLE TO CONTROL THE FLOW OF HIS OWN POWERS?
REGRETTABLY, LORD SAFFRON HATCHED BEFORE THIS CONTROLLING FUNCTION COULD FORM. MAKING HIM RATHER LIKE...
A FLAME THROWER WITHOUT A SAFETY VALVE!!
WHAT?!

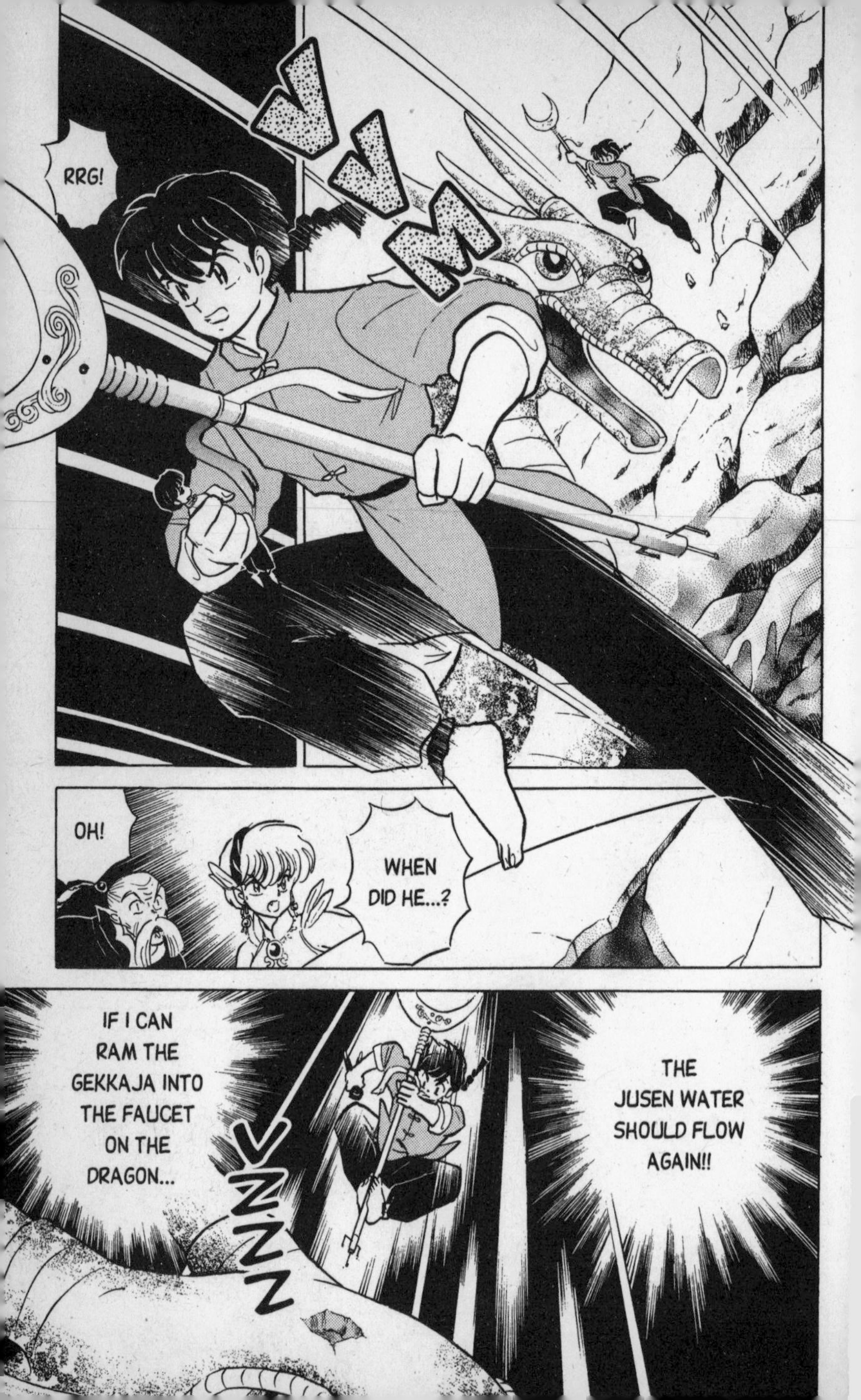
VVVM
RRG!
OH!
WHEN DID HE...?
IF I CAN RAM THE GEKKAJA INTO THE FAUCET ON THE DRAGON...
VNNN
THE JUSEN WATER SHOULD FLOW AGAIN!!

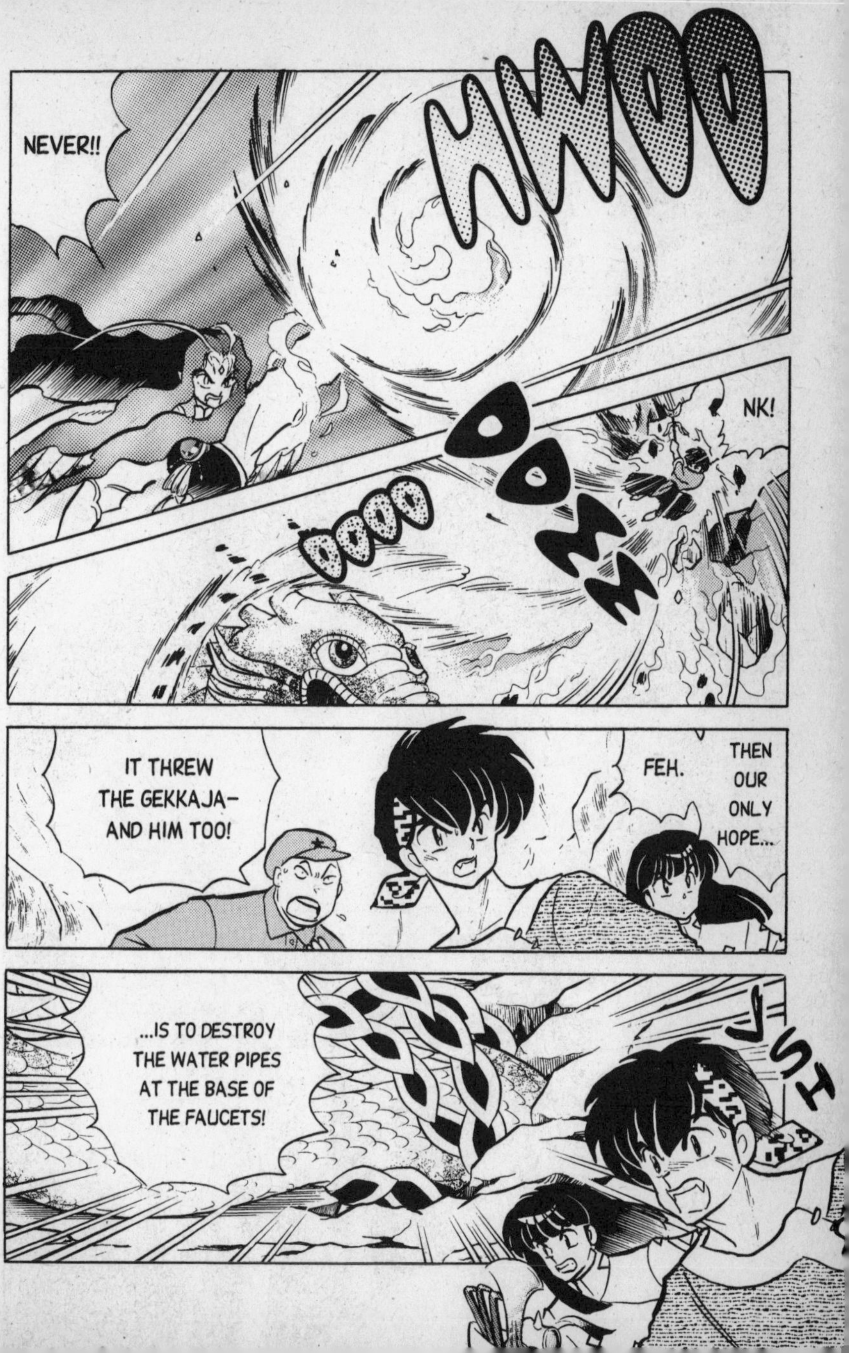
NEVER!!
HWOO
NK!
IT THREW THE GEKKAJA— AND HIM TOO!
FEH.
THEN OUR ONLY HOPE...
...IS TO DESTROY THE WATER PIPES AT THE BASE OF THE FAUCETS!

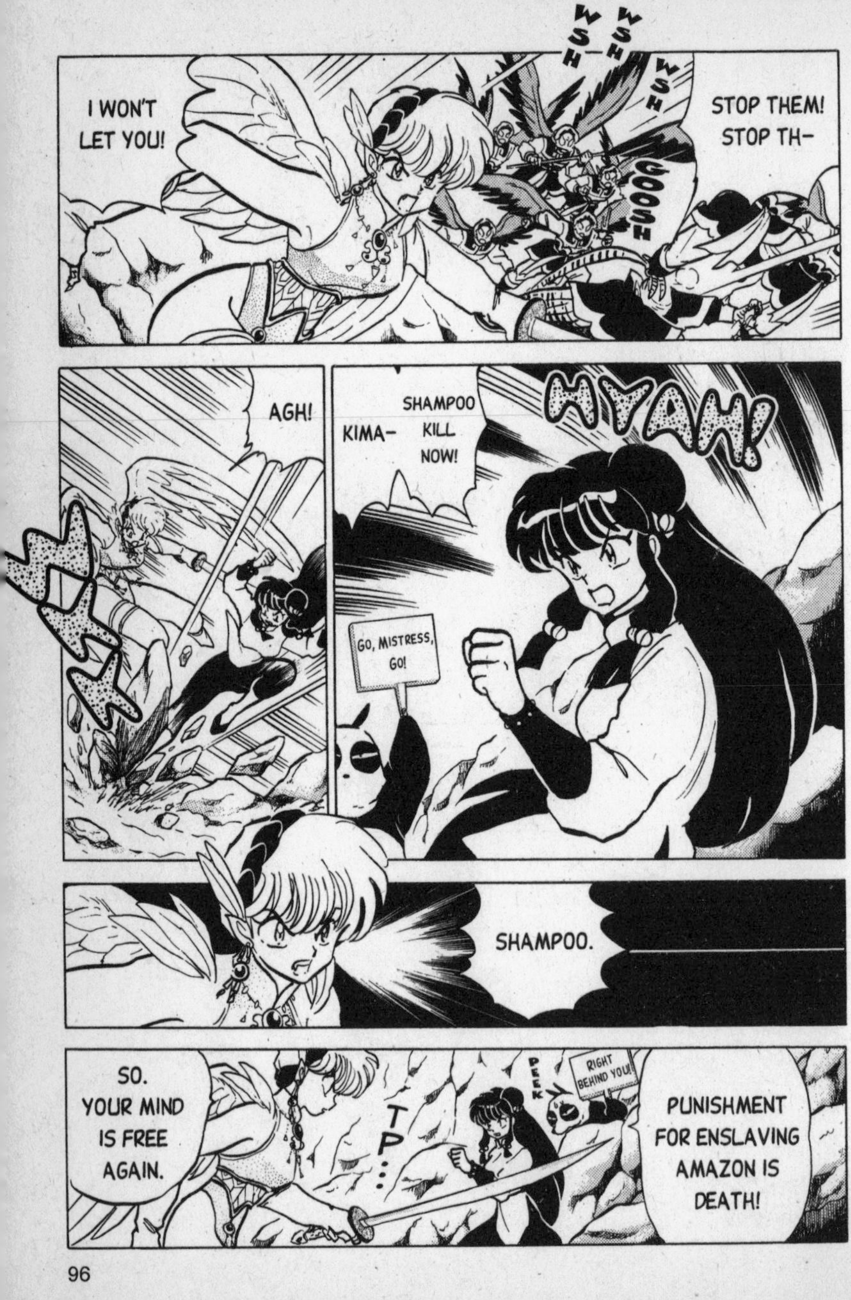
WSH WSH WSH
I WON'T LET YOU!
STOP THEM! STOP TH-
GOOSH
AGH!
KIMA-
SHAMPOO KILL NOW!
HYAH!
GO, MISTRESS, GO!
SHAMPOO.
SO. YOUR MIND IS FREE AGAIN.
TP...
PEEK
RIGHT BEHIND YOU!
PUNISHMENT FOR ENSLAVING AMAZON IS DEATH!

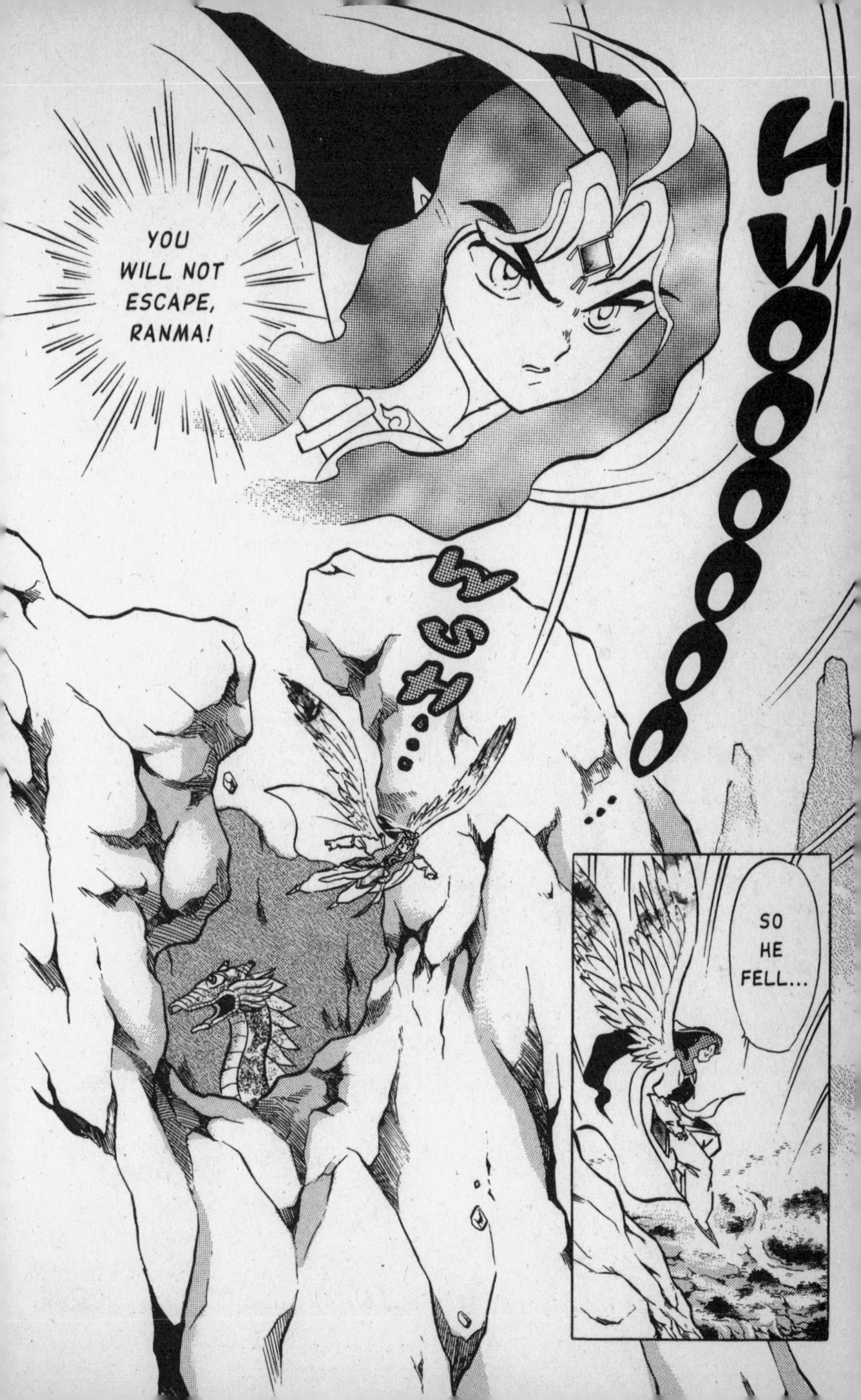

YOU WILL NOT ESCAPE, RANMA!
WHOOOOOOOO
WSH...
...
SO HE FELL...

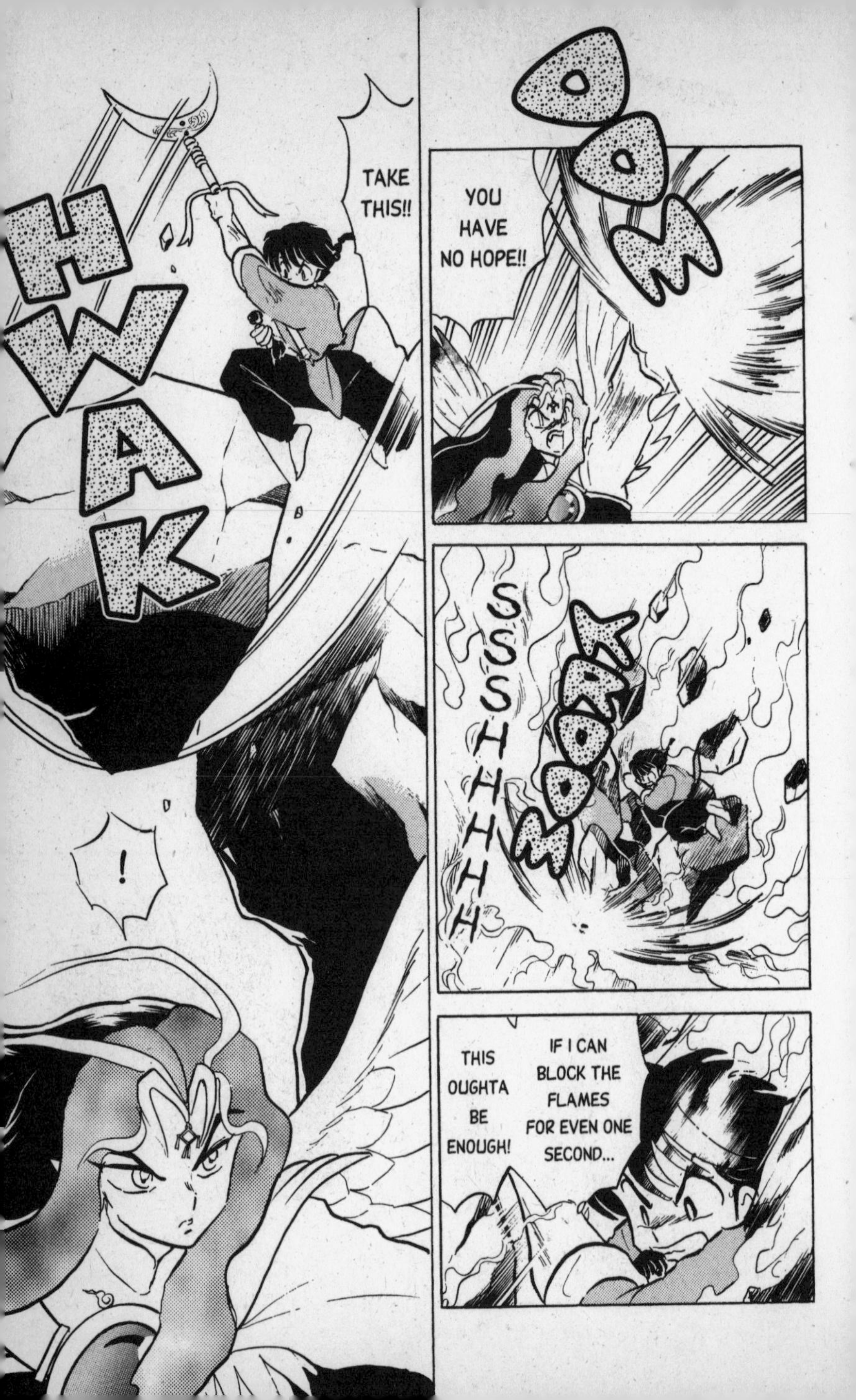
TAKE THIS!!
HWAK
!
DOOM
YOU HAVE NO HOPE!!
SSSHHHHHHH
KRADOOM
IF I CAN BLOCK THE FLAMES FOR EVEN ONE SECOND...
THIS OUGHTA BE ENOUGH!

YOU'RE
GROUNDED!!

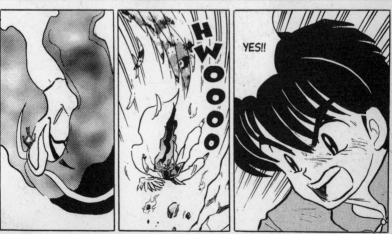

HWOOOO

YES!!

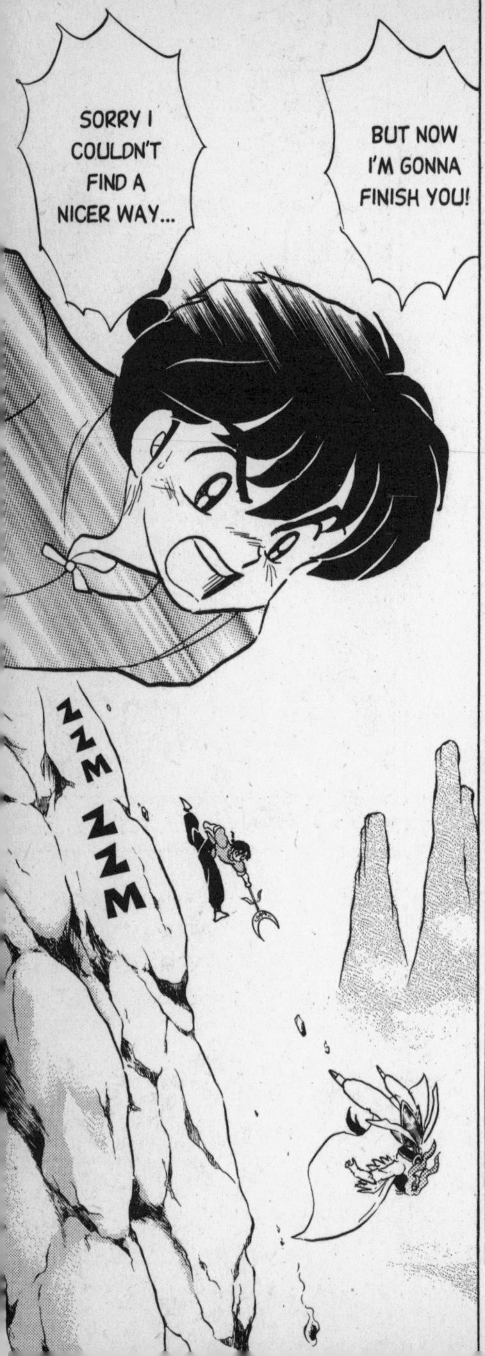
SORRY I COULDN'T FIND A NICER WAY...
BUT NOW I'M GONNA FINISH YOU!
ZZM ZZM
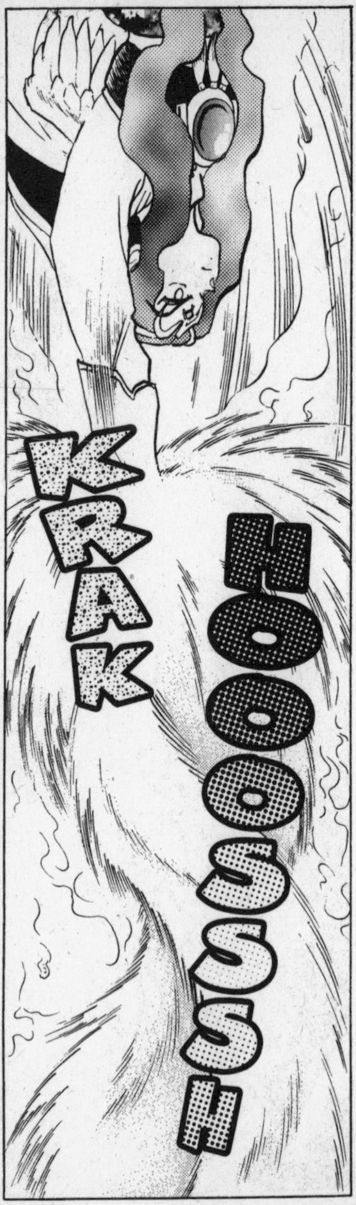
KRAK
HOOOSSSH

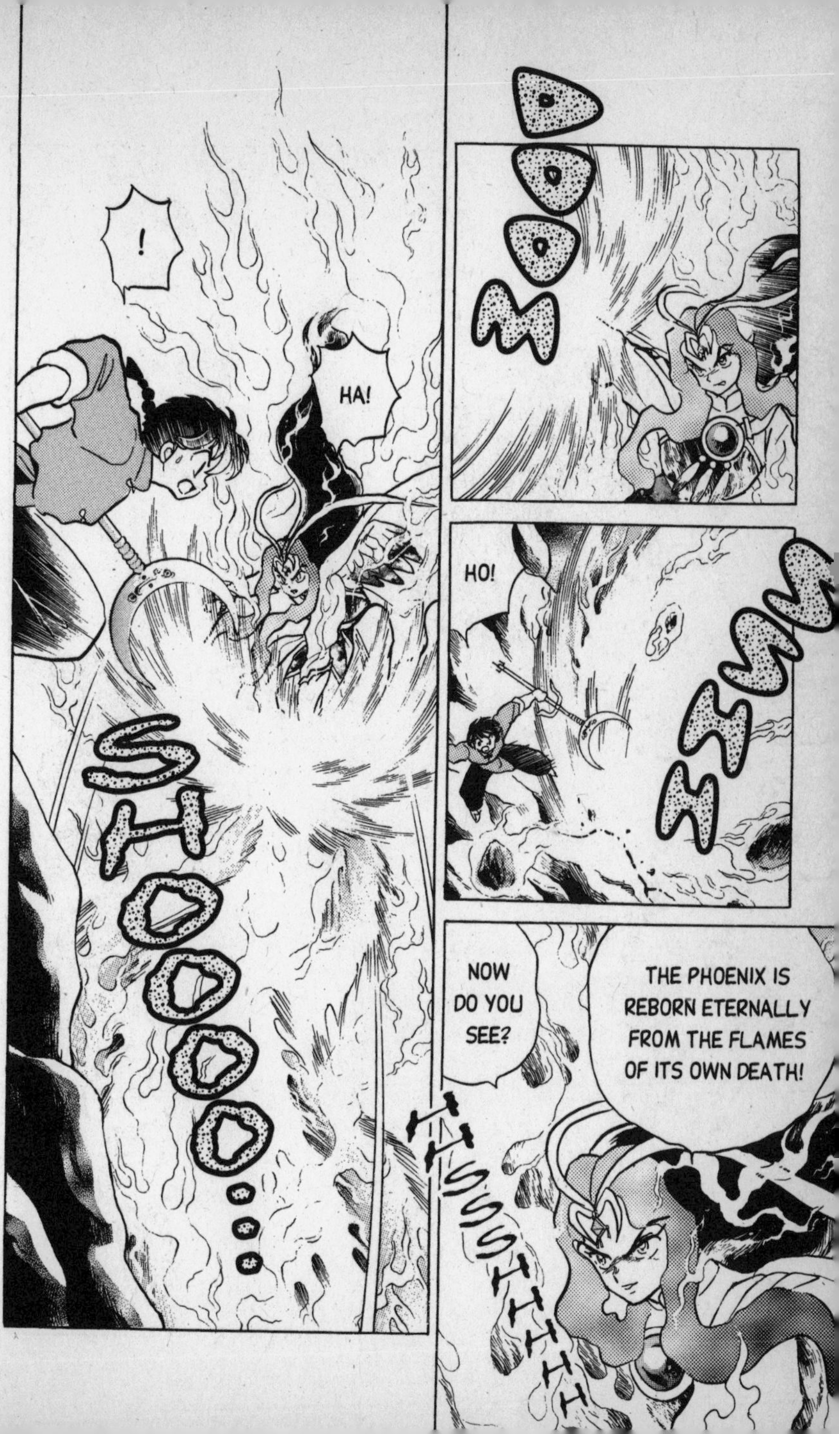
!
HA!
SHOOOOO...
DOOOM
HO!
NOW DO YOU SEE?
THE PHOENIX IS REBORN ETERNALLY FROM THE FLAMES OF ITS OWN DEATH!

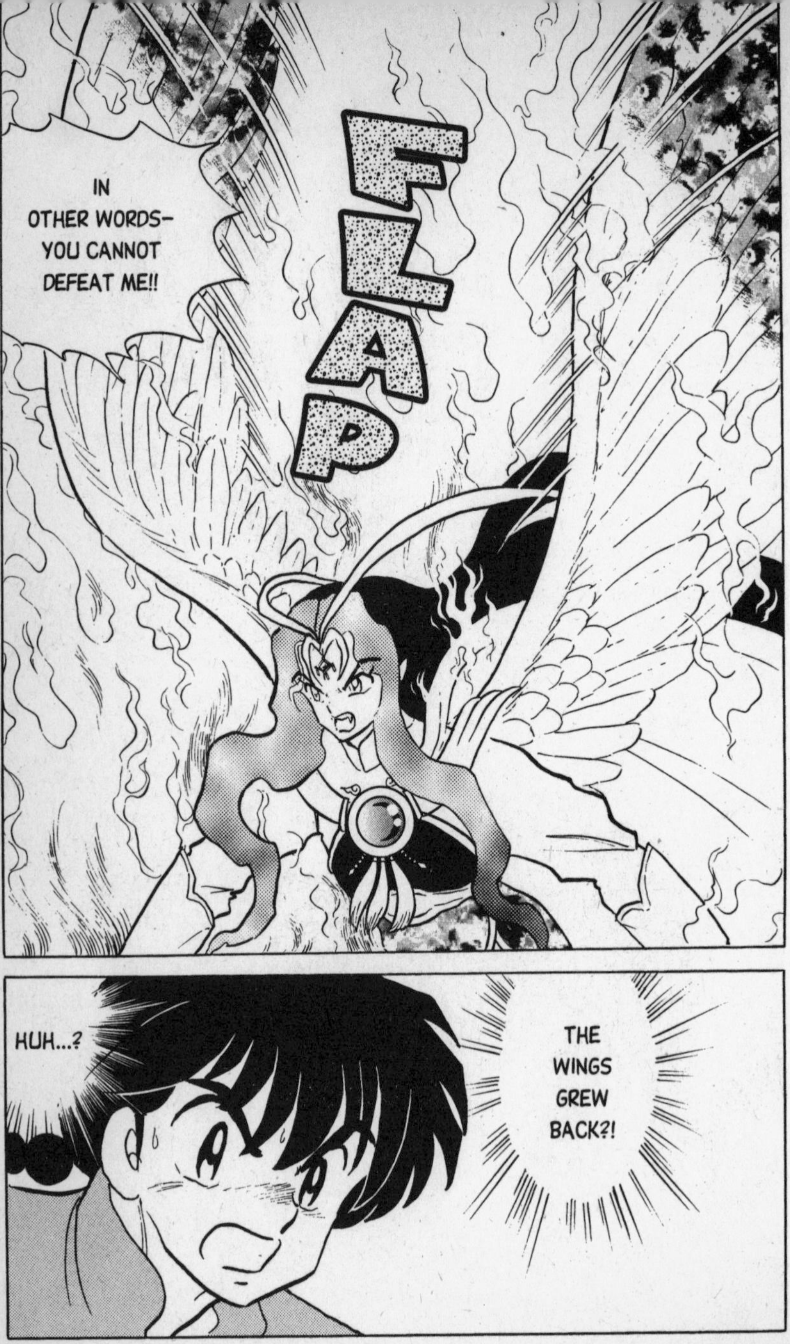
IN OTHER WORDS-YOU CANNOT DEFEAT ME!!
FLAP
HUH...?
THE WINGS GREW BACK?!

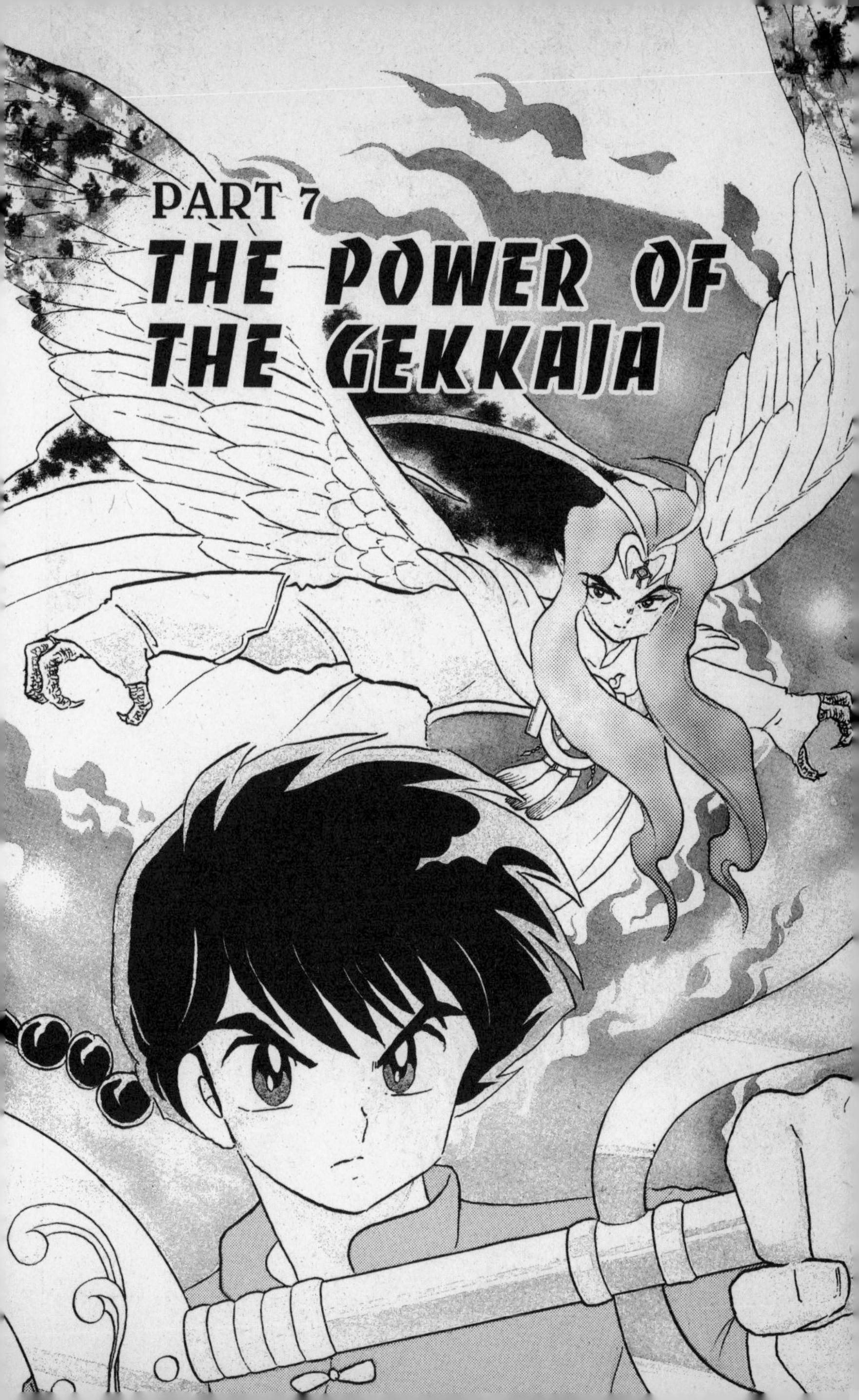
PART 7
THE POWER OF THE GEKKAJA

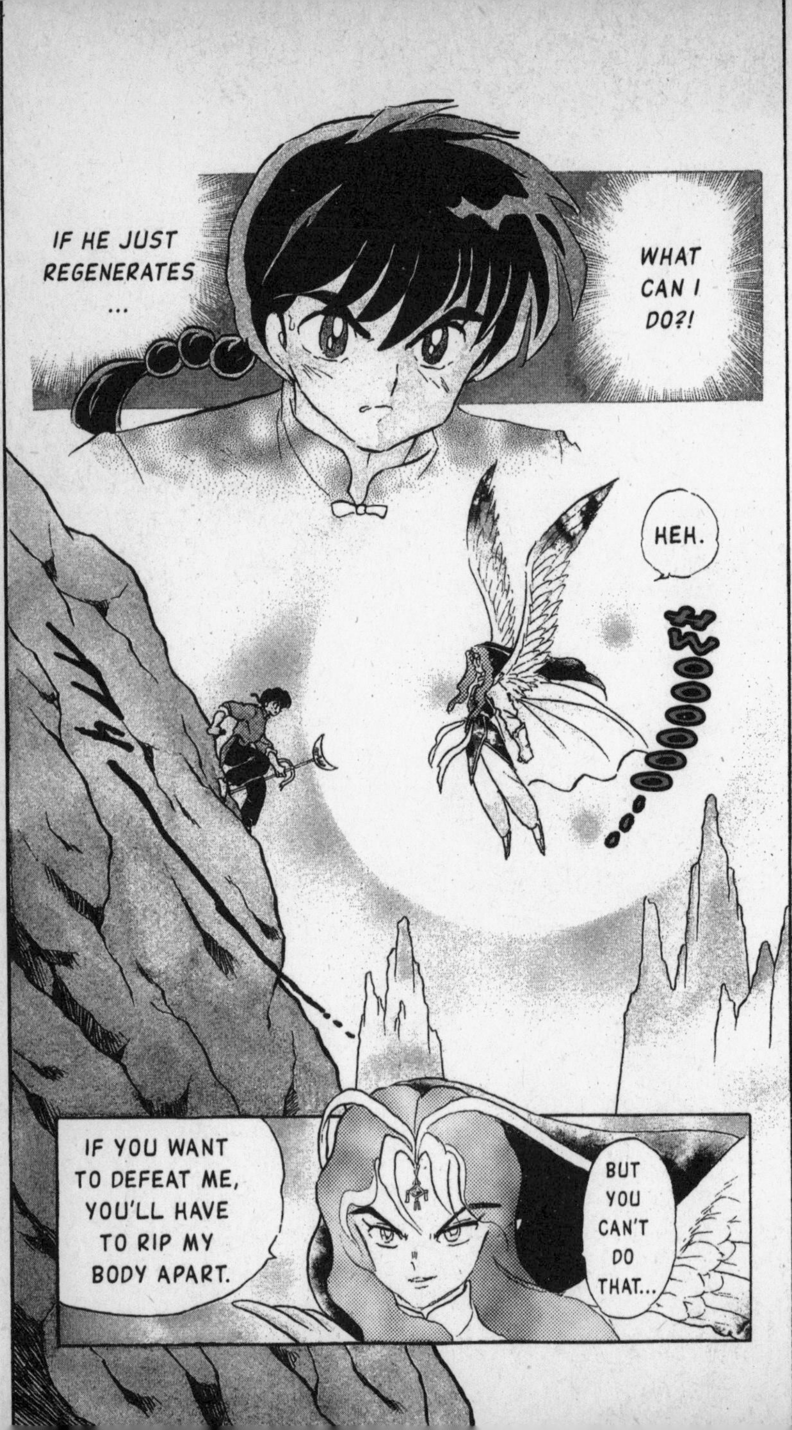
IF HE JUST REGENERATES ...
WHAT CAN I DO?!
HEH.
FWOOOOOOOO...
IF YOU WANT TO DEFEAT ME, YOU'LL HAVE TO RIP MY BODY APART.
BUT YOU CAN'T DO THAT...

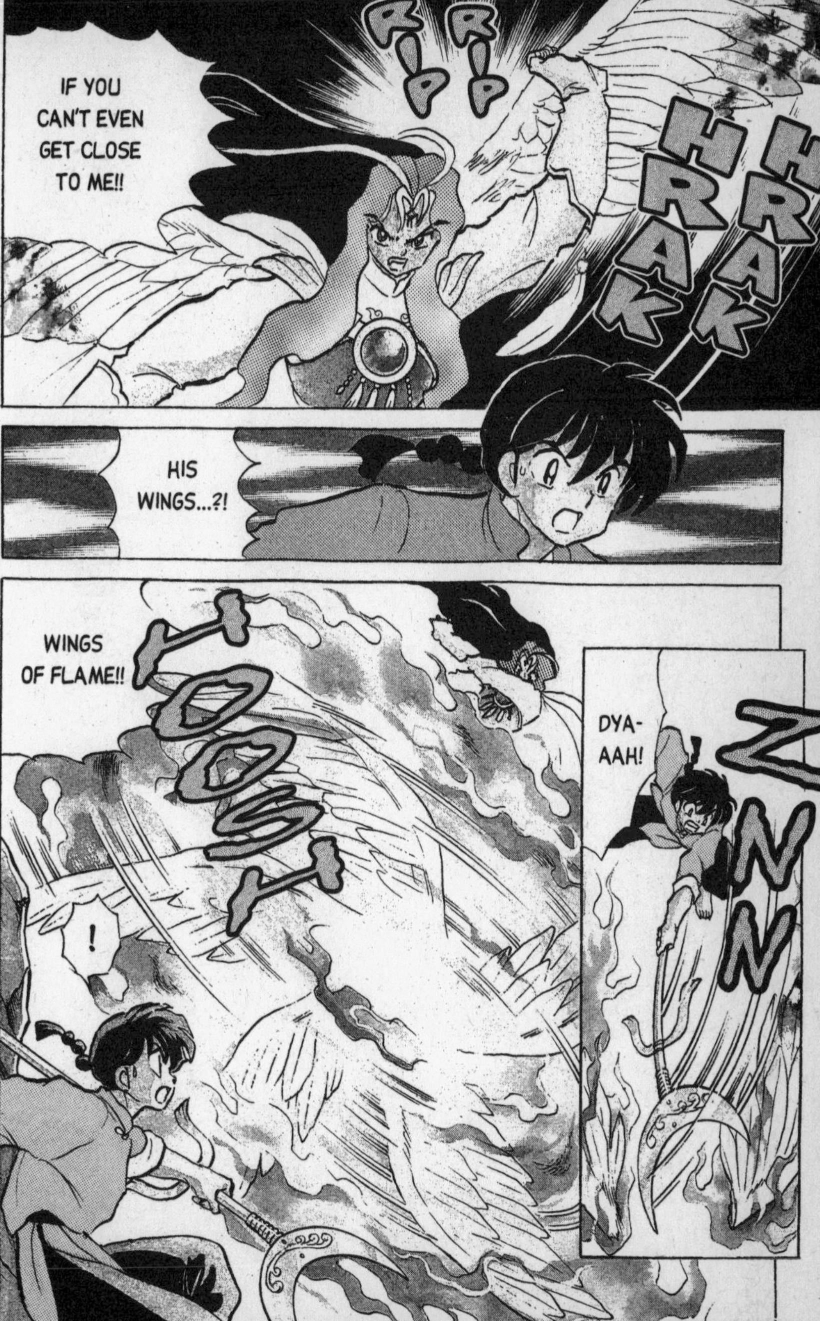
RIP RIP
IF YOU CAN'T EVEN GET CLOSE TO ME!!
HHRAK HHRAK
HIS WINGS...?!
WINGS OF FLAME!!
FOOSH
!
DYA-AAH!
ZNNN

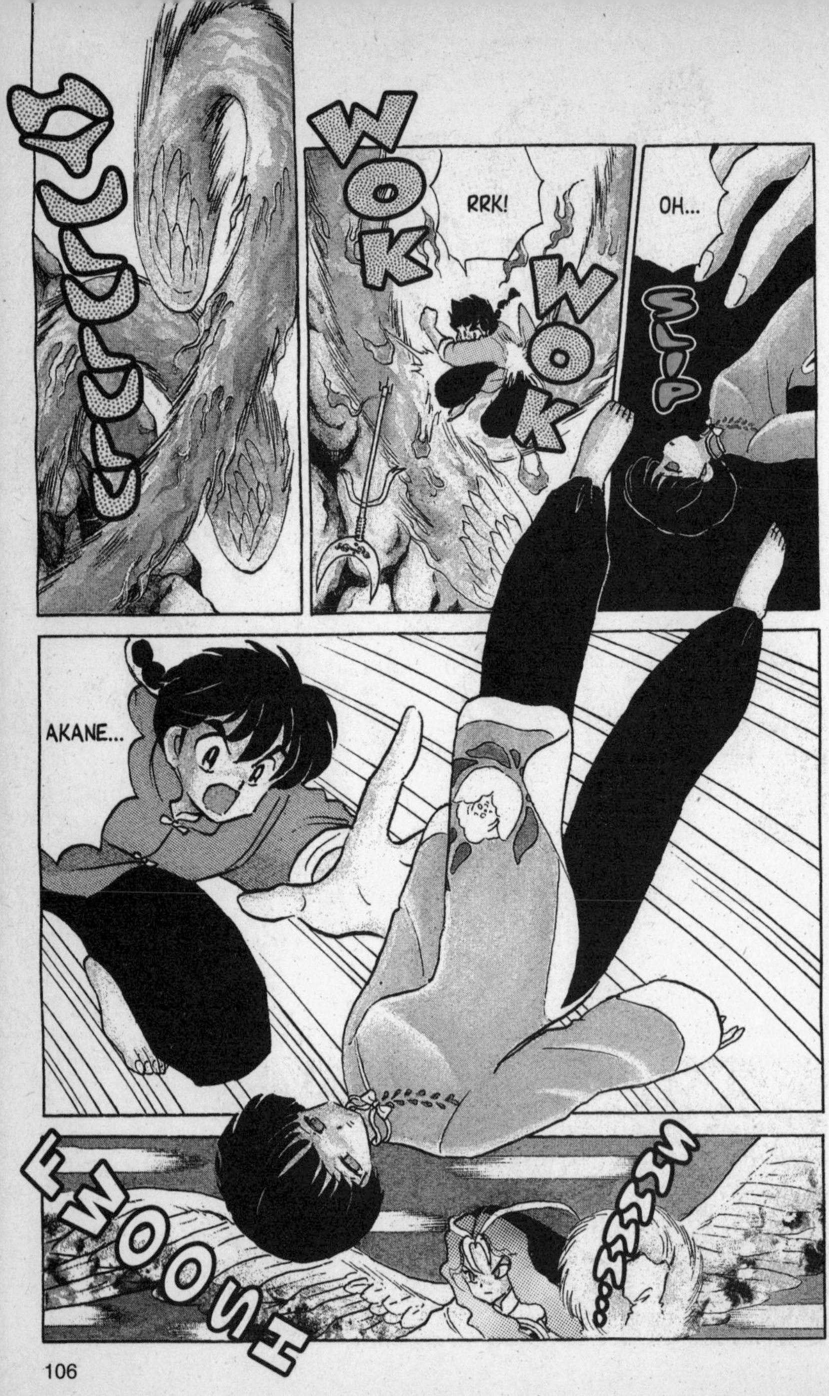
OH...
SLIP
RRK!
WOK WOK
WOK WOK
AKANE...
FWOOSH

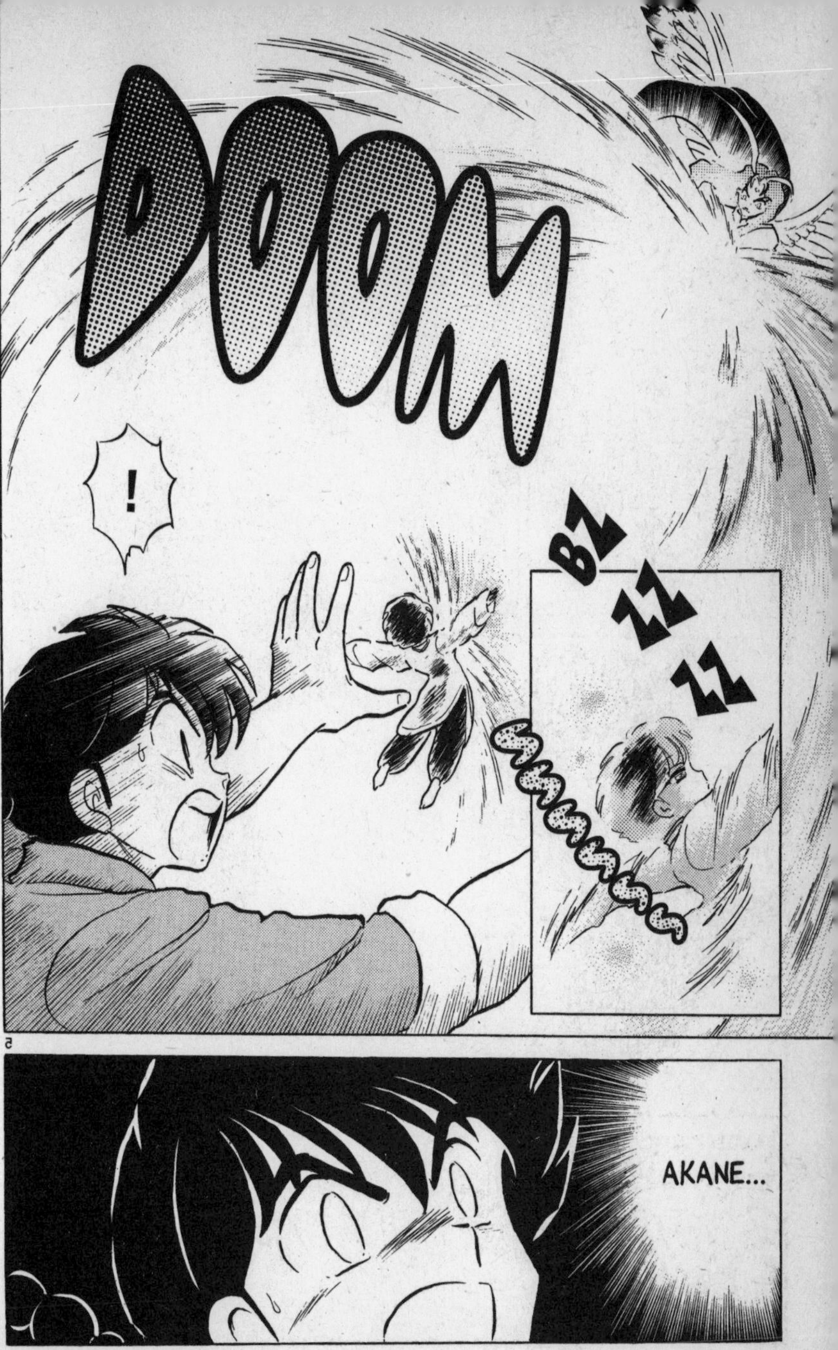
DOOM
!
BZ
ZZ
ZZ
AKANE...

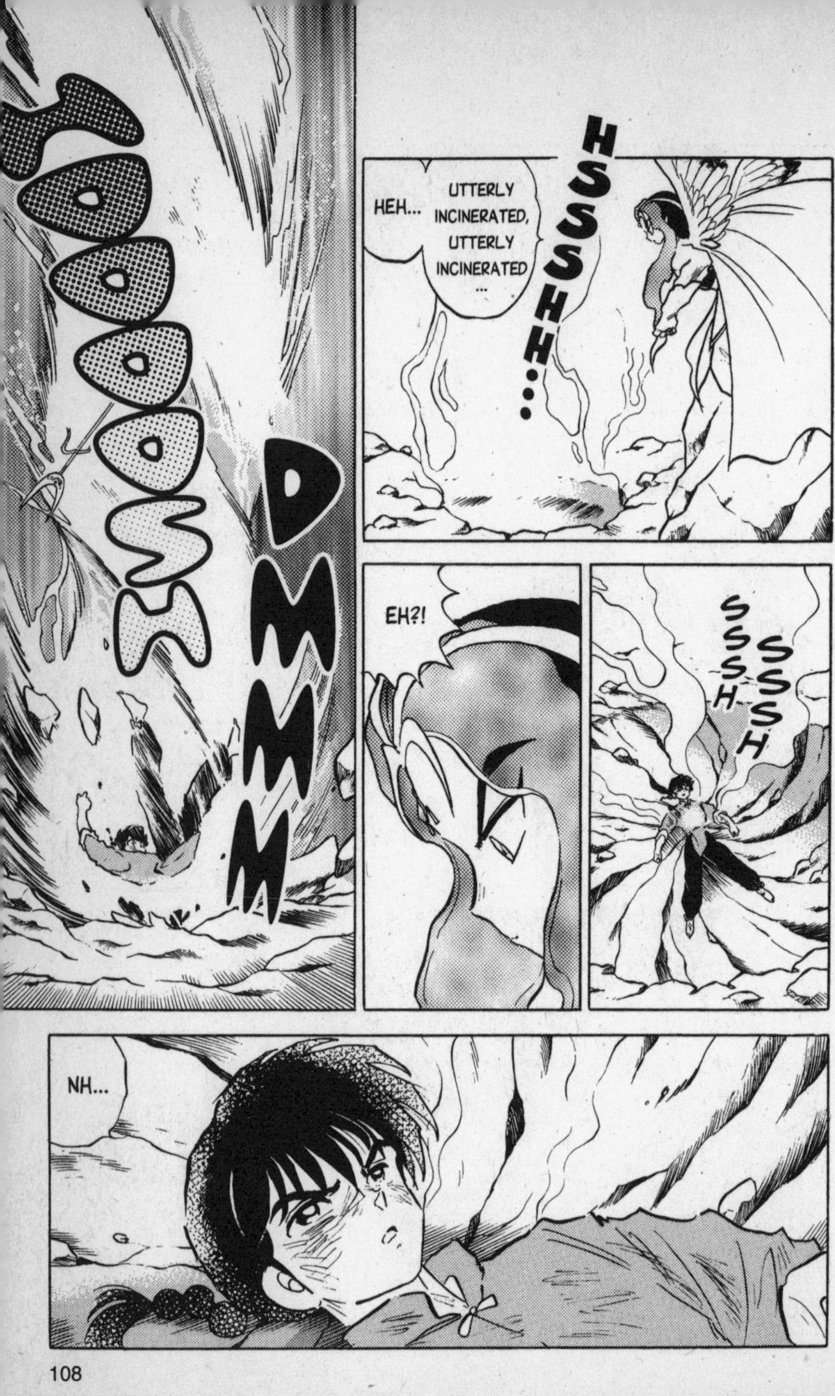
DMMMM
HSSSHH...
HEH...
UTTERLY INCINERATED, UTTERLY INCINERATED ...
EH?!
SSSH
SSSSH
NH...

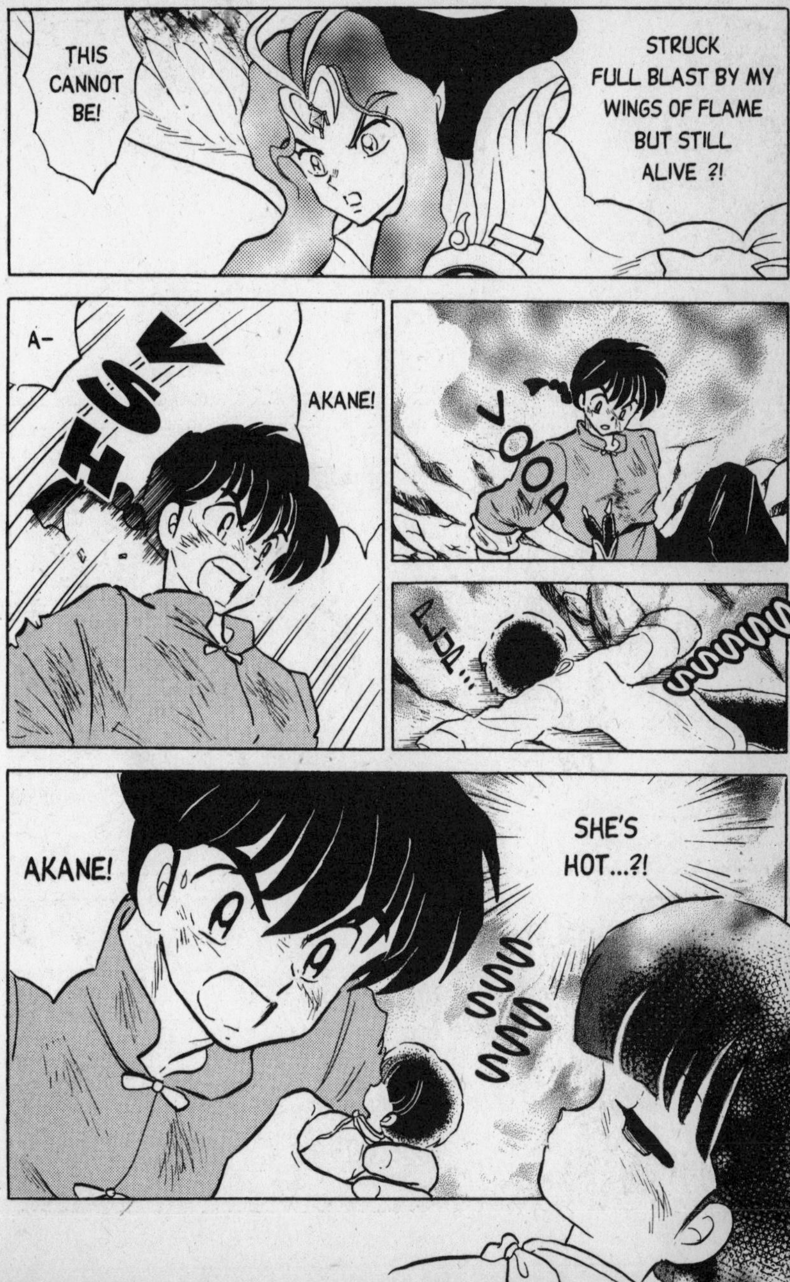
THIS CANNOT BE!
STRUCK FULL BLAST BY MY WINGS OF FLAME BUT STILL ALIVE ?!
A-
AKANE!
AKANE!
SHE'S HOT...?!

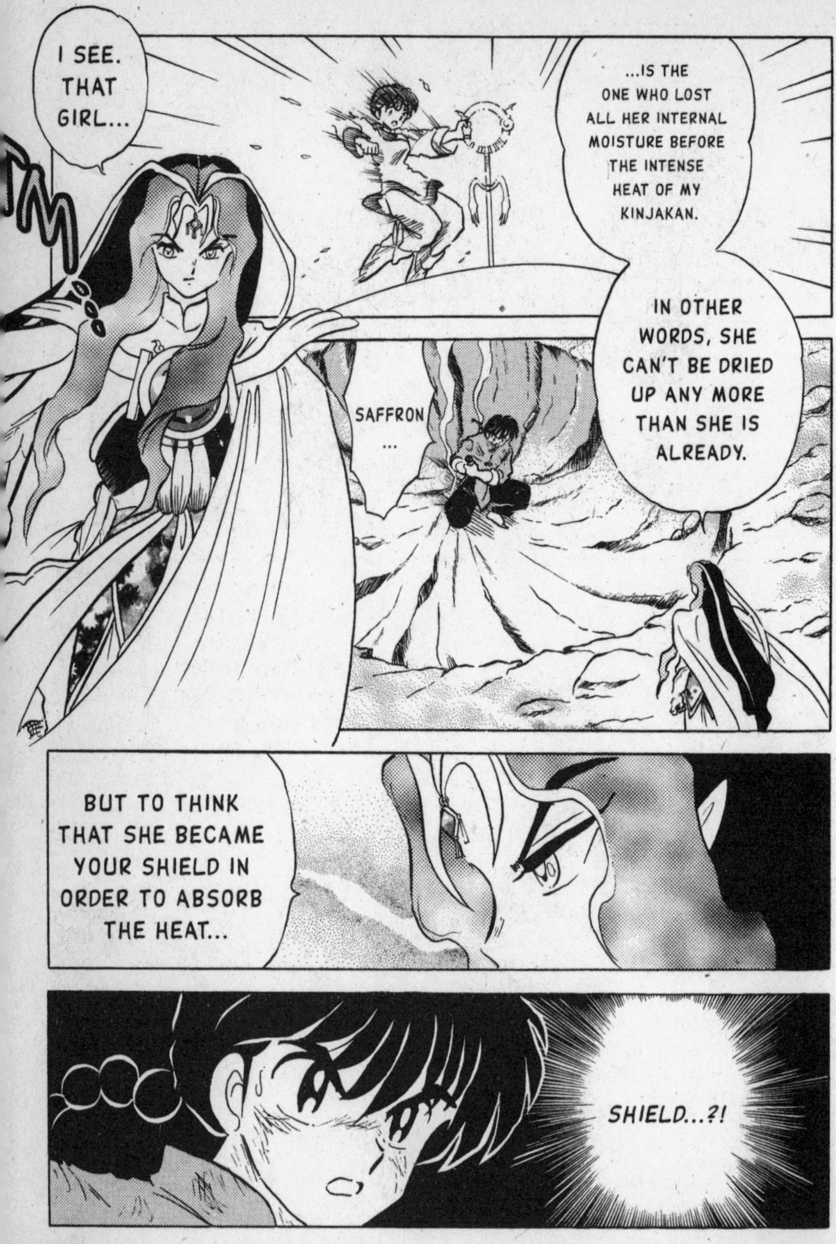
I SEE. THAT GIRL...
...IS THE ONE WHO LOST ALL HER INTERNAL MOISTURE BEFORE THE INTENSE HEAT OF MY KINJAKAN.
SAFFRON ...
IN OTHER WORDS, SHE CAN'T BE DRIED UP ANY MORE THAN SHE IS ALREADY.
BUT TO THINK THAT SHE BECAME YOUR SHIELD IN ORDER TO ABSORB THE HEAT...
SHIELD...?!

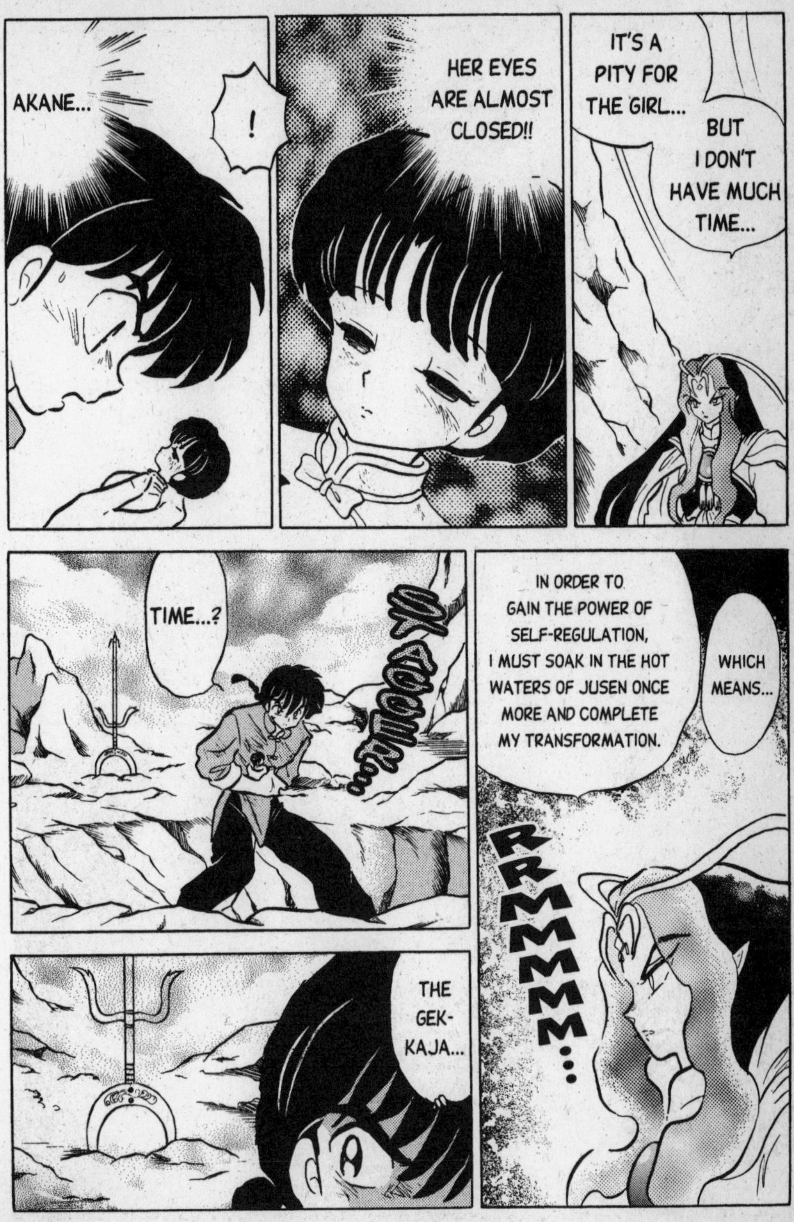
AKANE...
!
HER EYES ARE ALMOST CLOSED!!
IT'S A PITY FOR THE GIRL...
BUT I DON'T HAVE MUCH TIME...
TIME...?
THE GEK-KAJA...
IN ORDER TO GAIN THE POWER OF SELF-REGULATION, I MUST SOAK IN THE HOT WATERS OF JUSEN ONCE MORE AND COMPLETE MY TRANSFORMATION.
WHICH MEANS...
RRMMMMM...

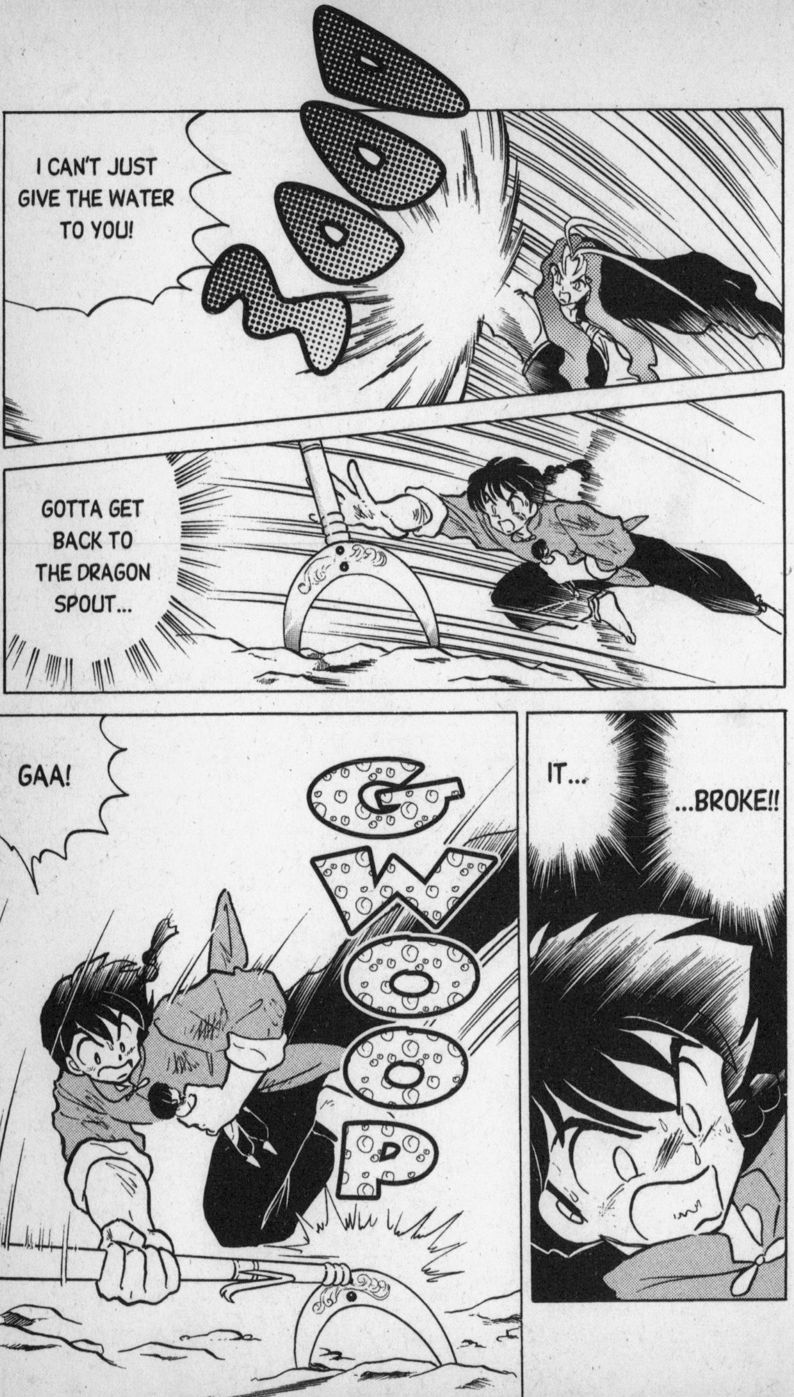
I CAN'T JUST GIVE THE WATER TO YOU!
GOTTA GET BACK TO THE DRAGON SPOUT...
GAA!
GWOOOP
IT...
...BROKE!!

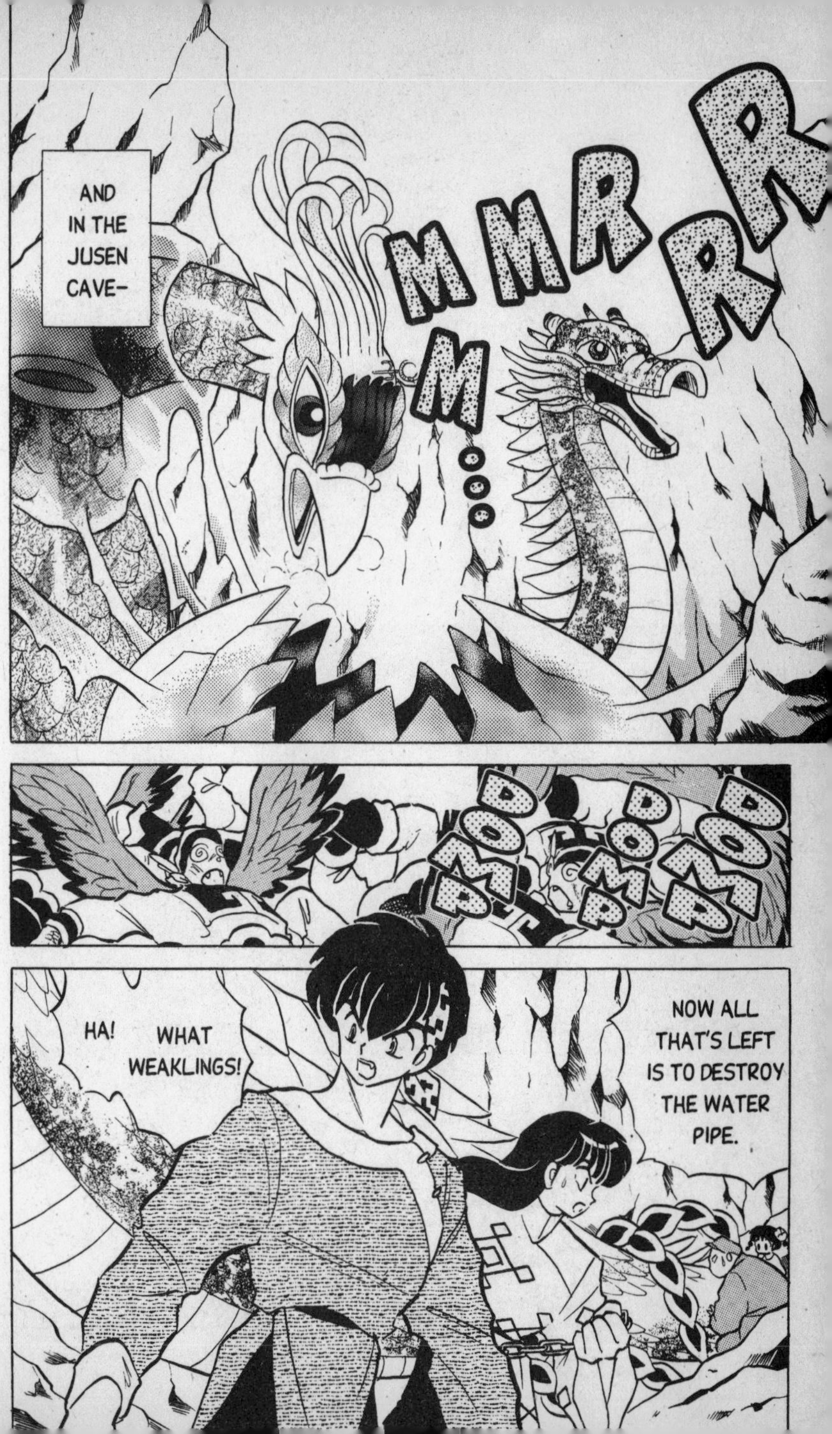

AND IN THE JUSEN CAVE–
MMMRRRR
MMM...
DOMP DOMP DOMP
HA!
WHAT WEAKLINGS!
NOW ALL THAT'S LEFT IS TO DESTROY THE WATER PIPE.

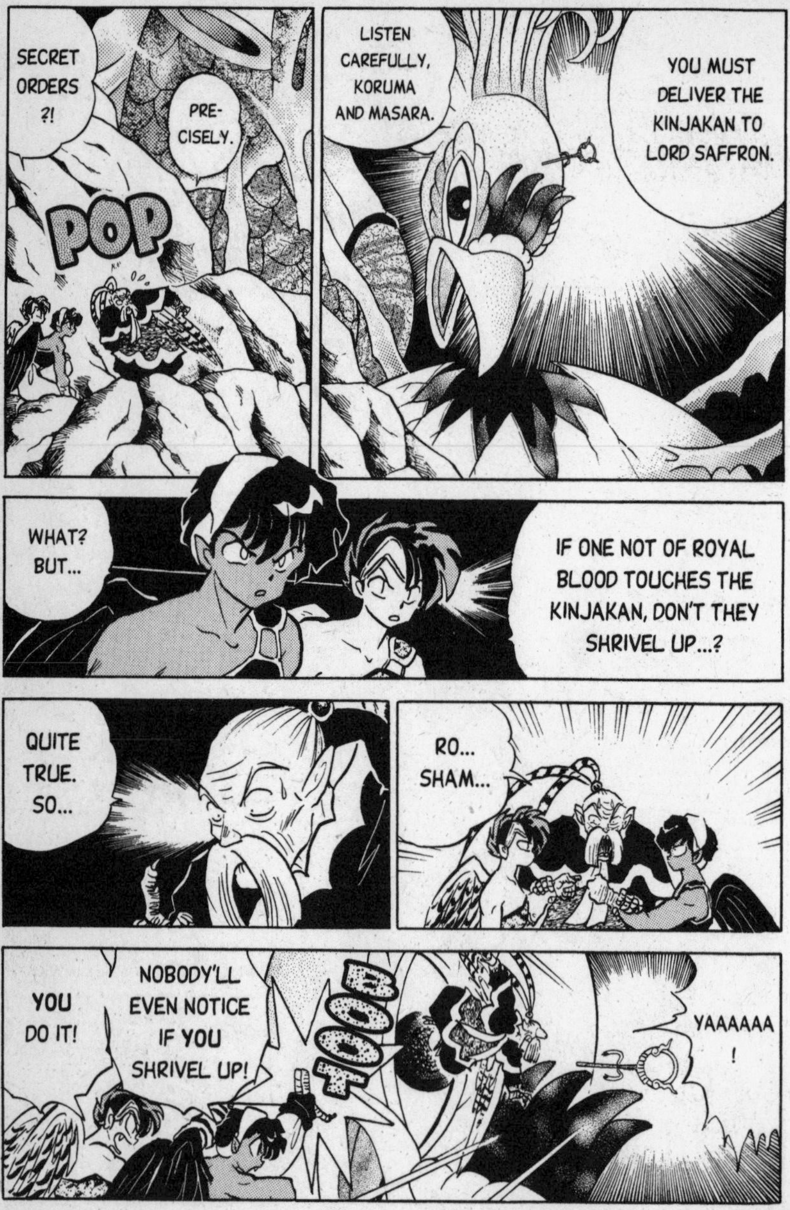
SECRET ORDERS ?!
PRE-CISELY.
POP
LISTEN CAREFULLY, KORUMA AND MASARA.
YOU MUST DELIVER THE KINJAKAN TO LORD SAFFRON.
WHAT? BUT...
IF ONE NOT OF ROYAL BLOOD TOUCHES THE KINJAKAN, DON'T THEY SHRIVEL UP...?
QUITE TRUE. SO...
RO... SHAM...
YOU DO IT!
NOBODY'LL EVEN NOTICE IF YOU SHRIVEL UP!
BOOT
YAAAAAA !

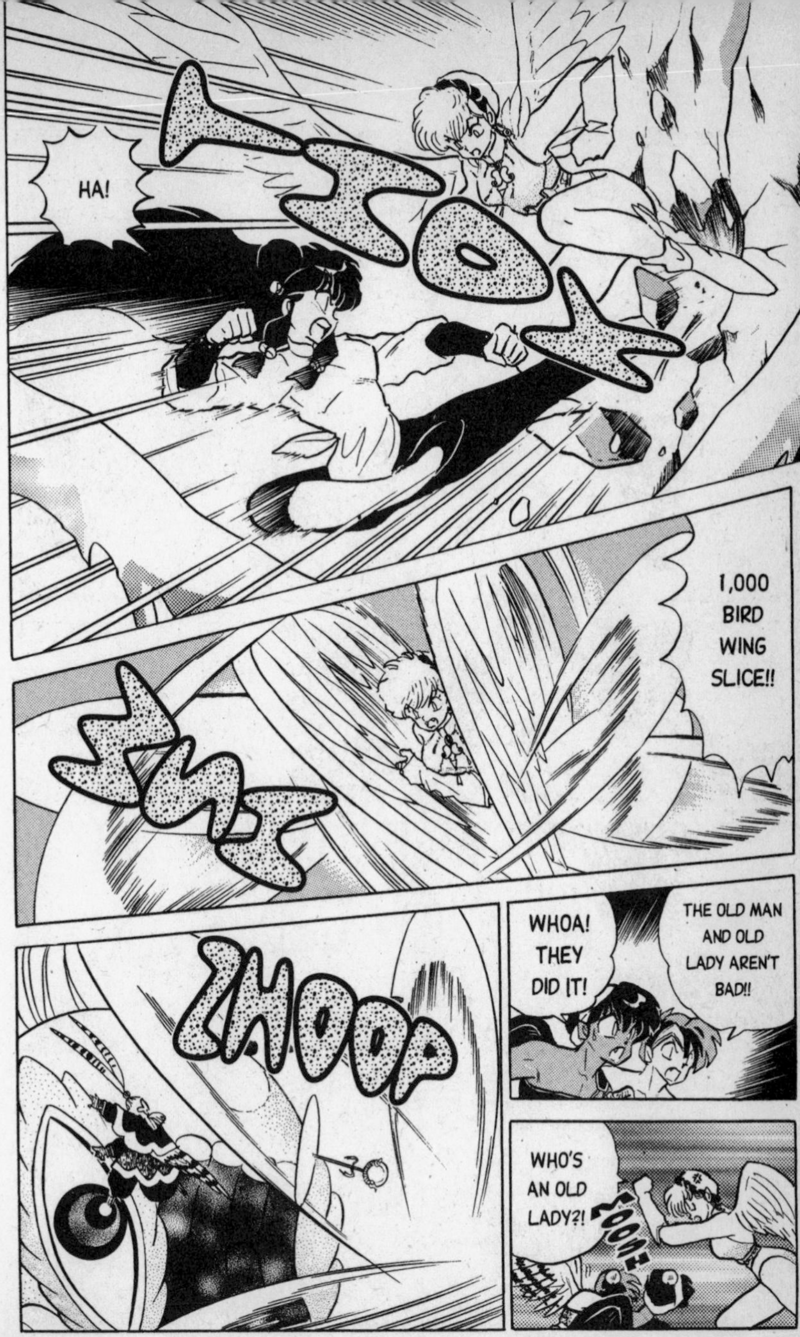
HA!
1,000 BIRD WING SLICE!!
ZHOOP
WHOA! THEY DID IT!
THE OLD MAN AND OLD LADY AREN'T BAD!!
WHO'S AN OLD LADY?!
ZOOSH

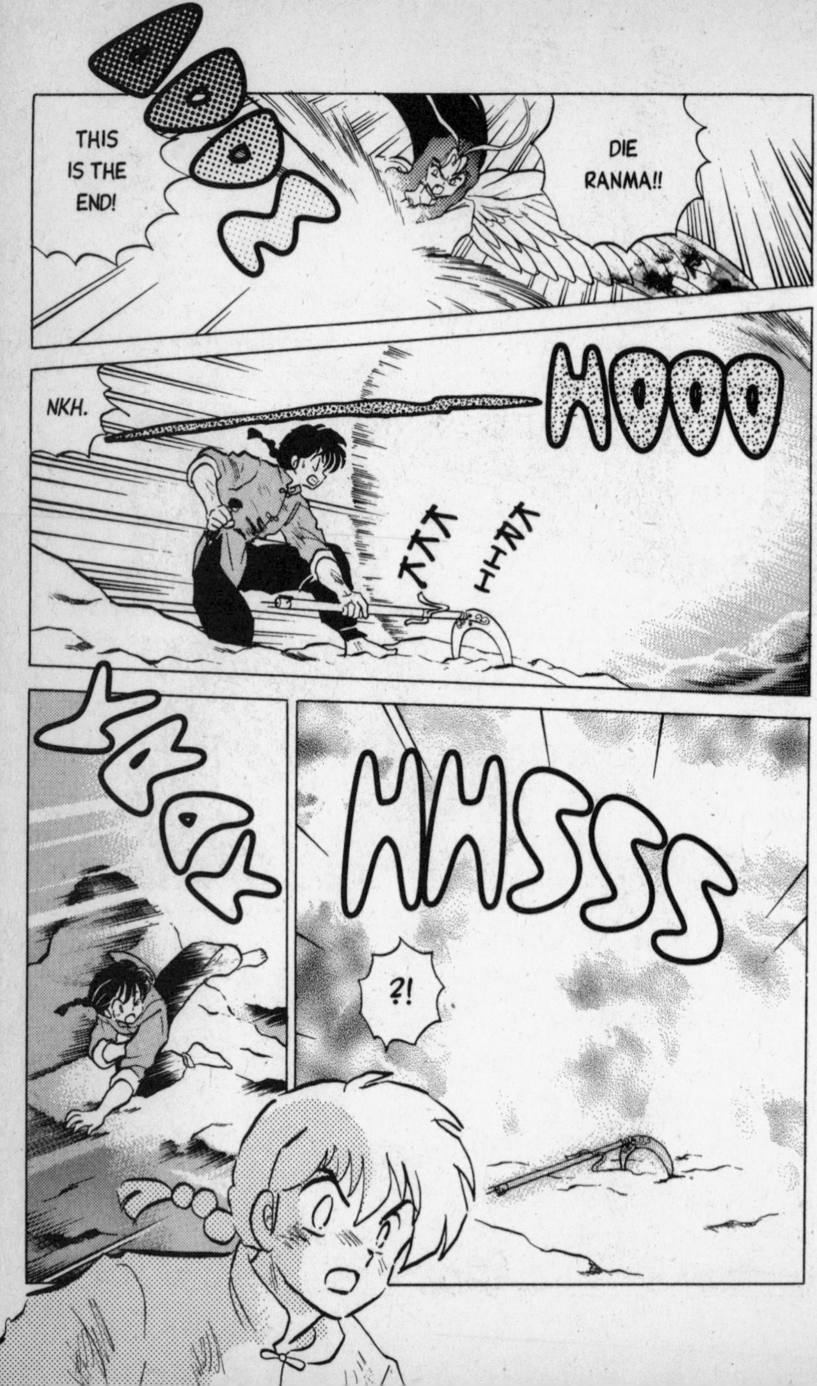
THIS IS THE END!
DIE RANMA!!
NKH.
?!

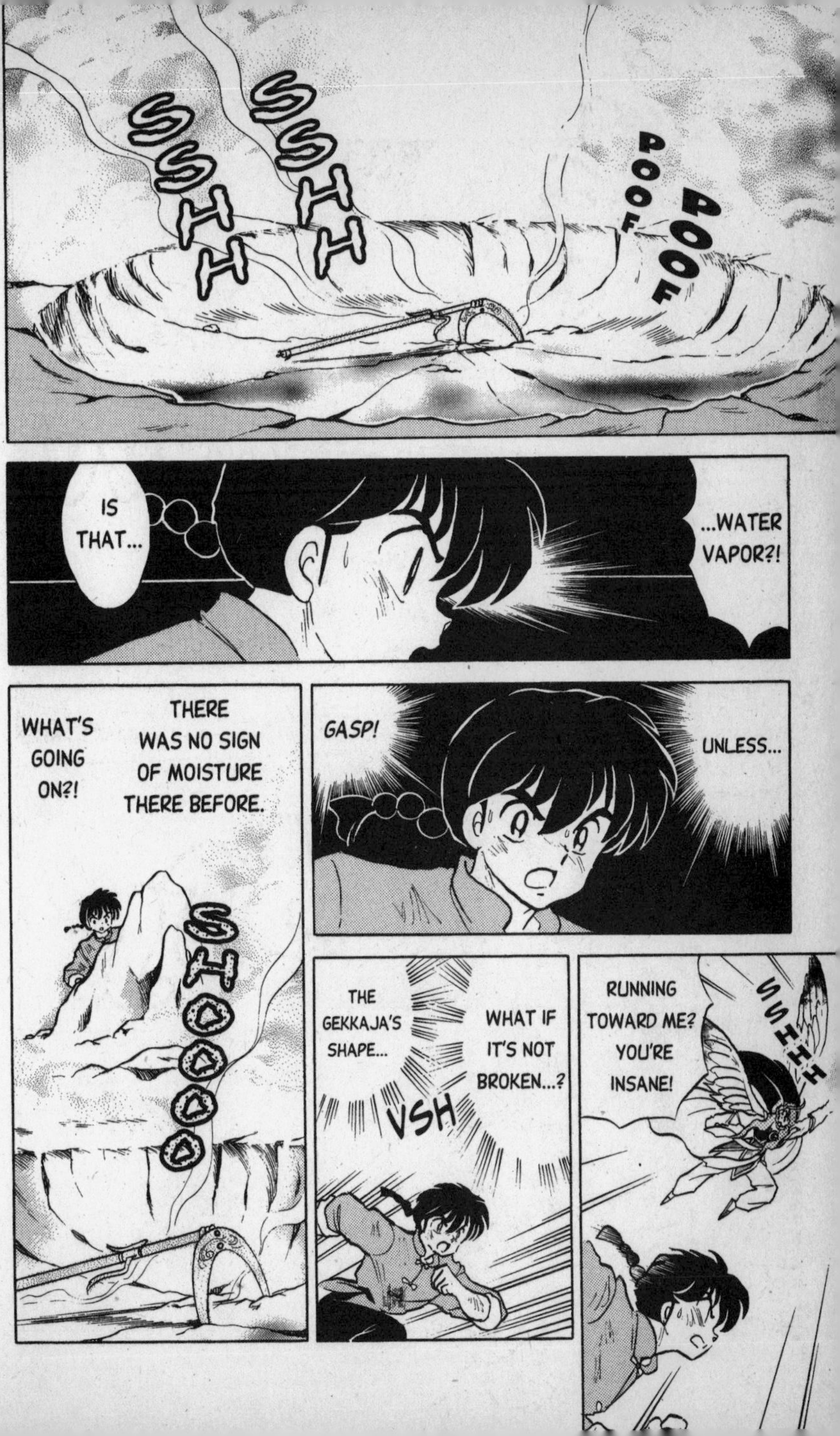
SSHH
SSHH
POOF
POOF
IS THAT...
...WATER VAPOR?!
WHAT'S GOING ON?!
THERE WAS NO SIGN OF MOISTURE THERE BEFORE.
SHOOOO
GASP!
UNLESS...
THE GEKKAJA'S SHAPE...
WHAT IF IT'S NOT BROKEN...?
VSH
RUNNING TOWARD ME? YOU'RE INSANE!
SSHHH

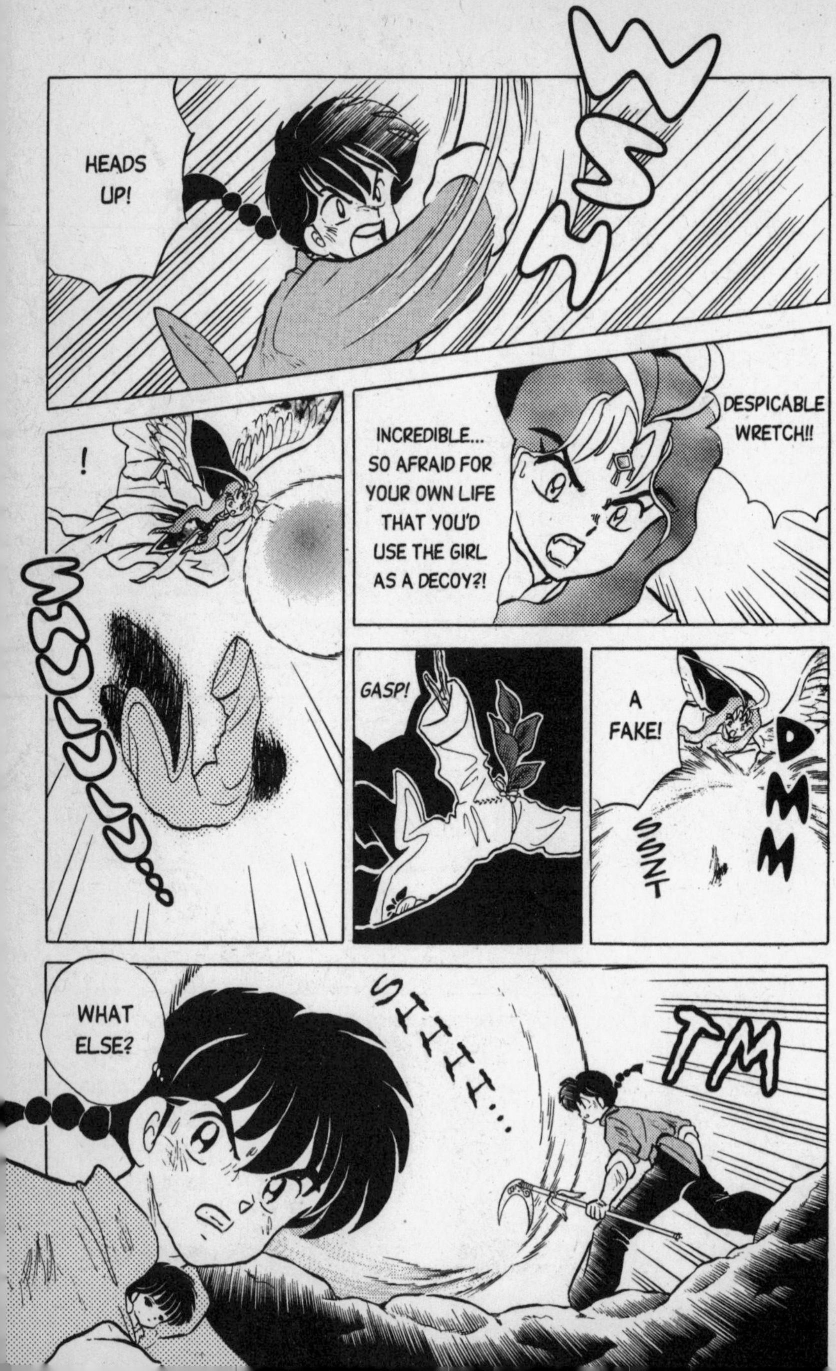

HEADS UP!
!
INCREDIBLE... SO AFRAID FOR YOUR OWN LIFE THAT YOU'D USE THE GIRL AS A DECOY?!
DESPICABLE WRETCH!!
GASP!
A FAKE!
DMMM
SSNT
WHAT ELSE?
SIIIII...
TM

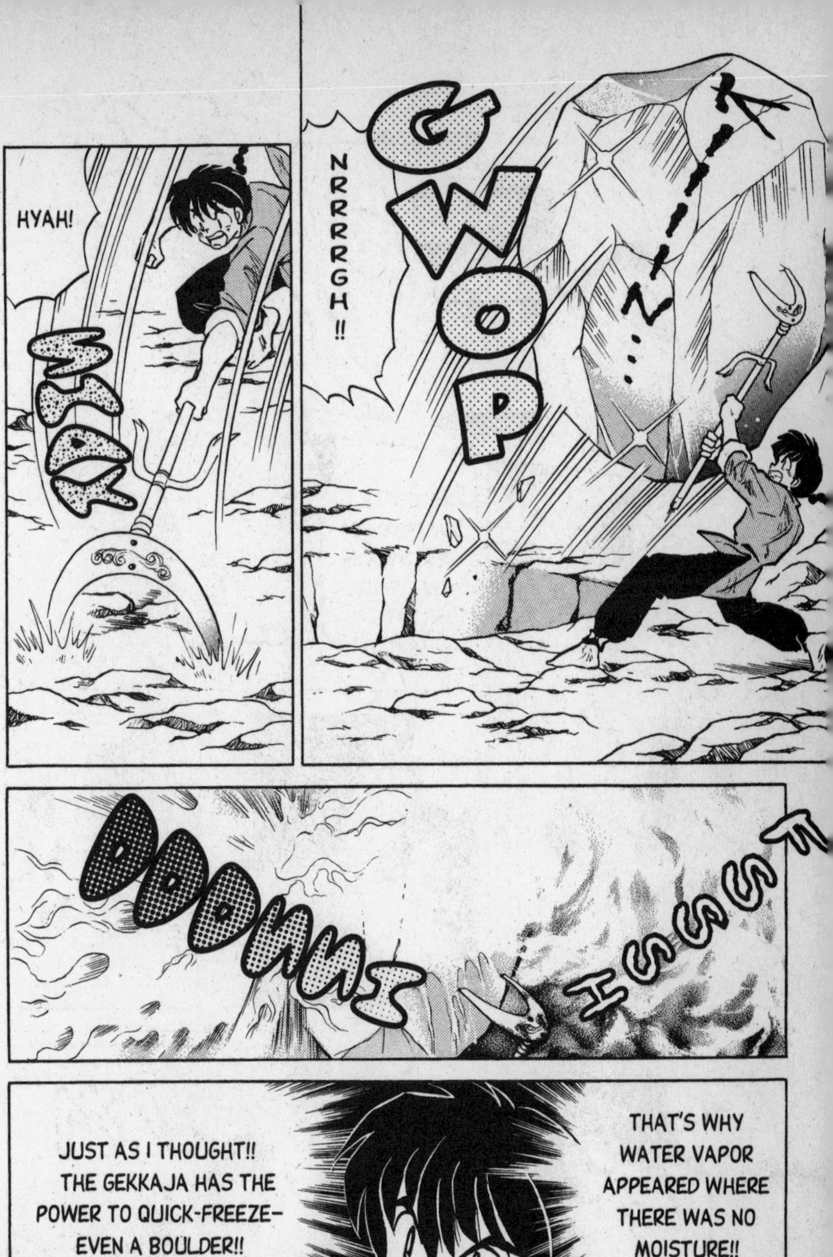
HYAH!
NRRRRGH!!
GWOP
JUST AS I THOUGHT!! THE GEKKAJA HAS THE POWER TO QUICK-FREEZE—EVEN A BOULDER!!
THAT'S WHY WATER VAPOR APPEARED WHERE THERE WAS NO MOISTURE!!

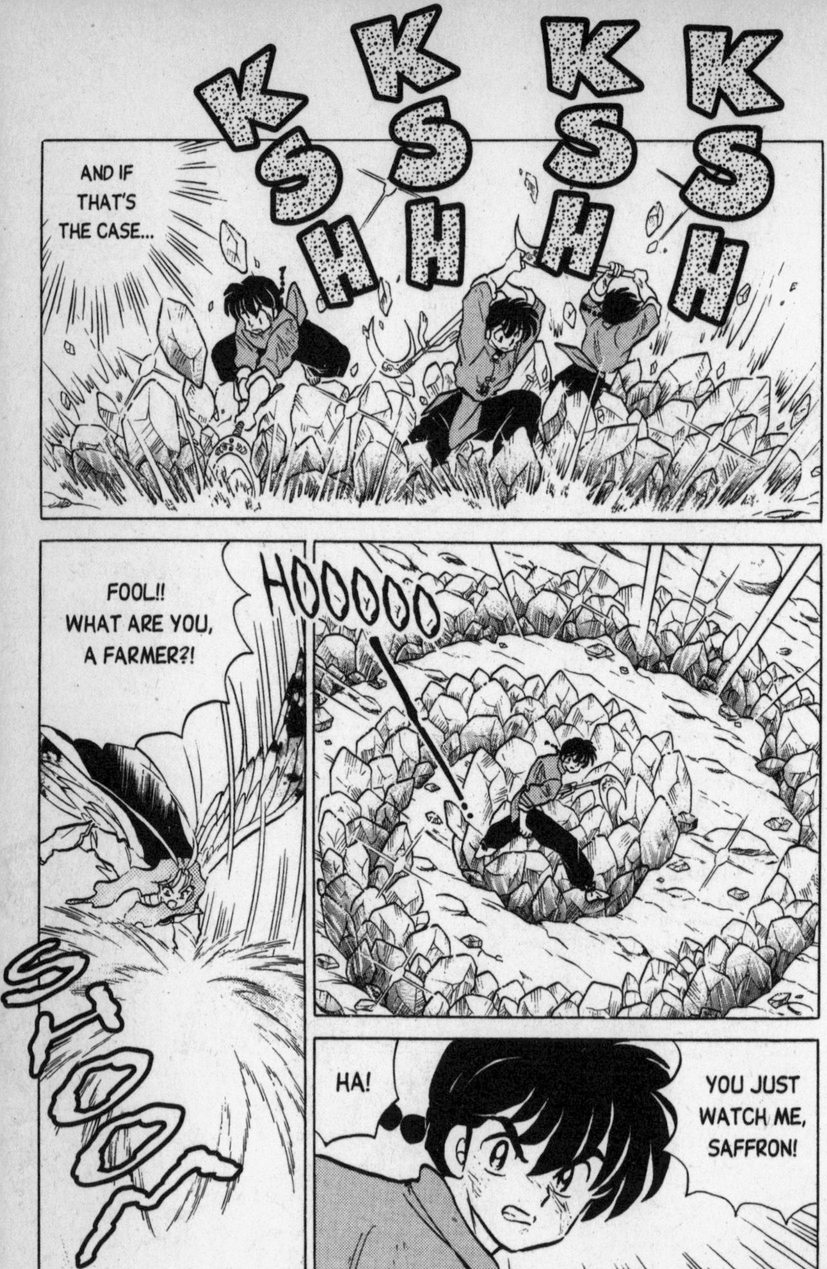
AND IF THAT'S THE CASE...
KSH KSH KSH KSH
FOOL!! WHAT ARE YOU, A FARMER?!
STOOO
HOOOOO
HA!
YOU JUST WATCH ME, SAFFRON!

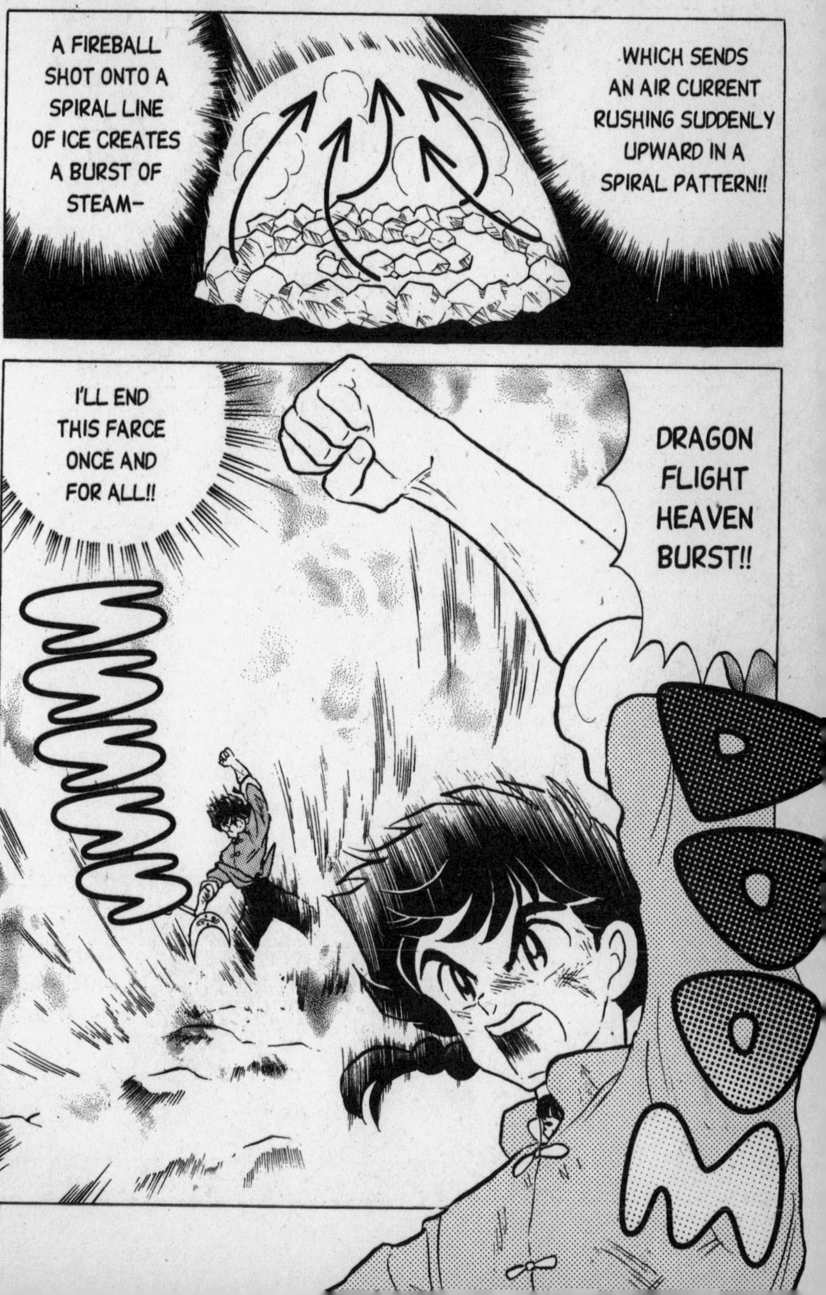
A FIREBALL SHOT ONTO A SPIRAL LINE OF ICE CREATES A BURST OF STEAM—
WHICH SENDS AN AIR CURRENT RUSHING SUDDENLY UPWARD IN A SPIRAL PATTERN!!
I'LL END THIS FARCE ONCE AND FOR ALL!!
DRAGON FLIGHT HEAVEN BURST!!

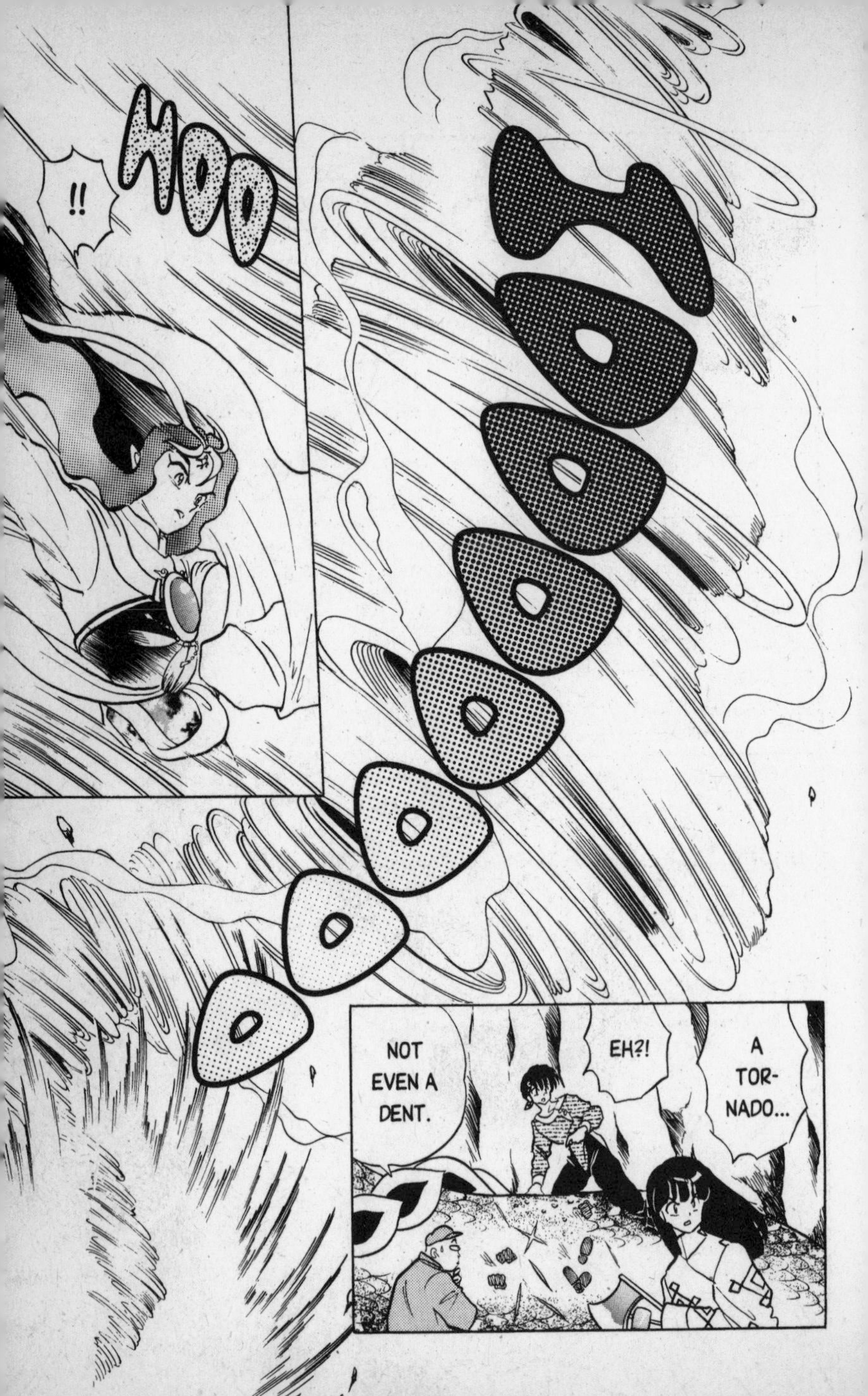
!!
HOO
HOOOOOOO
NOT EVEN A DENT.
EH?!
A TOR-NADO...

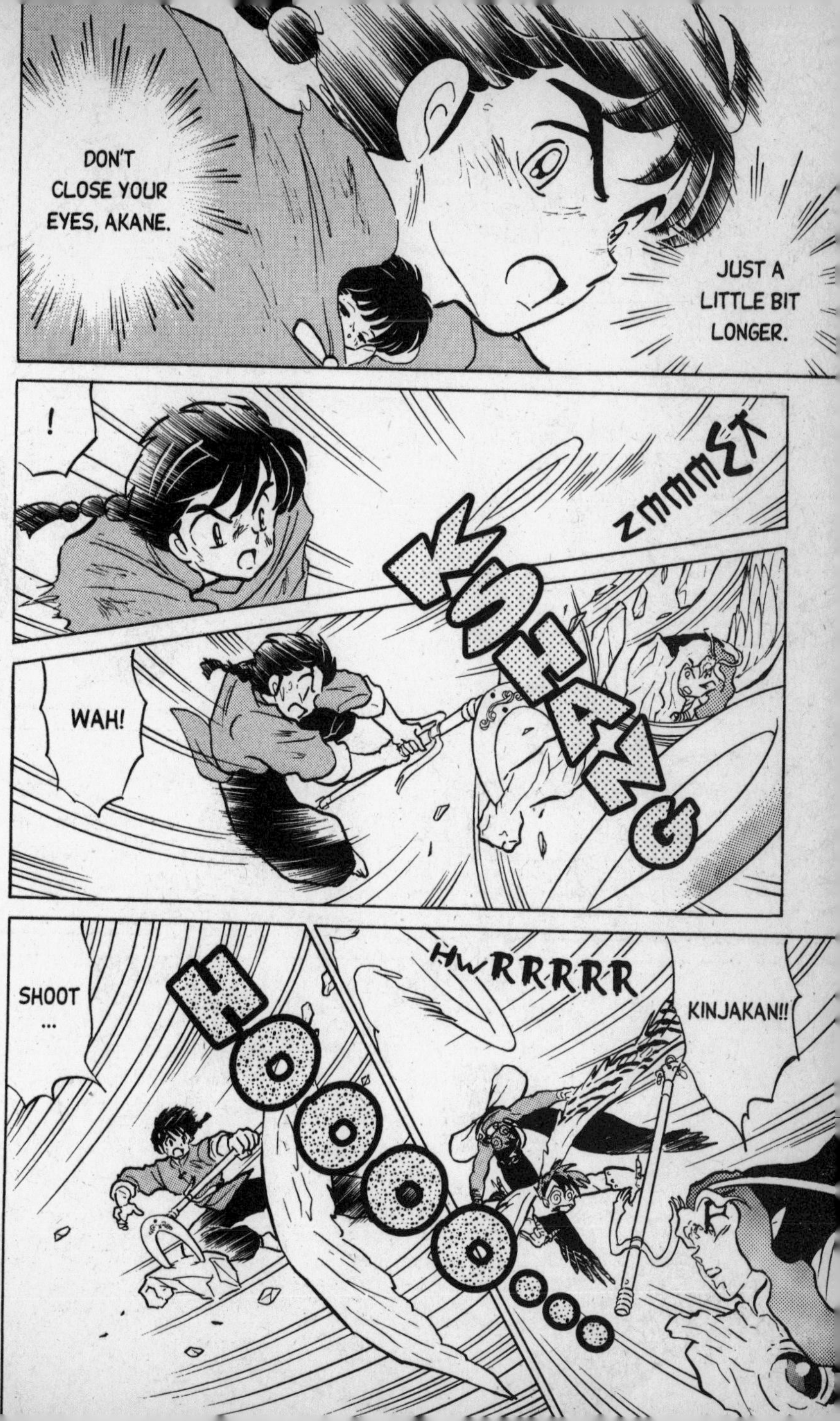
DON'T CLOSE YOUR EYES, AKANE.
JUST A LITTLE BIT LONGER.
!
ZMMMMM
KSHANG
WAH!
SHOOT ...
HWRRRRRR
KINJAKAN!!
HOOOOO....

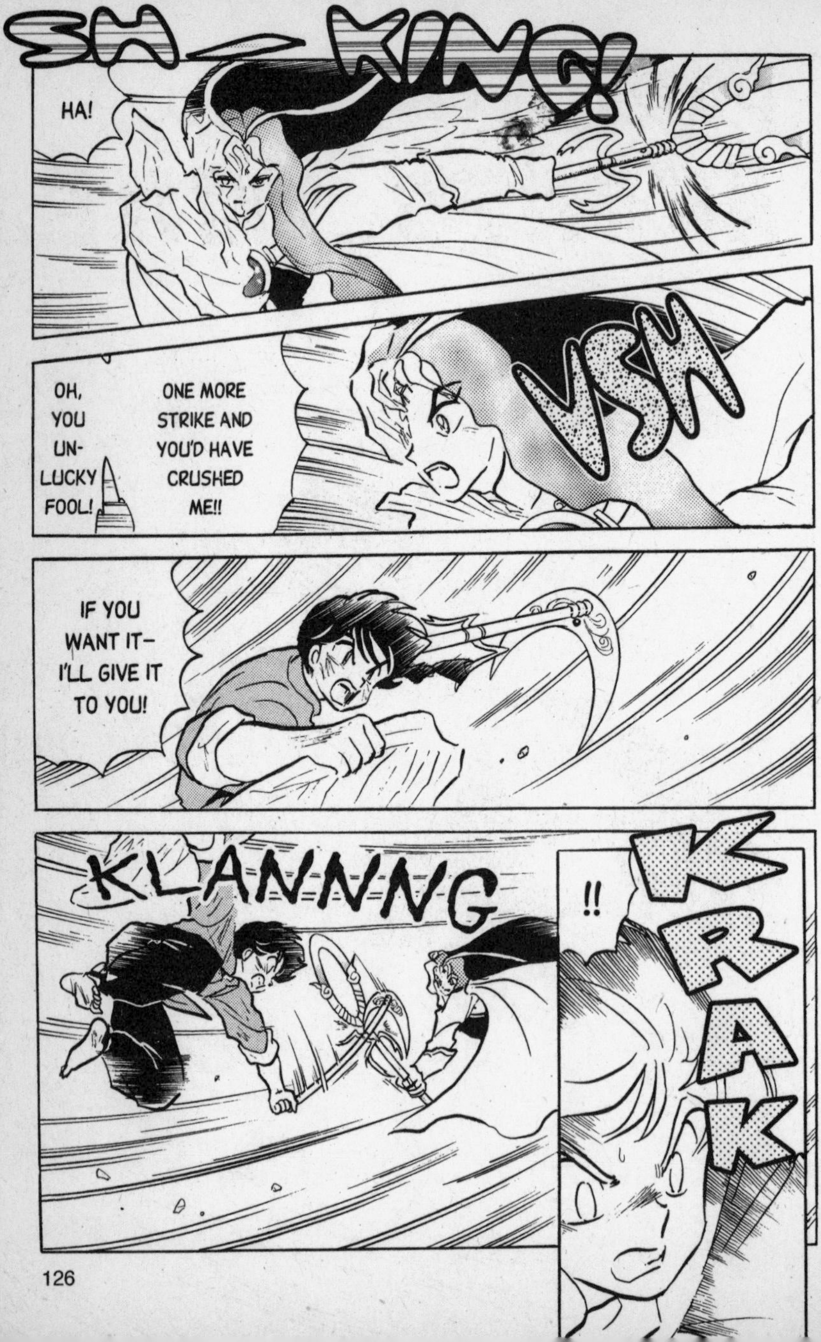
SH—KING!
HA!
OH, YOU UN-LUCKY FOOL!
ONE MORE STRIKE AND YOU'D HAVE CRUSHED ME!!
VSH
IF YOU WANT IT— I'LL GIVE IT TO YOU!
KLANNNG
!!
KRAK

PART 8
AKANE'S SMILE

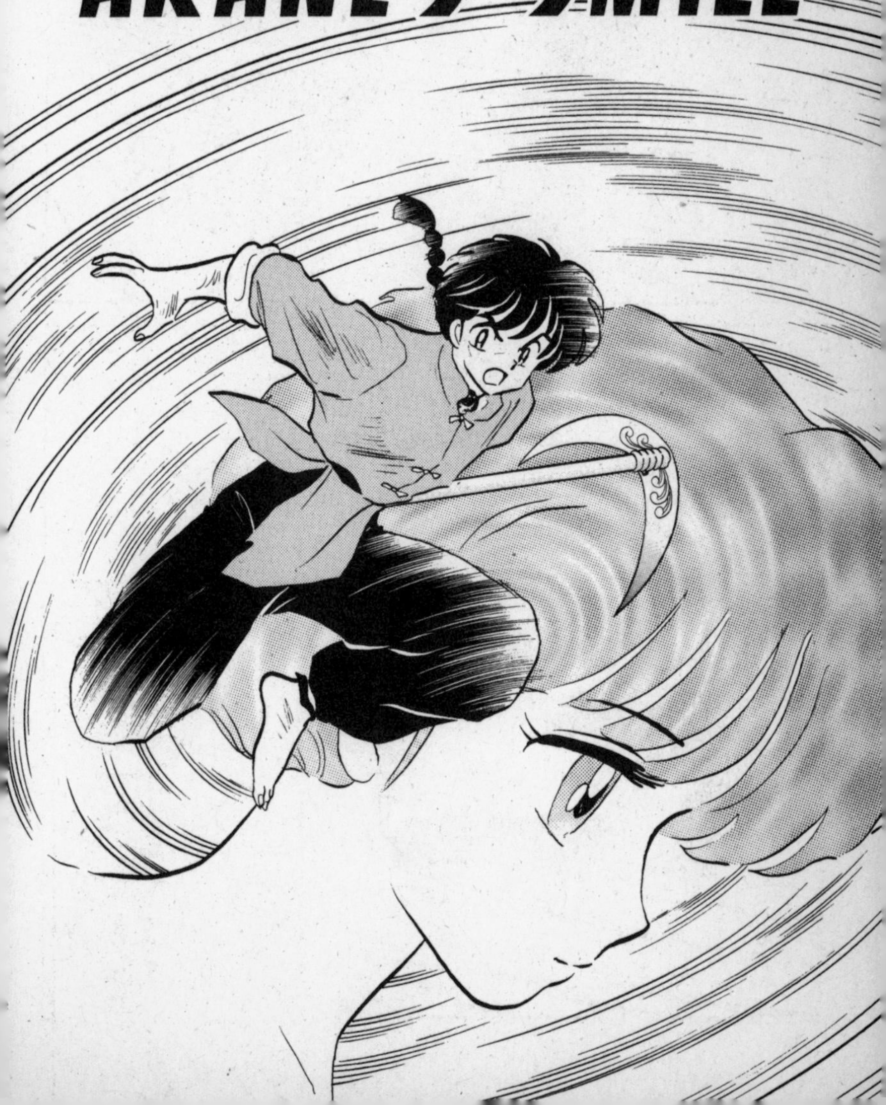

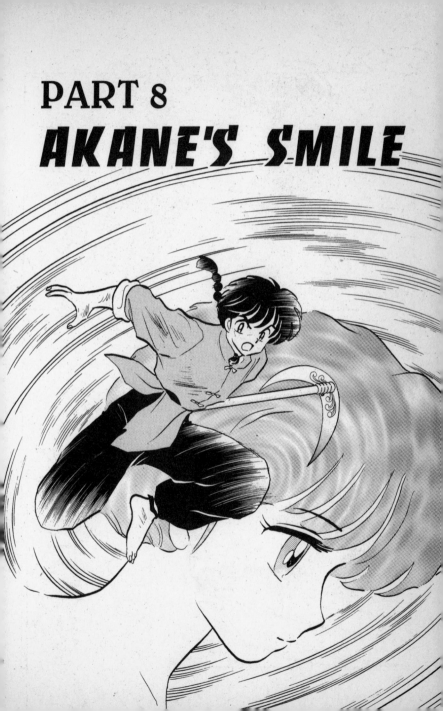

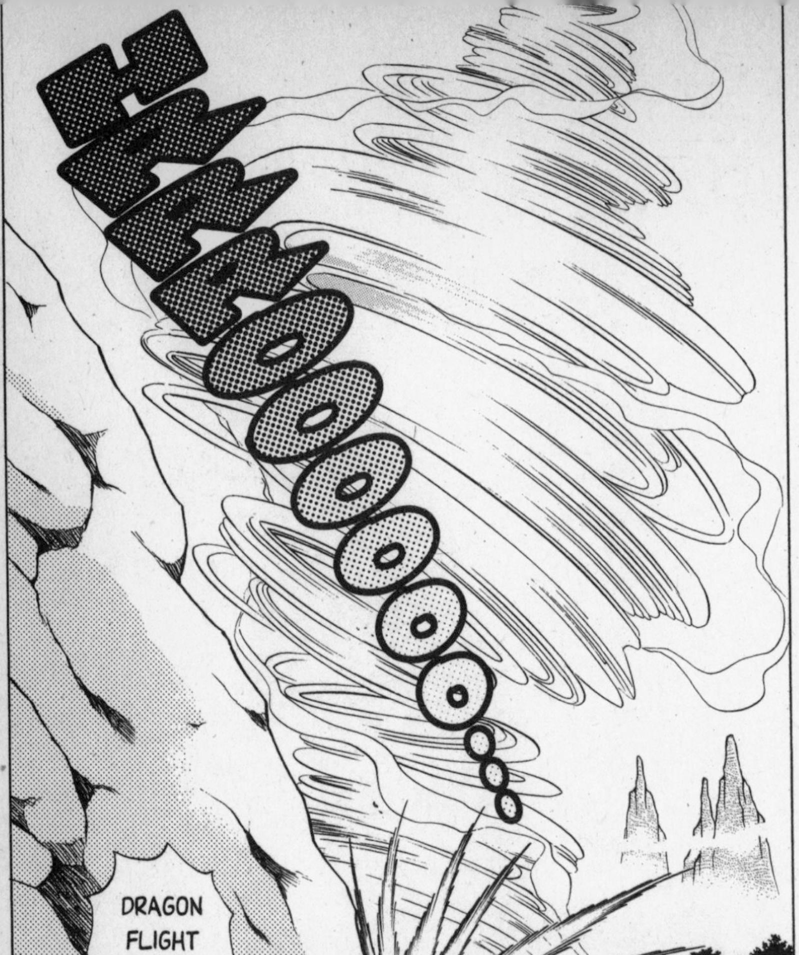
ZZZWOOOOOOOO...
DRAGON FLIGHT HEAVEN BURST!!

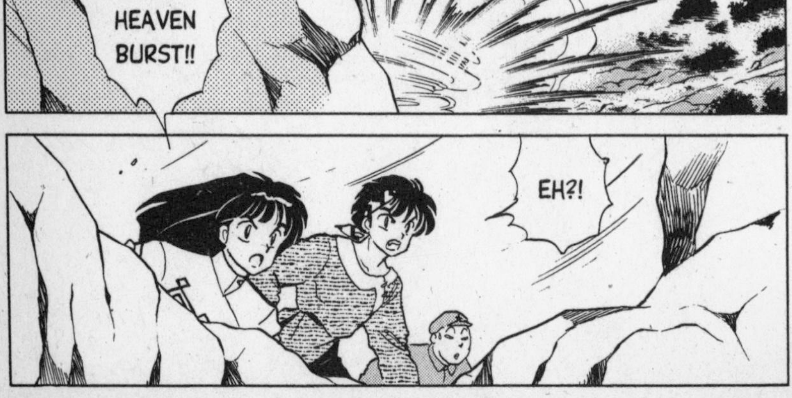
EH?!

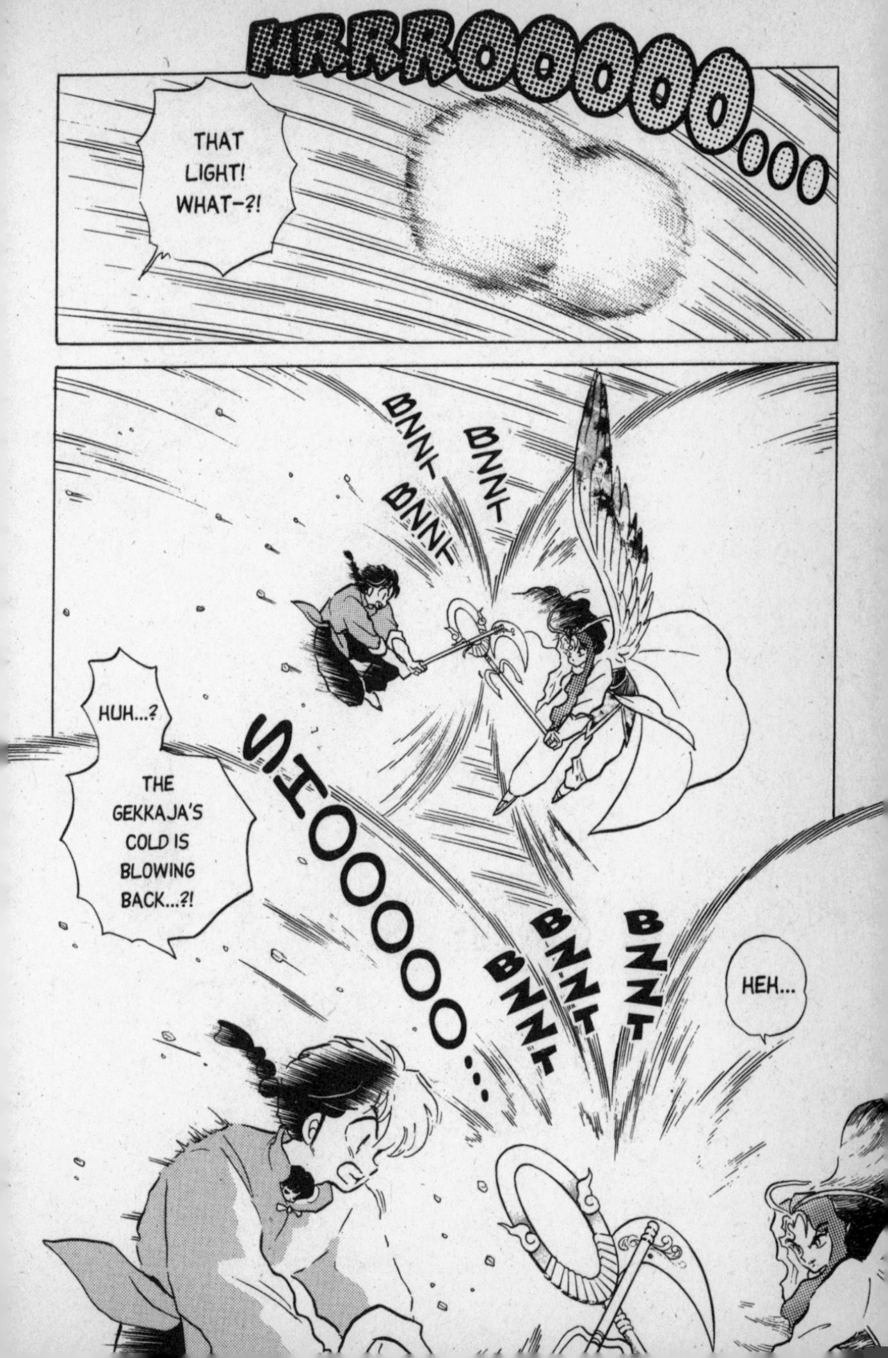
KRRROOOOOOO....
THAT LIGHT! WHAT-?!
BZZZT BZZZT BZZZT
HUH...?
THE GEKKAJA'S COLD IS BLOWING BACK...?!
SHOOOOO...
BZZZT BZZZT BZZZT
HEH...

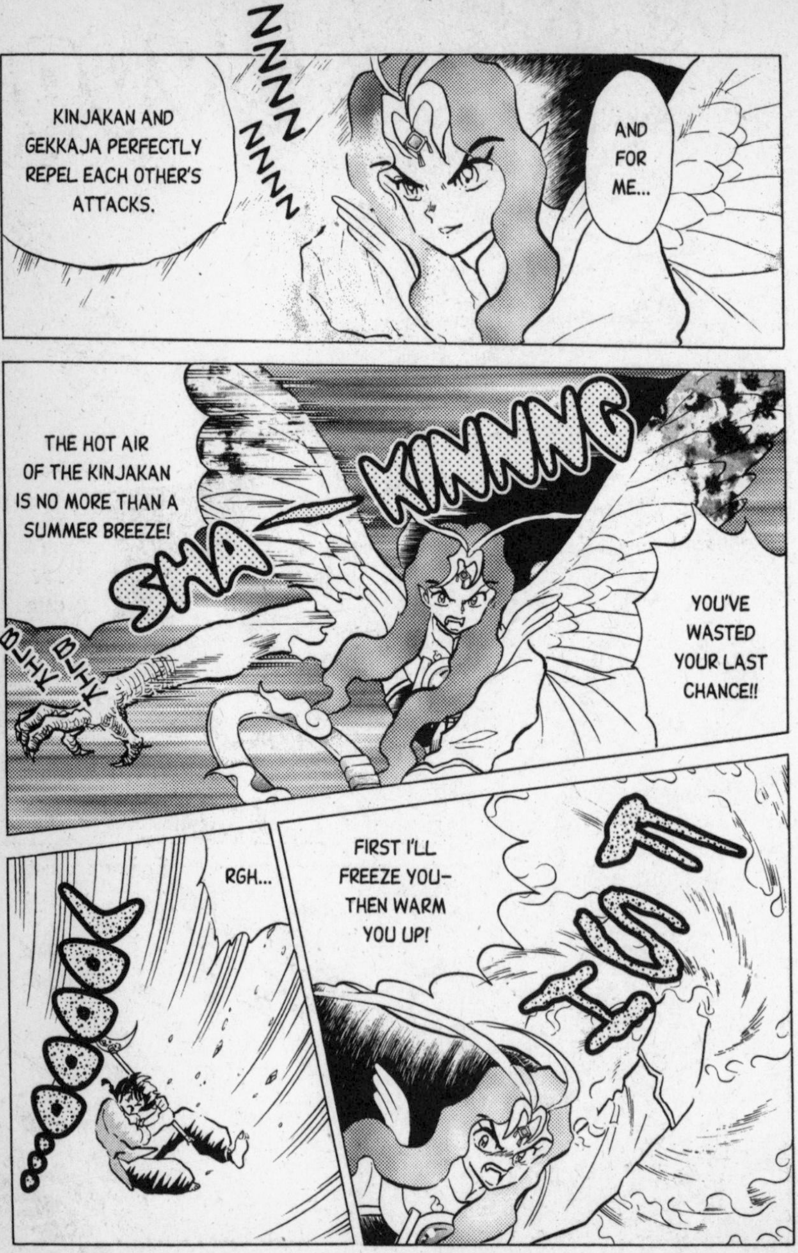
KINJAKAN AND GEKKAJA PERFECTLY REPEL EACH OTHER'S ATTACKS.
AND FOR ME...
THE HOT AIR OF THE KINJAKAN IS NO MORE THAN A SUMMER BREEZE!
SHA—KINNNG
YOU'VE WASTED YOUR LAST CHANCE!!
RGH...
FIRST I'LL FREEZE YOU— THEN WARM YOU UP!

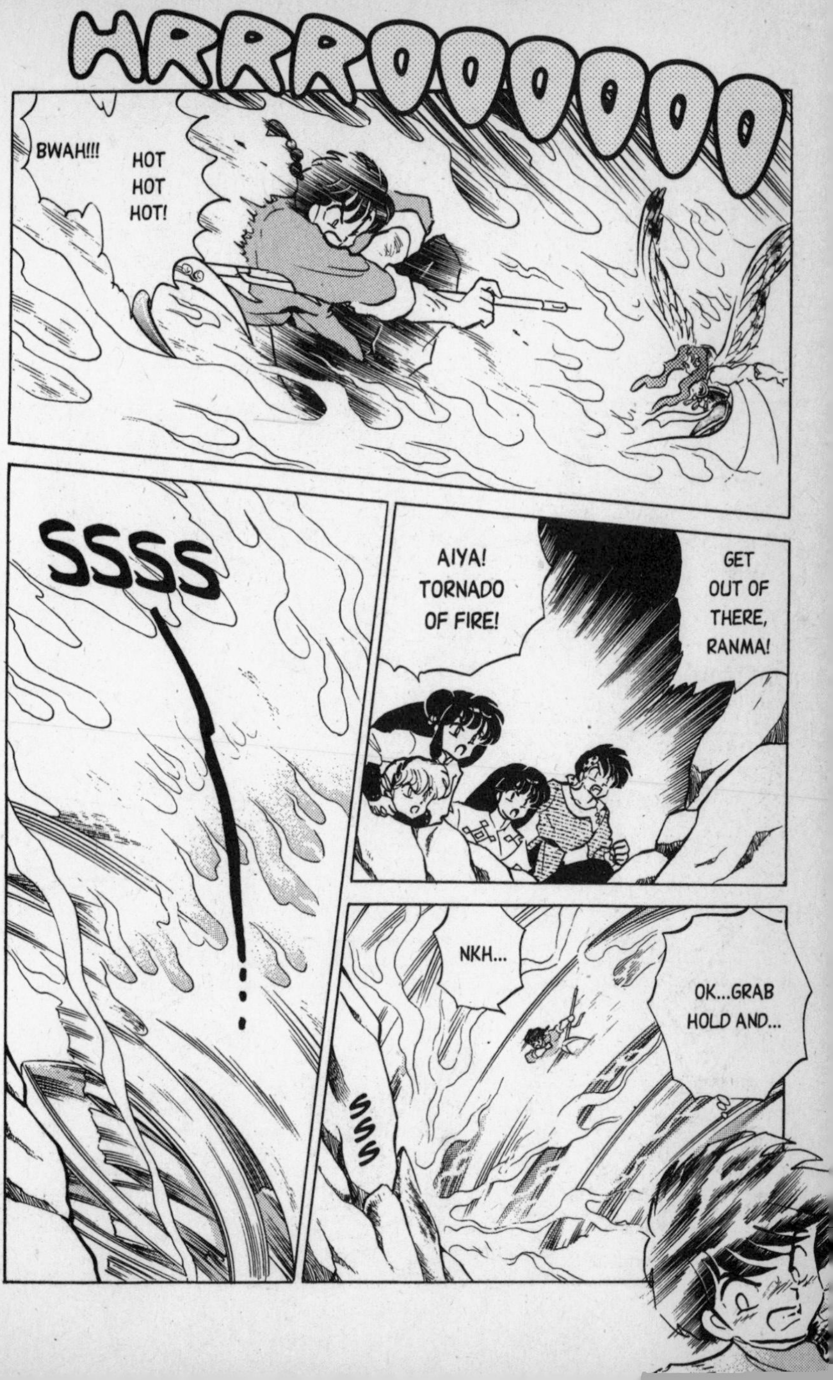
HRRROOOOOOO
BWAH!!!
HOT HOT HOT!
SSSS
AIYA! TORNADO OF FIRE!
GET OUT OF THERE, RANMA!
NKH...
OK...GRAB HOLD AND...
SSS

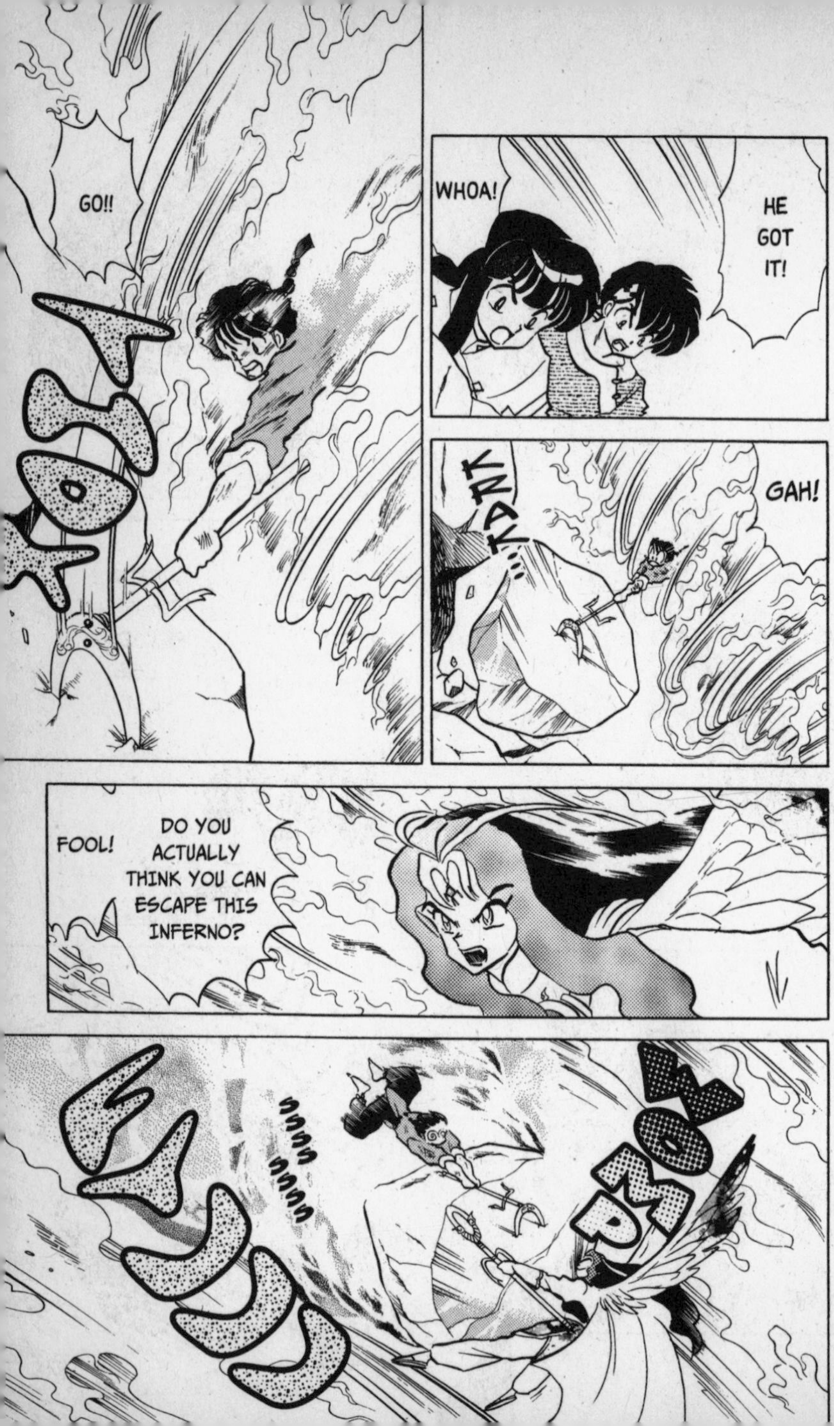
GO!!
WHOA!
HE GOT IT!
KRAK!!
GAH!
FOOL!
DO YOU ACTUALLY THINK YOU CAN ESCAPE THIS INFERNO?

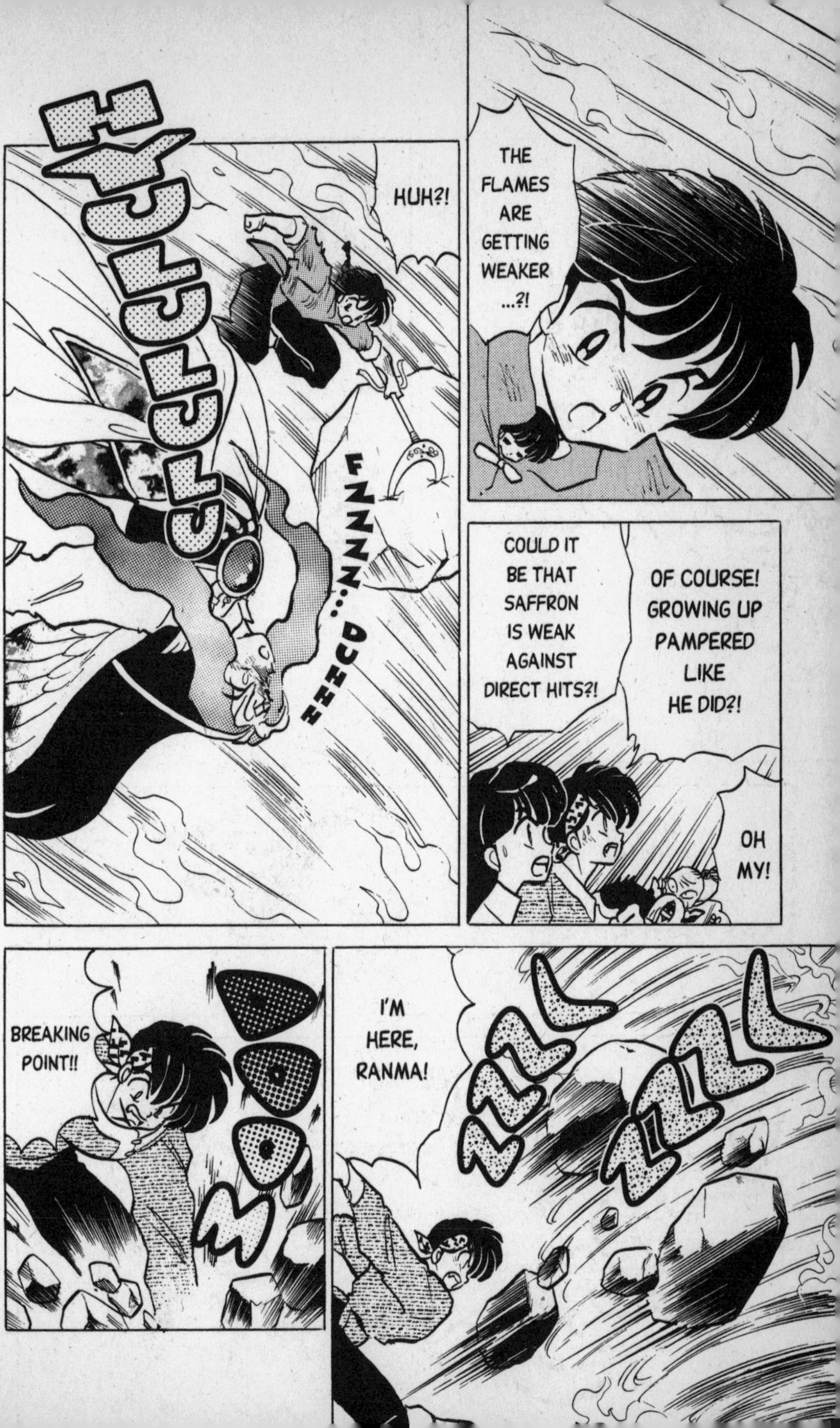
HUH?!
FZZZZ...DUHHH
THE FLAMES ARE GETTING WEAKER ...?!
COULD IT BE THAT SAFFRON IS WEAK AGAINST DIRECT HITS?!
OF COURSE! GROWING UP PAMPERED LIKE HE DID?!
OH MY!
BREAKING POINT!!
I'M HERE, RANMA!

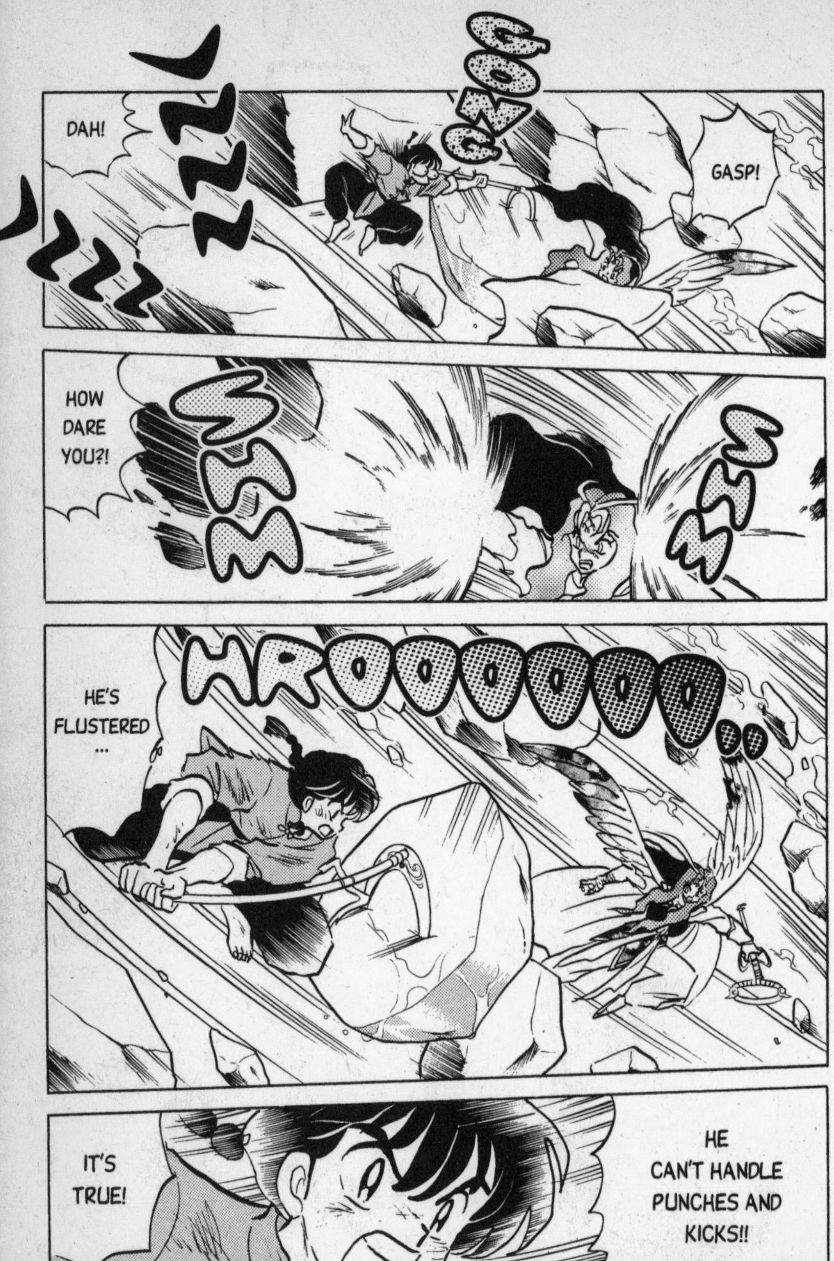
DAH!
ZZZZ
ZZZZ
GONG
GASP!
HOW DARE YOU?!
SHM
SHM
HE'S FLUSTERED ...
HROOOOOOO..!!
IT'S TRUE!
HE CAN'T HANDLE PUNCHES AND KICKS!!

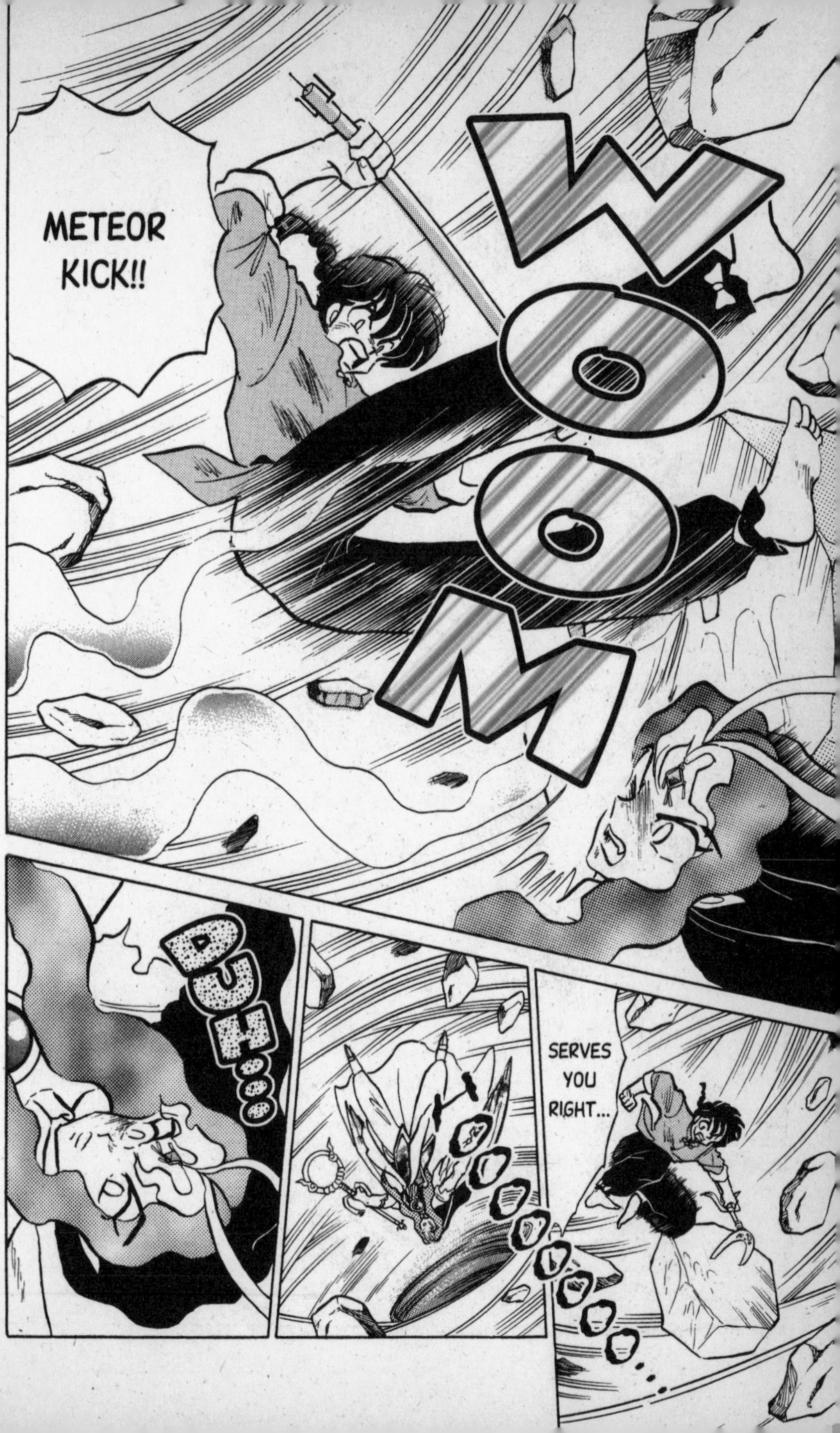
METEOR KICK!!
WOOM
DUH...
SERVES YOU RIGHT...

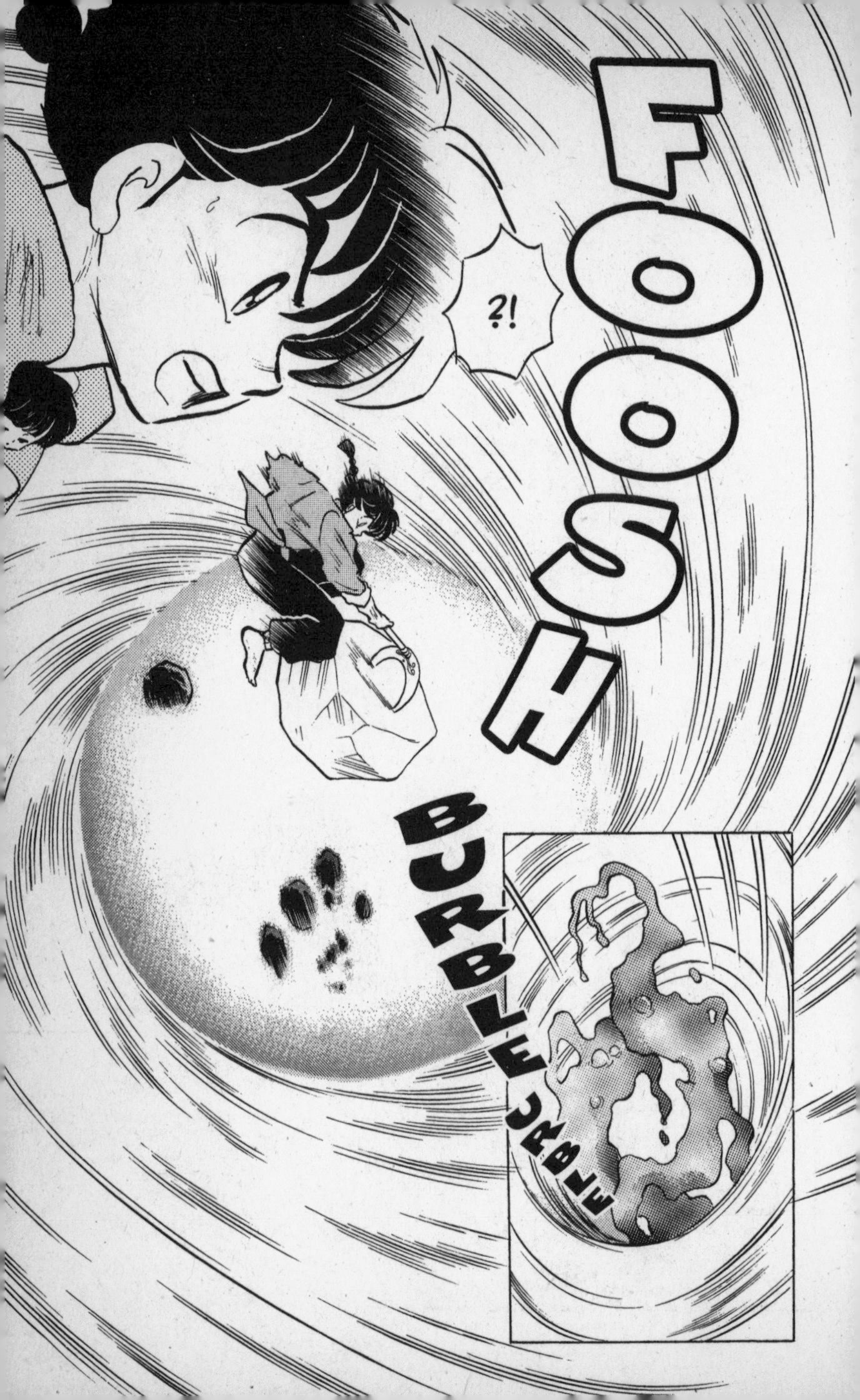

?!
FOOSH
BURBLE
BURBLE

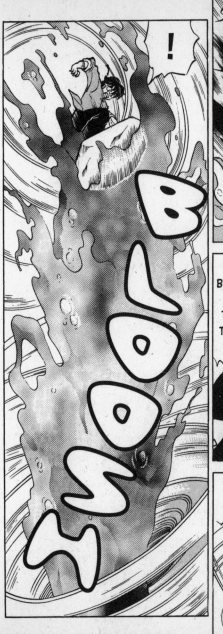

!

B
O
O
M

SSHH

THE BOULDER—IT'S TURNING TO LAVA!

BUT THERE WASN'T ENOUGH HEAT!

HA!

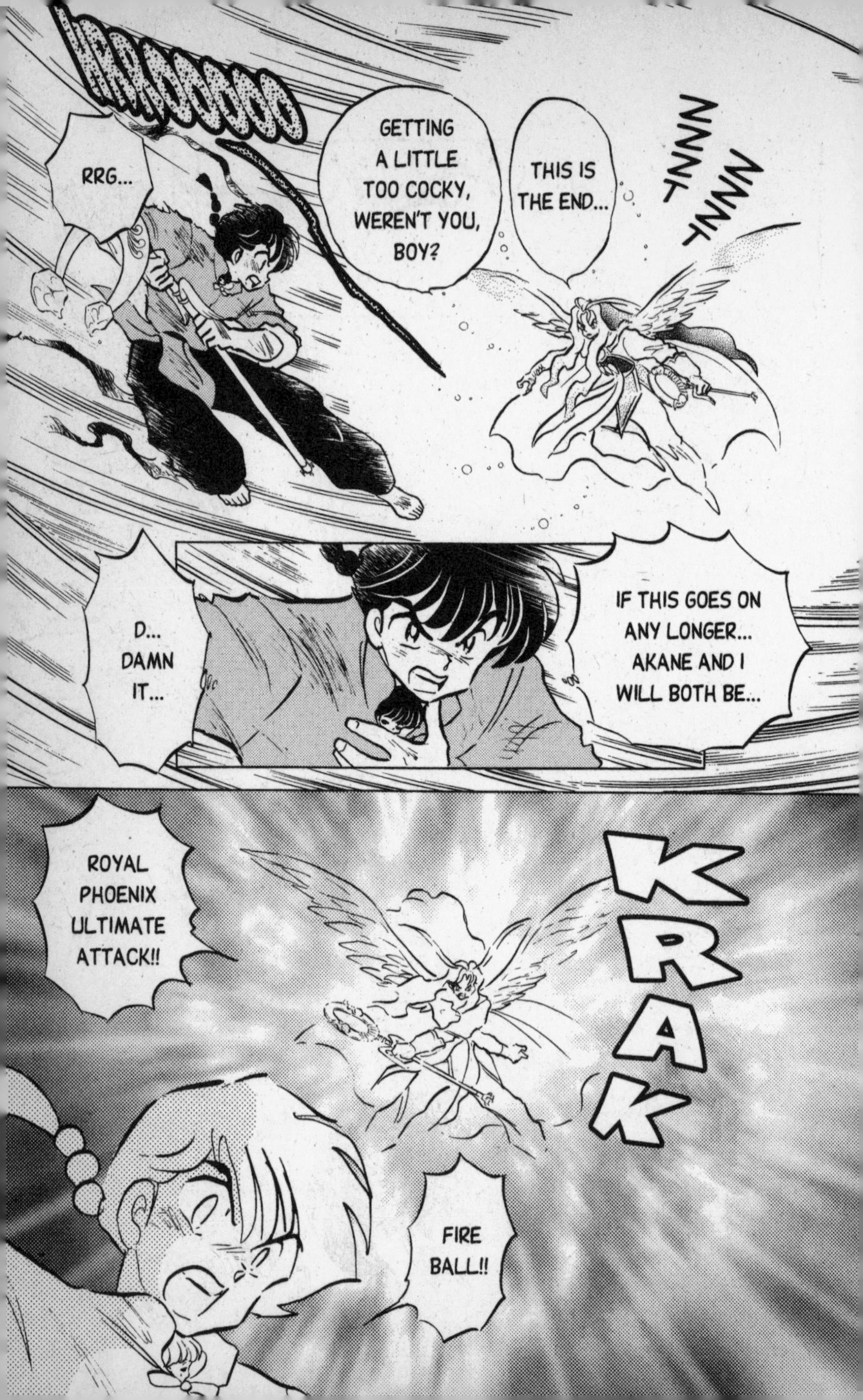
RRG...
GETTING A LITTLE TOO COCKY, WEREN'T YOU, BOY?
THIS IS THE END...
D... DAMN IT...
IF THIS GOES ON ANY LONGER... AKANE AND I WILL BOTH BE...
ROYAL PHOENIX ULTIMATE ATTACK!!
KRAK
FIRE BALL!!

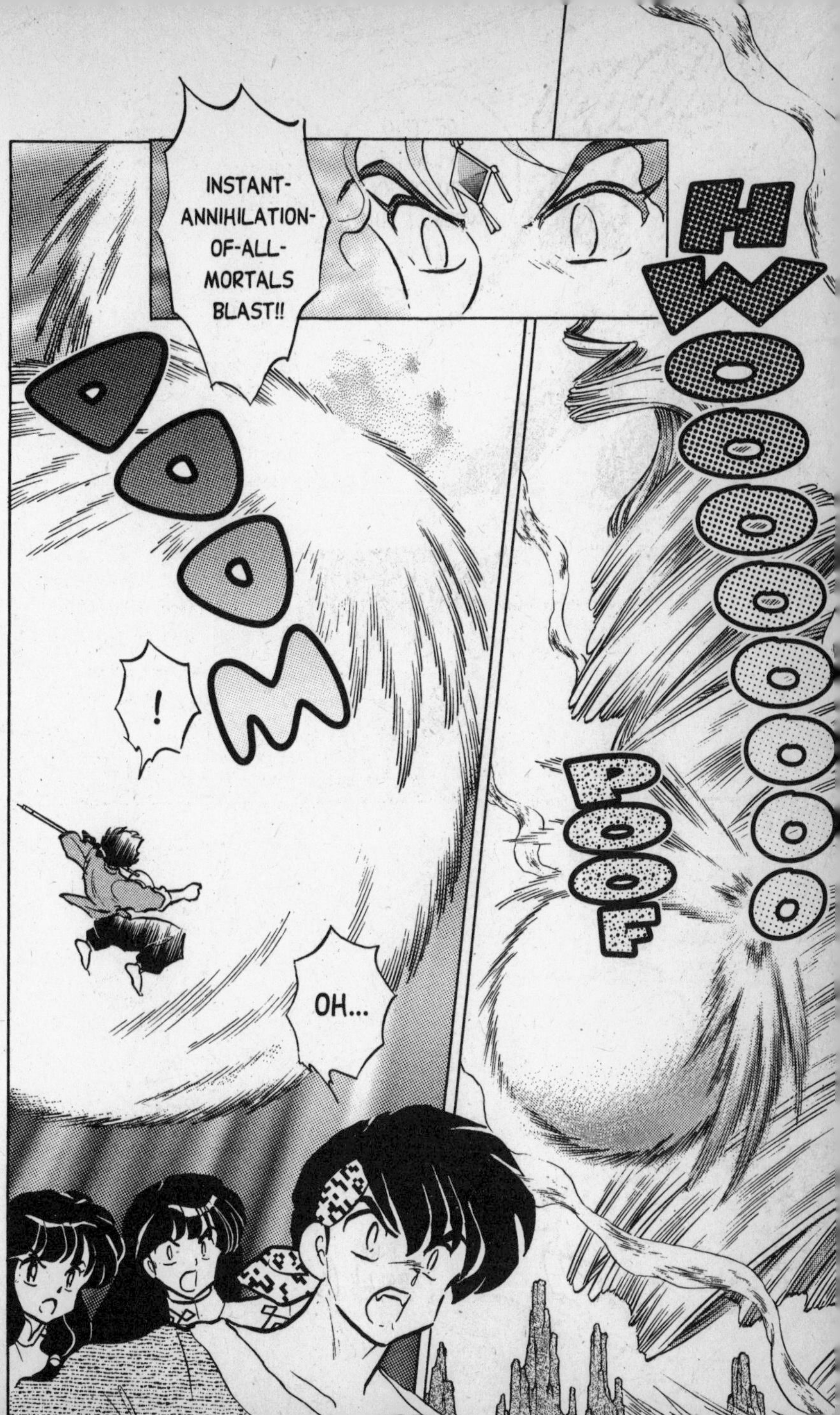

INSTANT-ANNIHILATION-OF-ALL-MORTALS BLAST!!
DOOOM
!
OH...
HWOOOOOOOO
POOF

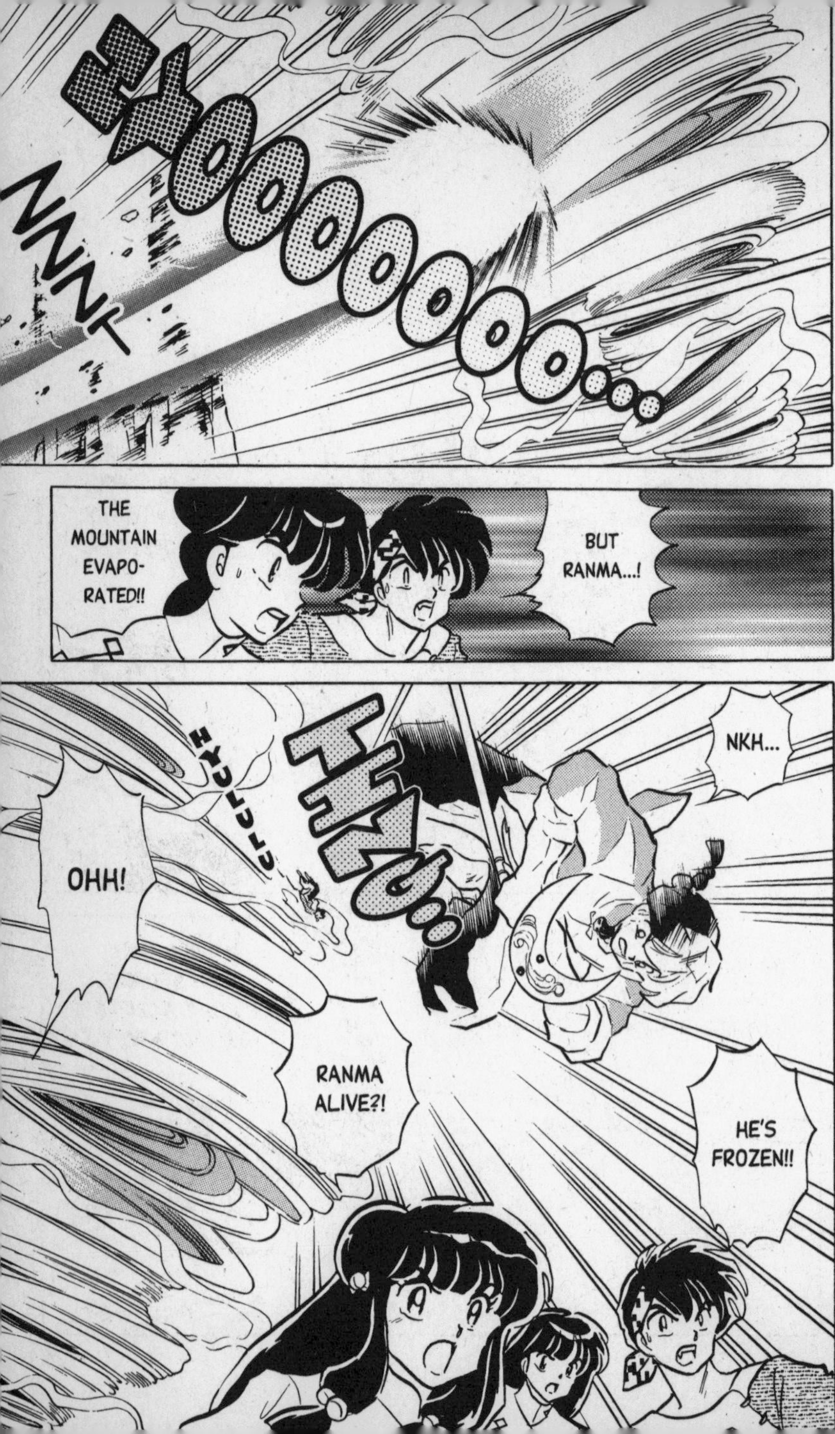
ZYOOOOOOOO...
NNNT
THE MOUNTAIN EVAPORATED!!
BUT RANMA...!
HYULULU
OHH!
NKH...
RANMA ALIVE?!
HE'S FROZEN!!

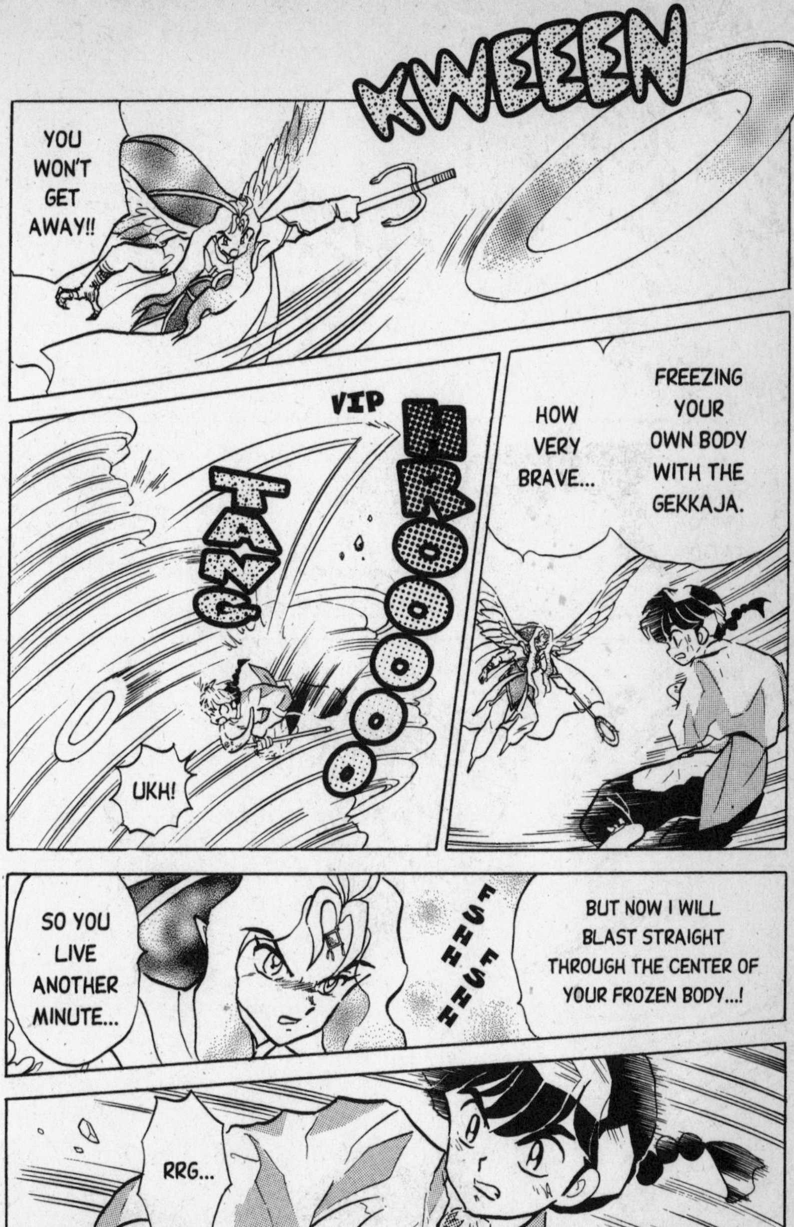
KWEEEN
YOU WON'T GET AWAY!!
VIP
TANG
HROOOOOOO
UKH!
HOW VERY BRAVE...
FREEZING YOUR OWN BODY WITH THE GEKKAJA.
SO YOU LIVE ANOTHER MINUTE...
FSHHH
FSHH
BUT NOW I WILL BLAST STRAIGHT THROUGH THE CENTER OF YOUR FROZEN BODY...!
RRG...

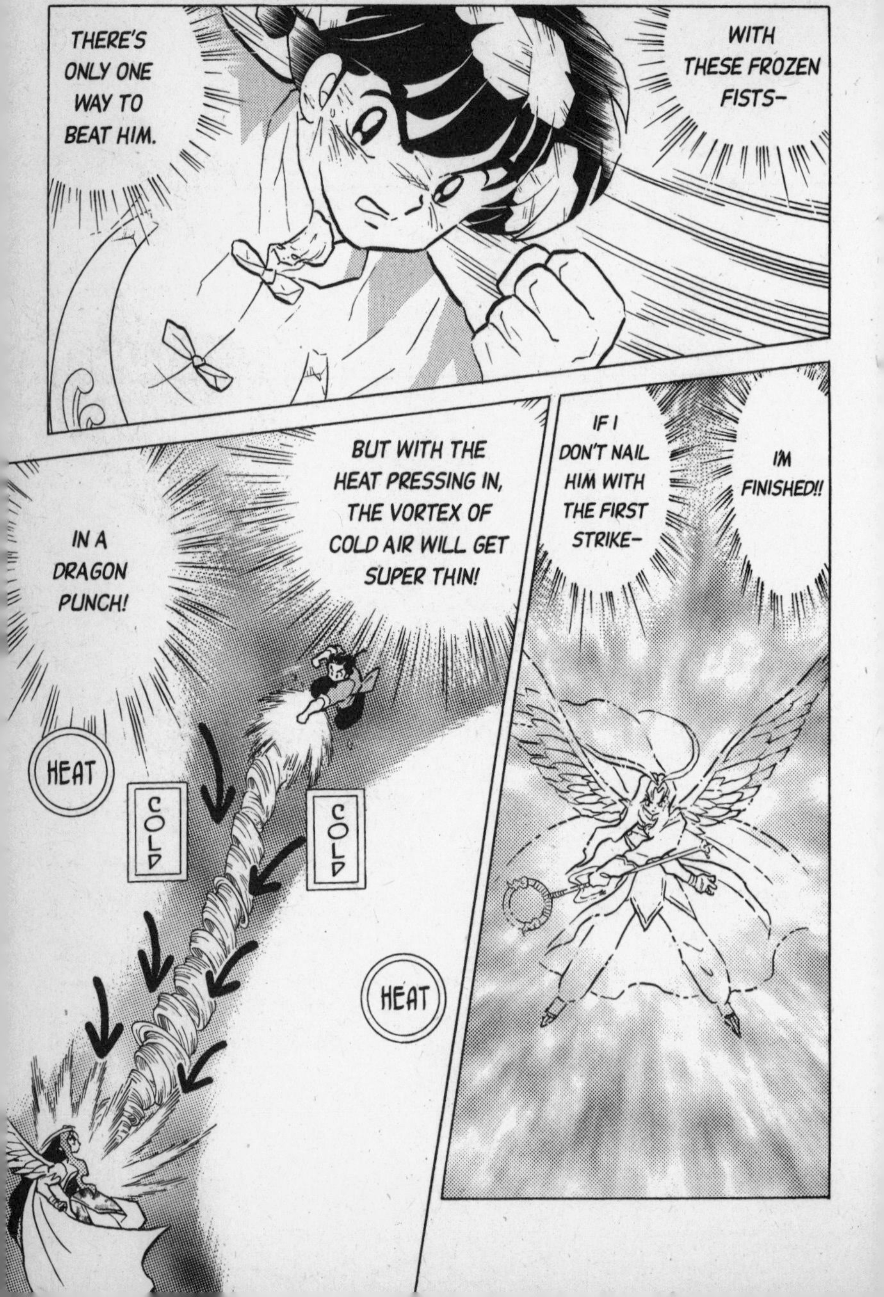
THERE'S ONLY ONE WAY TO BEAT HIM.
WITH THESE FROZEN FISTS-
IN A DRAGON PUNCH!
BUT WITH THE HEAT PRESSING IN, THE VORTEX OF COLD AIR WILL GET SUPER THIN!
HEAT
COLD
COLD
HEAT
IF I DON'T NAIL HIM WITH THE FIRST STRIKE-
I'M FINISHED!!

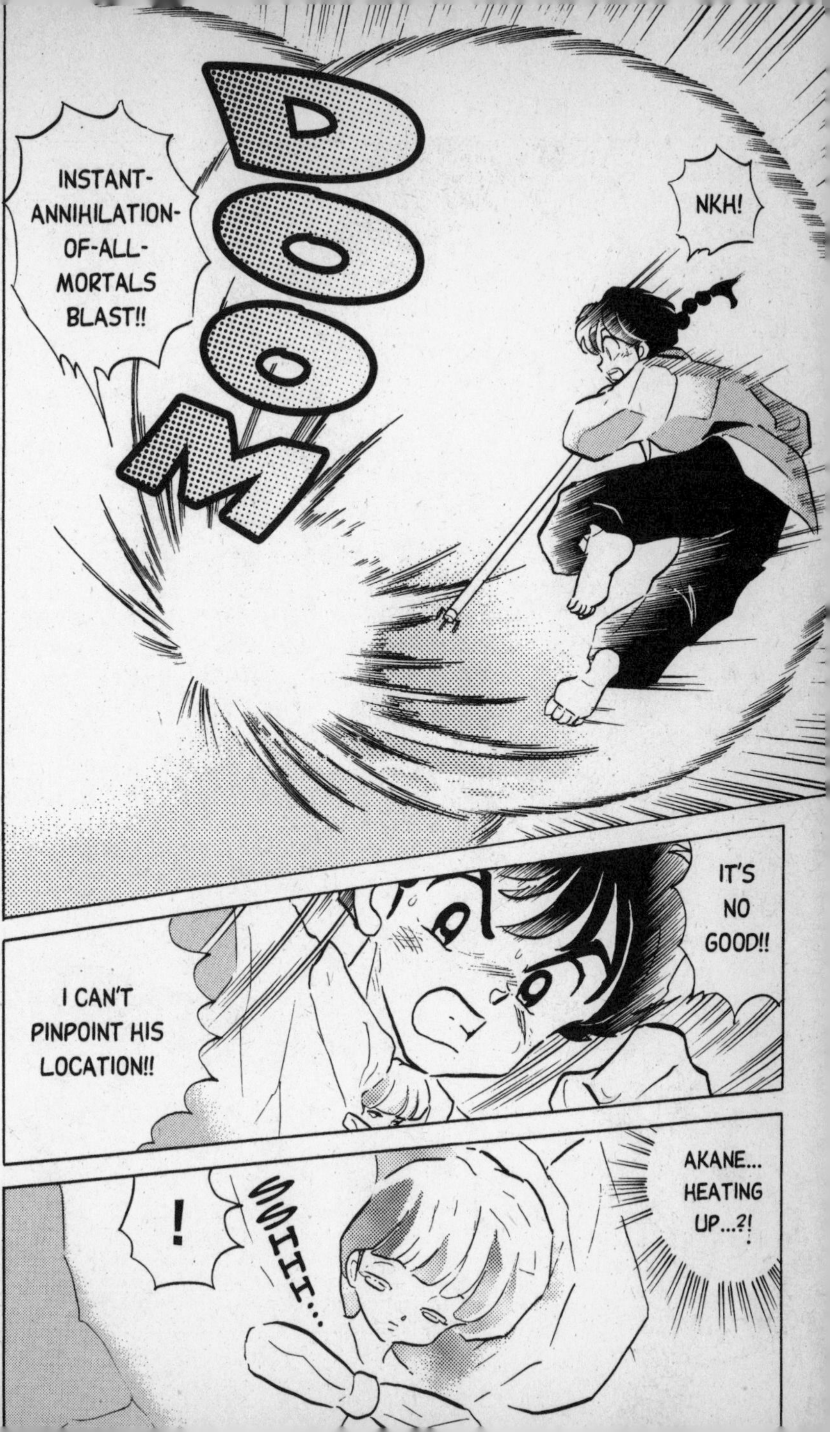

INSTANT-ANNIHILATION-OF-ALL-MORTALS BLAST!!
DOOM
NKH!
IT'S NO GOOD!!
I CAN'T PINPOINT HIS LOCATION!!
!
SSHHH...
AKANE... HEATING UP...?!

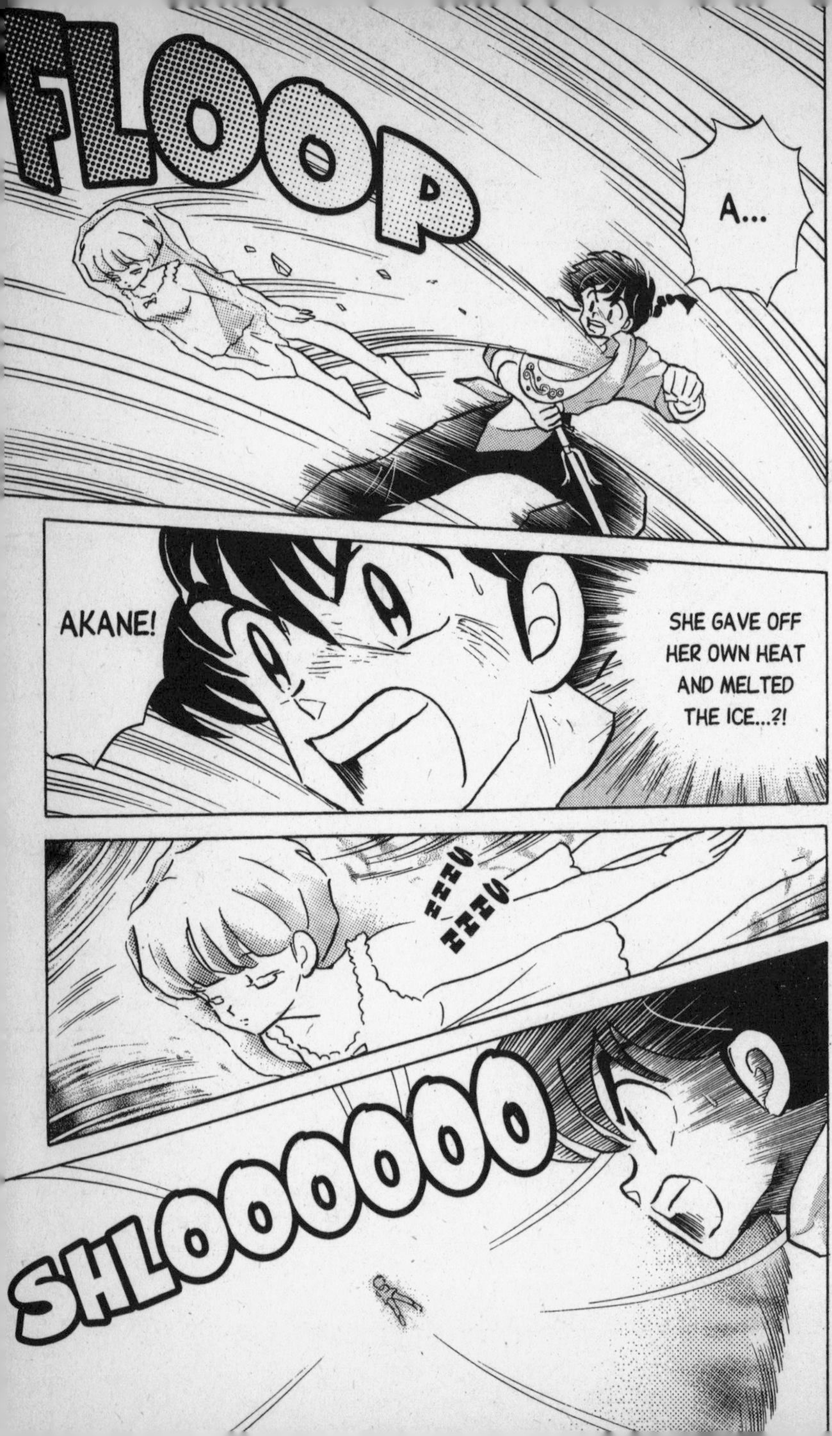
FLOOP
A...
AKANE!
SHE GAVE OFF HER OWN HEAT AND MELTED THE ICE...?!
SHIIII
SHIIII
SHLOOOOOOO

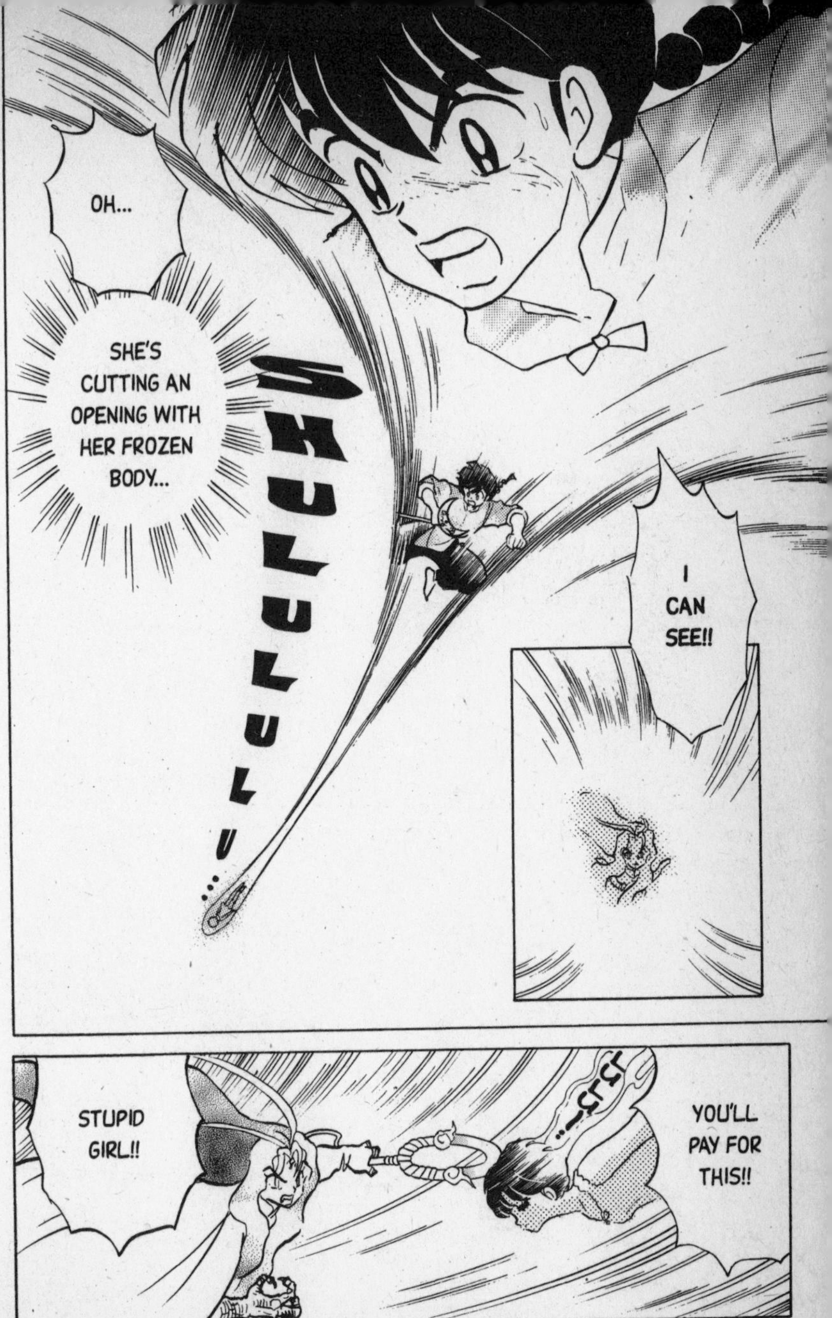
OH...
SHE'S CUTTING AN OPENING WITH HER FROZEN BODY...
SHULULULU...
I CAN SEE!!
STUPID GIRL!!
YOU'LL PAY FOR THIS!!

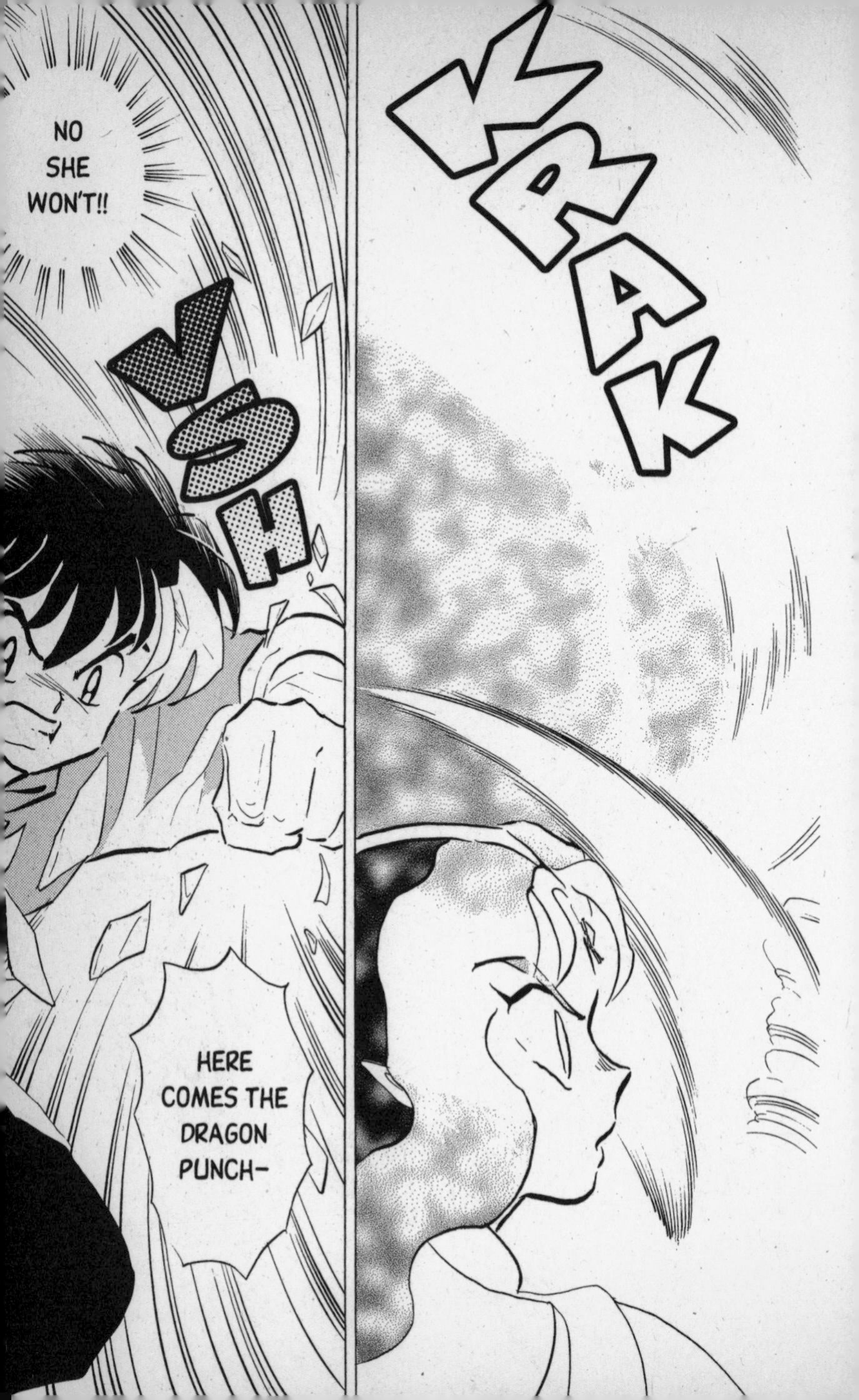
NO SHE WON'T!!
VOOSH
HERE COMES THE DRAGON PUNCH-
KRAK

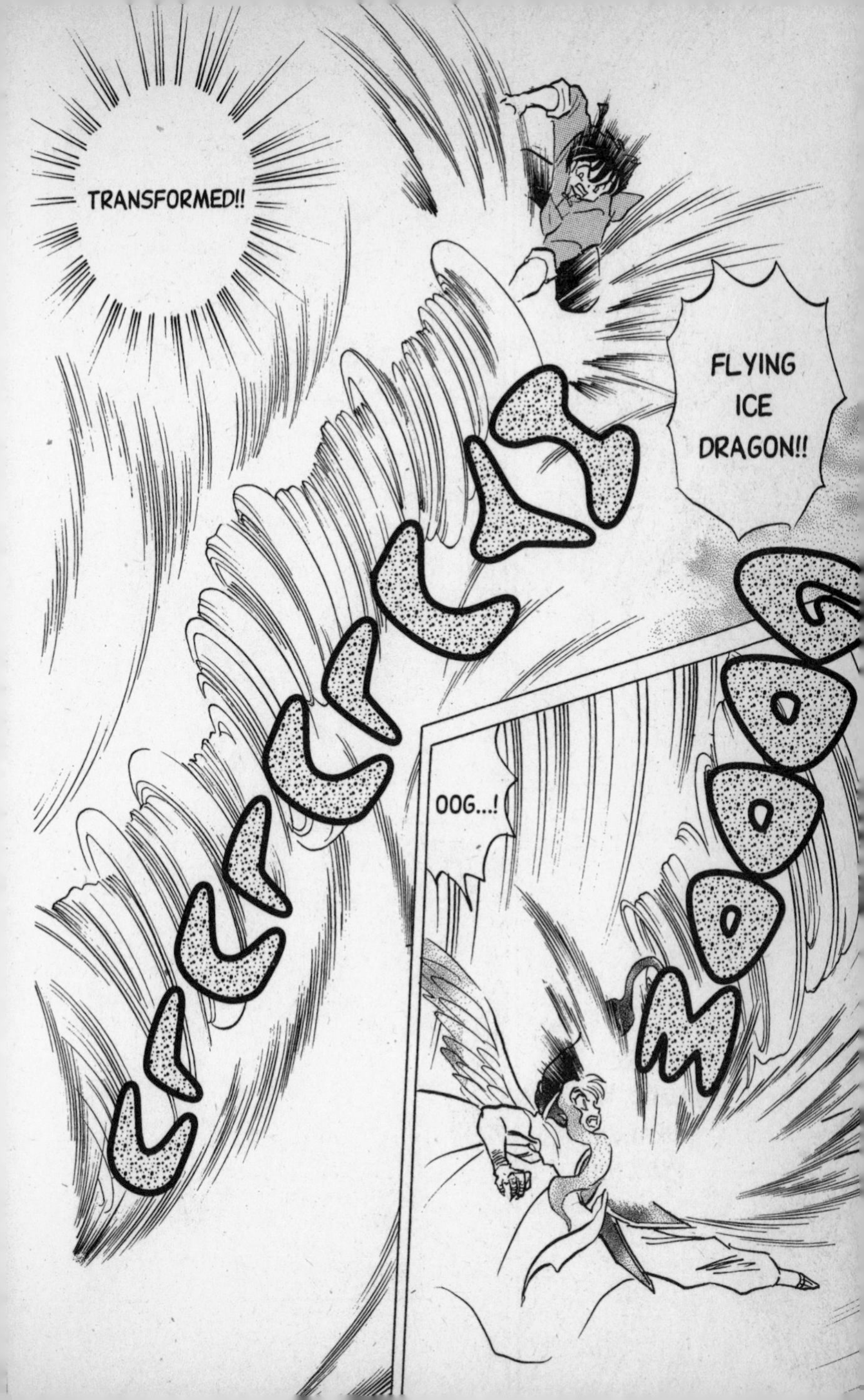
TRANSFORMED!!
FLYING ICE DRAGON!!
OOG...!

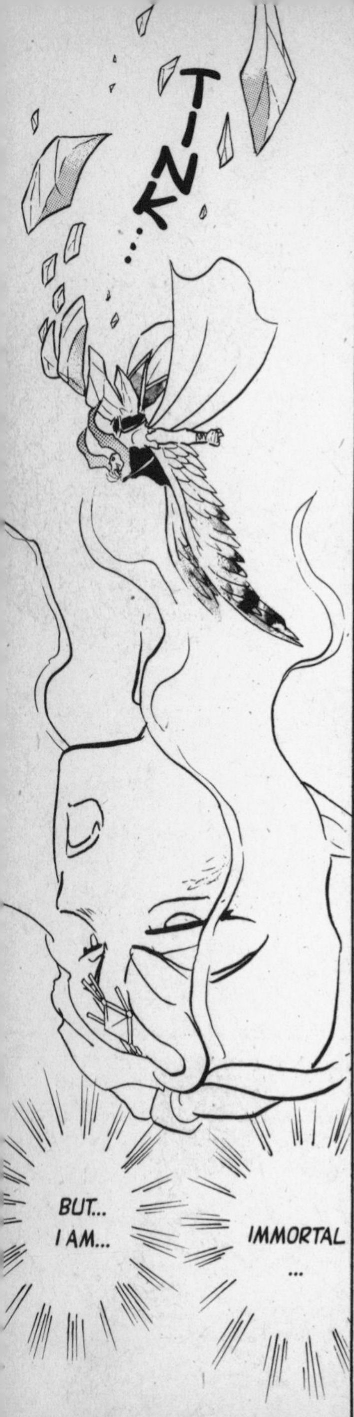
TINK...
BUT...
I AM...
IMMORTAL
...

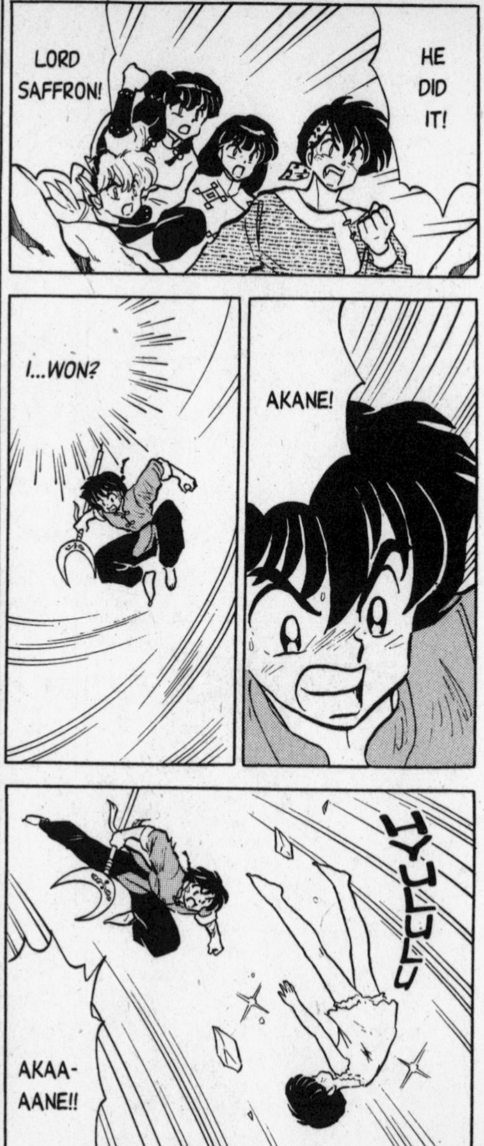
LORD SAFFRON!
HE DID IT!
I...WON?
AKANE!
HYULULU
AKAA-
AANE!!

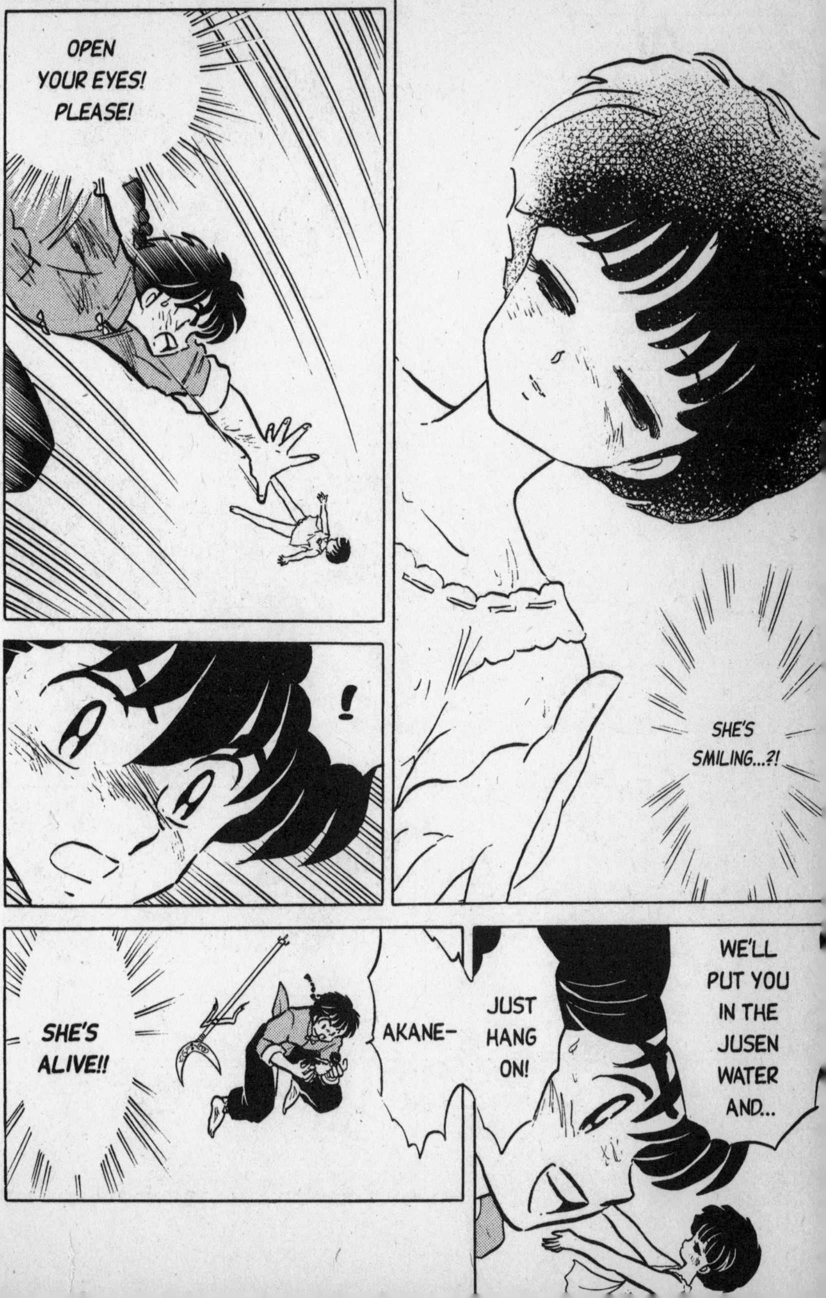
OPEN YOUR EYES! PLEASE!
!
SHE'S SMILING...?!
SHE'S ALIVE!!
AKANE-
JUST HANG ON!
WE'LL PUT YOU IN THE JUSEN WATER AND...

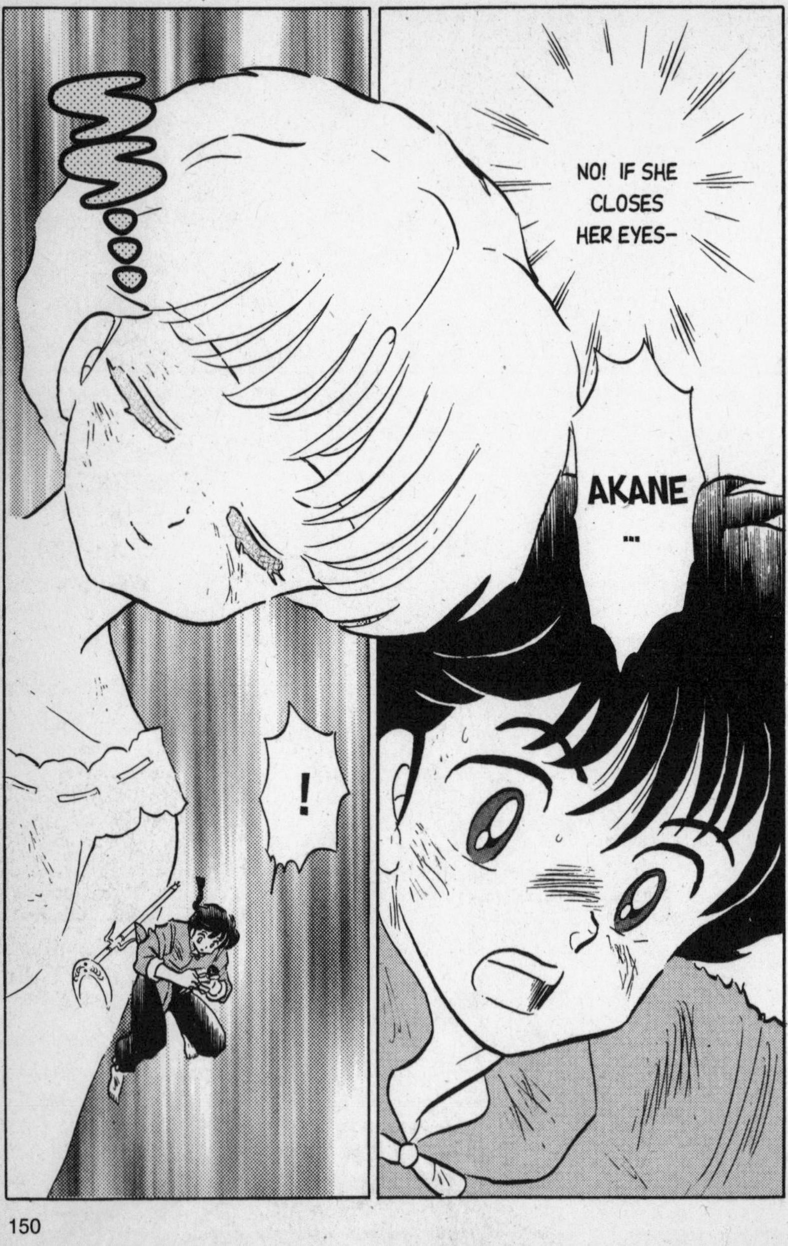
!
NO! IF SHE CLOSES HER EYES–
AKANE ...

-IT'LL BE TOO LATE!
THERE'S NO TIME JUST TO WAIT FOR US TO FALL!!
RRG!
WSH
AKANE!!
NEXT: THE FINAL CHAPTER

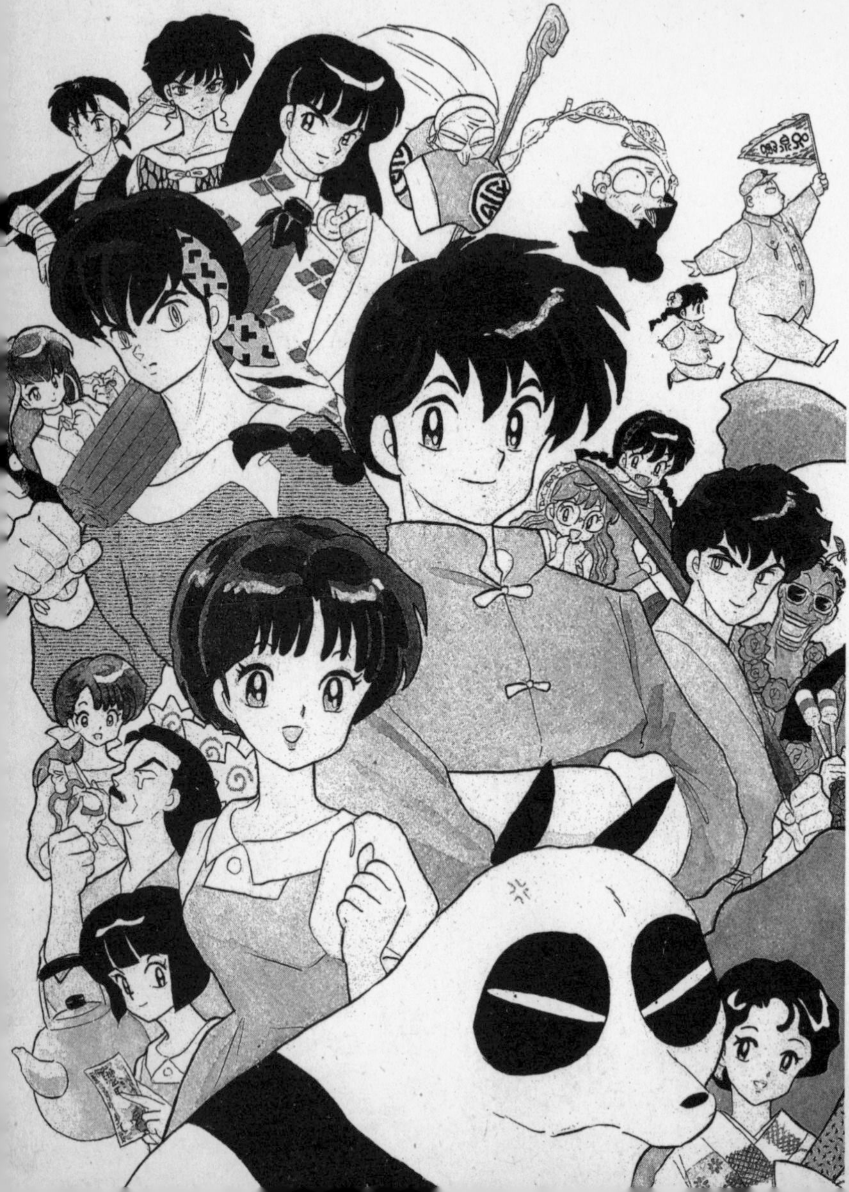

THE FINAL CHAPTER

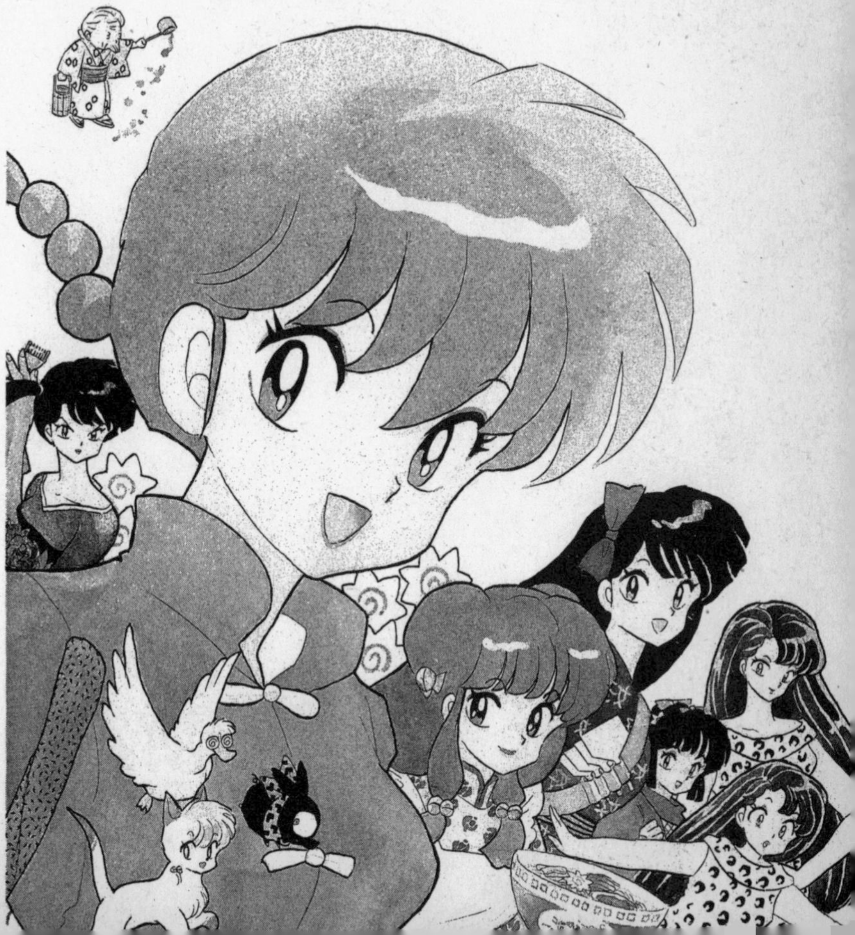

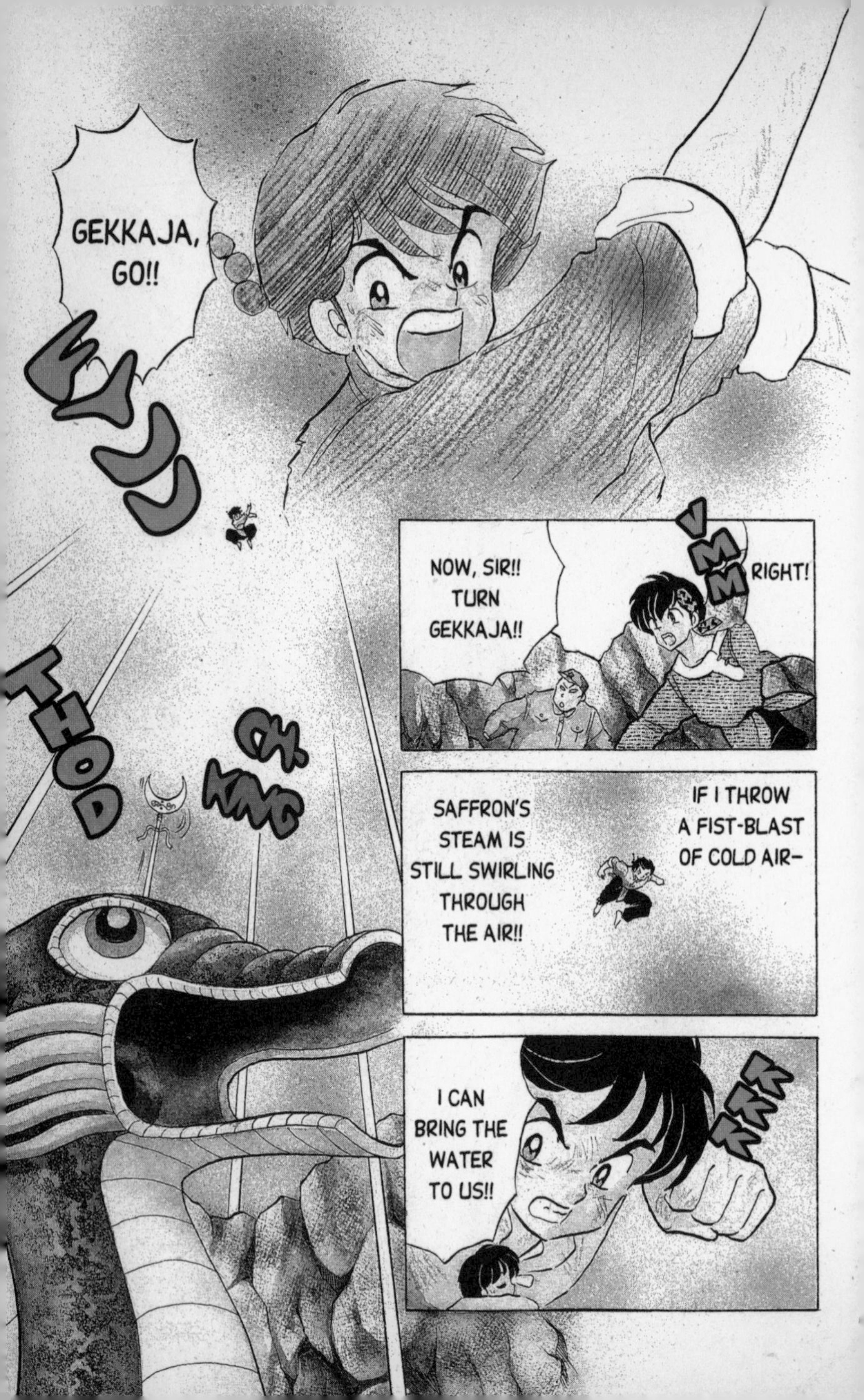
GEKKAJA, GO!!
THOD
CHKING
NOW, SIR!! TURN GEKKAJA!!
VMM
RIGHT!
SAFFRON'S STEAM IS STILL SWIRLING THROUGH THE AIR!!
IF I THROW A FIST-BLAST OF COLD AIR–
I CAN BRING THE WATER TO US!!
KKK

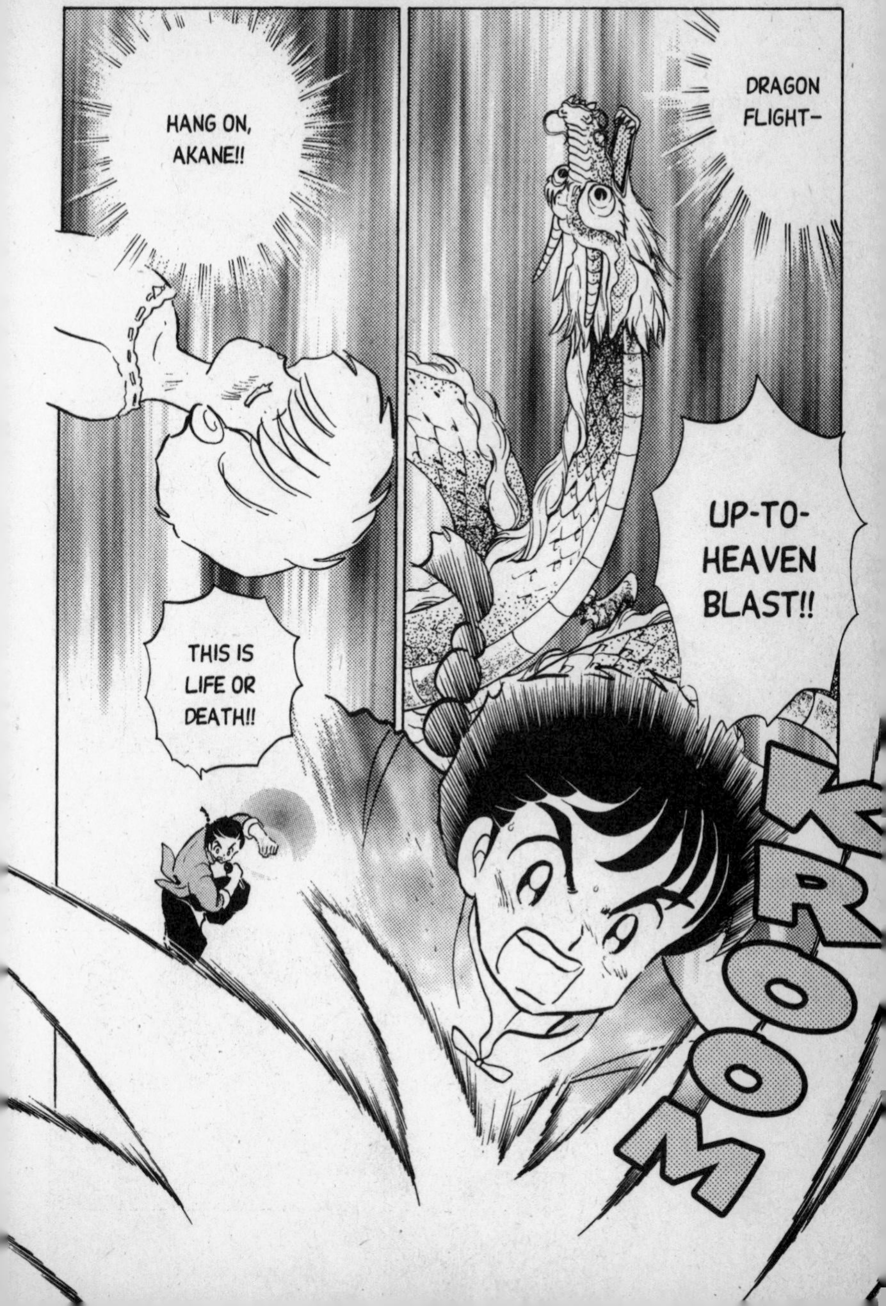
HANG ON, AKANE!!
THIS IS LIFE OR DEATH!!
DRAGON FLIGHT–
UP-TO-HEAVEN BLAST!!
KRROOOM

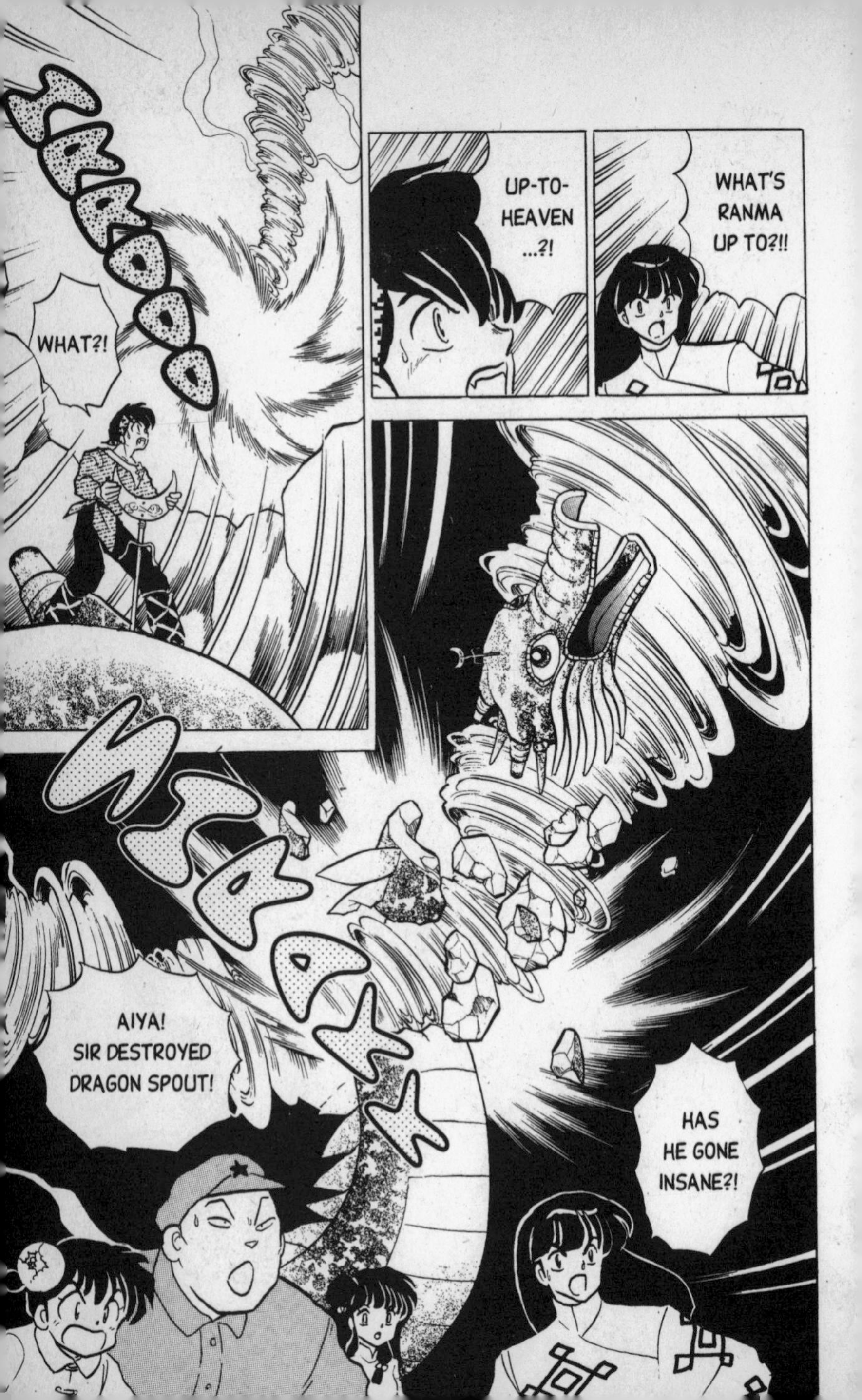

WHAT?!
UP-TO-HEAVEN ...?!
WHAT'S RANMA UP TO?!!
AIYA! SIR DESTROYED DRAGON SPOUT!
HAS HE GONE INSANE?!

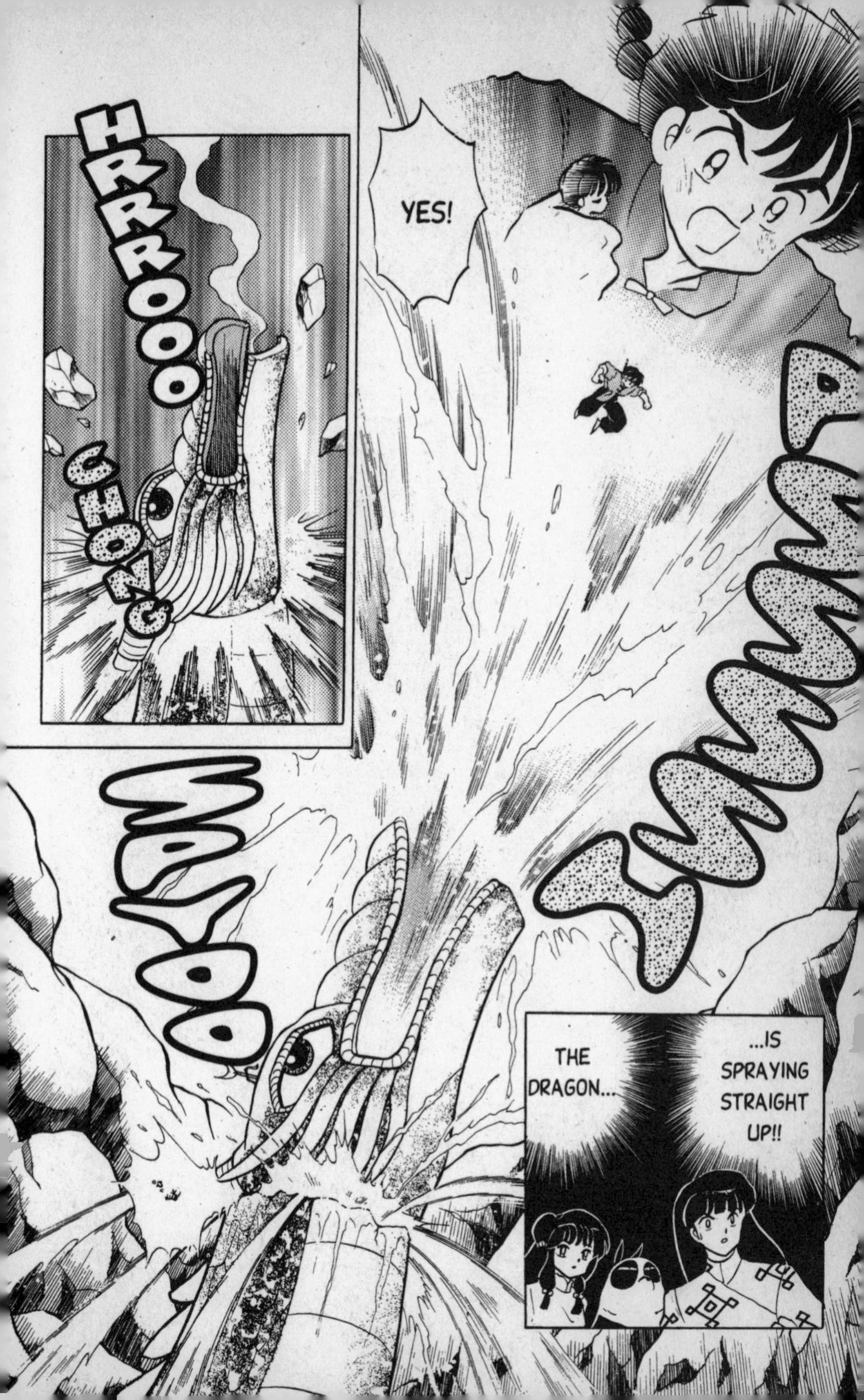
HRRROOO
CHONG
YES!
THE DRAGON...
...IS SPRAYING STRAIGHT UP!!

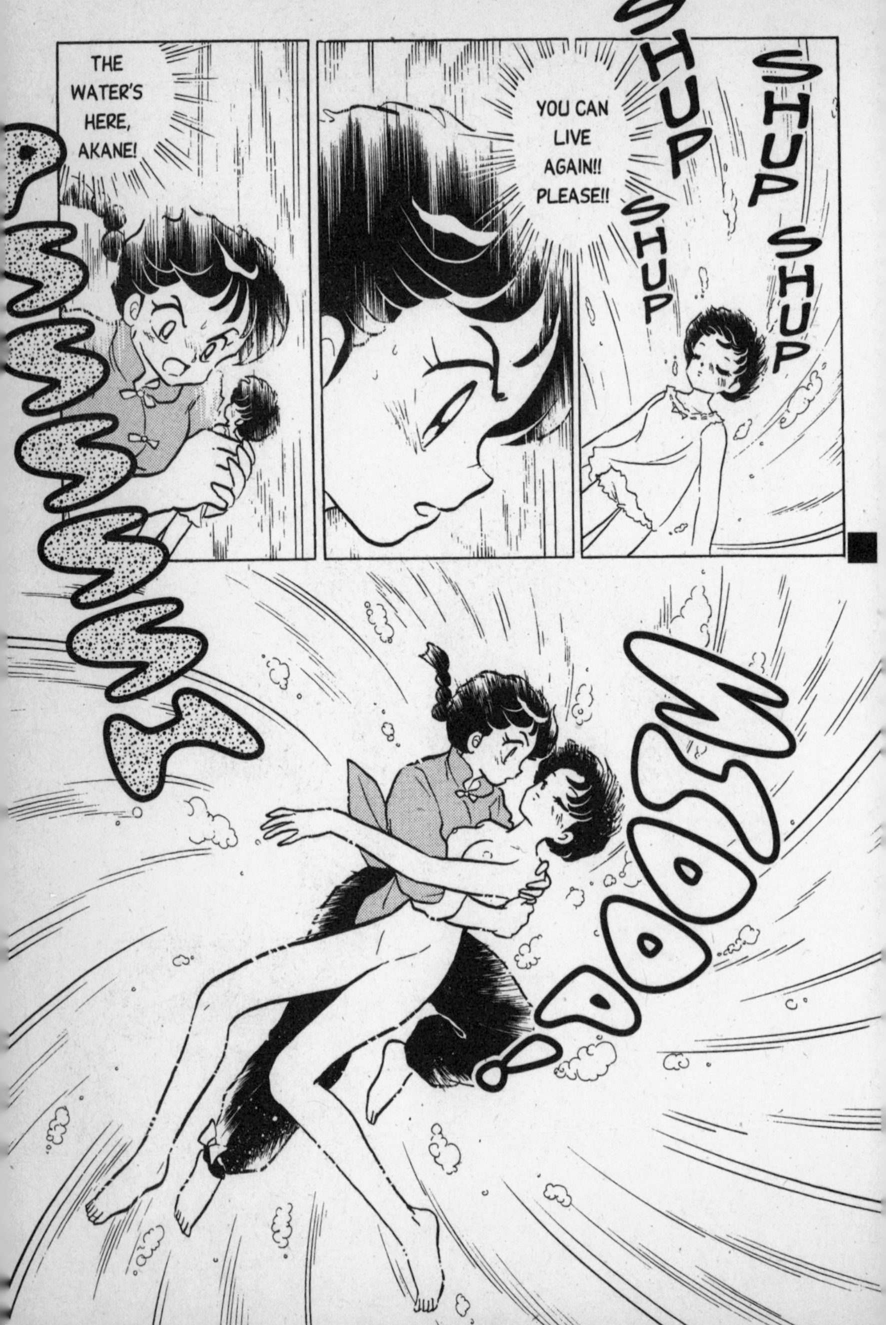
THE WATER'S HERE, AKANE!
PWSSSSH
YOU CAN LIVE AGAIN!! PLEASE!!
SHUP SHUP
SHUP SHUP
POOOM

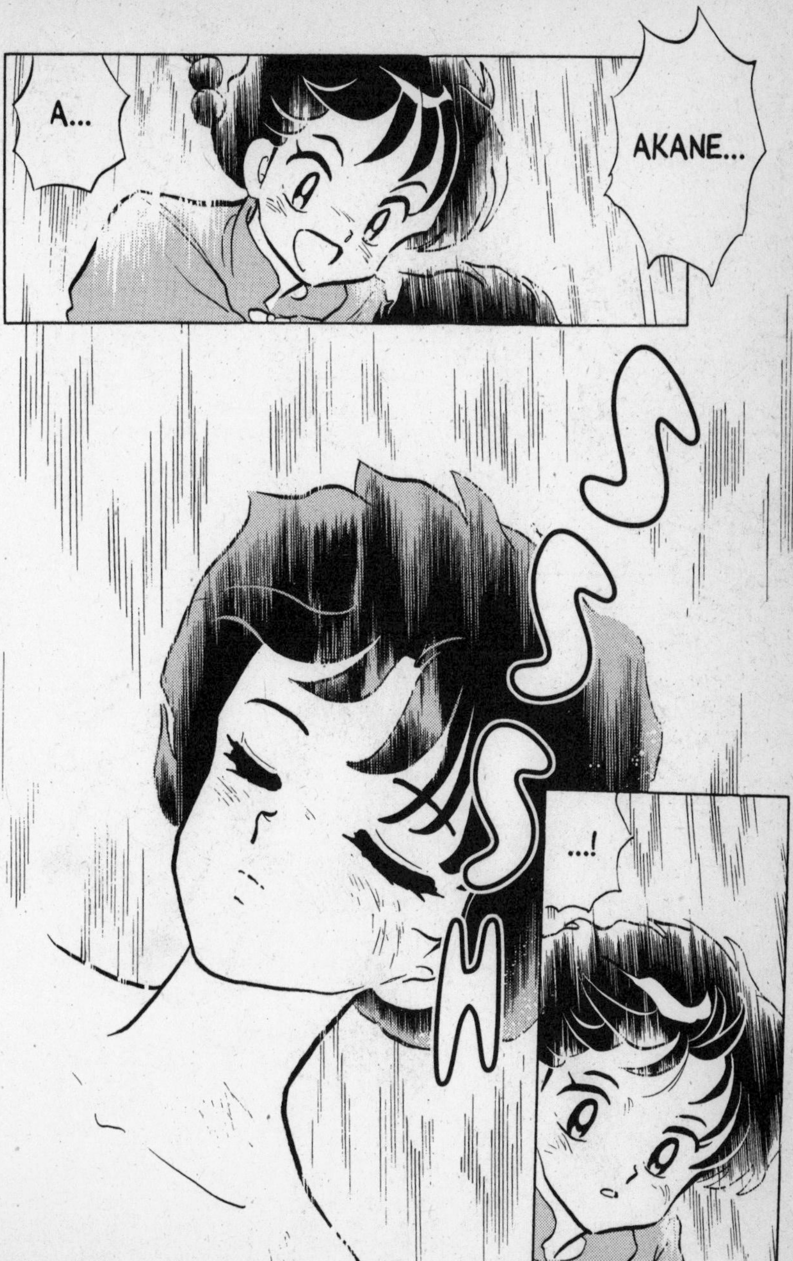
A...
AKANE...
...!

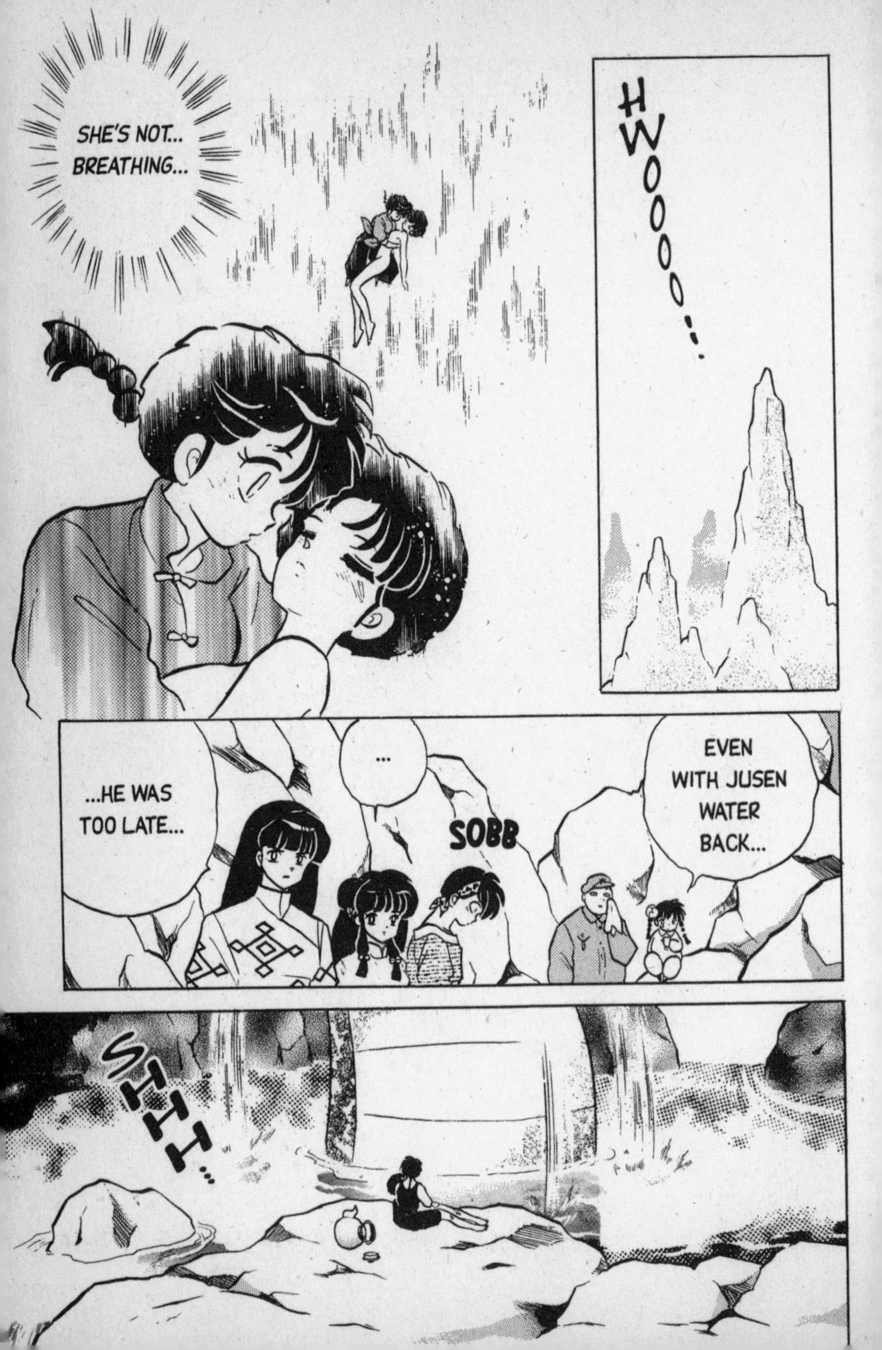
SHE'S NOT... BREATHING...
HWOOOO...
...HE WAS TOO LATE...
...
SOBB
EVEN WITH JUSEN WATER BACK...
SHIII...

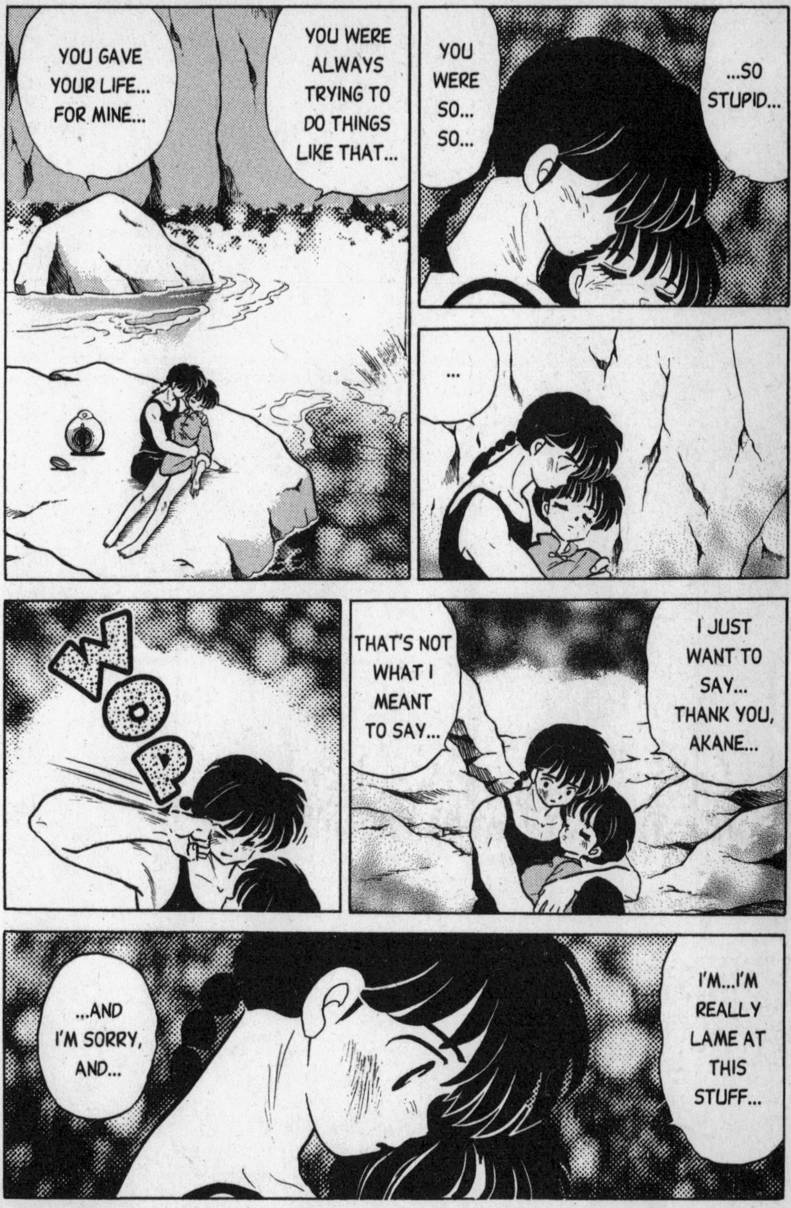
YOU GAVE YOUR LIFE... FOR MINE...
YOU WERE ALWAYS TRYING TO DO THINGS LIKE THAT...
YOU WERE SO... SO...
...SO STUPID...
...
WOP
THAT'S NOT WHAT I MEANT TO SAY...
I JUST WANT TO SAY... THANK YOU, AKANE...
...AND I'M SORRY, AND...
I'M...I'M REALLY LAME AT THIS STUFF...

I NEVER... ..TOLD YOU WHAT I REALLY FELT...

AKANE, CAN YOU HEAR ME?

I WANT TO TELL YOU SOMETHING.

PLEASE...

...BE ABLE TO HEAR ME, AKANE...

I JUST MADE YOU MAD AND HURT YOU...

...

PLUP PLUP

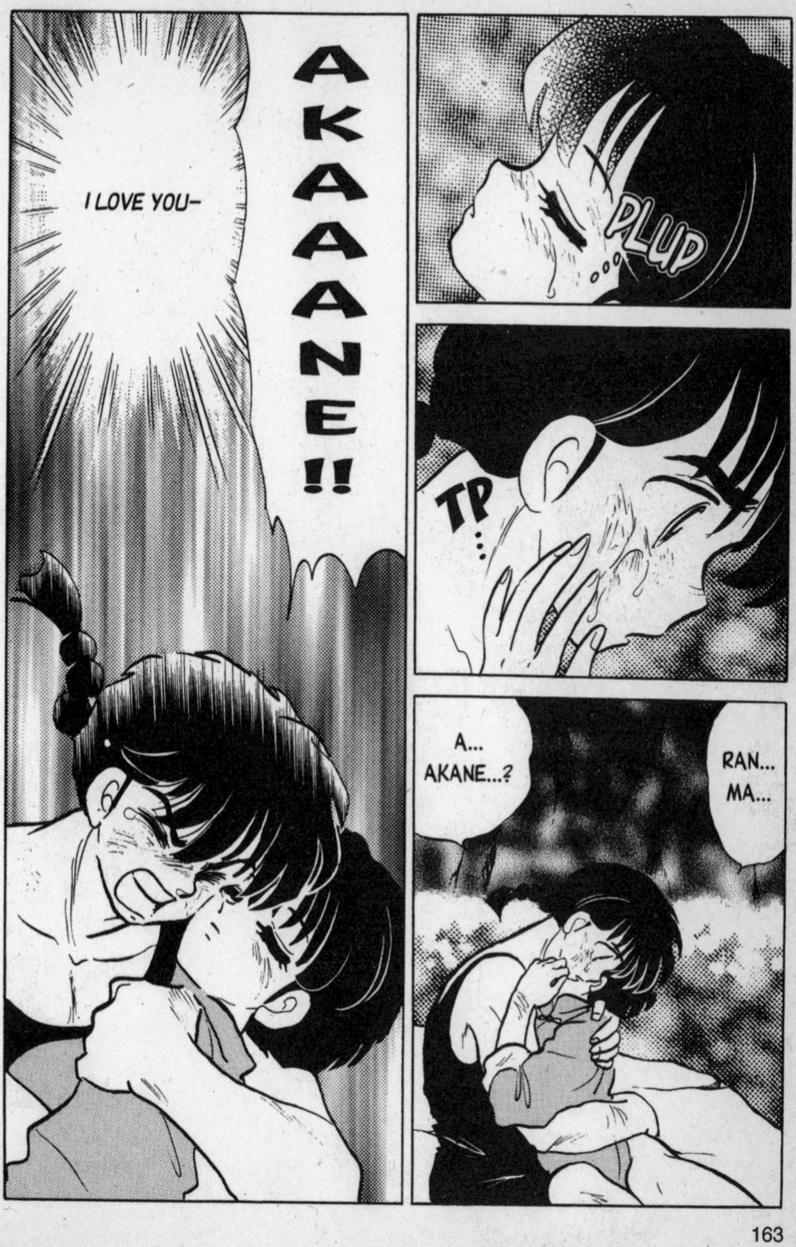
I LOVE YOU-
AKAAANE!!
PLUP
TP...
A... AKANE...?
RAN... MA...

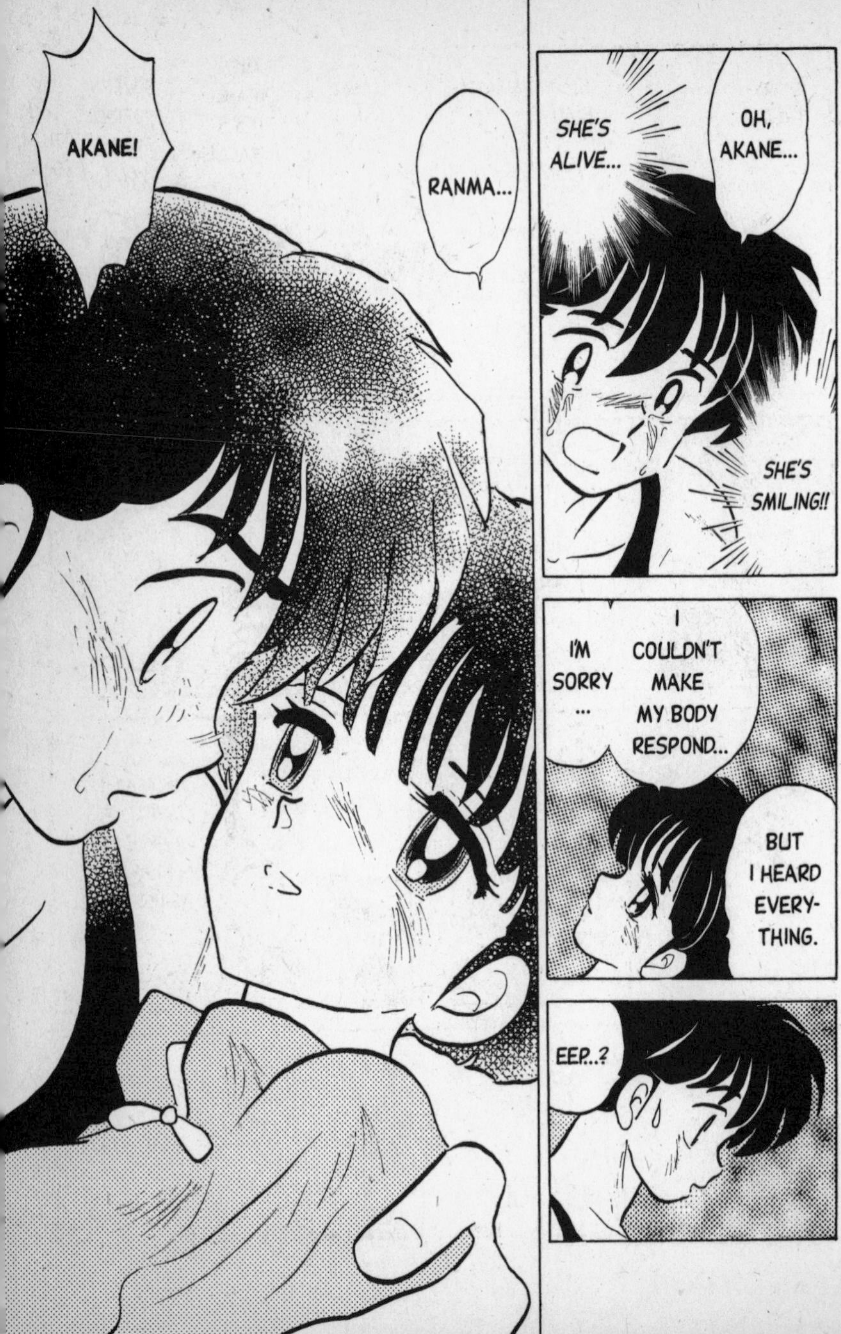
AKANE!
RANMA...
SHE'S ALIVE...
OH, AKANE...
SHE'S SMILING!!
I'M SORRY ...
I COULDN'T MAKE MY BODY RESPOND...
BUT I HEARD EVERYTHING.
EEP...?

EVERY-
THING?!

BLUSH

UH-
HUH!

WHAT?

WHAT?

WHAT
DID I
SAY?

MISS
AKANE!
IT'S A
MIRACLE!

SORRY I
WORRIED
EVERY-
BODY.

TOO
STUPID
TO DIE.

THIS IS SO
DISTRESSING!

DEAR
LORD
SAFFRON...

SAF-
FRON...?

YOU MEAN...
THAT EGG...?

SIIIGH

PWAK

PCH

PCH

PCH

POP

WAAAAAA!

AND THAT UGLY
LITTLE BABY...?

LORD SAFFRON
USED UP ALL
OF HIS ENERGY
IN HIS BATTLE
AGAINST YOU.

NOW WE'VE
LOST ALL
REASON
TO FIGHT.

LET'S GO
HOME TO
HO'O PEAK.

165

THIS TIME RAISE HIM TO BE A NICER PERSON!

WAIT A SECOND... ...DOES THAT MEAN...

SKRTCH SKRTCH

OH, MISTRESS!

...WHEN IT'S TIME FOR SAFFRON'S NEXT TRANSFORMATION...

...THEY'LL ATTACK THE JUSEN CAVES AGAIN?

BUT AT HO'O PEAK—

WATER!

BLOOOSH!

WATER IS FLOWING!

SUCH FORCE...

BUT... IT'S BEEN DRY SO LONG...

SSSSSH

INDEED. ONE CAN ONLY SUPPOSE...

...THAT THE BATTLE BETWEEN LORD SAFFRON AND RANMA...

...SOMEHOW WROUGHT A CHANGE TO THE CAVE'S SUBTERRANEAN WATER CHANNEL.

AT LAST, HO'O PEAK IS SECURE...

AOWWW

WATER FOWL

SIIIIGH

THEN THE BATTLE WAS NOT IN VAIN...

DUHHH...

SO GLAD TO HEAR THAT...

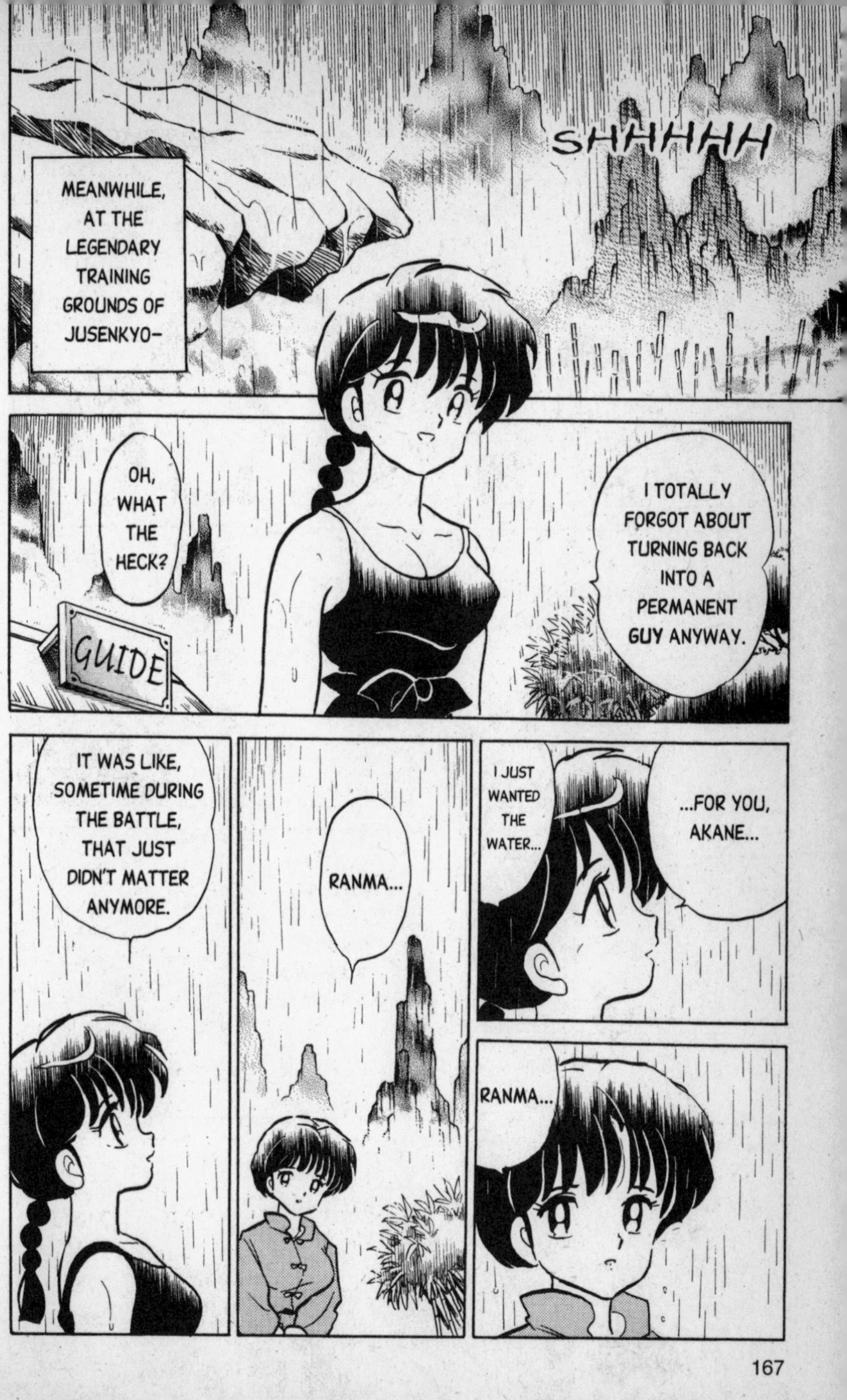
MEANWHILE, AT THE LEGENDARY TRAINING GROUNDS OF JUSENKYO–
SHHHHH
OH, WHAT THE HECK?
GUIDE
I TOTALLY FORGOT ABOUT TURNING BACK INTO A PERMANENT GUY ANYWAY.
IT WAS LIKE, SOMETIME DURING THE BATTLE, THAT JUST DIDN'T MATTER ANYMORE.
RANMA...
I JUST WANTED THE WATER...
...FOR YOU, AKANE...
RANMA...

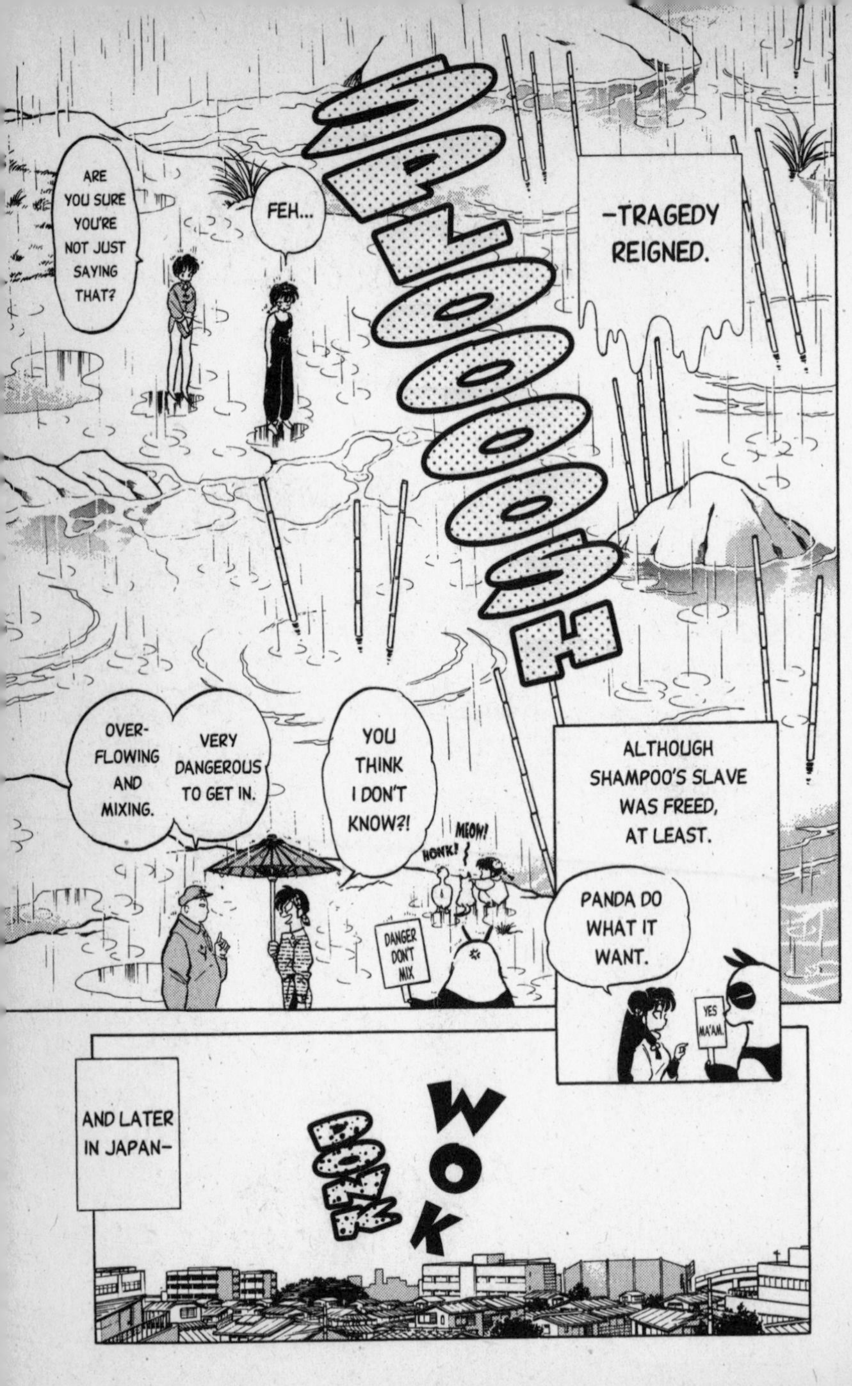
ARE YOU SURE YOU'RE NOT JUST SAYING THAT?
FEH...
—TRAGEDY REIGNED.
OVER-FLOWING AND MIXING.
VERY DANGEROUS TO GET IN.
YOU THINK I DON'T KNOW?!
HONK!
MEOW!
DANGER DON'T MIX
ALTHOUGH SHAMPOO'S SLAVE WAS FREED, AT LEAST.
PANDA DO WHAT IT WANT.
YES MA'AM.
AND LATER IN JAPAN—
WOK

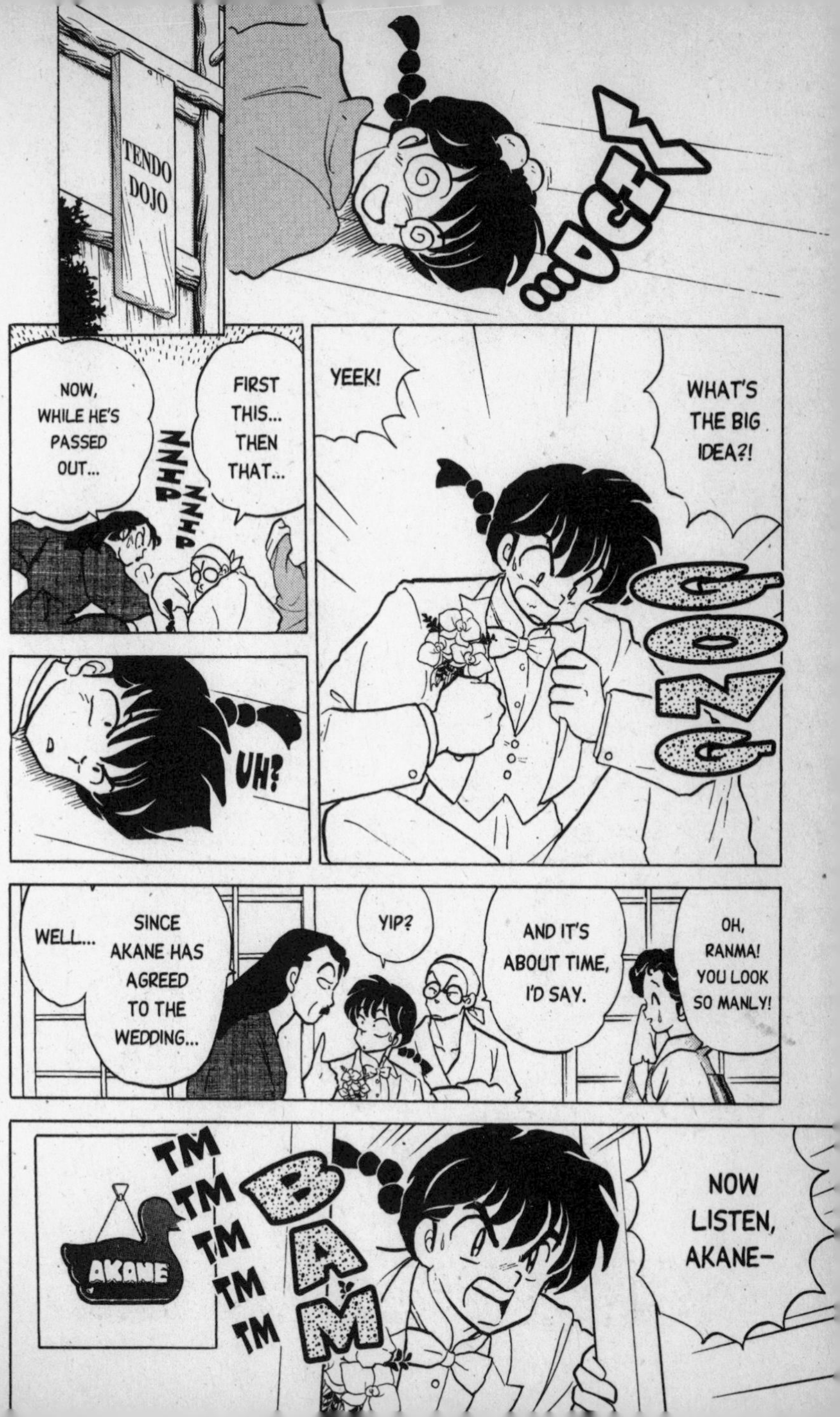
TENDO DOJO
...DGEY
NOW, WHILE HE'S PASSED OUT...
FIRST THIS... THEN THAT...
ZZHIP ZZHIP
UH?
YEEK!
WHAT'S THE BIG IDEA?!
GONG
WELL...
SINCE AKANE HAS AGREED TO THE WEDDING...
YIP?
AND IT'S ABOUT TIME, I'D SAY.
OH, RANMA! YOU LOOK SO MANLY!
AKANE
TM TM TM TM TM
BAM
NOW LISTEN, AKANE—

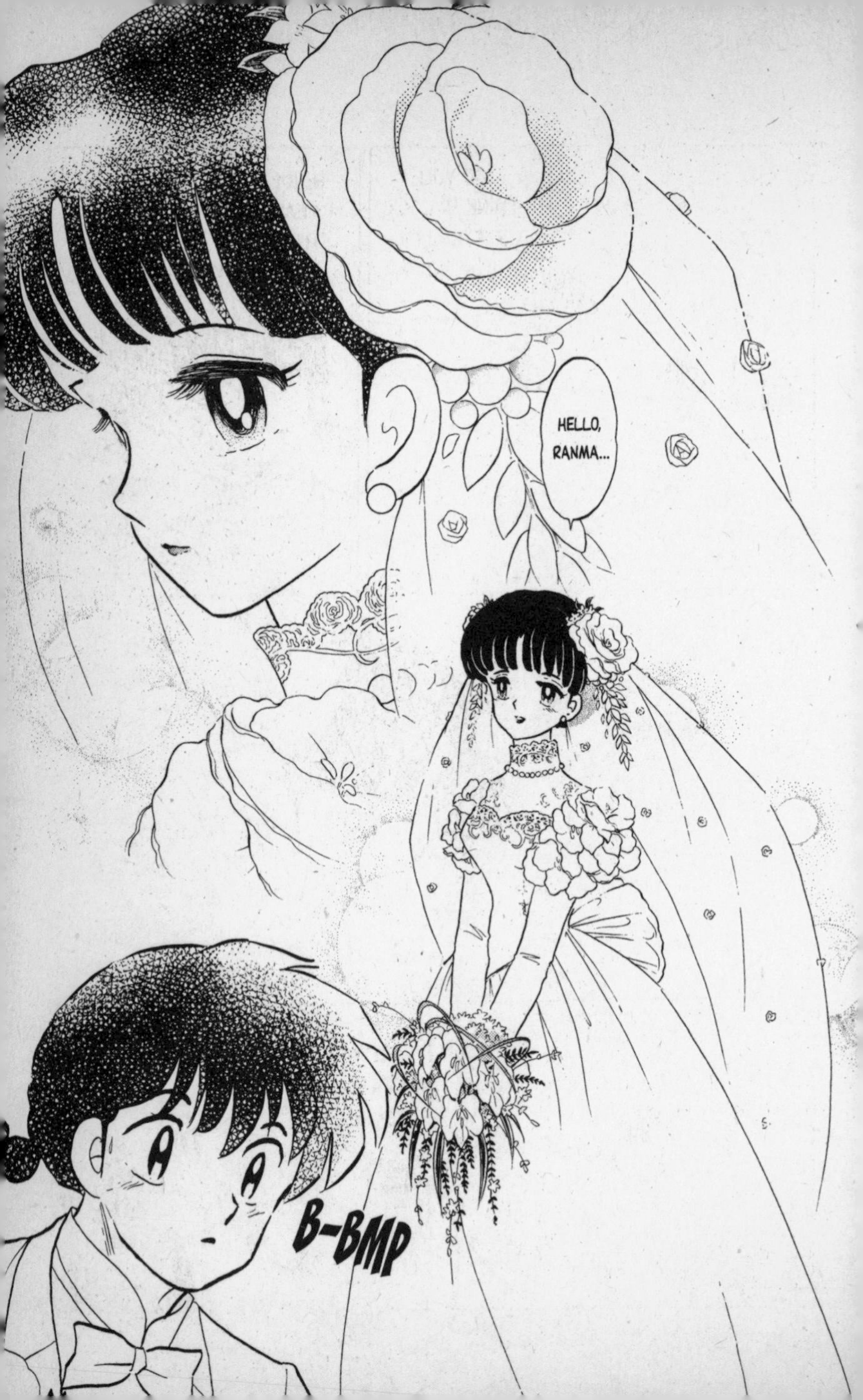
HELLO, RANMA...
B-BMP

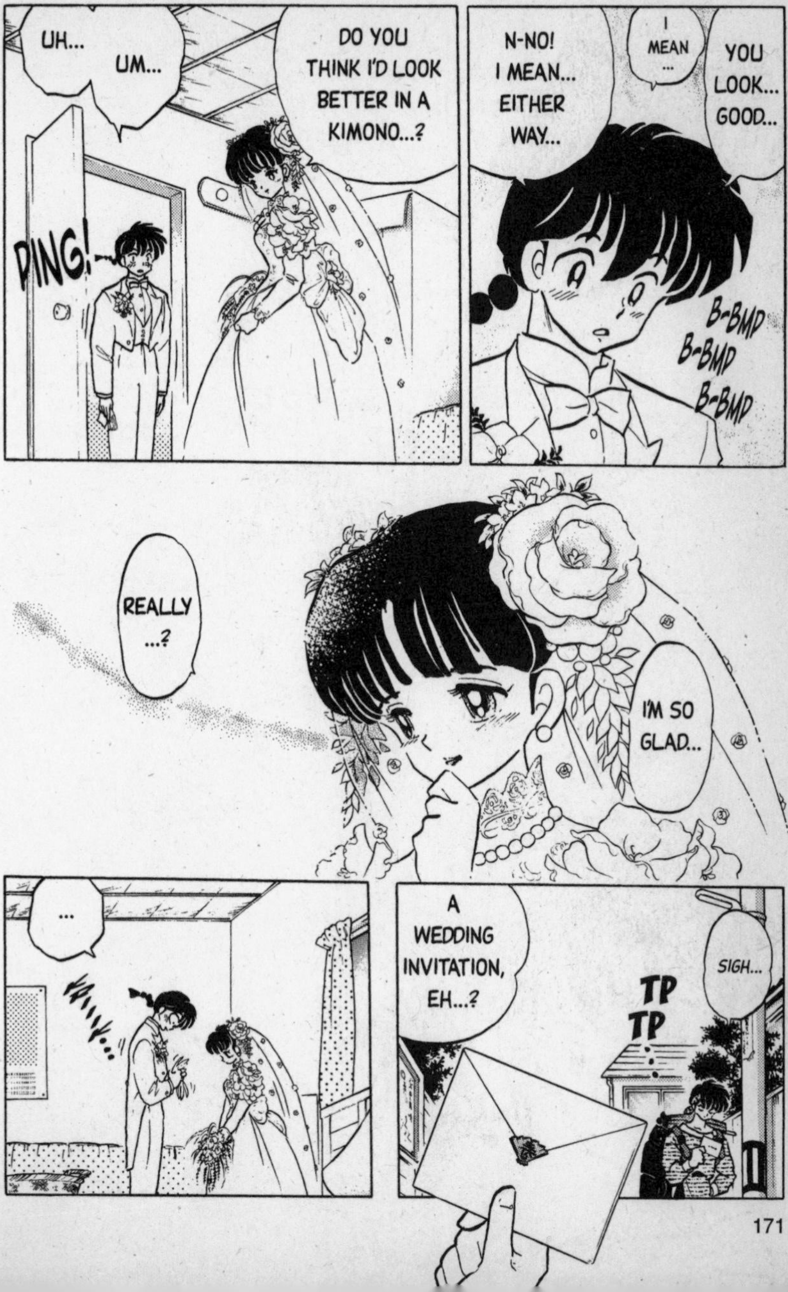
UH... UM...
DO YOU THINK I'D LOOK BETTER IN A KIMONO...?
DING!
N-NO! I MEAN... EITHER WAY...
I MEAN...
YOU LOOK... GOOD...
B-BMP
B-BMP
B-BMP
REALLY...?
I'M SO GLAD...
...
A WEDDING INVITATION, EH...?
TP
TP
SIGH...

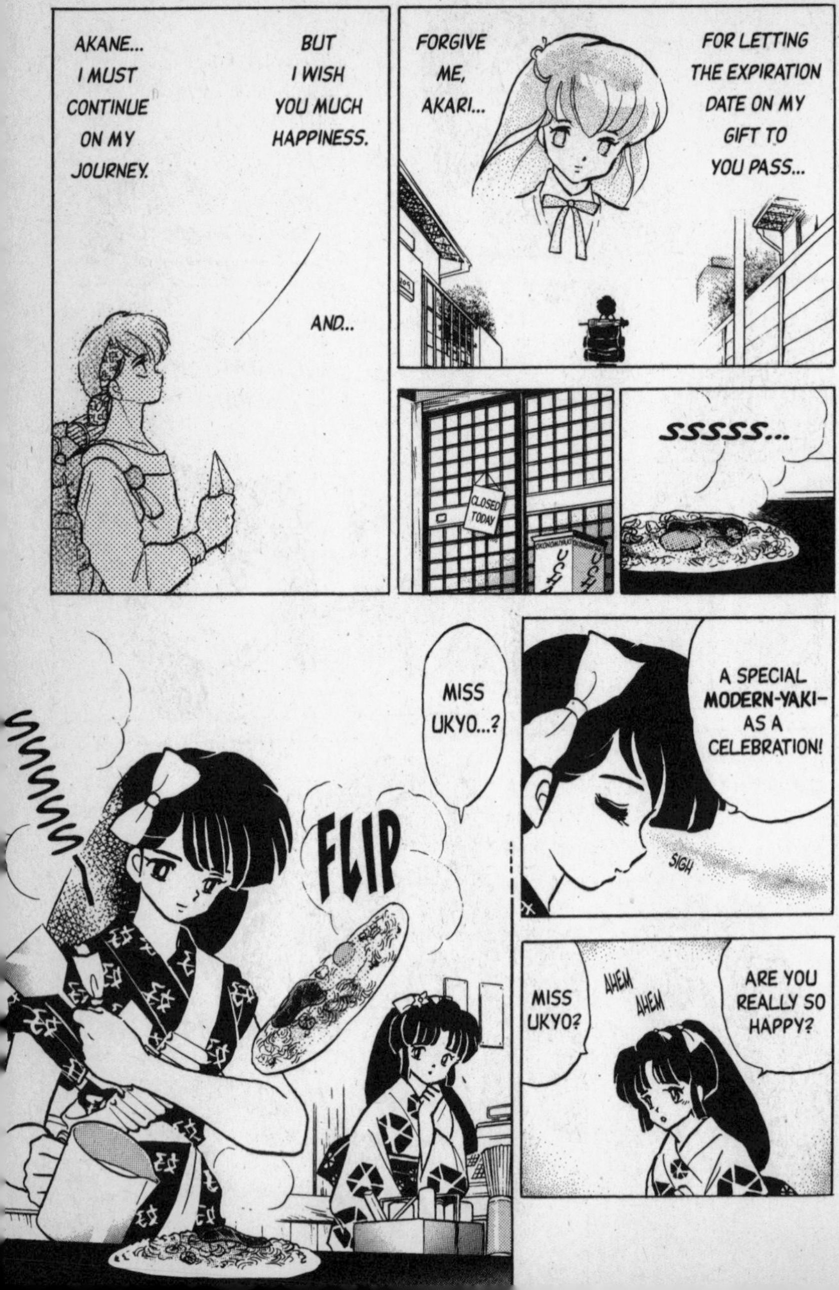
AKANE... I MUST CONTINUE ON MY JOURNEY.
BUT I WISH YOU MUCH HAPPINESS.
AND...
FORGIVE ME, AKARI...
FOR LETTING THE EXPIRATION DATE ON MY GIFT TO YOU PASS...
CLOSED TODAY
SSSSS...
FLIP
MISS UKYO...?
A SPECIAL MODERN-YAKI— AS A CELEBRATION!
SIGH
MISS UKYO?
AHEM
AHEM
ARE YOU REALLY SO HAPPY?

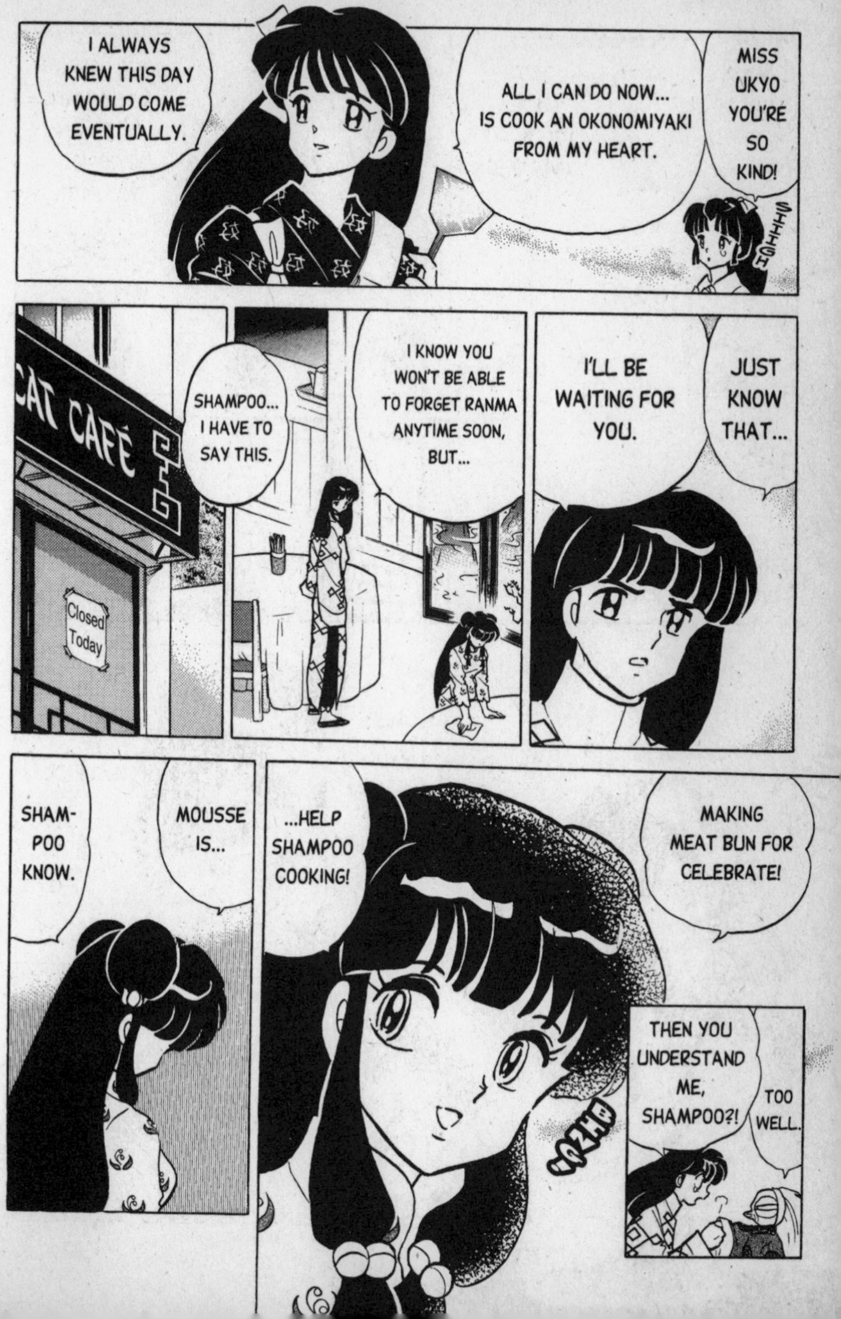
I ALWAYS KNEW THIS DAY WOULD COME EVENTUALLY.
ALL I CAN DO NOW... IS COOK AN OKONOMIYAKI FROM MY HEART.
MISS UKYO YOU'RE SO KIND!
SIIIGH
CAT CAFÉ
Closed Today
SHAMPOO... I HAVE TO SAY THIS.
I KNOW YOU WON'T BE ABLE TO FORGET RANMA ANYTIME SOON, BUT...
I'LL BE WAITING FOR YOU.
JUST KNOW THAT...
SHAM-POO KNOW.
MOUSSE IS...
...HELP SHAMPOO COOKING!
MAKING MEAT BUN FOR CELEBRATE!
THEN YOU UNDERSTAND ME, SHAMPOO?!
TOO WELL.

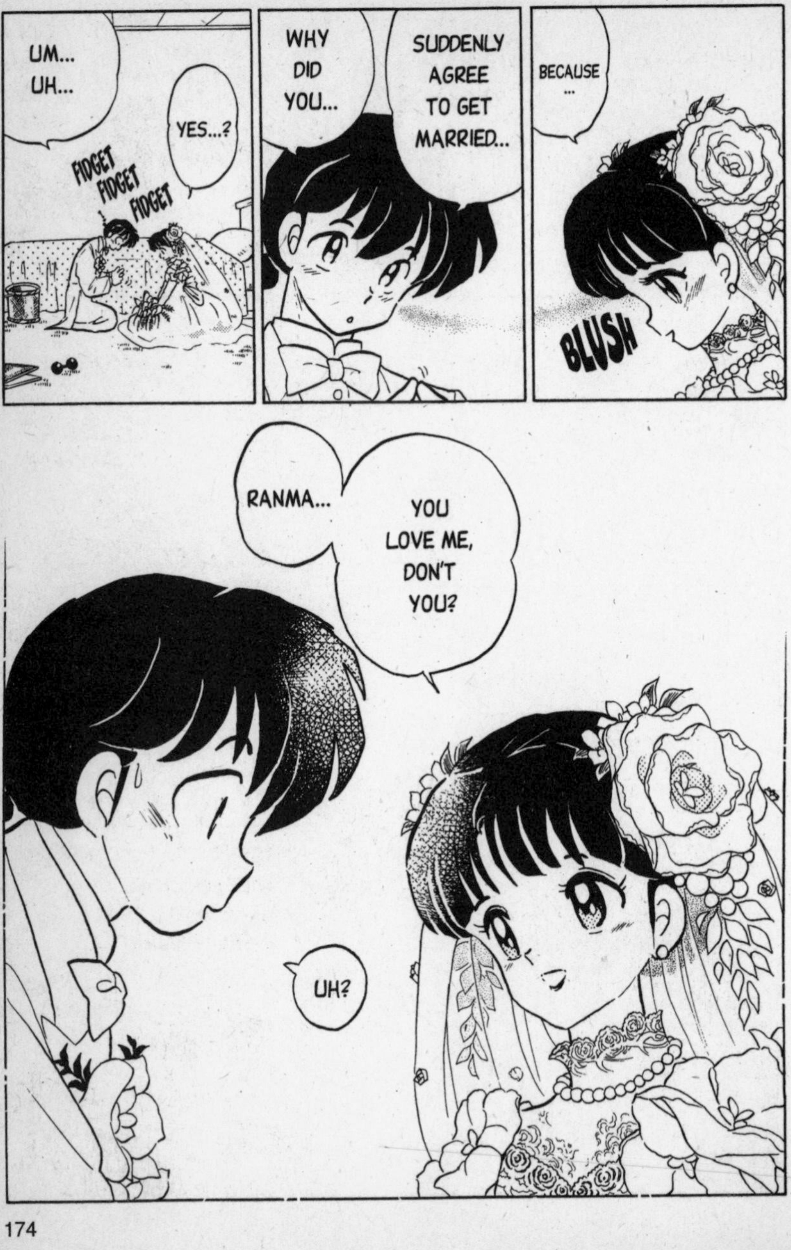
UM... UH...
YES...?
FIDGET FIDGET FIDGET
WHY DID YOU...
SUDDENLY AGREE TO GET MARRIED...
BECAUSE ...
BLUSH
RANMA...
YOU LOVE ME, DON'T YOU?
UH?

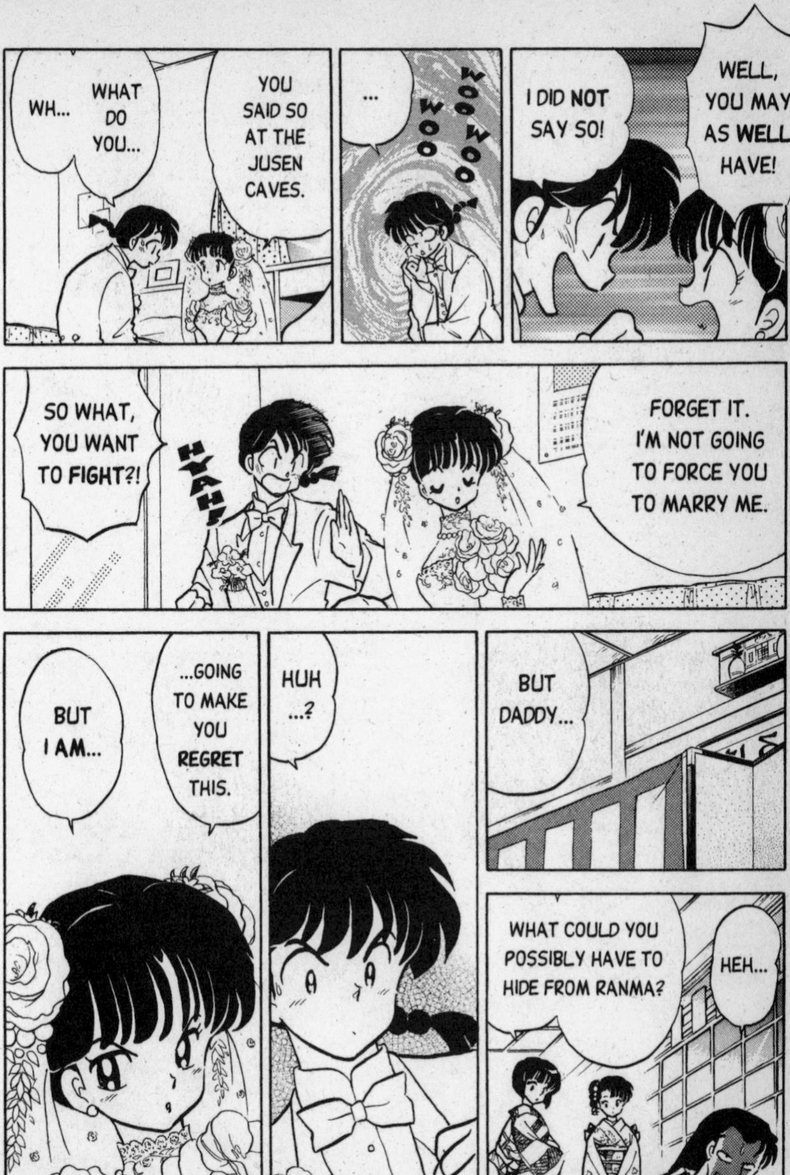
WH...
WHAT DO YOU...
YOU SAID SO AT THE JUSEN CAVES.
...
WOO
WOO WOO
I DID NOT SAY SO!
WELL, YOU MAY AS WELL HAVE!
SO WHAT, YOU WANT TO FIGHT?!
HYAH!
FORGET IT. I'M NOT GOING TO FORCE YOU TO MARRY ME.
BUT I AM...
...GOING TO MAKE YOU REGRET THIS.
HUH ...?
BUT DADDY...
WHAT COULD YOU POSSIBLY HAVE TO HIDE FROM RANMA?
HEH...

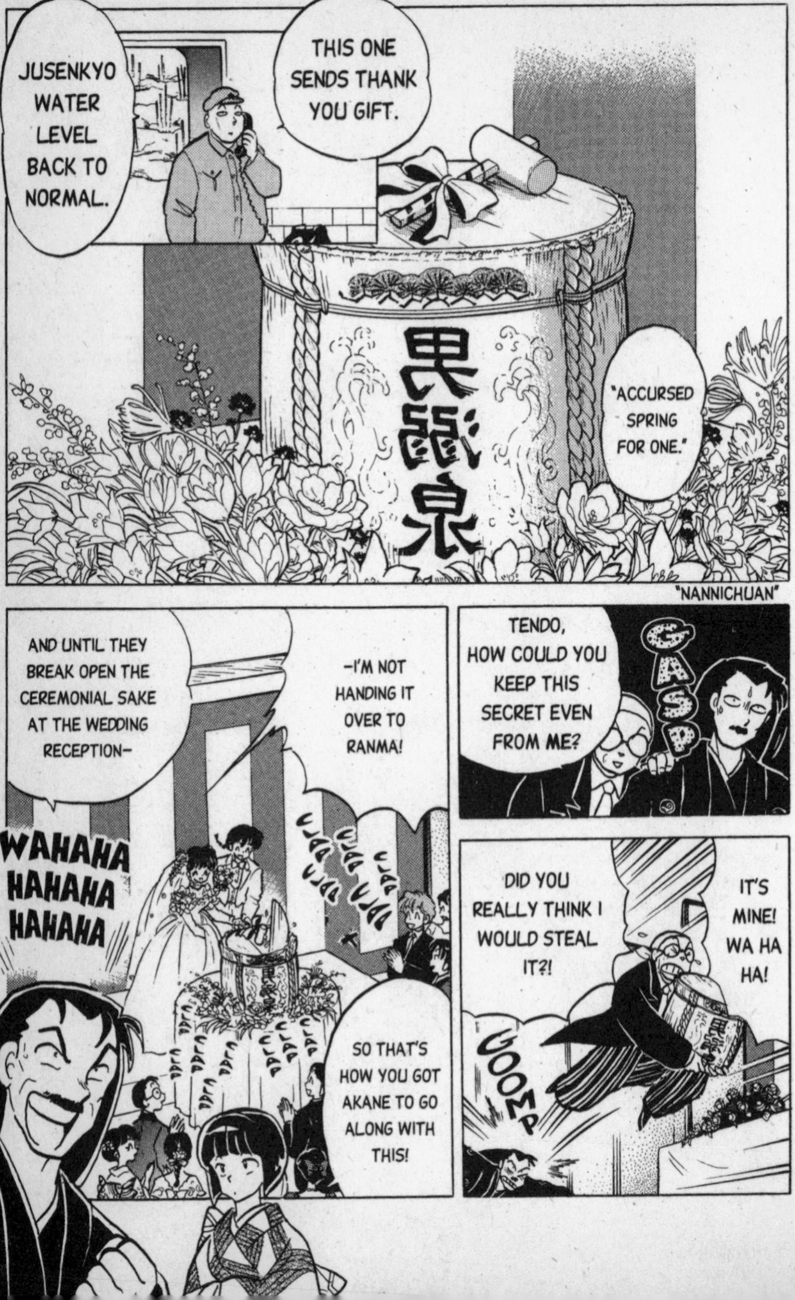
JUSENKYO WATER LEVEL BACK TO NORMAL.
THIS ONE SENDS THANK YOU GIFT.
男溺泉
"ACCURSED SPRING FOR ONE."
"NANNICHUAN"
AND UNTIL THEY BREAK OPEN THE CEREMONIAL SAKE AT THE WEDDING RECEPTION—
—I'M NOT HANDING IT OVER TO RANMA!
WAHAHA HAHAHA HAHAHA
CLAP CLAP CLAP CLAP CLAP CLAP
CLAP CLAP CLAP CLAP CLAP CLAP CLAP CLAP
SO THAT'S HOW YOU GOT AKANE TO GO ALONG WITH THIS!
TENDO, HOW COULD YOU KEEP THIS SECRET EVEN FROM ME?
GASP
DID YOU REALLY THINK I WOULD STEAL IT?!
IT'S MINE! WA HA HA!
GOOMP

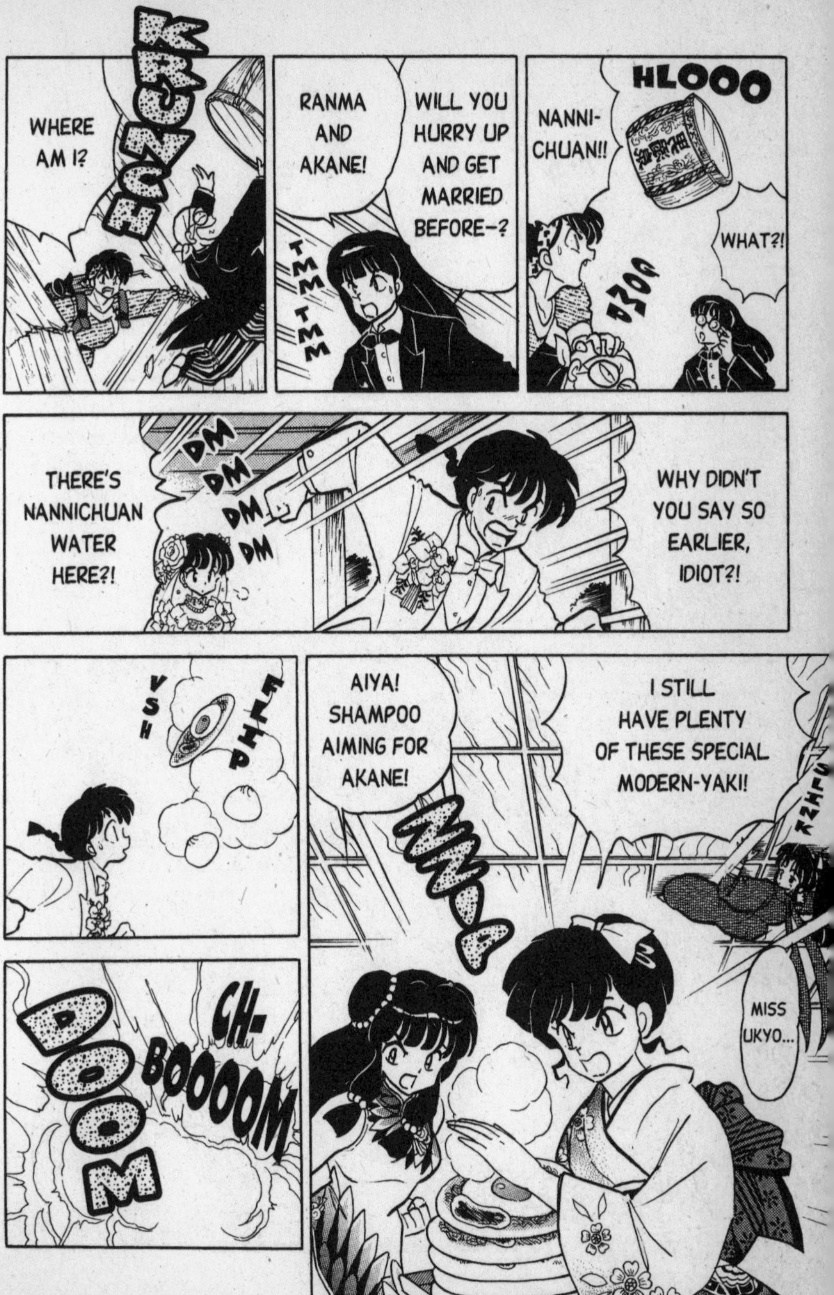
KRUNCH
WHERE AM I?
RANMA AND AKANE!
WILL YOU HURRY UP AND GET MARRIED BEFORE-?
TMM TMM
NANNI-CHUAN!!
HLOOO
WHAT?!
DM DM DM DM
THERE'S NANNICHUAN WATER HERE?!
WHY DIDN'T YOU SAY SO EARLIER, IDIOT?!
VSH
AIYA! SHAMPOO AIMING FOR AKANE!
I STILL HAVE PLENTY OF THESE SPECIAL MODERN-YAKI!
MISS UKYO...
CH-BOOOOM

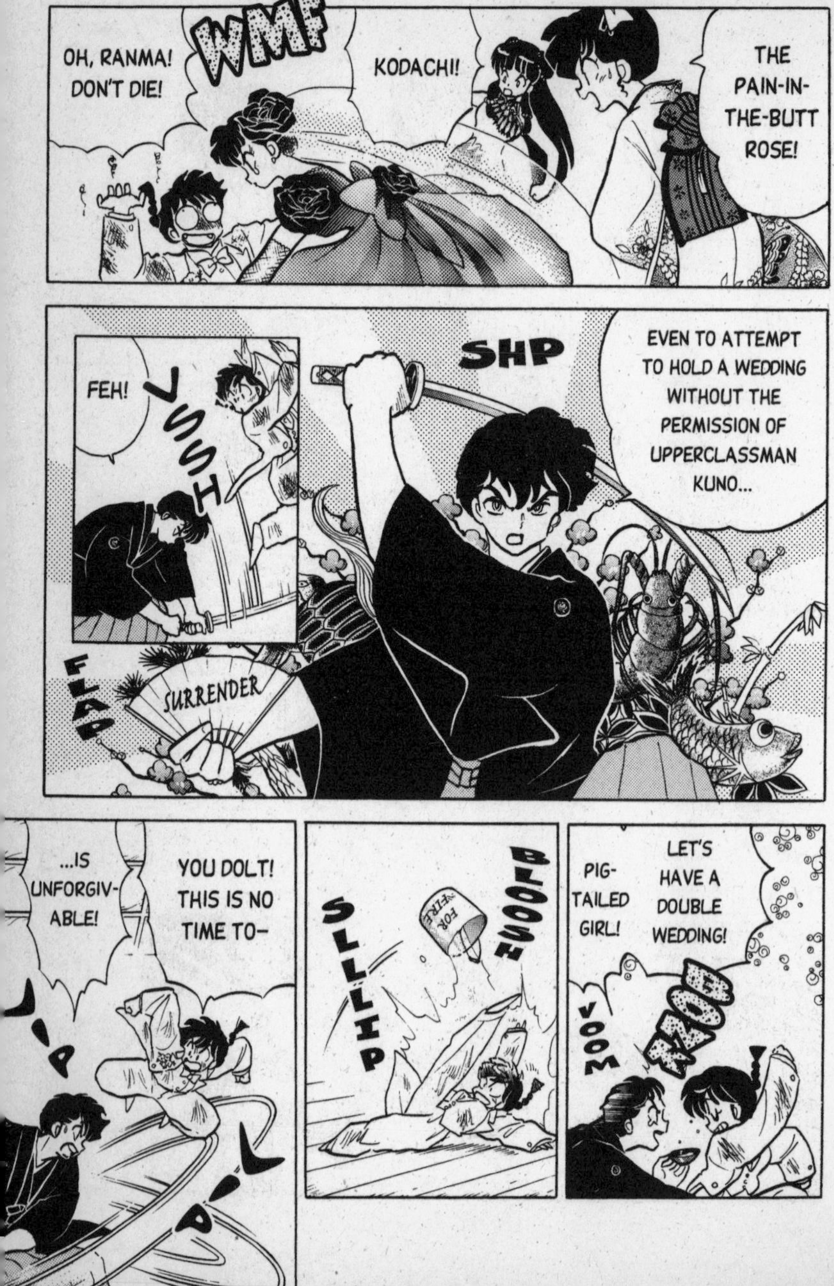
OH, RANMA! DON'T DIE!
WMF
KODACHI!
THE PAIN-IN-THE-BUTT ROSE!
FEH!
VSSH
SHP
EVEN TO ATTEMPT TO HOLD A WEDDING WITHOUT THE PERMISSION OF UPPERCLASSMAN KUNO...
FLAP
SURRENDER
...IS UNFORGIV-ABLE!
YOU DOLT! THIS IS NO TIME TO—
SLLLIP
FOR FIRE
BLOOSH
PIG-TAILED GIRL!
LET'S HAVE A DOUBLE WEDDING!
VOOM

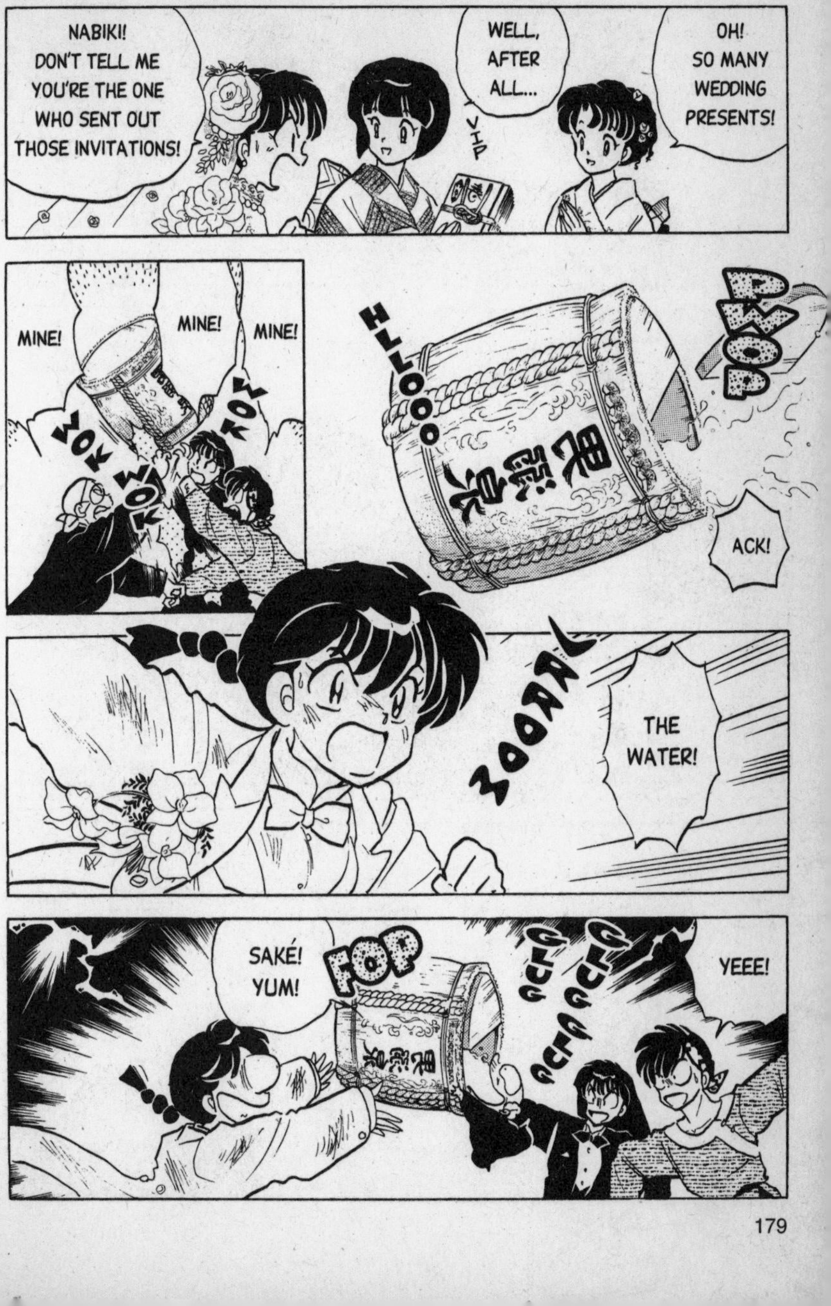
NABIKI! DON'T TELL ME YOU'RE THE ONE WHO SENT OUT THOSE INVITATIONS!
WELL, AFTER ALL...
VIP
OH! SO MANY WEDDING PRESENTS!
MINE!
MINE!
MINE!
WOK
WOK
WOK
WOK
HLLOOO
PWOP
ACK!
WOORRL
THE WATER!
SAKÉ! YUM!
FOP
GLUG GLUG
GLUG GLUG
YEEE!

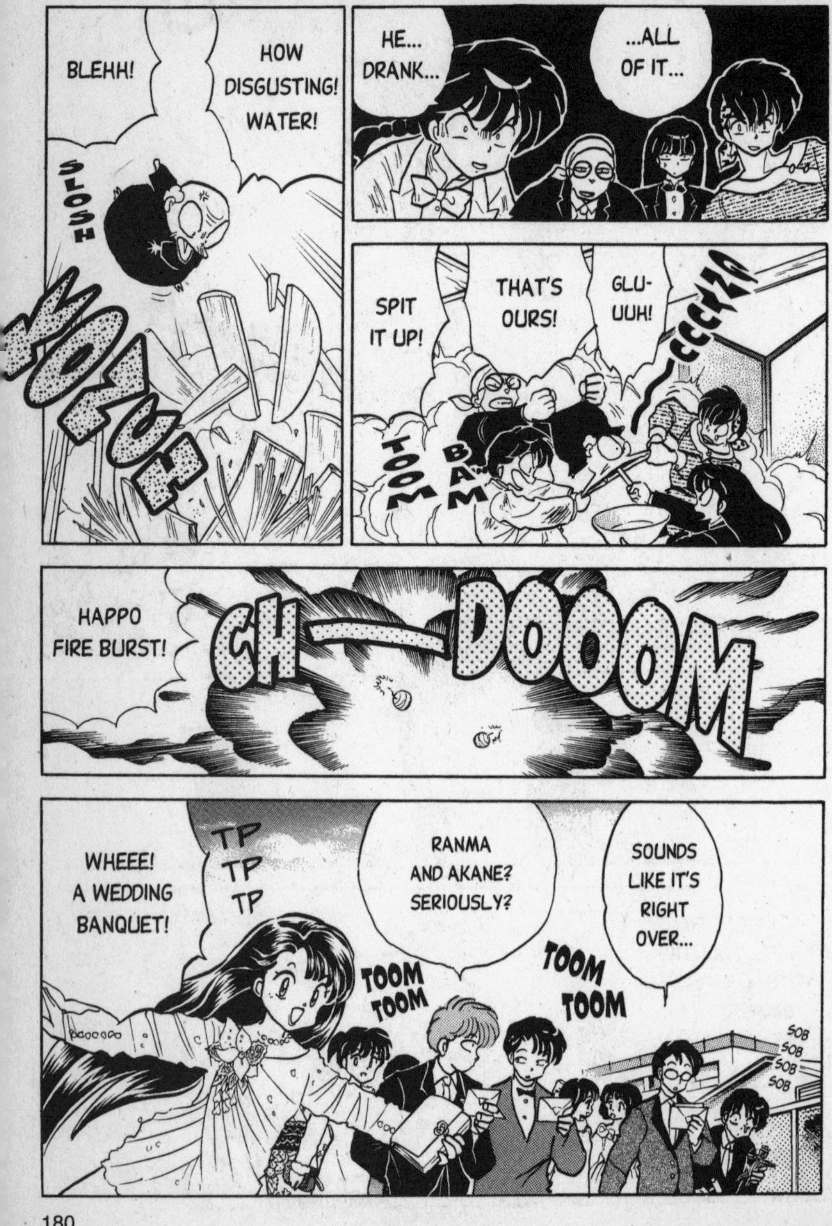

BLEHH!
HOW DISGUSTING! WATER!
SLOSH
HE... DRANK...
...ALL OF IT...
SPIT IT UP!
THAT'S OURS!
GLU-UUH!
TOOM
BAM
HAPPO FIRE BURST!
CH—DOOOM
WHEEE! A WEDDING BANQUET!
TP TP TP
RANMA AND AKANE? SERIOUSLY?
SOUNDS LIKE IT'S RIGHT OVER...
TOOM TOOM
TOOM TOOM
SOB SOB SOB SOB

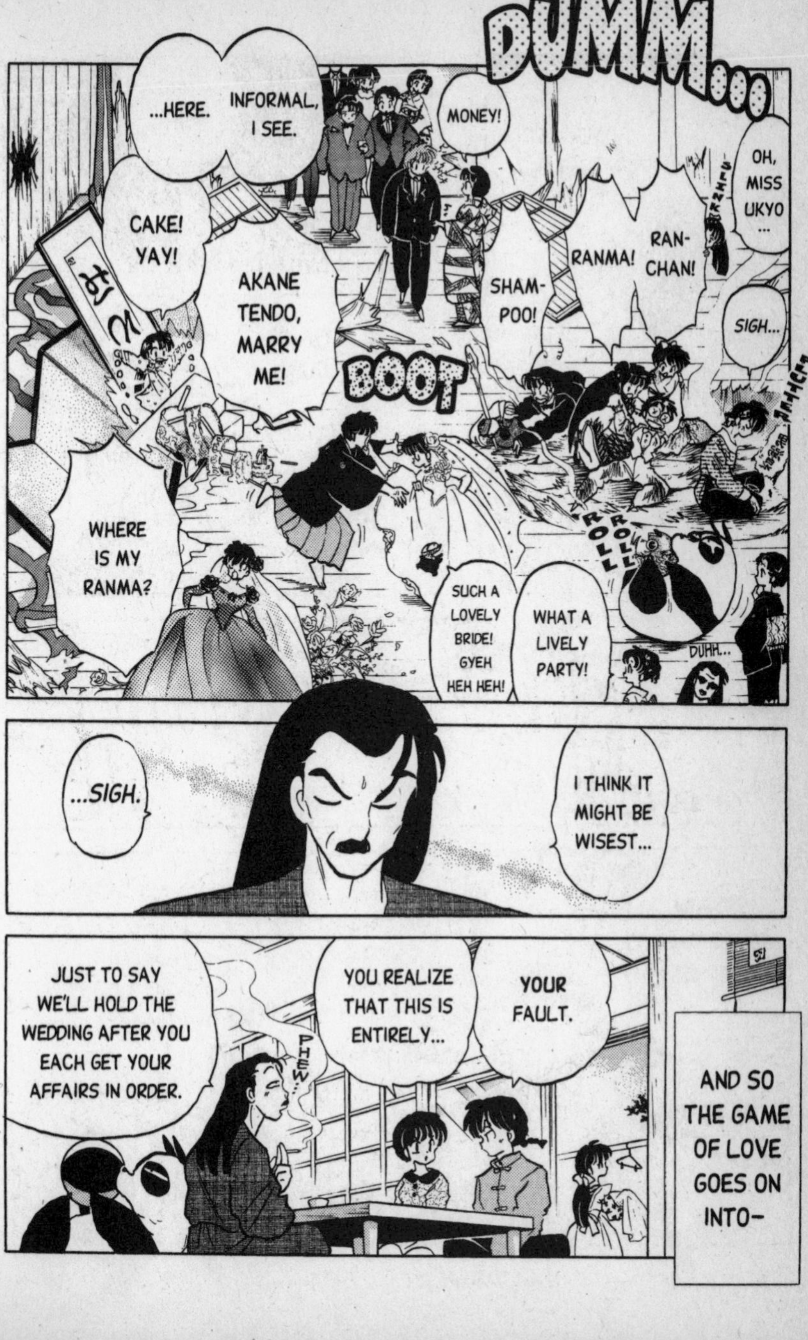
...HERE.
INFORMAL, I SEE.
MONEY!
DUMM...
OH, MISS UKYO...
SLINK
CAKE! YAY!
SHAM-POO!
RANMA!
RAN-CHAN!
AKANE TENDO, MARRY ME!
SIGH...
BOOT
WHERE IS MY RANMA?
ROLL ROLL
SUCH A LOVELY BRIDE! GYEH HEH HEH!
WHAT A LIVELY PARTY!
DUHH...
...SIGH.
I THINK IT MIGHT BE WISEST...
JUST TO SAY WE'LL HOLD THE WEDDING AFTER YOU EACH GET YOUR AFFAIRS IN ORDER.
PHEW...
YOU REALIZE THAT THIS IS ENTIRELY...
YOUR FAULT.
AND SO THE GAME OF LOVE GOES ON INTO—

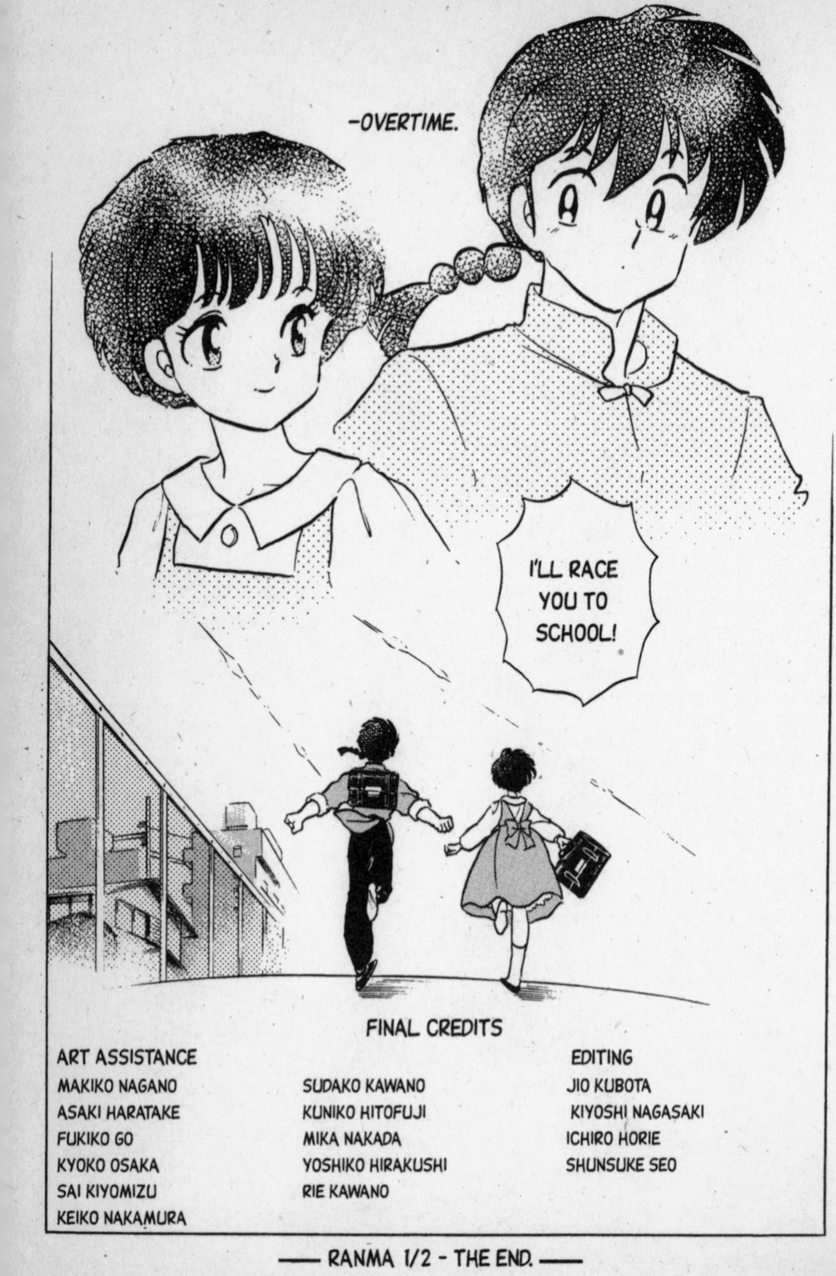
-OVERTIME.
I'LL RACE YOU TO SCHOOL!

FINAL CREDITS

ART ASSISTANCE

MAKIKO NAGANO
ASAKI HARATAKE
FUKIKO GO
KYOKO OSAKA
SAI KIYOMIZU
KEIKO NAKAMURA
SUDAKO KAWANO
KUNIKO HITOFUJI
MIKA NAKADA
YOSHIKO HIRAKUSHI
RIE KAWANO

EDITING

JIO KUBOTA
KIYOSHI NAGASAKI
ICHIRO HORIE
SHUNSUKE SEO

—— RANMA 1/2 - THE END. ——

Thank you so much for reading all the way to the end. I'm so glad that *Ranma 1/2* was able to cross national boundaries and that people were able to enjoy it. I would be so happy if the characters from *Ranma 1/2* would stay in your hearts and remain your friends for life.

-Rumiko Takahashi, 2006

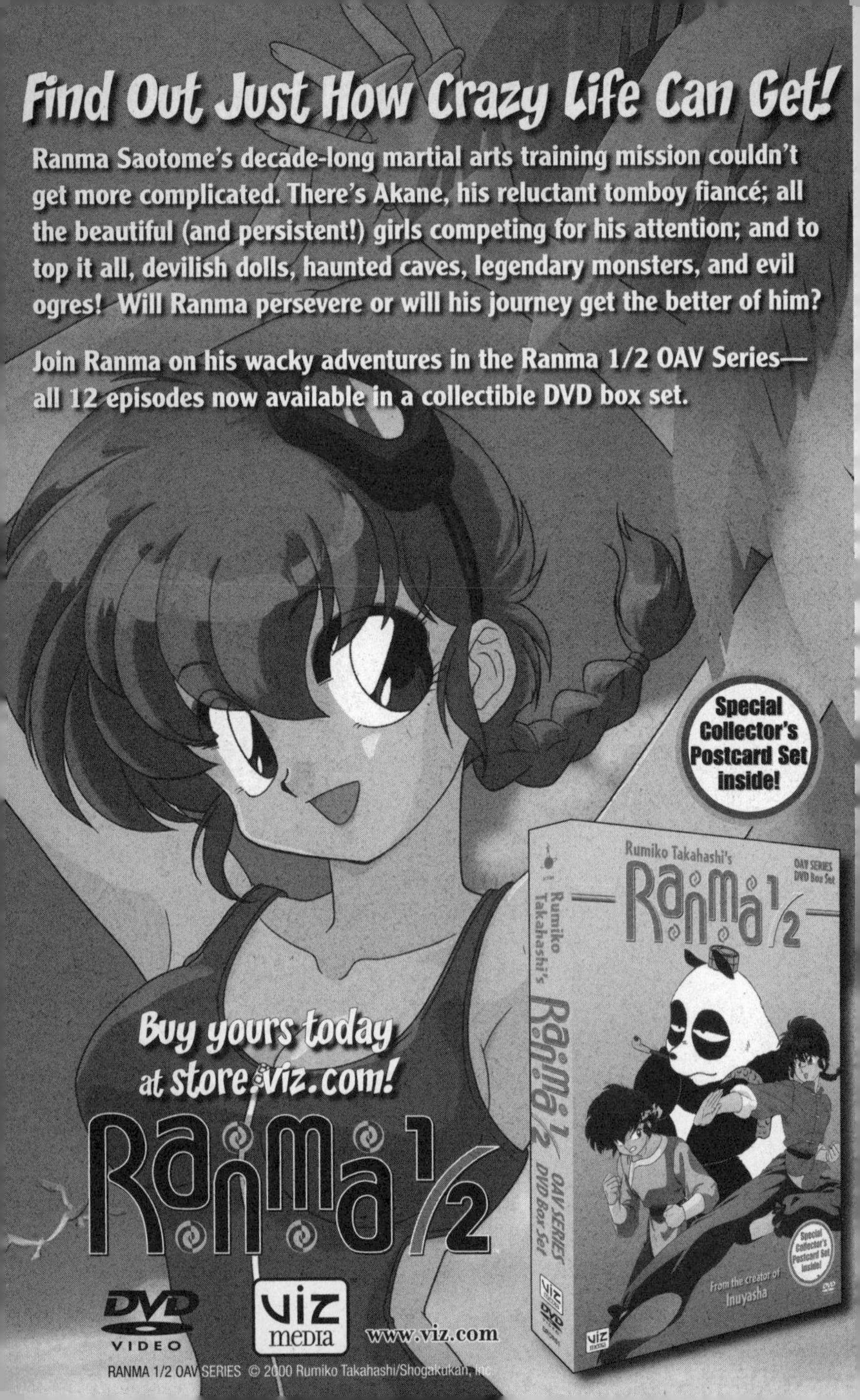

Find Out Just How Crazy Life Can Get!
Ranma Saotome's decade-long martial arts training mission couldn't get more complicated. There's Akane, his reluctant tomboy fiancé; all the beautiful (and persistent!) girls competing for his attention; and to top it all, devilish dolls, haunted caves, legendary monsters, and evil ogres! Will Ranma persevere or will his journey get the better of him?
Join Ranma on his wacky adventures in the Ranma 1/2 OAV Series—all 12 episodes now available in a collectible DVD box set.
Special Collector's Postcard Set inside!
Rumiko Takahashi's
Ranma 1/2
OAV SERIES DVD Box Set
From the creator of Inuyasha
Buy yours today at store.viz.com!
Ranma 1/2
DVD VIDEO
VIZ media
www.viz.com
RANMA 1/2 OAV SERIES © 2000 Rumiko Takahashi/Shogakukan, Inc.

Half Human, Half

When Kagome discovers a well that transports her to feudal era Japan, she unwittingly frees a half-demon, Inuyasha, and shatters the sacred Jewel of Four Souls. Now they must work together to restore the jewel before it falls into the wrong hands...

InuYasha

The manga that inspired a phenomenon!

FULL COLOR adaptation of the TV series!

Only $9.95!

Only $11.95!

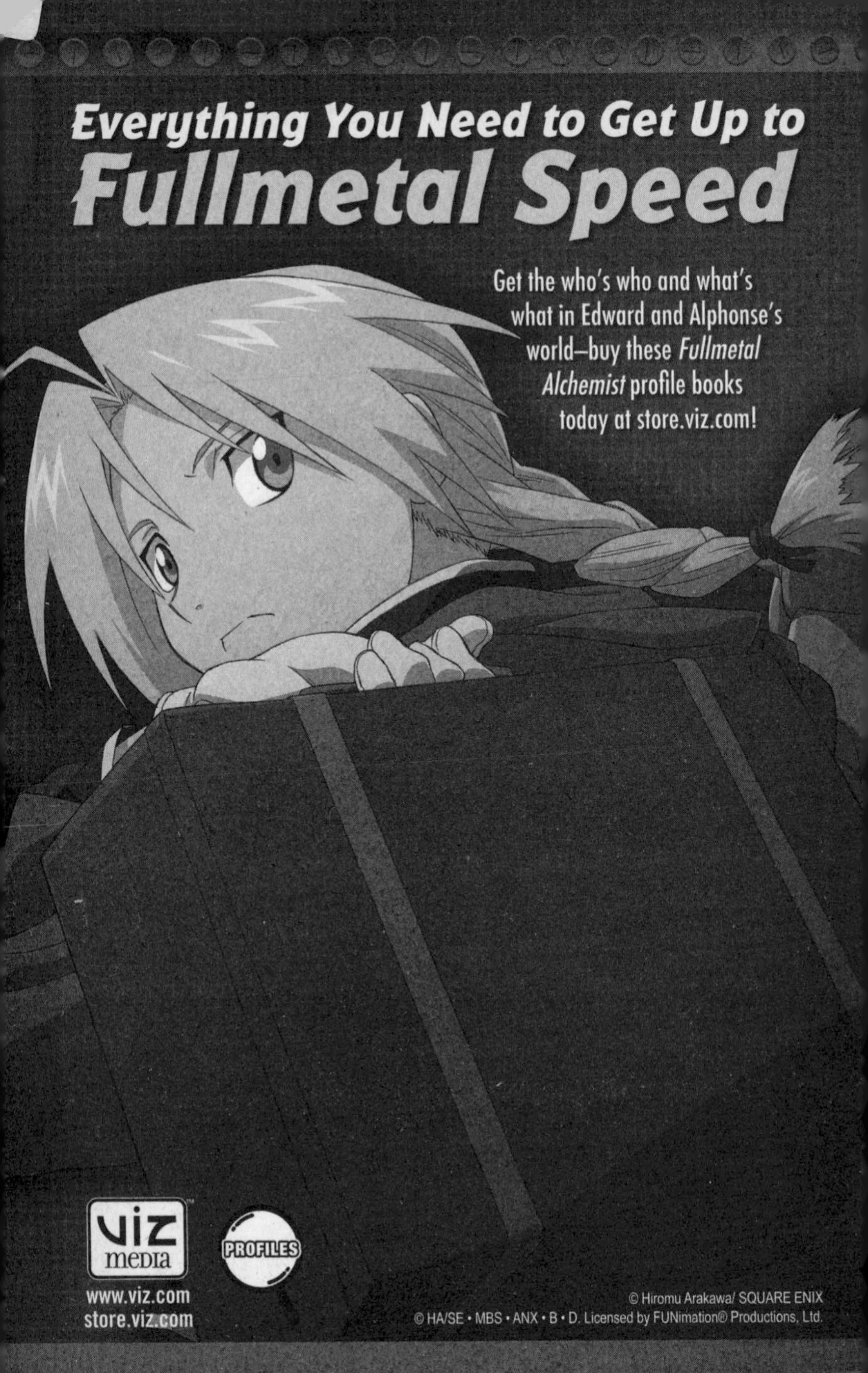
Everything You Need to Get Up to
Fullmetal Speed
Get the who's who and what's what in Edward and Alphonse's world—buy these Fullmetal Alchemist profile books today at store.viz.com!
viz media
PROFILES
www.viz.com
store.viz.com
© Hiromu Arakawa/ SQUARE ENIX
© HA/SE • MBS • ANX • B • D. Licensed by FUNimation® Productions, Ltd.